Three cheers for the unemployed

Three cheers for the unemployed describes the beginnings and development of unemployment reform up to the New Deal. As a consequence of the large-scale industrialization after the Civil War, joblessness could no longer be considered to be caused by character defects, but had to be ascribed to societal forces. It became clear that traditional remedial measures could not cope with the problem adequately. In times of depression, the large number of unemployed far exceeded the aid capacity of private philanthropies and civic authorities. And the continuous expansion of the labor market made it obvious that local action would remain insufficient, especially if prevention could take the place of the less-desirable solution.

By the time the United States entered World War I, reformist thinkers had devised the major tools that were later used to deal with unemployment. After the war and during most of the 1920s, these tools underwent thorough examination and refinement. The early years of the Great Depression saw them used tentatively. On the eve of the New Deal, a well-reasoned and successfully tested group of social programs was available.

This book essentially refutes a social-control explanation for this process. It demonstrates that the unemployment measures of the New Deal emanated from the reformist endeavors of the Progressive Age.

Three cheers for the unemployed

Government and unemployment before the New Deal

UDO SAUTTER

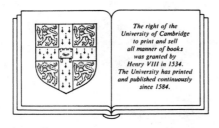

The right of the
University of Cambridge
to print and sell
all manner of books
was granted by
Henry VIII in 1534.
The University has printed
and published continuously
since 1584.

Cambridge University Press

Cambridge
New York   Port Chester   Melbourne   Sydney

Published by the Press Syndicate of the University of Cambridge
The Pitt Building, Trumpington Street, Cambridge CB2 1RP
40 West 20th Street, New York, NY 10011, USA
10 Stamford Road, Oakleigh, Melbourne 3166, Australia

First published 1991

Printed in Canada

Library of Congress Cataloging-in-Publication Data

Sautter, Udo, 1934-
Three cheers for the unemployed : government and unemployment
before the New Deal / Udo Sautter.
p.   cm.
Includes bibliographical references and index.
ISBN 0-521-40041-4
1. Unemployment – United States – History.   2. Unemployment –
Government policy – United States – History.   3. Unemployed – United
States – History.   4. United States – Full employment policies –
History.   I. Title.
HD5724.S32   1991
331.13'7973 – dc20   91-24805
                                                                            CIP

A catalog record for this book is available from the British Library.

ISBN 0-521-40041-4 hardback

Contents

Figures and tables

vii

Tables

Abbreviations used in the text or footnotes

AALL	American Association for Labor Legislation
AAPEO	American Association of Public Employment Offices
ACWA	Amalgamated Clothing Workers of America
AFL	American Federation of Labor
ALLR	*American Labor Legislation Review*
AMA	American Management Association
Annals	American Academy of Political and Social Science. *Annals*
ASA	American Statistical Association
COS	Charity Organization Society (New York City)
CR	*Congressional Record*
CUBC	President's Conference on Unemployment. Committee on Unemployment and Business Cycles
CWA	Civil Works Administration
ERCA	Emergency Relief and Reconstruction Act
FERA	Federal Emergency Relief Administration
FESB	Federal Employment Stabilization Board
G.P.O.	[United States] Government Printing Office
IAPES	International Association of Public Employment Services
IAU	International Association on Unemployment
ILO	International Labour Organization
MLR	*Monthly Labor Review*
NAM	National Association of Manufacturers
NCCC	National Conference of Charities and Correction
PACE	President's Advisory Committee for Employment
PECE	President's Emergency Committee for Employment
POUR	President's Organization on Unemployment Relief
PWA	Federal Administration of Public Works
RFC	Reconstruction Finance Corporation

TERA	Temporary Emergency Relief Administration
USES	United States Employment Service
WMA	Wisconsin Manufacturers' Association
WPA	Works Progress Administration

Acknowledgments

This book has been many years in gestation. Its writing was facilitated with the assistance of many people to whom I am sincerely grateful. At the Leddy Library and the Law Library of the University of Windsor, my home ground, the reference librarians came up with many unexpected finds and leads; the circulation, documents, and interlibrary loan staff always listened cheerfully to my many requests, some quite outlandish, and actually met most of them. I received similar kind attention at the Detroit Public Library as well as at the various libraries of Wayne State University and the University of Michigan, all of which accorded me free access to their rich holdings. Over several years the Harlan Hatcher Graduate Library at the latter institution also granted me free borrowing privileges, without which the collection of many materials would have been a considerably more arduous task. I was made equally welcome at the archives I visited, a number of them several times – the United States National Archives, the Library of Congress (Manuscript Division), and the Georgetown University Archives in Washington, D.C.; the Herbert Hoover Library in West Branch, Iowa; the State Historical Society Archives in Madison, Wisconsin; the Walter P. Reuther Archives in Detroit; the Franklin D. Roosevelt Library in Hyde Park, New York; and the New York State Library of Industrial and Labor Relations in Ithaca, New York. At all of them the staff was most courteous and supportive; mention should be made of Richard Strasberg at Ithaca, whose gracious assistance made my sojourn at Cornell particularly fruitful.

Thanks are also due to the Social Science and Humanities Research Council of Canada and the German Research Council (Deutsche Forschungsgemeinschaft). The latter helped to get the unemployment project under way. The former supported it during its most intensive research phase. Additional aid came from the University of Windsor; several small research grants helped to bridge gaps in major funding; the Department of History gave me use of its research office when the sprawling source materials collection began to submerge its collector; and the Dean of Social Science put a microcomputer in that office at a time when such a device still conferred on its user something of an avant-gardist nimbus. I also feel indebted to a number of colleagues, both in the United States and in Germany, whose interest and considerateness helped to sustain my hope over the years that the project would finally reach its intended end. The manuscript itself benefited from the good advice generously offered by two anonymous readers for Cambridge University Press. Ronald Cohen did a marvelous job of smoothing out the all too numerous stylistic edges and grooves of the original manuscript. Special thanks go to Frank Smith, the social science editor at Cambridge University Press, without whose understanding and helpfulness the book would not have appeared in this form.

Most of the time my family was keenly aware that this work was in the making. I always deeply appreciated the patience and goodwill they showed, especially my wife Hilla's encouragement and cheerfulness, which were invaluable. Our children, Andreas and Sabine, have presently reached crucial crossroads in their studies; Claudia will soon follow suit. I am not sure whether the existence of this book can mean anything in particular to them. But it has grown with them, and it is to them, as well as to Hilla, that I dedicate it.

Windsor, Ontario

There was a rich banquet, and after the toasts were over one gentleman rose to make a few remarks. He said: "When I came to this beautiful banquet hall, and looked around at these gorgeous draperies, and these fine furnishings, and saw this expensive linen and silverware – I looked about and I thought of the poor unfortunate persons in Chicago – and I thought of the poor unemployed persons in Chicago – and – and I am so overcome with feeling for the poor unfortunate persons in Chicago who are unemployed – I am so overcome that – that I sit down." And he sat down. Another diner arose and said, "I also couldn't help thinking all the time of the poor unemployed persons in Chicago. But I do not sit down! I move that we do something for the poor unemployed persons in Chicago! I move that we give – three cheers for the poor unemployed persons in Chicago!"[1]

1 "General Discussion," *ALLR* 4:2 (May 1914), 346.

1. Introduction

This is a book about some of the cheers that American society gave on behalf of the unemployed in the two generations straddling the turn of the twentieth century.

More precisely, the book discusses the evolution of unemployment reform up to the end of the Hoover presidency. It does not deal extensively with the well-known measures of the New Deal period, which for the first time aimed at combating joblessness in America on a large scale. It looks rather at the far less understood process that led up to these measures. The unemployment action of the New Deal and its precedents during the Hoover administration had a long history stretching over more than a half century. It was the experience of the depression of the 1870s that initiated the rethinking of accepted laissez-faire rules and engendered a development that reached maturation during the economic downturn of the 1930s. By the time the New Deal began, the important prerequisites of effective action – public acceptance of large-scale governmental involvement and an informed understanding of what specific measures constituted viable propositions – were in place as a result of the laborious toil of decades of dedicated reform work.

With advancing industrialization, unemployment had taken on a new quality. It had probably always been wrong to assume that everybody who wanted work would find it. But in a society predominantly oriented toward agriculture – even more so if that society still disposed of vacant land to which the plow could be put – genuine joblessness had been a relatively rare phenomenon. At any rate, there had seemed to exist ample justification for ascribing an individual's idleness to his own disposition and choice. The advent of manufacturing under industrial circumstances, however, wrought profound changes in this idea. Workers who were increasingly at the mercy of employment conditions that they did not control could no longer be held responsible for finding themselves without jobs.

1

It is the nascence and growth of the idea that government should assume responsibility for the economic welfare of these unemployed that forms the subject of this book. [The term "government," when used in this book without further qualification, is understood to mean "senior government" (state and/or federal).]

An arbitrary decision had to be made as to the boundaries of the field to be investigated. Even during the decades under consideration, when administrative services were of a smaller dimension than in a later era, government engaged in a great number of dealings that touched in one way or another upon the fate of the unemployed. Some of them, like currency management or tariff legislation, did so quite unintentionally as a rule. Other activities were pursued with a growing awareness of their potential impact upon the employment scene. Support of vocational education probably belonged in this category; fiscal behavior in general definitely did. For the purposes of this study it appeared reasonable, though, to concentrate upon those governmental measures that the advocates of reform themselves considered to be the most promising prospects. This focus naturally excludes any extended excursions into questions of economic reform and public finance, of business reorganization or trade unionism. Not all of the specific goals after which the reformers aspired proved attainable; others did not fulfill the hopes they had carried. Seen from a distance, however, it is clear that it was the endeavors that aimed to realize these aspirations that prepared the ground for the more informed measures of a later age.

Probably the most intriguing question about the drive for unemployment reform is the one concerning the motivation of those who advanced the cause. Given the vast array of people involved, a global answer cannot fittingly be ventured. The most valid observation, even if this does not qualify as a particularly distinctive description, is perhaps the statement that it was mainly progressive minds that guided the reform effort. This assertion, of course, pushes the boundaries of what is usually called the Progressive Era backward as well as forward by a considerable number of years, but it is clearly borne out by the evidence. Most of the traits that are commonly seen as typical of the movement as a whole can also readily be identified in the particular efforts that promoted unemployment reform, and this not only during the period between the turn of the century and World War I, but also in the years before and after it. The will to ameliorate the conditions of industrial life, the optimistic assumption that governmental intervention could achieve this, the faith in the power of scientific solutions, and the nationwide presence of concern were all sooner or later among the dominant characteristics of the pertinent advocacy.[2]

Like other social justice movements – and it was this also – unemployment reform had a certain number of left-wing radicals among its supporters. But socialists did not dominate the scene. Center stage was rather held by the more moderate element, of which the membership of the American Association for Labor Legislation (AALL) was representative. Academics of various stripes supplied their analytical and auctorial skills. Many of them taught at the university, with Columbia professors, strategically placed in New York close to the AALL headquarters, easily putting the biggest single contingent into the field. The developing disciplines of political economy and sociology naturally showed the greatest interest, but more than a sprinkling of law teachers and lawyers provided much needed structure and form to various inchoate proposals.

These people had much in common, in outlook as well as in dedication, with that other group that also figured prominently in the promotion of unemployment reform – the emerging profession of social workers. Not all of them favored governmental intervention unequivocally, and originally the unemployment matter was not a conspicuous item on their agenda. But over time their preoccupation grew with the cause, and by the early 1930s it clearly dominated their program. The profession's organ, *The Survey*, formerly *Charities*, ranked second only to the AALL's *American Labor Legislation Review* (*ALLR*) as a voice of concern. The social workers' forte was the advocacy of action rather than seminal thought, but in this their part was indispensible because of the unmatched intimacy of their acquaintance with the relief scene. Of the diverse institutes and institutions that aided in the campaign, the Russell Sage Foundation acted as the closest ally, furnishing expertise and financial support for assorted research projects and publications.

If academics and social workers could consider social analysis and the search for remedial solutions as part of their vocation, it is less clear why some profit-oriented entrepreneurs displayed interest in reform experiments. Humanitarian inclination may have contributed to their activism,

---

2 For a recent summary listing of these traits see Richard L. McCormick, *The Party Period and Public Policy: American Politics from the Age of Jackson to the Progressive Era* (New York: Oxford University Press, 1986), 269–72. See also Daniel T. Rodgers, "In Search of Progressivism," *Reviews in American History* 10:4 (Dec. 1982), 113–32, in particular 123–32.

but overall it appears to have been the insight, spreading slowly but inexorably, that the "American system" needed modification if it was to survive that fostered an increasing acceptance of the need for social action. It is true that the number of businessmen who would confess to such views remained relatively small up to the end of our period, and that those who actively sought to translate this kind of thought into reality were even fewer. It has also to be stated that the ones who did, generally preferred business action, be it under governmental guidance, over direct governmental involvement. But it is manifest, on the other hand, that by acting as the spearheads of welfare capitalism in this respect, they played a signal role in opening a breach in the solid front of conservative resistance.

Legislative action, however tentative, could not take place without the participation of law makers. As a rule, most of those who took unemployment reform initiatives in their respective chambers had to be coaxed and cajoled to do so. Before the war, reformers found some more willing assistance among legislators close to Theodore Roosevelt's Progressive party. But it was only with the advent of the Great Depression, when commitment to the cause promised better political returns, that readiness and dedication increased noticeably. Interestingly, party membership proved a less distinguishing factor than reform-mindedness. Whereas the Democrats more consistently endorsed the unemployment reform cause in their national platforms, Republican insurgents played at least as great a role as Democrats, if not a greater one, in advancing pertinent legislation in Congress.

The unemployed themselves, perhaps not too strangely, figured most of the time as the objects of the solicitude of others. Instances when some of them tried to advance the cause of unemployment reform, in other ways than by writing letters to the authorities or voicing occasional protests in the streets, were infrequent and generally not very significant.[3] The spirit of associationalism did not reach them in a meaningful manner. One reason was certainly that joblessness, whatever its definition, usually constituted an unstable condition, not lending itself to easy organization and political operation. The more oppressive unemployment fell upon the least educated and articulate who lacked the requisite capability –

3 An attempt to link unemployment and protest behavior has recently been made by Harold R. Kerbo and Richard A. Shaffer, "Unemployment and Protest in the United States, 1890–1940: A Methodological Critique and Research Note," *Social Forces* 64:4 (June 1986), 1046–56.

and often the expectant optimism – to formulate their grievances in more than rudimentary form. This goes far to explain the ambiguous attitude of the established trade unions. Representing preponderantly skilled workers who were perhaps less subject to the vagaries of an unstable labor market, and in any event had not as much competition to fear as the unskilled, they usually contented themselves with expressing regret for the fate of the less fortunate. On occasion, ulterior considerations produced a more active concern, most significantly the fear that too much labor available might be detrimental to their own aspirations. But in general, and this is especially true of the American Federation of Labor (AFL) during the first three decades or so of its existence, the unions disliked the idea of government interference in the social sphere, and behaved accordingly.

The quest for unemployment reform thus remained for the most part a kind of middle class, if not a WASP, affair. What motivated individuals to participate, marginally or with substantial engagement, depended, of course, very much on particular personal circumstances. Humanitarianism certainly occupied an important place in the oratory of the proponents of reform; it appears to have been a genuine concern with many. The understanding that the rise of industrialism was perverting the American dream and that corrective measures were needed if the promise of the Declaration of Independence was to be kept achievable also dwelled in numerous minds.

There surely were less lofty stimuli as well. Whether the Hofstadterian notion of status fear really played a significant role is difficult to decide. A prosopographical study would probably reveal that few of the reform activists had, in that sense, much status to lose, although the specter of looming social unrest occasionally entered their rhetoric. On a more mundane level, however, the intent to use welfare advocacy as a vehicle for different political pursuits, as well as the wish to secure bureaucratic positions or influence, were indeed incentives significant enough with some of the proponents of reform to deserve mention here.

Obviously one must distinguish between those who advocated the implementation of remedial measures and those who wielded the power to effect this implementation. With regard to the latter, on the face of it the evidence presented could be taken by some to suggest, as perhaps most notably Piven/Cloward have done, that relief measures expand in times of mass unemployment for purposes of social control (in the sense in which the "new social history" uses this expression) rather than for any other important reason.[4] The second part of this argument – that relief performance contracts during spans of prosperity so as to enforce work – cannot be observed in our period for lack of any significant government measures before 1933 to be reduced; but one can maintain that government *interest* in providing such measures in fact behaved in a cyclical pattern.

At further glance one may wonder, however, whether the social control explanation does full justice to the development described in this book. Even if one acknowledges "the economic and political functions of relief-giving,"[5] it appears that governmental concern was not just ebbing and flowing in quantitative terms, but that qualitative changes of a one-directional nature took place. Governmental attitudes, on both the state and federal levels, were very different in the depression of 1921 than in the 1890s, and they had again changed enormously by the early 1930s.

It is of course possible to argue that the involvement of senior governments – this constituted the major shift – merely meant that the latter took over the control functions that had formerly been the preserve of lower level or private institutions, and that the effect remained the same. But this view sidetracks the essential fact that the primary role of unemployment reform, as seen by the commanding majority of those who advanced it, was not to secure control of the masses but to safeguard, through the inclusion of a disadvantaged segment of industrialized society,

4 Frances Fox Piven and Richard A. Cloward, *Regulating the Poor: The Functions of Public Welfare* (New York: Pantheon Books, 1971). See also idem, *Poor People's Movements: Why They Succeed, How They Fail* (New York: Pantheon Books, 1977). A similar argument is put forth by Henry L. Allen, "A Radical Critique of Federal Work and Manpower Programs, 1933–1974," in Betty Reid Mandell, ed., *Welfare in America: Controlling the "Dangerous Classes"* (Englewood Cliffs, N.J.: Prentice-Hall, 1975), 23–38. For a critical discussion of the thesis advanced by Piven/Cloward see the articles by John K. Alexander, Raymond A. Mohl, Muriel W. Pumphrey and Ralph E. Pumphrey, W. Andrew Achenbaum, and James Leiby in Walter I. Trattner, ed., *Social Welfare or Social Control? Some Historical Reflections on Regulating the Poor* (Knoxville: University of Kentucky Press, 1983), and the response of Piven/Fox ibid., 114–45. See also David A. Rochefort, "Progressive and Social Control Perspectives on Social Welfare," *Social Service Review* 55:4 (Dec. 1981), 568–92. More positive is Michael B. Katz, *Poverty and Policy in American History* (New York: Academic Press, 1983), 230–35. The argument by Gaston V. Rimlinger, "Welfare Policy and Economic Development: A Comparative Historical Perspective," *Journal of Economic History* 26:4 (Dec. 1966), 556–71, repeated in idem, *Welfare Policy and Industrialization in Europe, America, and Russia* (New York: Wiley, 1971), 337–38 that welfare measures for workers were adopted when labor became scarcer, appears difficult to sustain with regard to the development of American unemployment policies before the New Deal.

5 Piven and Cloward, *Regulating the Poor*, xvi.

the latter's continued functioning for the benefit of the whole. The story is not really one of the oppressors seeking ways to keep the oppressed in line. The final, factual acknowledgement of a governmental obligation to care for the unemployed represented rather the recognition by the leading political forces – and this implicitly includes, in our case, general public opinion as well as the bureaucracy – that a modern, increasingly integrated society cannot operate according to superannuated principles. It is the inception and growth of this insight upon which our interest has to focus. If this organizational explanation largely excludes the parts of villains and victims from the piece, it does not deny that the advent of governmental unemployment care happened in conjunction with, and at the cost of, plenty of human suffering, nor that the mass of the unemployed had but little say in the matter; it seeks to demonstrate that a development took place whose purpose transcended the narrow interest of any one segment of the population.

The lengthy and inconstant course of unemployment reform in the United States was obviously an intrinsic part of the broader adaptation process through which American society adjusted to life under industrial conditions. The shift of responsibility for the care of the disadvantaged from the local to the governmental level seems to have been characteristic of this process, reflecting the increasing integration of the social components. Unemployment reform largely paralleled the related quests for workmen's compensation, for legislation on wages, hours, or child labor, for public health programs and old age provision. It shared with them at the outset the lack of a clear understanding of the precise way to be pursued or the chances of success. It suffered, as some of the other reforms did, from the constitutional uncertainty characteristic of the transition to the industrial age. Many of the people who promoted the other reforms, or opposed them, were also involved in the unemployment cause.

Among these kindred concerns, the challenge posed by unemployment was in a way the social problem most genuinely industrial. Accidents at the workplace may have shared some of this genuineness, but the trouble they caused easily ceded precedence to joblessness in terms of sheer numerical magnitude. Because the difficulty was a product of the unfolding industrial age, it is not surprising that from the beginning in the decades before the turn of the century the quest for solutions was to a large degree, and perhaps even chiefly so, motivated by intentions germane to that period. Humanitarianism and the desire to ensure social stability may be found in any era. A reading of the evidence shows, however, that

that most potent of progressive urges, the will to arrange things in a rational and efficient way, conspicuously permeated, and often dominated, the reform proponents' advocacy. Specifically, the loss that involuntary idleness means to economic productivity and the deterioration of character it wreaks upon manpower, therewith lowering the latter's future potential, were constant themes in the reformers' pleadings. This fact not only reveals the reformers' own thinking, if it really does that, but perhaps more important is the necessary conclusion that they would not have expressed themselves in such terms had they not believed that the public at large, and politicians as well as bureaucrats in particular, might respond positively to the proposition that order should be brought into a chaotic situation. If it soon seemed reasonable to eliminate waste on the shop floor and streamline the production process through "scientific" management, it appeared equally reasonable and progressive to ensure that unemployed members of society be kept in good standing. The profit would be society's as well as theirs.

This process of societal reorganization with the goal of integrating the unemployed was clearly not finished with what is commonly regarded as the end of the Progressive Era. Much necessary spadework had indeed been accomplished by the American entry into World War I, most significantly concerning the delineation of the problem and the conception of the most useful remedial approaches. The war, however, did not effectively stifle the ameliorative impetus, but rather furnished two essential ingredients of further development. The widespread acceptance of governmental social action during the emergency of the armed conflict set a precedent for similar activities in different, but equally taxing circumstances. Moreover, the federal government's assumption of a leading role in this respect implicitly acknowledged that social problems increasingly transcended state lines.

Because the war did not effect a lasting change in the material conditions that had earlier produced the quest for unemployment reform, the postwar decade continued to witness reform endeavors, in many instances by people who had been active in this area before the war. "Intellectual progressivism," Arthur S. Link has noted, "not only survived in the 1920's but actually flourished in many fields."[6] The consequence

---

6 Arthur S. Link, "What Happened to the Progressive Movement in the 1920's?" *American Historical Review* 64:4 (July 1959), 844. Link stresses the need to investigate the growth of welfare activities during the period. Ibid., 849; 851.

in our context was a growing appreciation of the demands of the political environment as well as considerable refinement and augmentation of the existing intelligence regarding remedial procedures. It is true that few new ideas appeared, a fact that proved the thoroughness of the prewar investigation; but much debate and some tenacious legislative exertion rendered the period one of reform-oriented growth rather than stagnation or regression.

When startlingly strong joblessness occurred in the winter of 1927–28 as a precursor of the Depression, a lean and well-reasoned reform program was ready as a result of the diligent work done in the previous years. It was in the crucible of the first Depression years that this concept underwent the ultimate test. The challenge of pervasive and large-scale unemployment gauged the practical usefulness and political viability of its components. As a result, by the end of Hoover's presidential term the challenge that unemployment in American industrial society constituted was clearly understood. The need for substantial government action was widely recognized, and so was the obligation of the federal government to assume a leadership role in this respect. It had also become evident which measures held the most promise and in what form implementation should be ventured. Unemployment reform had reached the stage of maturity and could provide the New Deal with a workable blueprint.

In view of the historical and contemporary relevance of unemployment, it is somewhat surprising that only a few inquiries have been conducted into the subject matter of this book. The place of unemployment reform within the general movement toward the welfare state has long been recognized.[7] But there is an astonishing scarcity of specific studies. About the only older treatments deserving mention in this respect are Irwin Yellowitz's seminal article in *Labor History* (1968), the pertinent chapter in Roy Lubove's book on the advent of social security (1968), and Daniel Nelson's very helpful examination of the adoption of unemployment insurance, published in 1969.[8] These works grew out of the decade that

7 See for instance Robert H. Bremner, *From the Depths: The Discovery of Poverty in the United States* (New York: New York University Press, 1956), 73–74; 134–35; 160–61; Clarke A. Chambers, *Seedtime of Reform: American Social Service and Social Action 1918–1933* (Minneapolis: University of Minnesota Press, 1963), 143–46; 170–250.
8 The paucity of unemployment reform studies is paralleled by a general lack of historical investigations of unemployment as such, which has mostly left the field, in Keyssar's words, "to ahistorical social science." Alexander Keyssar, "Unemployment before and after the Great Depression," *Social Research* 54:2 (Summer 1987), 201. – Irwin Yellowitz, "The Origins of Unemployment Reform in the United States," *Labor History* 9:3 (Fall

witnessed the "War on Poverty." Perhaps because of the abatement of reform enthusiasm in the following years, no immediate sequels were forthcoming. It was only in 1978 that John A. Garraty again drew attention to the historical importance of joblessness, providing useful background with his survey of the ways in which different societies over the ages perceived and dealt with the phenomenon.[9] Different in approach, offering a view of unemployment "from the bottom up," is Alexander Keyssar's doctoral dissertation, published in revised form in 1986; it investigates in considerable detail the new unemployment and its social repercussions in one American state.[10] Another dissertation, by Jeffrey Singleton, makes an effort to pull together the relief measures of the early 1930s, but it ignores any developments preceding the Great Depression.[11] Similarly restricted in its time frame, though more circumspect in other regards, is William R. Brock's treatment of welfare in the New Deal, which has a few early chapters on the preceding years.[12]

Three Cheers for the Unemployed reflects this state of affairs. There was, of course, no reason to cover at length areas that have already received adequate treatment elsewhere. The development of unemployment insurance legislation and some aspects of the relief efforts of the early 1930s are therefore only outlined, although in given instances supplementary detail is furnished. In principle, the investigation relies throughout upon primary materials. As a consequence, much of this book is exploratory

1968), 338–60. This study is somewhat supplemented, but not superseded, by Peter Seixas, "Unemployment as a 'Problem of Industry' in Early-Twentieth-Century New York," *Social Research* 54:2 (Summer 1987), 403–30. – Roy Lubove, *The Struggle for Social Security 1900–1935* (Cambridge, Mass.: Harvard University Press, 1968), 144–74; Daniel Nelson, *Unemployment Insurance: The American Experience 1915–1935* (Madison: University of Wisconsin Press, 1969). [– is used throughout to indicate a new reference.]

9 John A. Garraty, *Unemployment in History: Economic Thought and Public Policy* (New York: Harper & Row, 1978).

10 Alexander Keyssar, *Out of Work: The First Century of Unemployment in Massachusetts* (New York: Cambridge University Press, 1986).

11 Jeffrey C. Singleton, "Unemployment Relief and the Welfare State: 1930–1935" (Boston University Ph.D., 1987).

12 William R. Brock, *Welfare, Democracy, and the New Deal* (Cambridge, Engl.: Cambridge University Press, 1988). To these works may be added some of the author's [Sautter's] own articles, notably Udo Sautter, "North American Labor Agencies before World War One: A Cure for Unemployment?" *Labor History* 24:3 (Summer 1983), 366–93; idem, "Unemployment and Government: American Labour Exchange before the New Deal," *Histoire Sociale – Social History* 18:36 (Nov. 1985), 335–58; idem, "Government and Unemployment: The Use of Public Works before the New Deal," *Journal of American History* 73:1 (June 1986), 59–86.

in nature, and it raises perhaps more questions than it offers answers. Among the important problems that will need further examination and reflection are the ones about the influence of the environment upon the inception and growth of unemployment reform. To what extent did changing conceptions of the nature of the state influence the reform movement? What was the relationship of unemployment reform to other reform quests? To what degree did the latter's success or failure affect it, and vice versa? What was the influence of specific local or regional conditions? It seems logical that heavily industrialized Massachusetts played a guiding role, at least initially, but why did Ohio move more quickly than Pennsylvania? If the degree of industrialization was not necessarily the most powerful determinant, what other elements have to be considered? Was the reform tradition of a state a significant factor? The political constellation? The presence or absence of personalities with leadership qualities? The relative or absolute number of unemployed? Was the overrepresentation of rural areas in many state legislatures a substantial obstacle to reform? Was the latter's progress expedited or hindered by the federative character of the nation's constitution? What was the composition of the coalitions that formed in Congress for and against the reformers? What role did the strength of the opposing camp play? What were its true motivations? To such questions the story in the following pages, which basically constitutes a first survey of the field, can all too often propose tentative answers at best, if any at all. Many further studies have to be undertaken, especially about the local and regional detail, before firm opinions can be ventured.

The same holds true with regard to considerations of the genesis of the governmental response. How did administrations on the state and federal levels really arrive at the positions they took? Governmental actions and reactions obviously depended not only upon the disposition of politicians but also on the cooperation of bureaucratic individuals as well as on the structures of government. Did bureaucrats enjoy a degree of autonomy in their actions? If yes, to what ends did they use their discretionary power? Were they subject to what has recently been called "regime imperatives," meaning economic market place pressures?[13] What role did

---

13 For the evolution and meaning of the term "regime imperatives" see Ellis W. Hawley, "Social Policy and the Liberal State in Twentieth Century America," in Donald T. Critchlow and Ellis W. Hawley, *Federal Social Policy: The Historical Dimension* (University Park: Pennsylvania State University Press, 1988), 117–39, in particular 123–25. See

patronage-thinking play? What were the governmental structures like? Did the process of policy formulation influence the result; in other words, did similar processes beget similar responses? Moreover, did the reform drive conversely influence the governmental set-up? If yes, what did this mean for unemployment reform?

Another set of intriguing questions, ones that could not be broached at all in this book, concerns the international dimension. A quick look abroad suggests that many other comparable countries did experience a similar development. Not only did unemployment reform advance in Great Britain, Belgium, France, Germany, and various other nations during roughly the same decades, but the outcome was most often essentially the same as in the United States. Although some cross-fertilization of ideas occurred, it can by no means be claimed that foreign influences were strong enough to push, or even only to guide, the American development toward its eventual goal. The converse also seems to be true. Can one conclude that industrial growth, at least in societies organized along Western principles, was prone to give rise in these societies to analogous unemployment problems, and that there was some inherent necessity about the kind of solutions that were sought and ultimately adopted? Which were the constants, which the variables of this process? To what degree were the political institutions, the "political culture" of individual states, determinants? Do the differences in process and result really matter much? In other words, is there room for an exceptionalist view that emphasizes American distinctiveness? There do not seem to be any comparative studies as yet that include the American unemployment reform experience in a substantial way, although their desirability is obvious.[14]

also Gerald N. Grob, "Reflections on the History of Social Policy in America," *Reviews in American History* 7:3 (Sept. 1979), 293–306.

14 The classical statement of the comparative problem in general is Asa Briggs, "The Welfare State in Historical Perspective," *European Journal of Sociology* 2:2 (1961), 221–58. More distinctly written from a social science perspective are the articles in Peter Flora and Arnold J. Heidenheimer, eds., *The Development of Welfare States in Europe and America* (New Brunswick: Transaction Books, 1981); and Theda Skocpol and John Ikenberry, "The Political Formation of the American Welfare State in Historical and Comparative Perspective," *Comparative Social Research* 6 (1983), 87–148. An interesting and testworthy model for comparative analysis is proposed in Hawley, "Social Policy and the Liberal State," 125–26. Equally suggestive is James T. Patterson, "Comparative Welfare History: Britain and the United States, 1930–1945," in Wilbur J. Cohen, ed., *The Roosevelt New Deal: A Program Assessment Fifty Years After* ([Richmond:] Virginia Commonwealth University, 1986), 125–43. See also Saundra K. Schneider, "The

At any rate, by the mid-1930s, not only in most industrial countries abroad, but very much in the United States as well, unemployment reform had reached maturity in the sense that large, increasing segments of the working population could feel confident that the specter of joblessness was losing its dreadfulness. The significant point, for workers and in historical perspective, was not so much that specific remedies had been developed. The shape of the available measures would clearly change over time. Of essential importance was the fact that the insufficiency of the average individual's resources to overcome unemployment had been recognized, that government had been singled out as the sole agency possessing the ability to come to the rescue, and that a governmental obligation to do so had been established.

Superficial observation on the eve of the New Deal might still perceive that nothing, except perhaps a few decibels, had changed from the days when the Chicago welfare crowd gave three cheers to the unfortunate unemployed. But this impression was misleading. The difference was that the cheering now came from the government side, indicating the latter's readiness for action. In America, the reform-minded had had to fight a long, arduous, and not always promising struggle to achieve this goal. Learning about the various theaters of operations in which these contests took place, and understanding the protagonists' maneuvers as well as their and the bystanders' motivations, can take us a good step further in the quest to comprehend the steps, and perhaps the reasons, that led to what is commonly called the twentieth-century welfare state.

Evolution of the Modern Welfare State: A Comparative Analysis of the Development of Social Welfare Programs in the United States, Canada, and Western Europe" (State University of New York at Binghampton Ph.D., 1980), in particular 187–88; 205–208; 234–38.

2. Perceiving the problem: 1870s to the entry into World War I

The generation before the outbreak of World War I experienced what has been called "the discovery of unemployment."[1] Joblessness had certainly existed earlier but had been perceived in a different way. In American society throughout most of the nineteenth century the conviction had prevailed that natural laws cannot be tampered with and that consequently government action in the social sphere would ultimately fail. The belief in the merits of competition postulated the individual's self-reliance. By the time of the American entry into the world war, however, a perceptible change had occurred. Although laissez-faire tenets still very much informed governmental behavior toward the jobless, their validity was increasingly being challenged. Advancing industrialization and the concomitant spells of mass unemployment induced reform-oriented thinkers and progressive activists to question the justification of administrative reserve. They laid the seed for future governmental involvement by articulating the problem, devising possible solutions, and broadcasting the need for action. Palpable successes were few as yet, but there could be no doubt that by 1916 a broad public had become acquainted with the issue and governments had grown uneasy about their traditional inertia.

I   Growing awareness

A new perspective

According to preindustrial convictions, reflected in adherence to the principles of the English Poor Law of 1601 and its modification in 1834, the

---

1 Thus the title of a chapter in John A. Garraty, *Unemployment in History: Economic Thought and Public Policy* (New York: Harper & Row, 1978), 102–28. The phrase is also used by Paul T. Ringenbach, *Tramps and Reformers 1873–1916: The Discovery of Unemployment in New York* (Westport: Greenwood Press, 1973).

14

individual was responsible for his own welfare. It was understood that work was available to those who looked for it, and idleness of employable persons was caused by character deficiencies. In the view of classical economists and Social Darwinists, lack of employment was thus the result of intemperance, ignorance, laziness, incompetence, or unwillingness or incapacity to do the work that was waiting to be done.[2]

Much of the economic thinking of the nineteenth century supported this attitude. Economist Henry C. Carey in his *Principles of Social Science* (1858–59) gave what may be called an early American theory of unemployment. Refuting Malthus's contention that population can outstrip the means of subsistence, he claimed that man's reproductive power "diminishes as his various faculties are more and more stimulated into action – as employments become more diversified – as the societary action becomes more rapid." In Carey's view, the accelerating "rapidity of circulation" of societary action produced a continuity of motion without uncomfortable ups and downs, and the "unceasing waste of labor" characteristic of early society was replaced by an equal distribution of employment throughout the year. The idea that increased industrial activity would ultimately produce a harmonious arrangement could still be found four decades later in the 1890 edition of Francis Bowen's *American Political Economy*. Harking back to Adam Smith, he asserted that high wages compensated for irregularity of employment, rendering remedial action unnecessary. This kind of thinking was propped up, if not prompted, by the widely accepted view that a certain amount of unemployment was not only inevitable, but actually necessary for the normal functioning of the economy; it was this "reserve army" of the unemployed that in good times allowed the boosting of economic output beyond average levels.[3]

The classical understanding postulated that a person impecunious as a result of joblessness had to be classified with the poor at large. Private charity and the aid of local authorities, grudgingly given and as a rule

2 Sidney Fine, *Laissez Faire and the General-Welfare State: A Study of Conflict in American Thought 1865–1901* (Ann Arbor: University of Michigan Press, 1956), 62.
3 H. C. Carey, *Principles of Social Science.* 3 Vols. (Philadelphia: Lippincott, 1858–65), vol. III, 28; in general 17–232; 308; Francis Bowen, *American Political Economy, Including Strictures on the Management of the Currency and the Finances since 1861* (New York: Scribner's, 1890), 192–93. Bowen was economics professor at Harvard University. For a discussion of the concept of the reserve army, Marxian and other, see Garraty, *Unemployment in History*, 104–06. See also Alexander Keyssar, *Out of Work: The First Century of Unemployment in Massachusetts* (Cambridge: Cambridge University Press, 1986), 69–76.

wholly inadequate, were the most that those out of work could count upon. There was no entitlement to even this kind of help. Francis Wayland, president of Brown University and a distinguished economist, in 1840 attacked the Poor Laws as contrary to the fundamental principles of government, refuting any notion that "the rich are under obligation to support the poor." His younger Harvard colleague J. Laurence Laughlin more than a generation later asserted that governmental help lowered self-respect and tended "to make all individual energy weak and flabby, because it teaches one to rely on an outside power." While regretting the depression unemployment of the 1890s, New York Governor Roswell P. Flower emphatically felt that "it is not the province of the government to support the people." This persuasion held that all that society should really do was to try and change the individual's deficient habits. By inculcating religion, morality, sobriety, and industry into the presumed loafer, malign influences could be eliminated and betterment attained.[4]

Even people who had second thoughts about some aspects of the classical doctrine contested the value of governmental assistance. Francis A. Walker, a noted teacher at the Massachusetts Institute of Technology and first president of the American Economic Association, although doubtful of the ability of the worker to obtain justice for himself in an unregulated economy, nevertheless questioned the appropriateness of substantial state action on the worker's behalf. Carroll D. Wright, first federal commissioner of labor and a pioneer of labor reform, still held that the prevalent cause of poverty was a lack of personal competence. His interest was less the unemployed worker than the unenlightened one, and he gave little attention to the personal and social problems arising from joblessness.[5]

Under the impact of industrialization in the decades around the turn of the century, however, a tendency to reappraise the place of the individual in society made itself felt. The organizational revolution in business,

4 Francis Wayland, *The Elements of Political Economy* (Boston: Gould, Kendall, Lincoln, 1840), 127; J. Laurence Laughlin, *The Elements of Political Economy: With Some Applications to Questions of the Day* (New York: Appleton, 1887), 266. Flower is quoted in Samuel Rezneck, "Unemployment, Unrest, and Relief in the United States during the Depression of 1893–97," *Journal of Political Economy* 61:4 (Aug. 1953), 332. – Walter I. Trattner, *From Poor Law to Welfare State: A History of Social Welfare in America* (New York: Free Press, 1974), 63.

5 Francis A. Walker, *Political Economy*. 3d ed. (New York: Holt, 1888), 363; James Leiby, *Carroll Wright and Labor Reform: The Origin of Labor Statistics* (Cambridge, Mass.: Harvard University Press, 1960), 200.

creating behemoths that dwarfed the employee and reduced him to practical anonymity, engendered deepening reflection. Insightful observers came to realize the growing interdependence of the varied social components. As a result, "a more conscious sense of individual helplessness," as Robert Wiebe has expressed it, began to spread. This reevaluation, equally observable in the fields of sociology and psychology, meant with regard to the interpretation of poverty that the old hostility toward pauperism gradually gave way to an acknowledgment of the existence of undeserved want. As Robert H. Bremner has observed, "unemployment, low wages, and high living costs took the central place [formerly] assigned to idleness, improvidence, and intemperance in the moralistic view of the problem."[6]

The revision of ingrained beliefs did not come overnight. It was the increasingly widespread unemployment during economic downturns in the decades after the Civil War that caused the beginning of reorientation. During the preceding two generations, an important shift had occurred in the system of labor relations. Whereas at the threshold of the nineteenth century most of the free manpower had been self-employed on the farm or in the trades, by the last decades of the century over half of the labor force depended upon wage employment. In Massachusetts, at least 70 percent of the males and most working females were wage or salary earners by 1875. The economic downturn of the 1870s thus created for the first time the national specter of large groups of workers deprived of their means of livelihood. Continuously strong immigration, peaking occasionally when cyclical unemployment reached higher levels, appears to have accounted for much of the excess labor thereafter.[7]

6 Robert H. Wiebe, *The Search for Order 1877–1920* (New York: Hill and Wang, 1967), 187; Richard Hofstadter, *Social Darwinism in American Thought* (Boston: Beacon Press, 1955), 156–61. For the beginning of mass unemployment see also Keyssar, *Out of Work*, 7; 35–38. – Robert H. Bremner, *From the Depths: The Discovery of Poverty in the United States* (New York: New York University Press, 1956), 134. See also John H. Ehrenreich, *The Altruistic Imagination: A History of Social Work and Social Policy in the United States* (Ithaca: Cornell University Press, 1985), 62–63. The emerging drive for reform regarding social ills other than unemployment is described in Hace Sorel Tishler, *Self-reliance and Social Security 1870–1917* (Port Washington: Kennikat Press, 1971). For a good case study of the emergence of a new, more concerned civic mood in general see David P. Thelen, *The New Citizenship: Origins of Progressivism in Wisconsin, 1885–1900* (Columbia, Mo.: University of Missouri Press, 1972).
7 David M. Gordon, Richard Edwards, and Michael Reich, *Segmented Work, Divided Workers: The Historical Transformation of Labor in the United States* (Cambridge: Cambridge University Press, 1982), 53; 104; 230; 252, note 2. The part of the labor force employed

Over time, acceptance of the new view inexorably gained momentum. Shortly after the panic of the mid-1870s, David A. Wells, a popular writer on natural sciences and economics, professed his belief that the chief cause of unemployment was technological improvement. Henry George wrote of "the enforced idleness of large numbers of would-be producers, which wastes the productive force of advanced communities." The insight that joblessness did not necessarily spring from a character defect soon spread beyond the circle of visionaries. Sixty percent of his clientele, the superintendent of the New York (State) Free Employment Bureau wrote in 1896, "are willing and able to work, but are unemployed simply because 'No man hath hired them.' " After the turn of the century, this understanding became official when the federal Industrial Commission acknowledged in 1902 that the "causes of unemployment are as varied as the entire industrial and social conditions of the people" and proposed to distinguish between "personal, climatic [i.e. seasonal], and industrial causes."[8]

Thus the new understanding did not exclude the notion that human insufficiency might play a part in bringing about want and destitution, but it was nevertheless based upon the conviction that social rather than individual conditions were the primary causes of poverty. Prominent social worker Robert Hunter had no doubts that unemployment was commonly brought about by "the brutal power of the economic forces." In his well-received book *Misery and Its Causes* (1909), Edward T. Devine, Schiff Professor of Social Economy at Columbia University and general secretary of the New York (City) Charity Organization Society (COS), asserted that misery, rather than being caused by moral defects, "is economic, the result of maladjustment." On the eve of World War I this notion had become a generally accepted tenet in reform circles. Julia E. Johnsen, after surveying much of the pertinent literature, summed it up by stating

in agriculture sank from 53% in 1870 to 43% in 1890 and to 31% in 1910. U.S. Bureau of the Census, *Historical Statistics of the United States, Colonial Times to 1970: Bicentennial Edition, Part 1* (Washington: G.P.O., 1975), 139. – Keyssar, *Out of Work*, 16.

8 David A. Wells, "How Shall the Nation Regain Prosperity?" *North American Review* 125:256 (July-Aug. 1877), 125–26; Henry George, *Progress and Poverty: An Inquiry into the Cause of Industrial Depressions and of Increase of Want with Increase of Wealth: The Remedy* (New York: Sterling, 1879), 259. See also similarly T. V. Powderly, "The Army of Unemployed," in George E. McNeill, ed., *The Labor Movement: The Problem of Today* (Boston: Bridgman, 1887), 576. See also Edward Bellamy's testimony in Massachusetts. Board to Investigate the Subject of the Unemployed, *Report*. 5 Vols. (Boston: Wright and Potter, 1895), vol. III, 110. – New York (State). Bureau of Statistics of Labor, *Report, 1897*, 1027; U.S. Congress. House, *Final Report of the Industrial Commission*. H.Doc. 380, 57 Cong., 1 sess. (1902), vol. XIX, 746.

that the causes of unemployment were to be found in the mass character of industrialized society. "The multiplication of large capitalized establishments and the consequent reduction of independent industrial effort," she maintained, "have made the welfare of those without assured means of support depend upon every economic change in the nation, state, municipality, and private business."[9]

The shift from insistence on the individual's responsibility to a recognition of the influence of environmental forces was paralleled by a change in the prevailing concept of the nature of labor. Much of the earlier lack of public concern was due to a view that emphasized labor's economic function. "We must take labor abstractly," Wright wrote on one occasion, meaning that it had to be considered as essentially a commodity. Like other commodities it was "governed by the imperishable laws of demand and supply," as the *Watchman and Reflector* put it in 1874, asking, "what is labor but a matter of barter and sale?"[10]

Gradually, however, demands for a recognition of the individuality of the worker began to be voiced. Christian reformers played a major role in stressing the inherent human value of the laborer. Social gospelers argued that the employee should not be considered merchandise from which to make a profit, but should be understood to be a child of God whose welfare must be a constant concern. "The labor of the nation is the life of the nation," Congregational minister Washington Gladden exhorted the American public in 1886 from Columbus, Ohio, wondering whether labor should be regarded as "a commodity to be bought in the cheapest market and sold in the dearest?" John R. Commons, then a young professor of economics at Indiana University and secretary of

---

9 Robert Hunter, *Poverty: Social Conscience in the Progressive Era* (New York: Harper & Row, 1965), 27; 318. The original edition appeared in 1904. – Edward T. Devine, *Misery and Its Causes* (New York: Macmillan, [1909] 1913), 11. For a similar, but more tentative statement see his earlier *The Principles of Relief* (New York: Macmillan, 1904), 151–53; 161. On Devine's thought in general see Sandra Sidford Cornelius, "Edward Thomas Devine 1867–1948: A Pivotal Figure in the Transition from Practical Philanthropy to Social Work" (Bryn Mawr Ph.D., 1976). A brief appreciation of Devine's role in unemployment reform can be found in Peter Seixas, "Unemployment as a 'Problem of Industry' in Early-Twentieth-Century New York," *Social Research* 54:2 (Summer 1987), 408–16. The adoption of an environment-oriented viewpoint in the emerging social work profession is described in Clarke A. Chambers and Andrea Hinding, "Charity Workers, the Settlements, and the Poor," *Social Casework* 49:2 (Feb. 1968), 96–101. – Julia E. Johnsen, ed., "Introduction," in idem, *Selected Articles on Unemployment* (White Plains, N.Y.: Wilson, 1915), 1–2.

10 Wright is quoted in Leiby, *Carroll Wright*, 200; *Watchman and Reflector* is quoted in Henry F. May, *Protestant Churches and Industrial America* (New York: Harper, 1949), 55.

Wisconsin sociologist Richard T. Ely's newly formed American Institute of Christian Sociology, asserted that "involuntary idleness and irregular employment are the Antichrist of today." In his plea for a "living wage," accepted as a doctoral thesis at the Catholic University of America, budding social reformer Father John A. Ryan affirmed the existence of a generic right of the laborer to a decent livelihood, which he saw "based upon his intrinsic worth as a person, and on the sacredness of those needs that are essential to the reasonable development of personality." This ethical emphasis was echoed in labor circles, where the "moral centrality of work" found increasing avouchment, and where quests for recognition of the "dignity of labor" and the worth of those who did the world's "real" work began to be common.[11]

The new appreciation of the value of labor brought with it the realization that idleness, when recognized as involuntary, needed a new name. It was thus no mere coincidence that the very word "unemployment," as Garraty has pointed out, came into use in the late 1880s, supplanting terms like "non-employment" or "lack of employment." The status of joblessness obviously acquired a new quality. The same change occurred with regard to designations of the persons involved. "The term *unemployed* as used today is a new term in our economic vocabulary," the chairman of the Massachusetts Board to Investigate the Subject of the Unemployed wrote in 1894, affirming that it corresponded "to new conditions." More than two decades later, Frederick C. Mills, formerly Garth Fellow in Eco-

---

11 Charles Howard Hopkins, *The Rise of the Social Gospel in American Protestantism 1865–1915* (New Haven: Yale University Press, 1940), 93; Washington Gladden, *Applied Christianity: Moral Aspects of Social Questions* (Boston: Houghton Mifflin, 1886), 52; John R. Commons, "The Church and the Problem of Poverty in Cities," *Charities Review* 2:7 (May 1893), 351. On Commons' social thought during this period see Mary O. Furner, *Advocacy & Objectivity: A Crisis in the Professionalization of American Social Science, 1865–1905* (Lexington: University Press of Kentucky, 1975), 198–204. The larger picture of the influence of social Christianity on social thinking is sketched in David B. Danbom, *"The World of Hope": Progressives and the Struggle for an Ethical Public Life* (Philadelphia: Temple University Press, 1987), 63–111. See also the still-valuable remarks by Harold Underwood Faulkner, *The Quest for Social Justice 1898–1914* (New York: Macmillan, 1931), 219–28. – John A. Ryan, *A Living Wage: Its Ethical and Economic Aspects* (New York: Macmillan, 1906), 324. For the background of Ryan's argument see Francis L. Broderick, *Right Reverend New Dealer John A. Ryan* (New York: Macmillan, 1963), 39–45. See also in this context Daniel T. Rodgers, *The Work Ethic in Industrial America 1850–1920* (Chicago: University of Chicago Press, 1974), 174; 181. - Nell Irvin Painter, *Standing at Armageddon: The United States, 1877–1919* (New York: Norton, 1987), 173; 186.

nomics at Columbia University, could still write that "until quite recently the blanket terms for the unemployed of this country have been 'tramp' and 'vagrant.' " Language thus recognized the change of perspective. Adoption of the new environmental viewpoint shifted the emphasis of humanitarian reform from the cold dispensation of charity to an examination and treatment of the social origins of poverty.[12]

Society's task

If society caused distress, it was society's task to alleviate it. In 1906, Devine, then president of the National Conference of Charities and Correction (NCCC), gave clear expression to this altered concept when he declared that modern philanthropy must seek out and strike effectively "at those particular causes of dependence and intolerable living conditions which are beyond the control of the individuals whom they injure and whom they too often destroy." Humanitarianism alone, of course, did not fully account for the change in outlook. It was mainly the American middle class that shrank from the principle of competition that had been glorified during the preceding decades, and it instigated the search for remedies that were now recognized as necessary for the cure of social ills.[13]

Thus, another of the reformers' incentives appears to have been the desire for social control. As Tamara Hareven has put it, they felt that society had to choose between "child labor reform or juvenile delinquency, adequate housing or tuberculosis, the protection of women workers or prostitution, humane working conditions or crime." The memory of the social upheavals of the eighties and nineties, Samuel P. Hays has noted, hung "like a pall over the minds of the articulate public," and alleviating the distress of "the other half" could ensure the maintenance of the existing order. Henry R. Seager, professor of political economy at Columbia University, was a prominent and outspoken member of the charity

---

12 Garraty, *Unemployment in History*, 109, note 12; Davis R. Dewey, "Irregularity of Employment," in American Economic Association, *Publications* 9:5–6 (1894), 528. For an early attempt to understand the phenomenon of unemployment see Powderly, "The Army of Unemployed," 575–84. – Frederick C. Mills, *Contemporary Theories of Unemployment and of Unemployment Relief* (New York: Longmans, Green, 1917), 129; Samuel P. Hays, *The Response to Industrialism 1885–1914* (Chicago: University of Chicago Press, 1957), 79.

13 Edward T. Devine, "The Dominant Note of the Modern Philanthropy," NCCC, *Proceedings 1906* (n.p., n.d.), 3; Richard Hofstadter, *Social Darwinism in American Thought* (Boston: Beacon, rev. ed. 1955), 202.

scene in New York. "More good men," he wrote in his *Social Insurance* (1910), the first American book to deal extensively with unemployment, "have been transformed into embittered advocates of social revolution by unemployment than by any other single cause." If nothing appropriate was done, Representative H. Robert Fowler (D-Illinois) told his colleagues in Congress a few years later, "a large military force [will have] to subdue the unemployed and hold them in proper check to prevent revolution."[14]

Although there can be little question regarding the genuineness of this concern about the stability of the existing social order, it is possible to discern still another motivation. The thought of a society plagued by strife and waste vexed many progressive reformers. The industrial organization of the United States, Seager complained, "is wasteful, unintelligent, even chaotic." The Employers' Liability Commission, established in New York (State) in 1909 under its chairman J. Mayhew Wainwright as a result of the preceding depression, was appalled at finding the labor market "completely unorganized, unsystematized, uncentralized." Reform thus was to ensure "a frictionless operation" of society aimed at maximum returns for a minimum outlay of time and effort. This was humanitarianism in an elevated sense. "Efficient and good," Samuel Haber has remarked, "came closer to meaning the same thing in these years than in any other period of American history."[15]

Established society could apparently no longer shrink from accepting

---

14 Tamara K. Hareven, "Societal Problems," in Clarke A. Chambers, ed., *A Century of Concern 1873–1973* (Columbus: National Conference on Social Welfare, n.d.), 69; Hays, *Response to Industrialism*, 84; Henry Rogers Seager, *Social Insurance: A Program of Social Reform* (New York: Macmillan, 1910), 84. On Seager see Joseph Dorfman, *The Economic Mind in American Civilization.* 5 vols. (New York: Viking, 1959), vol. IV, 267–72. Specifically on his role in unemployment reform see Seixas, "Unemployment as a 'Problem of Industry,' " 416–21. – *CR*, 63 Cong., 3 sess., 4 March 1915, p. 834.

15 Seager, *Social Insurance*, 93. Similarly John Price Jackson, "Relation of the State to Unemployment," *ALLR* 5:2 (June 1915), 438; similarly Massachusetts. Public Employment Offices, *10th Annual Report, 1916*, 5. – New York (State). Commission to Inquire into the Question of Employers' Liability and Other Matters, *Third Report: Unemployment and Lack of Farm Labor* (Albany: J. B. Lyon, 1911), 15. See similarly Chicago. Municipal Markets Commission, *Report to the Mayor and Aldermen on a Practical Plan for Relieving Destitution and Unemployment in the City of Chicago* (Chicago: Municipal Markets Commission, 1914), 20. - Wiebe, *Search for Order*, 155–56; similarly James Gilbert, *Designing the Industrial State: The Intellectual Pursuit of Collectivism in America, 1880–1940* (Chicago: Quadrangle, 1972), 288. – Samuel Haber, *Efficiency and Uplift: Scientific Management in the Progressive Era 1890–1920* (Chicago: University of Chicago Press, 1964), ix.

the task of alleviating individual distress. The magnitude of the problem, however, more and more exceeded the capacity of private initiative and local institutions to handle it. It seemed logical to seek the help of the government. There was nothing too revolutionary in this kind of quest, as during the decades before and around the turn of the century various states had increasingly assumed responsibilities in the social sphere. Massachusetts, which at the time was the most industrialized state in the union, took the lead by creating the nation's first state board of charities in 1863 and establishing the first bureau of labor statistics in 1869.[16] Discussion concerning areas of possible social legislation picked up momentum after the Civil War. It layed the groundwork for a number of measures such as workmen's compensation (first enacted in Maryland, 1902), the ten-hour day for women (Oregon, 1903), widows' pensions (Missouri, 1911), or the Massachusetts minimum wage law of 1912. Even on the federal level some readiness to confront the social tasks of the industrial age could be discerned in the establishment of the federal Bureau of Labor (1884), of the Interstate Commerce Commission (1887), the passage of laws like the Sherman Antitrust Act (1890) and the Pure Food and Drug Act (1906), or the creation of the Children's Bureau (1912). Demands for governmental intervention on behalf of the unemployed were thus part of the greater reform movement aimed at adjusting living conditions to the exigencies of industrialization.

Voices pleading for governmental help for the jobless were increasingly heard, particularly as a result of the depression experience of the mid–1890s. Academics and social gospelers figured prominently, even though no new fully developed theory of unemployment emerged as yet. As early as 1889, the Episcopalian minister R. Heber Newton advocated government aid to cope with unemployment. Ely requested that the state assume the responsibility for public employment offices and emergency work and that it perhaps even guarantee the right to a job. A decade later, Gladden wanted the state to find creative remedies for unemployment and to remove the structural roots of destitution. Similar ideas were held by

16 On the agitation for bureaus of labor at the time see John Lombardi, *Labor's Voice in the Cabinet: A History of the Department of Labor from Its Origins to 1921* (New York: Columbia University Press, 1942), 15–43. See also Wendell D. Macdonald, "The Early History of Labor Statistics in the United States," *Labor History* 13:2 (Spring 1972), 267–78; Ewan Clague, *The Bureau of Labor Statistics* (New York: Praeger, 1968), 3–11. The prehistory of the Massachusetts Board of State Charities is described in Robert W. Kelso, *The History of Public Poor Relief in Massachusetts 1620–1920* (Boston: Houghton Mifflin, 1922), 121–42.

political economists like Henry Carter Adams or Westel W. Willoughby who wanted government at least to ensure fair competition. The sociologists Lester Frank Ward, then with the U.S. Geological Survey, and Edward A. Ross at Stanford regretted the helplessness of the unemployed, who, in Ward's words, in the "soulless struggle for existence and scramble for gain are crowded to the wall," and indicated a growing receptiveness in America for the idea of public action.[17]

Over the years the call for such intervention grew more articulate. Seager was blunt. "We need not freedom from governmental interference," he asserted in 1910, "but... an aggressive program of governmental control and regulation." Unemployment caused by trade conditions, the Wainwright Commission concluded in 1911, "is a matter with which the State should concern itself." Princeton professor William F. Willoughby, president of the AALL in 1913 and Westel's brother, saw the problem from a constitutional perspective. To him the old laissez-faire order had outlived its justification. "Fundamentally there exists throughout modern society the juristic paradox that liberty is many times sacrificed by laws conferring freedom," he told the members of his association in 1913. In his view, a reversal of legislative thinking in the direction of regulation and government intervention was necessary; the United States, being "far in the rear of most of our great competitors in respect to social legislation," ought to make increased efforts to fulfill the prime function of a constitutional government, namely "the protection of the individual against oppression and the guaranteeing to him of the fullest possible enjoyment of life." Charles F. Gettemy, director of the Massachusetts Bureau of Labor Statistics, put it more simply. Joblessness "for which the worker is in no wise to blame and of which the employer is too often the victim, while society as a whole pays the penalty in times

---

17 Fine, *Laissez Faire*, 183; Richard T. Ely, *Socialism: An Examination of Its Nature, Its Strength and Its Weakness, with Suggestions for Social Reform* (New York: Crowell, 1894), 331–33; Jacob Henry Dorn, *Washington Gladden: Prophet of the Social Gospel* ([Columbus]: Ohio State University Press, 1966), 281–82; Henry Carter Adams, "Relation of the State to Industrial Action," in idem, *Two Essays: Relation of the State to Industrial Action & Economics and Jurisprudence*, Joseph Dorfman, ed. (New York: A. M. Kelley, 1969), 90–98; Westel Woodbury Willoughby, *Social Justice: A Critical Essay* (New York: Macmillan, 1900), 304–11; Lester F. Ward, *Dynamic Sociology or Applied Social Science as Based upon Statical Sociology and the Less Complex Sciences.* 2 Vols. (New York: Appleton, 1883), vol. I, 30; Edward Alsworth Ross, *Social Control: A Survey of the Foundations of Order* (New York: Macmillan, 1901), esp. 411–31. For other voices asking for governmental action see Douglas W. Steeples, "The Panic of 1893: Contemporary Reflections and Reactions," *Mid-America* 47:3 (July 1965), 155–75.

of industrial depression," he asserted at the eve of the American entry into the world war, "has created a problem with which the state alone can successfully cope."[18]

Economic conditions transcended state lines, however. Although social matters lay traditionally within the purview of state legislation, by about 1914 the intricacy and magnitude of the unemployment question brought the "recognition of unemployment as a national problem," as Leah Hannah Feder has expressed it. In other words, many reformers arrived at the conviction that nothing short of federal intervention would be satisfactory. This opinion was even voiced in Congress. In 1914, Representative Victor A. Murdock (R-Kansas) asserted that "unemployment is a matter which no state can adequately treat," since the means of the states were "altogether insufficient to cope with a problem that is in no sense local, but national." For this reason the legislatures of California and Nevada, prompted by the experience of the harsh 1914–15 winter, addressed resolutions to Congress asking for exploration of the unemployment problem by federal authorities.[19]

The articulation and dissemination of this kind of thinking was in no small degree due to the efforts of concerned individuals writing in reform-dedicated journals and organizing in like-minded groupings. They expressed, and at the same time profited from, what John Milton Cooper, Jr., has recently called the age's "middle-class sympathy towards expressions of social discontent." The depression experience of the mid-nineties served as a kind of catalyst for the debate on unemployment. Many publications carried articles examining the causes and extent of the evil as well as on the necessity of and responsibility for remedial action – general interest or reform magazines like the *Arena*, the *Forum*, the *Nation*, or the *Atlantic Monthly*, later the *Survey* and the *New Republic*, but also learned periodicals such as the *Quarterly Journal of Economics*, the *Annals* of the American Academy of Political and Social Science, or the newly established *American Journal of Sociology*. When the economy improved, interest usually flagged, but it revived with increased vigor in periods of

---

18 Seager, *Social Insurance*, 5; New York (State). Commission to Inquire [etc.], *Third Report*, 8; W. F. Willoughby, "The Philosophy of Labor Legislation," *ALLR* 4:1 (March 1914), 40; 42; 46; Massachusetts. Public Employment Offices, *10th Annual Report, 1916*, 5.

19 Leah Hannah Feder, *Unemployment Relief in Periods of Depression: A Study of Measures Adopted in Certain American Cities, 1857 through 1922* (New York: Russell Sage Foundation, 1936), 218; *CR*, 63 Cong., 2 sess., 1 May 1914, p. 416 (Victor A. Murdock). See similarly *CR*, 63 Cong., 3 sess., 4 March 1915, p. 834 (Robert Fowler); "Unemployment," *ALLR* 5:4 (Dec. 1915), 763.

renewed joblessness. William Hard, a reformer-journalist on the staff of *Everybody's Magazine* and formerly active in the settlement movement, counted eight articles on unemployment published in important American magazines between 1900 and 1904; in the years 1905 to 1909, which included the depression year of 1908, their number jumped to sixty-four articles, of which forty discussed American conditions.[20]

These voices were still widely scattered and lacked focus. An estimable attempt at integrating various efforts and providing a kind of support unit for its advocacy, however, was made in the years preceding the war by the AALL. Following the precedent of the establishment of the International Association for Labor Legislation in Paris in 1900, some interested economists, among them Seager and Ely, founded the AALL in New York in 1906. Its originally small membership increased quickly, from 271 at the end of 1908 to 903 a year later. It was prestigious, comprising many academics, journalists, government officials, some progressive businessmen, and also a sprinkling of labor leaders. Functioning very much in the manner of older reform groupings like the National Consumers' League or the National Civil Service Reform League, the AALL, operating out of headquarters in New York, brought together reform-minded personalities; by raising funds and spending them on research, publicity work, and lobbying activities, it sought to lay the ground work for appropriate legislation. In exemplary manner it employed the techniques of the reform movements of the age, which meant, in the words of Clarke A. Chambers, to "keep on the firing line, study and agitate and propagandize, beat tactical retreats when necessary, engage in flank attacks, never for a moment surrender the initiative, and wait for the breaks."[21]

The association's original purpose, according to its constitution, was the encouragement of the study of labor conditions. But under the vigorous leadership of John B. Andrews, a Commons pupil who was made AALL executive secretary the year after completing his doctorate at the University of Wisconsin in 1908, it broadened its concerns. The asso-

20 John Milton Cooper, Jr., *Pivotal Decades: The United States 1900–1920* (New York: Norton, 1990), 83; William Hard, "Unemployment as a Coming Issue," *ALLR* 2:1 (Feb. 1912), 93.
21 AALL, *Third Annual Meeting New York, N.Y., Dec. 28–30, 1909: Proceedings, Reports, Addresses* (New York: AALL, 1910), 34; Clarke A. Chambers, *Seedtime of Reform: American Social Service and Social Action 1918–1933* (Minneapolis: University of Minnesota Press, 1963), 89.

ciation soon worked toward the implementation of workmen's compensation, minimum wage boards for men and women, and health and safety legislation. Its quarterly journal, the *ALLR*, skillfully directed from its inception in 1911 by Andrews, quickly established itself as the primary organ advocating social legislation in the United States.[22] To be able to marshall as many forces as possible for the promotion of its various causes, the AALL maintained officially a nonpartisan attitude. The direction of its endeavors naturally implied some rapport with the radical element, and socialists like insurance expert Isaac M. Rubinow or New York congressman Meyer London found the ranks of the association as well as the pages of the *ALLR* open to them. But their presence was more than balanced by the moderate majority, for which the era's label "progressive" was possibly the most fitting overall designation. Occasional animosity between members over differences of opinion do not seem to have materially affected the group's functioning.[23]

The AALL would evidently have been pleased to cooperate with organized labor in many instances. It invited union leaders to its meetings, printed their utterances, and noted union concerns in its periodical. Prom-

22 "General Session on the American Association for Labor Legislation 1907–1942: Held in Great Hall of Memorial Union," in John B. Andrews Memorial Symposium on Labor Legislation and Social Security, University of Wisconsin, 1949, *Proceedings* ([Madison], [n.d.]), 81–88; Chambers, *Seedtime of Reform*, 11–12; Irwin Yellowitz, *Labor and the Progressive Movement in New York State, 1897–1916* (Ithaca: Cornell University Press, 1965), 55–58; James Leiby, *A History of Social Welfare and Social Work in the United States* (New York: Columbia University Press, 1978), 201. Commons was the first secretary of the AALL after this position was created in December 1908. AALL, *Proceedings of the Second Annual Meeting* (Madison, 1909), 1; 12.

23 The most noteworthy example was the jealous relationship between Andrews and William M. Leiserson, the former on occasion complaining to Commons of Leiserson's "disagreeable attacks upon me" dictated by "his own selfish interest." Andrews to Commons, 13 Jan. 1915, microfilm, reel 13, Andrews Papers. See also Andrews to Fred MacKenzie, 27 Jan. 1915, ibid.; and John A. Fitch to Leiserson, 28 June 1913, Box 14, Leiserson Papers. Fitch was industry editor of the *Survey*. Rubinow was a former medical practitioner with socialist convictions who had once worked for the federal Bureau of Labor before turning insurance statistician. See on him J. Lee Kreader, "Isaac Max Rubinow: Pioneering Specialist in Social Insurance," in Frank R. Breul and Steven J. Diner, eds., *Compassion and Responsibility: Readings in the History of Social Welfare Policy in the United States* (Chicago: University of Chicago Press, 1980), 288–311; and idem, "America's Prophet for Social Security: A Biography of Isaac Max Rubinow" (University of Chicago Ph.D., 1988). For the difference between "statists" and "voluntarists" see Donald J. Murphy, "John B. Andrews, the American Association for Labor Legislation, and Unemployment Reform, 1914–1929," in Jerold E. Brown and Patrick D. Reagan, eds., *Voluntarism, Planning, and the State* (New York: Greenwood, 1988), 1–2.

inent AALL member Charles R. Henderson, a professor of sociology at the University of Chicago, admitted in private that he would love "to awaken and keep [AFL president Samuel Gompers'] interest." Some labor leaders, among them John Mitchell of the United Mine Workers, whose union significantly included unskilled as well as skilled workmen, on occasion complied. But Gompers, for one, remained suspicious of the association's advocacy of governmental action and probably also of its middle-class provenance. He generally preferred to stay aloof, persuaded that the interests of the skilled trades that he represented were better served by his own organization's exertion. This attitude of "pure and simple" unionism implicitly recognized the fact that unemployment before World War I was mainly a problem of the unskilled worker, who was not only more likely to be out of work, but also less able to pursue his interests in an organized and articulate way. Gompers' main concern in this respect was "the real menace which a body of unemployed workers constitutes to the standards of wages, working conditions, and living of those who are employed." But he did not consider the menace threatening enough to advocate anything more unorthodox than the enhancement of public construction and a shorter working day.[24]

Unemployment reform was recognized as a target meriting the attention of the AALL when the British parliament passed the National Insurance Act in late 1911, establishing the first governmental unemployment insurance system in the world. At its December 1911 annual meeting, the association held a session on "The Unemployment Problem in America." Andrews perceived unemployment to be "not only the most difficult but the most important problem with which we will have to deal in the coming years." In his keynote paper, Hard contended that it was the task of organizations such as the AALL to make available "the information which the public will need in legislating about unemployment."[25] In order to

24 Henderson to Max Lazard, 5 March 1910, microfilm, reel 2, Andrews Papers. For the lack of organization of the unskilled see Sanford M. Jacoby, *Employing Bureaucracy: Managers, Unions, and the Transformation of Work in American Industry, 1900–1945* (New York: Columbia University Press, 1985), 30–34. Keyssar, *Out of Work*, 55 contends that skilled and unskilled suffered equally during economic downturns, but he quotes evidence that the greater supply of unskilled laborers made their overall chance to have work smaller. See also page 5. - AFL. 33d Annual Convention, *Proceedings 1913*, 89; Keyssar, *Out of Work*, 181–84. For the progress of the shorter hours argument and its questionableness see ibid., 191–202.

25 Andrews to T. N. Carver, 9 Nov. 1912, microfilm, reel 8, Andrews Papers; Hard, "Unemployment as a Coming Issue," 93. Murphy, "John B. Andrews, the American

better fulfill this mandate, in December 1912 the AALL joined the International Association on Unemployment (IAU), which had been founded in Paris two years earlier.[26] But adherence to this organization subsequently proved to be a formality, as litte cooperation came of it.

The AALL itself, however, took the unemployment task seriously enough and kept busy in presenting the matter to the public. More or less everybody active in unemployment reform during those years could be found on the membership list of the association. Its most important instruments in fulfilling its mandate were the organization of conferences and the sponsorship of studies. On 6–7 June 1913, the AALL held an American Conference on Social Insurance in Chicago, where Henderson gave a paper on unemployment insurance. When unemployment increased in the winter of 1913–14 to unusual proportions for the first time since 1907–08, the AALL issued a call for the First National Conference on Unemployment, which convened in New York on 27–28 February 1914. During four sessions delegates from fifty-nine cities and twenty-five states discussed causes, the question of responsibility, European experiences, and remedies. A set of resolutions urged the federal and state governments to take action. Andrews found reasons to consider the proceedings a success. Over 2,000 people had attended a big public meeting at Cooper Union and, as he happily reported to IAU headquarters in Paris, "newspapers throughout the United States," among them the *New York Times*, had given the affair welcome exposure. As a result, he later confided to a correspondent, he was able to gather a "quite substantial fund to continue the work started under such favorable circumstances."[27]

The downturn in the economy during 1914, aggravated by the outbreak of the war in Europe, rendered the unemployment problem even more

Association for Labor Legislation, and Unemployment Reform, 1914–1929," 1–23 gives a factual summary of the subsequent involvement of the AALL in unemployment reform.
26 "Conference on Unemployment," *Survey* 23:15 (8 Jan. 1910), 495; John B. Andrews, "Introductory Note: Organization to Combat Unemployment," *ALLR* 4:2 (May 1914), 214–16. On the IAU see International Association on Unemployment, *Statutes of the International Association and of the National Sections* (n.p., n.d. [1911]), 21–22.
27 Charles Richmond Henderson, "Insurance against Unemployment," *ALLR* 3:2 (June 1913), 172–82; "General Discussion," ibid., 183–87. For growing concern about unemployment see Fitch to Leiserson, 17 Dec. 1913, Box 14, Leiserson Papers. – Invitational letter, signed by Seager and Andrews, dated January 1914, in Box 1, Leiserson Papers. Proceedings of the Conference are printed in *ALLR* 4:2 (May 1914), 209–354. – Andrews to Lazard, 12 March 1914, microfilm, reel 11, Andrews Papers; Andrews to Samuel McCune Lindsay, 16 March 1914, ibid.; Andrews to Danziger, 25 March 1914, ibid.; *New York Times*, 22 Feb. 1914, V, p. 6; ibid., 1 March 1914, II, p. 3.

urgent. Andrews commissioned several studies on specific subjects such as the seasonality in industry, public works practices, and the British unemployment insurance system. Insights gained through these investigations and the results of former deliberations were compressed into a twenty-page pamphlet distributed in December 1914 with the title *A Practical Program for the Prevention of Unemployment in America*. This pamphlet contained the gist of the wisdom acquired by American unemployment reformers during the preceding generation. It constituted a sort of manifesto that opposed the creed of social responsibility to the laissez faire ideology now considered hurtful. "The time is past," Andrews wrote in his preface, "when the problem of unemployment could be disposed of either by ignoring it, as was the practice until recent years in America, or by attributing it to mere laziness and inefficiency. We are beginning to recognize that unemployment is not so much due to individual causes and to the shiftlessness of 'won't-works,' as social and inherent in our present method of industrial organization."[28]

The pamphlet itself was divided into four major parts, dealing respectively with the establishment of public employment exchanges, the systematic distribution of public work, the regularization of industry, and unemployment insurance. It was characteristic of the reformers' thinking that three of these implied governmental action. Only the regularization of industry, by which was meant the smoothing out of the business cycle through conscious producer and consumer behavior, relied entirely on private initiative. Significantly, it was the remedy that over time proved to be the least successful. Andrews knew that his program had no chance of immediate implementation. Its primary purpose was educational, he disclosed to an acquaintance, "in order that the people throughout the country may begin to visualize the problem in all its complexities." On this point he apparently made some headway, as the *Program* went through four separate printings totaling 22,000 copies over the next few months.[29]

Encouraged by such interest, the AALL organized a Second National Conference on Unemployment in Philadelphia on 28–29 December 1914. Attendance was not as good as at the first meeting ten months earlier, but the main theme of the necessity of governmental involvement again

28 [John B. Andrews], "Foreword," *ALLR* 5:2 (June 1915), 173.
29 John B. Andrews, "A Practical Program for the Prevention of Unemployment in America," *ALLR* 5:2 (June 1915), 171–92; Andrews to J. Lionberger Davis, 10 Feb. 1915, microfilm, reel 13, Andrews Papers; John B. Andrews, "Introductory Note," *ALLR* 5:2 (June 1915), 168.

dominated the proceedings. The most forceful presentation was made by Pennsylvania Commissioner of Labor and Industry John P. Jackson, who entered a strong plea for the creation of "the proper machinery" to care for the unemployed in a paper entitled "Relation of the State to Unemployment." He denounced those who construed this "as in the nature of paternalism" and insisted that "the serious importance of unemployment as a state and a national economic problem" demanded innovative action.[30]

Meanwhile, the AALL kept working at that problem in its own way. The misery of the winter of 1914–15 was deep and extensive enough to warrant a further large-scale enterprise. "In order that [its] painful lessons ... may be utilized and not forgotten," the association undertook a survey of what had been done in 115 American communities, including the principal cities. The result was a report of some 120 pages, outlining the distressing inadequacy of the prevailing relief system. "Standard Recommendations," drafted in order to assist the municipalities in future emergencies, culminated in the demand for state and federal aid in the form of legislation and appropriations. When this piece of assiduous fact collection reached the public in November 1915, however, the pace of the economy was already picking up momentum in response to increased demands from the belligerents in Europe, and for the next few years the prospects for long-term action against unemployment receded accordingly.[31]

Various theories

The reflective and admonitory work of those concerned with unemployment reform profited substantially from insights gained elsewhere. References to experiences abroad appeared continuously in the literature on the subject, whereas Americans contributed to the body of theory only to a lesser degree. The reason may have been the comparative lateness of the American endeavor. From the 1890s, at any rate, a search for inspiration from overseas was quite evident. In 1893, John Graham Brooks, an expert in the federal Bureau of Labor and first president of the National Consumers' League, described relief actions in German cities. The 1894

---

30 Jackson, "Relation of the State to Unemployment," 439; 444. The proceedings of the Second National Conference are printed in ibid., 421–50.
31 John B. Andrews, "Introductory Note," *ALLR* 5:3 (Nov. 1915), 470; "Unemployment Survey," ibid., 475–593; "Standard Recommendations," ibid., 593–95.

report of the Massachusetts Bureau of Labor Statistics contained extensive accounts of the remedial use of public works in France and England,
of labor colonies in Germany, Holland, Belgium, France, Austria, Switzerland, England, and New Zealand, of public employment offices in England and France. In 1896, the *Annals* reviewed Georg Schanz's important
book on unemployment insurance just published in Germany, and in the
following year, Paul Monroe, a sociologist at the University of Chicago,
presented European unemployment insurance plans to the academic public. Commons discussed the merits of Herbert Spencer's and some French
theorists' views on the right to work. Gladden acquainted his audience
at the 1899 NCCC meeting with Charles Booth's and other investigations
in London.[32]

Over the years, attention focused on developments in the two countries
where the most remarkable improvements could be observed, Germany
and Great Britain. A German institution eagerly discussed by American
unemployment reformers was the system of federally assisted municipal
employment offices. As early as 1900, economics professor Ernest L.
Bogart of Indiana University, who held a Ph.D. from the German University of Halle, examined official German sources and concluded that
the German offices had met with good success, but that American industrial conditions were so different that little was to be learned from the
German experience. Henderson equally showed himself somewhat critical
at the founding meeting of the American Association of Public Employment Offices (AAPEO) in 1913. These views were questioned, however,
by others. Wainwright Commission member George A. Voss, a New York
(State) assemblyman who had traveled to Europe to observe the operation
of some of the 462 German offices then in existence, pronounced himself
more positively, and single-tax advocate cum urban reformer Frederic C.
Howe's presentation to the First National Conference on Unemployment
even offered an eloquent encomium of the German exchange system.
"The distinguishing thing about this legislation in Germany," Howe told
his listeners, "is its absolute sincerity." The United States Bureau of

32 John Graham Brooks, "The Unemployed in German Cities," *Quarterly Journal of Economics* 7:3 (April 1893), 353–58; Massachusetts. Bureau of Statistics of Labor, *24th
Annual Report, 1894*, 4–77; Emily Greene Balch, reviewing Georg Schanz, *Zur Frage
der Arbeitslosenversicherung* (Bamberg: Buchner, 1895), in *Annals* 7 (May 1896), 114–16;
Paul Monroe, "Insurance against Non-employment," *American Journal of Sociology* 2:6
(May 1897), 771–85; John R. Commons, "The Right to Work," *Arena* 21:2 (Feb. 1899),
131–42; Washington Gladden, "What to Do with the Workless Man," NCCC, *Proceedings 1899* (Boston: G. H. Ellis, 1900), 142–43.

Labor, for its part, in April 1915 translated an article from *Soziale Praxis* on efficiency measures in German employment agencies, and in 1916 it published a detailed account of the features and merits of the British and German systems.[33]

In an overall sense, more significant for American unemployment reform was the British example. Perhaps most importantly, British thinking could help to make up for the deficiencies in American theoretical deliberation. Despite occasional periods of severe unemployment and the more or less permanent problem of vagrancy, no serious American explanations were attempted in the decades after the Civil War beyond, as Frederick C. Mills put it, "generalizations of hobby-ridden individuals as to the causes of the phenomenon."[34] From the depressed 1890s, various writers sought to pinpoint origins and design remedies, but even then no thorough analysis of the problem under its new aspect surfaced. The theoretical works that did appear owed a heavy debt to contemporary British thought, which American reflection endeavored to adapt to conditions in the United States.

Of signal importance was the discussion engendered by the publication of William H. Beveridge's *Unemployment: A Problem of Industry*. This book preceded the introduction of the British unemployment insurance system, of which Beveridge became the first director. The study's attraction lay in its insistence that modern joblessness was a "problem of industry," not of the individual, and that therefore "the inquiry must be one into unemployment rather than into the unemployed." When the British National Insurance Act was passed in December 1911, the United States

---

33 E. L. Bogart, "Public Employment Offices in the United States and Germany," *Quarterly Journal of Economics* 14:3 (May 1900), 366–77. Quotation p. 77; New York (State). Commission to Inquire [etc.], *Third Report*, Appendix no. 2, 93–103; Charles R. Henderson, "Bureaus of Employment in Europe," AAPEO, Proceedings 1913, in U.S. Bureau of Labor Statistics, *Bulletin 192* (Washington: G.P.O., 1916), 16–23; Frederick C. Howe, "The German System of Labor Exchanges," *ALLR* 4:2 (May 1914), 301. For much the same opinion see also the statement of Dr. W.D.P. Bliss of the Religious Citizenship League in Hearings on H.R. 16130, pp. 33–34; 66. – Royal Meeker to Andrews, 6 April 1915, microfilm, reel 14, Andrews Papers; "Public Employment Offices in Great Britain and Germany," in U.S. Bureau of Labor Statistics, *Bulletin 192*, Appendix C, 146–62; B. Lasker, "The British System of Labor Exchanges," in U.S. Bureau of Labor Statistics, *Bulletin 206* (Washington: G.O.P., 1916), 5–67. See also Andrews' presentation, including exhibits, in Hearings on H.R. 16130, pp. 10–21. For the general interest in European developments see W.D.P. Bliss, "What Is Done for the Unemployed in European Countries," in U.S. Bureau of Labor Statistics, *Bulletin 76* (Washington: G.P.O., 1908), 741–934.
34 Mills, *Contemporary Theories*, 118.

government published the entire act, preceded by an introductory expose, in one of its bulletins. The psychological impact of the British developments on American reformers was immense. Beveridge's theory and program were compatible with the emphasis on prevention that was popular in the social reform and social insurance movements of the early twentieth century, and Beveridge moreover presented a credible alternative to more radical socialist solutions. The National Insurance Act provided a workable long-term program that could serve as a gauge for ideas in the United States, and in the following years numerous reports on and assessments of the British plan were published.[35]

As a consequence of the implementation of the British measures, references to the mother country of industry abounded in the writings of American unemployment reformers. The most noteworthy example was that of William M. Leiserson, a young economist tutored by Commons at the University of Wisconsin. After accompanying Voss to Europe in 1910 as a researcher for the Wainwright Commission, he wrote a report in which his position, as Garraty has noted, was "almost a carbon copy of Beveridge's." "The experience of every industrially developed European country shows," Leiserson observed, "that industry and unemployment go hand in hand." A few years later he praised Beveridge's treatment of the casual labor problem as a study that had "established the principles on which practical remedies can be based."[36]

There was a limit, of course, to the extent to which European theories could be appropriated in North America. Leiserson may in the main have been content to perceive American developments as being subject to universally valid determinants as outlined by British thinkers. Others,

35 W. H. Beveridge, *Unemployment: A Problem of Industry* (London: Longmans, 1909), 3; "British National Insurance Act, 1911," in U.S. Bureau of Labor Statistics, *Bulletin 102* (Washington: G.P.O., 1912), 7–87; Roy Lubove, *The Struggle for Social Security 1900–1935* (Cambridge, Mass.: Harvard University Press, 1986), 153–54; Daniel Nelson, *Unemployment Insurance: The American Experience 1915–1935* (Madison: University of Wisconsin Press, 1969), 11. Note also Walter E. Weyl, "Benefit Features of British Trade Unions," in U.S. Bureau of Labor Statistics, *Bulletin 64* (Washington: G.P.O., 1906), 699–848.

36 Garraty, *Unemployment in History*, 139–40. For Beveridge's influence on Leiserson see also Ringenbach, *Tramps and Reformers*, 151–53. – Brief considerations of Leiserson's role in unemployment reform are found in J. Michael Eisner, *William Morris Leiserson: A Biography* (Madison: University of Wisconsin Press, 1967), 30–35; and Seixas, "Unemployment as a 'Problem of Industry,' " 421–27. – New York (State). Commission to Inquire [etc.], *Third Report*, 27; W. M. Leiserson, "The Problem of Unemployment Today," *Political Science Quarterly* 31:1 (March 1916), 9.

however, took care to stress the need to complement those findings with considerations more reflective of the scene in the United States.

At least two specific factors were characteristic of the American situation – immigration and the migratory element. When unemployment entered into the public consciousness in the decades before World War I and the change in the ethnic composition of the stream of immigrants intensified old problems and created new ones, it became a popular perception that immigration constituted the basic cause of joblessness, or at least contributed to it in a major way. In 1902 the federal Industrial Commission claimed that "the presence of a large supply of immigrant workpeople" enhanced seasonal ups and downs in production activity. Nine years later the Immigration Commission wrote that "the influx is so continuous that... there has been created an over supply of unskilled labor." Not every student of the matter concurred, the notable example of a dissenter being Isaac A. Hourwich, a statistician with Marxist leanings, who tried to prove that immigration decreased when unemployment increased, and vice versa. But the federal commissioners found much sympathy for their view in labor quarters and elsewhere. John Mitchell noted "an inseparable relation between unemployment and immigration."[37] Prescott Farnsworth Hall, founder and secretary of the Immigration Restriction League, similarly held that "the displacement of large numbers of native workers by foreigners" increased the ranks of the unemployed. The remedy usually recommended was restriction of immigration. Such governmental action would have corresponded with the emphasis on prevention, and could be achieved with a minimum of fiscal exertion. Gompers submitted a statement to this effect to the federal Immigration Commission, and authors Jeremiah W. Jenks and W. Jett Lauck, both associated with that body, pleaded accordingly in 1913.[38]

---

37 *Final Report of the Industrial Commission*, vol. XIX, 751; U.S. Congress. Senate, *Abstracts of Reports of the Immigration Commission. Vol. I.* S.Doc. 747, 61 Cong., 3 sess. (1911), 39; Isaac A. Hourwich, *Immigration and Labor: The Economic Aspects of European Immigration to the United States* (New York: Putnam's, 1912), 137–39; U.S. Immigration Commission, *Reports* (Washington: G.O.P., 1911), vol. 41, 374. See also Alexander Keyssar, "Unemployment and the Labor Movement in Massachusetts, 1870–1916," in Herbert G. Gutman and Donald H. Bell, eds., *The New England Working Class and the New Labor History* (Urbana: University of Illinois Press, 1987), 243–44; idem, *Out of Work*, 77–90; 202–04. Regarding the strongly exclusionist attitude of the AFL, see ibid., 202–04.

38 Prescott F. Hall, *Immigration and Its Effects upon the United States* (New York: Holt, 1906), 135; similary New York (State). Commission to Inquire [etc.], *Third Report*, 7. – U.S. Immigration Commission, *Reports*, vol. 41, 369–431; Jeremiah Jenks and W. Jett

Another aspect of the unemployment scene peculiar to the United States was the enormous number of "floating laborers" migrating between unsteady jobs. They apparently became a notable problem with the depression of the 1870s. One estimate calculated that 3.5 million of the 10.4 million unskilled workers in 1910 had to be classified in this category. Traditionally, the vagrant had been seen as unwilling to find steady work. Quite telling was the experience that Coxey's Army had in 1894, when it was viewed by most newspapers and magazines as composed almost entirely of tramps. But as early as 1879, Henry George displayed a different understanding when he pointed at the connection between unemployment and tramps and denounced society for its failure to provide men with adequate means of securing a livelihood.[39]

The task, of course, was to separate the genuinely unemployed from the loafers. Even reform-minded contemporaries on occasion still held that the old-fashioned work test could be useful in this respect. In the opinion of Brooks, "adequate organized work tests" should be administered "not primarily to furnish work, but simply as tests." Gladden very much concurred, claiming that if any kind of aid were to be furnished by the state, some sort of work test had to be devised. Unsteadiness, he thereby implied, did not necessarily mean laziness. This view was fully accepted at the end of our period when the Industrial

Lauck, *The Immigration Problem: A Study of American Immigration Conditions and Needs* (New York: Funk & Wagnalls, 1913), 358–59. A dispassionate contemporary view of the situation can be found in Geza von Hoffmann, "L'immigrant et le chômage," in *Bulletin trimestriel de l'Association internationale pour la lutte contre le chômage* 3:2 (juillet-septembre 1912), 473–90. Von Hoffmann was Austro-Hungarian consul in the United States. The attitude of the AFL with regard to immigration in this period is described in Gwendolyn Mink, *Old Labor and New Immigrants in American Political Development: Union, Party, and State 1875–1920* (Ithaca: Cornell University Press, 1986), 195–97. For a modern interpretation of the historical relation between immigration and unemployment see Michael J. Piore, *Birds of Passage: Migrant Labor and Industrial Societies* (Cambridge: Cambridge University Press, 1979), 101–08.

39 Frank Leonard, " 'Helping' the Unemployed in the Nineteenth Century: The Case of the American Tramp," *Social Service Review* 40:4 (Dec. 1966), 429–34; Eric H. Monkkonen, "Introduction," in idem, ed., *Walking to Work: Tramps in America, 1790–1935* (Lincoln: University of Nebraska Press, 1984), 4–9; Carleton H. Parker, *The Casual Laborer and Other Essays* (New York: Harcourt, Brace and Howe, 1920), 17; Ringenbach, *Tramps and Reformers*, 43. For the generally hesitant and confused attitude of the public towards the unemployed see Keyssar, *Out of Work*, 253–56. – George, *Progress and Poverty*, book V, chap. II.

Relations Commission reported as a matter of fact that there were "large numbers of American workers, in all probability several millions, who are not definitely attached either to any particular locality or to any line of industry."[40]

Recognition of bona fide joblessness among migrant labor did not yet amount to solving the problem. The insight that repressive action alone could not suffice grew only slowly. Proposals for positive help were still scarce and included schemes like the establishment of a government-sponsored industrial army, as advocated in Congress from 1913 on, or the creation of farm colonies, both more extensively described later.[41] Also a touch above reality was the suggestion proffered by the Industrial Relations Commission to provide cheap transportation and the establishment of inexpensive workingmen's hotels. The sparse contemporary literature on the subject still concentrated upon the symptoms rather than seeking to find a cure through an explanation of the social causes of the phenomenon. "A definite attack and a definite solution," Mills felt at the time, had yet to be designed. But a conception of the matter's importance was dawning upon social thinkers. There can be little doubt, as Lubove has observed, that "awareness of the need for discrimination, joint with the emphasis upon the environmental and social origins of poverty," encouraged the subsequent adoption of new policies toward unemployment.[42]

40 John Graham Brooks, "The Future Problem of Charity and the Unemployed," *Annals* 5 (July 1894), 20; Gladden, "What to Do," 146. See also his *Social Salvation* (Boston: Houghton, Mifflin, 1902), 75–83. – U.S. Congress. Senate, *Industrial Relations: Final Report and Testimony Submitted to Congress by the Commission on Industrial Relations.* S.Doc. 415, 64 Cong., 1 sess. (1916), vol. I, 101. See also Mills, *Contemporary Theories,* 157–62; Donald L. McMurry, *Coxey's Army: A Study of the Industrial Army Movement of 1894* (Boston: Little, Brown, 1929), 12–20; Keyssar, *Out of Work,* 139–41; Eric H. Monkkonen, "Afterword," in idem, ed., *Walking to Work,* 241.
41 See pages 100–01; 104–06.
42 Commission on Industrial Relations, *Final Report* (Chicago: Barnard & Mills, 1915), 156–60; Alice Solenberger, *One Thousand Homeless Men: A Study of Original Records* (New York: Charities Publication Committee, 1911), 153–55; 235–37; Edmond Kelly, *The Elimination of the Tramp by the Introduction into America of the Labor Colony System Already Proved Effective in Holland, Belgium, and Switzerland, with the Modifications Thereof Necessary to Adapt This System to American Conditions* (New York: Putnam's, 1908). On Kelly's collectivist thinking as a background to his treatise see Gilbert, *Designing the Industrial State,* 125–58. – Frank J. Bruno, *Trends in Social Work 1874–1956: A History Based on the Proceedings of the National Conference of Social Work* (New York: Columbia

Nascent governmental awareness

Theoretical understanding of the task at hand thus grew in concerned circles, helped by pertinent insights adopted from abroad. But American governments were slow to acknowledge a corresponding obligation. During the decades under consideration, powerful interests, including the public at large, generally continued to be governed by traditional convictions, and refused to be swayed by the arguments of do-good reformers or radicals. They were fully aware that apart from the philosophical side of the issue with all its ethical and constitutional implications, prospective governmental activity in the social sphere also had a very practical side to it. Money was required, and an administrative apparatus to spend it. Both were not readily available, and their absence strengthened the reluctance of legislatures to embark upon unknown ventures. The men and women advocating unemployment reform thus fought a hard struggle, and the fact that by the time of the entry of the United States into World War I they had succeeded in making some sizable inroads into the public mind is testimony to the dedication and will to persevere that guided them.

If the steps through which governments approached the unemployment problem were hesitant, they nevertheless followed a certain logic. Obviously, comprehension of the phenomenon's manifestations and an understanding of its meaning could be viewed as prerequisites for any further considerations. As Josef Dorfman has remarked, the search for information and proper organization of control was an essential part of the attempt to reconcile free enterprise with government regulation. In other words, the unknown quality and extent of unemployment rendered study desirable before any solutions might be sought. Such investigative endeavors were timely enough in an age that saw, in Hays' words, "the rapid expansion of empirical inquiry for social change." Several states as well as the federal administration thus at one time or another sought to comprehend the configuration of the troubling matter.[43]

Massachusetts was first when it tried in the 1870s and 1880s in somewhat cursory fashion to assess the number of the unemployed. The severe economic and social dislocation from 1893 on caused more serious con-

University Press, 1957), 124–29; Mills, *Contemporary Theories*, 162; Lubove, *The Struggle for Social Security*, 146.

43 Dorfman, *Economic Mind*, III, 319; Samuel P. Hays, *American Political History as Social Analysis: Essays* (Knoxville: University of Tennessee Press, 1980), 247.

cern, and the government of the commonwealth made two earnest endeavors to explore the situation. One was a renewed counting exercise undertaken by the Bureau of Labor Statistics, which will be dealt with in greater detail later. More important because of its exhaustiveness was the study carried out in 1894–95 at the behest of the state's legislature by an exploratory board headed by Davis R. Dewey, professor of economics and statistics at the Massachusetts Institute of Technology. This investigation constituted a pioneering undertaking, and since its noncommittal pronouncements could be exploited in various ways, they were subsequently often referred to by friends and foes of governmental action alike. Carlos C. Closson of the University of Chicago saw reason to hail the study as "by far the most thorough work, both descriptive and critical, that has appeared in this country upon the problem of the unemployed." In five massive volumes bearing on relief measures, wayfarers and tramps, public works, and causes of joblessness, the board depicted in dispassionate terms the basic inadequacy of the existing arrangements for help. Its recommendations, however, did not go far beyond advice for local activities. The state itself was merely admonished to improve the collection of industrial information and to work toward a restriction of immigration.[44]

An investigation conducted in New York in the wake of the 1907–08 recession arrived at similarly cautious conclusions. The exploratory commission, headed by state senator Wainwright, immediately delegated the unemployment inquiry to a subcommittee chaired by Voss. Leiserson, who worked at the time at Columbia as a honorary fellow in political economy with commission member Seager, was appointed special investigator. He carried out the bulk of the research, in the course of which he not only studied the matter in New York and other states, but, as has been mentioned, in the summer of 1910 also undertook a tour of Great Britain, Belgium, Germany, and Switzerland. The result of this effort served as a basis for the commission's recommendations and was published in the appendix of its *Third Report*. Leiserson was also able to submit his findings to his department at Columbia, earning his degree in 1911 with this first American doctoral dissertation on unemployment.

44 Massachusetts. Bureau of Statistics of Labor, *24th Annual Report, 1894*, 3–267. For the counting effort of 1895 see page 44. – C[arlos] C. C[losson] reviewing *Report of the Massachusetts Board to Investigate the Subject of the Unemployed*, in *Journal of Political Economy* 3 (1895), 494. For the events that led to the establishment of the board see Keyssar, *Out of Work*, 224–28. - Massachusetts. House. Board to Investigate [etc.], *Report*, vol. I, xiii; ibid., vol. V, xxxvii-xxxviii; lxii.

The Wainwright Commission's own contribution to the cause of un-employment reform remained confined to the recognition of the existence of seasonal, cyclical, and "irregular" joblessness, and to the recommen-dation that a system of public employment offices be established.[45]

Leiserson's investigation, however, constituted the most thorough ex-amination of the problem made in North America since the Massachusetts study had been published in 1895. Circumspect, and for its time, ex-haustive, his report outlined the extent of unemployment, its causes and effects, and the existing relief mechanisms in the United States, Great Britain, and Germany. Leiserson also discussed possible remedies. His most important insight was doubtless the Beveridge-inspired conclusion that "remedial measures must be shaped toward prevention," which im-plied the conscious abandonment of the idea that relief handouts should be considered. The study established its author's reputation for ever. "I suppose," *Survey* editor Paul U. Kellogg lauded him, "now you are the expert of the country in the matter of unemployment."[46]

The investigative efforts of the Dewey and Wainwright commissions went as far as circumstances warranted at the time, and it appeared unlikely that their findings would be considerably altered through similar endeavors elsewhere. But the broadening official interest nevertheless caused some other public authorities to make comparable efforts. The harsh conditions of the 1913–14 winter that induced the AALL to or-ganize its First National Conference also served as a catalyst for the first in-depth investigation in the West. In January 1914, California governor Hiram W. Johnson, formerly vice-presidential candidate of the Progres-sive Party, asked the state's Commission of Immigration and Housing to

45 The commission was created according to 1909 *New York (State) Laws*, c. 518. See also Ringenbach, *Tramps and Reformers*, 150–54. The law seems to have been passed at the prompting of the Ethical Social League, a body that had been organized in New York (City) in February 1908 to unite churches and synagogues for the betterment of the community. See *New York Times*, 28 Feb. 1908, p. 6. – New York (State). Commission to Inquire [etc.], *Third Report*, 1; 25–69 (Appendix I); William Morris Leiserson, "Un-employment in the State of New York" (Columbia Ph.D., 1911); Eisner, *William Morris Leiserson*, 11–12; 30–31. The printed version of the dissertation is an offprint of the pertaining part of the commission report and has the same numbering. Another Ph.D. dissertation, finished at about the same time and dealing to some extent with unem-ployment, was that of Scott Nearing, "Social Cost and Economic Maladjustment" (University of Pennsylvania Ph.D., 1909), published as *Social Adjustment* (New York: Macmillan, 1911).

46 New York (State). Commission to Inquire [etc.], *Third Report*, 66; Paul U. Kellogg to Leiserson, 27 March 1911, Box 39, Leiserson Papers.

direct its attention to the situation in the labor market and to suggest "what, if any, remedy might be applied by the State." Subsequently the commission recommended, along the lines of the *Practical Program*, that the state government might open public labor exchanges and regulate private ones, and possibly provide public work and some form of out-of-work insurance. The commissioners admitted a debt to Leiserson, whom they quoted at length.[47]

Growing curiosity about unemployment was not confined to the state level. As early as 1880 the Bureau of the Census, prompted by the preceding depression, asked a question about joblessness. The first major undertaking of the federal Bureau of Labor, established in 1884, was an investigation into industrial depressions in which it found that a surplus of labor in the United States "rendered over-production easy." In subsequent years the bureau did not lose sight of this question again.[48]

Conspicuous federal recognition of the growing social importance of joblessness came through the Commission on Industrial Relations, created in 1912 "to discover the underlying causes of dissatisfaction in the industrial situation." During its extensive hearings, the Commission found that unemployment was "a prime cause of a burning resentment and a rising feeling of unrest among the workers" and that it was "one of the most important problems with which the country has to deal." Leiserson again exercised considerable influence, as Commons, one of the commissioners, had seen to it that the unemployment examination was entrusted to his former pupil. Leiserson shaped his proposals after the *Practical Program*, but the commission's conservative majority, reflecting federal hesitation about involvement, shrank from putting these ideas forward as its own. It contended itself with stating that the unemployment situation asked for the removal of "unjust distribution of wealth and monopolization of land and natural resources" and expressing the hope that Congress direct its attention to this task. A minority report, written by Commons,

47 California. Commission of Immigration and Housing, *Report on Unemployment* (Sacramento: State Printing Office, 1914), 6–7; 16–18.
48 U.S. Commissioner of Labor, *First Annual Report, 1886*, 291. For the federal Bureau of Labor's continued interest see, besides the annual departmental reports, its various pertinent publications cited in this chapter and U.S. Commissioner of Labor, *Seventh Special Report: The Slums of Baltimore, Chicago, New York, and Philadelphia* (Washington: G.P.O., 1894), 65–66; 502–505; U.S. Bureau of Labor, *Report on Conditions of Employment in the Iron and Steel Industry in the United States*. Vol. III: *Working Conditions and the Relations of Employers and Employees* (Washington: G.P.O., 1913), 205–08; 379–81.

however, took up Leiserson's suggestions and integrated them into its general recommendations.[49]

The investigations conducted in California and by the Industrial Relations Commission thus more or less confirmed the understanding achieved by 1911. Additional evidence was collected and similar conclusions were reached in surveys done during the 1914 depression in various cities, among which those in Chicago and New York were the most remarkable because of the wealth of material collected.[50] But these post-Wainwright studies did not produce any new insights. In the context of unemployment reform, their major merit was rather that they alerted a widely indifferent community to the existence of joblessness in its midst and invited reflection upon the public's role in this regard. These examinations, at any rate, were expressions of a sporadically appearing, still indeterminate inquisitiveness. The nascent governmental concern, however, manifested itself also in more specific and more tangible forms. Among them, the efforts to assess the precise extent of the unemployment phenomenon and to find remedies through manpower distribution, provision of public works, and social insurance deserve particular consideration.

II   Assessing the problem

Probing the survey

The awakening interest in unemployment naturally inspired the desire to know the number of persons afflicted by it. "Before the 'problem of unemployment' can be solved," the federal Bureau of Labor Statistics perceptively remarked, "it must first be stated."[51] The initiation of remedial measures did, of course, not necessarily depend on a full appreciation of the size of the evil, but the command of pertinent knowledge seemed a prerequisite for any substantial and sustained success of such action.

As everybody concerned with the question quickly came to realize, the

49 37 Stat. 351 (1912); U.S. Congress. Senate, *Industrial Relations: Final Report and Testimony*, I, 35–36; 38; 103–115; 200; 249–50. See also the statements of Leiserson and others, ibid., 345–70. – Idem. Commission on Industrial Relations, *1st Annual Report*, 42.
50 [Chicago.] Mayor's Commission on Unemployment, *Report* (Chicago, 1914); [New York (City).] Mayor's Committee on Unemployment, *Report* (New York, 1916).
51 "Unemployment in New York City, N. Y.," in U.S. Bureau of Labor Statistics, *Bulletin 172* (Washington: G.P.O., 1915), 5.

assignment asked for governmental involvement. Private charitable organizations might be inclined to dedicate care and good will, but the shapelessness and growing pervasiveness of unemployment clearly overtaxed their abilities. Municipalities attempted on occasion to assess the number of unemployed within their boundaries, but the constant fluctuation of the job seekers within a regional or even national labor market made such endeavors little more than exercises in futility. It thus fell to the state and federal governments to come to grips with the problem. The assignment was new and mostly unwelcome. Creating the necessary apparatus for counting asked for administrative experimentation and expenditure. More threatening still was the prospect that knowing the amount of unemployment would lead to having to care for those afflicted by it. Helpfully, though, another motivation besides humanitarian concerns also played a role in initiating counting procedures – namely, the upsurging interest in statistics that characterized the period. In Wiebe's words, "the bureaucratic thought" of the age, the urge to apply the "scientific method" of investigation with the goal of understanding society, clearly inspired the data-gathering efforts of state and federal officials.[52]

Two basic methods were tried out before World War I – the survey and the periodic report. The survey – an investigation of the census-taking type – enjoyed a certain popularity, as it was often the only means to arrive at any figures at all other than unverifiable estimates. The periodic report, on the other hand, provided figures at regular intervals, allowing the observation of trends. During the decades under consideration, both methods were thoroughly examined and tested. Their potential to yield useful unemployment data proved to be limited, however, and the United States had to wait for the implementation of unemployment insurance under the Social Security Act of 1935 before reliable information became available.[53]

The first governmental survey effort in the United States was made in Massachusetts in 1878 in the wake of the depression. As he lacked funds to conduct his own research, Wright, then chief of the state's Bureau of Labor Statistics, asked police and town assessors to make the necessary inquiries. When an aggregate number of 28,508 unemployed persons

52 Wiebe, *Search for Order*, 147. Wiebe mentions Wright. See also Bremner, *From the Depths*, 71–74.
53 The development of unemployment statistics does not seem to have received specific attention recently other than in Keyssar, *Out of Work*, 342–58, where some useful supplementary information can be found.

emerged, Wright considered this sufficient evidence to refute the "reckless and inconsiderate assertions... industriously circulated" that from 200,000 to 300,000 people had no jobs in the state. A repetition of the exercise in November showed a substantial decline over June, which the bureau, in view of the advance of the season, interpreted as an indication of returning prosperity.[54]

Opportunity for improvement came with the decennial state census of 1885. The bureau succeeded in getting two unemployment questions about the preceding twelve months into the census. As the census noted sex and occupations and sought to cover the entire population, a far more detailed analysis was possible than in 1878. Overall, the results, presented in December 1887, indicated that 29.6 percent of persons gainfully employed had been out of work at one time or another, and that the average duration of joblessness had been 4.11 months.[55]

The 1885 inquiry furnished "by far the most trustworthy basis for computing the extent of unemployment" available at the time, as one contemporary observer put it. But it had its deficiencies, among them the failure to secure information about the number of jobless persons at any specific time during the year. In the state census of 1895, therefore, a question was asked about the specific months of unemployment. The resulting computations indicated that 27.3 percent of the working population had known some unemployment during the preceding year. This figure was astonishing in view of the generally held assumption that the depression of the mid-1890s was far more severe than the recession of the early 1880s. Fortunately, some explanation could be found in the fact that the census of 1895 excluded certain professional classes that had been counted in 1885.[56]

The groundbreaking counting efforts made in Massachusetts were imitated with mixed results in two more states and at the federal level. In May–June 1888, the Colorado commissioner of labor statistics asked

---

54 Massachusetts. Bureau of Statistics of Labor, *10th Annual Report, 1879*, 3–13.
55 Carrol D. Wright, "The Value and Influence of Labor Statistics," *Engineering Magazine* 6:2 (Nov. 1893), 141; Massachusetts. Bureau of Statistics of Labor, *18th Annual Report, 1887*, 3–4; 294. Wright had thought at one point in 1885 that 7.5 percent of the total work force was out of work; other estimates amounted to twice as many. Samuel Rezneck, "Patterns of Thought and Action in an American Depression, 1882–1886," *American Historical Review* 61:2 (Jan. 1956), 287.
56 C[arlos] C. C[losson], "Unemployment," *Journal of Political Economy* 3 (1895), 489; Massachusetts, *Census of 1895*. Vol. VII: *Social Statistics and General Summaries* (Boston: Wright & Potter, 1900), 2–3; 102–06.

the county sheriffs of his state to survey the unemployed in their districts. The Rhode Island Bureau of Industrial Statistics used the state census in 1895 and the police inquiry method in 1908. In both states the results remained unconvincing.[57]

In the federal census as early as 1880 a question was included about the number of months individual persons had been unemployed. No results were tabulated, however, because the Census Bureau itself harbored "grave doubt as to the reliability of the information" it had collected. This hesitation proved amply justified when the results of the following censuses came in. Material gathered in 1890 showed that 16.0 percent of the male working population and 13.0 percent of the female had been unemployed during the preceding year. The census of 1900, by contrast, resulted in an aggregate figure of 22.3 percent. Because economic conditions at the time of the two latter censuses had been essentially similar, the enormous increase in percentage points was difficult to explain. When it felt equally uncertain about the data collected in the 1910 census, the bureau (as it did in 1880) refrained from printing them.[58]

In view of the doubtfulness of the census figures, Washington made some other attempts to approach the numbers problem. In 1901 the federal Bureau of Labor conducted an inquiry into the cost of living of 25,440 working-class families, distributed over 33 states, and also asked

57 Colorado. Bureau of Labor Statistics, *First Biennial Report, 1887–1888*, 366–67; Rhode Island. Commissioner of Industrial Statistics, *10th Annual Report, 1898*, 492. William Franklin Willoughby, "The Measurement of Unemployment: A Statistical Study." *Yale Review* 10 (Nov. 1901), 269 claims that the first Rhode Island investigation was "entirely different" from the Massachusetts one, because it showed month-to-month figures. However, the Massachusetts census clearly did this also. See tables in Massachusetts, *Census, 1895*. Vol. VII: *Social Statistics and General Summaries* (Boston: Wright & Potter, 1900), 90–91; Rhode Island. Commissioner of Industrial Statistics, *22d Annual Report, 1909*, 3–14; 18–19; Frank B. Sargent, "Statistics of Unemployment and the Work of Employment Offices," in U.S. Bureau of Labor Statistics, *Bulletin 109* (Washington: G.P.O., 1913), 27.

58 U.S. Dept. of Commerce and Labor. Bureau of the Census, *Special Report: Occupations at the Twelfth Census* (Washington: G.P.O., 1904), ccxxv; U.S. Census Office. 11th Census 1890, *Report on the Population of the United States at the Eleventh Census: Part I* (Washington: G.P.O., 1895), cxxxvi–cxl. The unemployment results of this census were discussed by Carroll D. Wright, "The Relation of Production to Productive Capacity – II." *Forum* 17 (Feb. 1898), 664–67. The 1910 results were not tabulated until 1948. U.S. Bureau of the Census, *Historical Statistics of the United States, Colonial Times to 1970: Bicentennial Edition, Part 1* (Washington: G.P.O., 1975), 122. Despite the questionableness of the census figures an effort was made to arrive at some usable estimates by combining them with other data in Paul H. Douglas, *Real Wages in the United States 1890–1926* (Boston: Houghton Mifflin, 1930), 409–16.

whether and how long the head of the family had been out of work during the last twelve months. Unfortunately, the results in many instances did not even come close to the census data of 1900. Another federal inquiry of the survey type was the 1905 Census of Manufactures. It basically furnished employment figures emanating from the payrolls of employers, allowing a crude guess at unemployment in the bad months.[59]

The absence of good counting procedures was particularly noticeable when the severe economic downturn caused by the outbreak of war in Europe brought an intensified and "widespread demand for information on the subject of unemployment throughout the United States," as the federal Bureau of Labor Statistics put it. Various municipalities such as Chicago, St. Louis, Detroit, and Providence struggled on their own to get a picture of the distress. In New York (City) the immensity of the problem induced the federal government to offer some assistance. At the request of the Mayor's Committee on Unemployment, and with the sponsorship of the federal Bureau of Labor Statistics, the Metropolitan Life Insurance Company, which was interested in underwriting unemployment insurance, secured unemployment data from its industrial policy holders in January 1915.[60] As the representativeness of its finding of 18 percent unemployment appeared doubtful, the bureau decided to make a survey of its own. In early 1915, a total of 54,849 families were questioned with the help of immigration agents rendered idle by the war. Among wage earners, 16.2 percent were found to be unemployed at the time of the inquiry, a result that the bureau in view of the advance of season judged satisfactorily close to that of the Metropolitan's investigation. As a consequence, then federal Commissioner of Labor Statistics Royal Meeker encouraged the Metropolitan to investigate continent-wide. Two inquiries in a total of twenty-eight cities in April and June/July 1915 found unemployment rates of 11.5 and 12.9 percent, respectively. In August and September, Meeker's bureau repeated its canvass, and in October the insurance company once more surveyed its New York (City) policy hold-

59 U.S. Bureau of Labor, *18th Annual Report, 1903: Cost of Living and Retail Prices of Food*, 11–17; 42–43; Bureau of the Census, *Special Report: Occupations at the Twelfth Census*, ccxxxv-ccxxxvi; table 5 in U.S. Dept. of Commerce and Labor. Bureau of the Census, *Bulletin 57: Census of Manufacturers: 1905, United States* (Washington: G.P.O., 1906), 23. Figures for the individual states are found in the bulletins dedicated to each.
60 U.S. Bureau of Labor Statistics, *Bulletin 172*, 6; [Chicago.] Mayor's Commission on Unemployment, *Report*, 14–16; "The Unemployment Crisis of 1914–1915," *ALLR* 5:3 (Nov. 1915), 480; [New York (City).] Mayor's Committee on Unemployment, *Report*, 7; 9–11; 23–26.

ers. The jobless rates that emerged – 6.7 and 9.1 percent, respectively – seemed at least to indicate that the employment situation was improving.[61]

It is easy to point out the inadequacy of the counting endeavors thus far described. In the first place, the collection methods were of questionable character. Police and town assessors were ill-suited helpers for the task, and even the official census canvassers used in the other inquiries certainly constituted a mixed lot. Moreover, the confusion that often admittedly existed about the specific meaning of the unemployment question cannot but have hampered uniformity. In this regard it is interesting to note that a major problem that was to cause headaches for future experts – namely, the proper definition of "unemployment" – apparently did not yet arouse any real concern among the investigators. "Out of work" or some similar term usually appeared sufficient to describe the condition in question. In addition, the reasons for joblessness, such as economic downturn, seasonal slack, or physical incapacity, knowledge of which would have been essential to any meaningful analysis, were not recorded. There was no means of knowing, as the Chicago Municipal Markets Commission wrote in 1914, "what per cent of these persons was idle from choice and what per cent wanted work and was unable to secure it."[62] The failure in many cases to distinguish between people such as independent businessmen and professionals on the one hand and wage workers on the other further added to the amorphousness of the results, as did the lack of recognition of the fact that in bad times job seekers might drop out of the labor market, becoming invisible to the assessor.

Not only was the information-gathering process wide open to criticism; the more fundamental question of the usefulness of the undertaking had to be asked. Even if the data collected had been satisfactorily detailed and reliable, the fact that they were available only after lengthy months

---

61 [New York (City).] Mayor's Committee on Unemployment, *Report*, 11–13; Hornell Hart, "Fluctuations in Unemployment in Cities of the United States, 1902 to 1917," *Studies from the Helen S. Trounstine Foundation* 1:2 (15 May 1918), 47; "Unemployment in New York City, New York," in U.S. Bureau of Labor Statistics, *Bulletin 172*, 7–8; Royal Meeker, "Some Recent Surveys of Unemployment," American Academy of Political and Social Science, *Annals* [hereafter *Annals*] 61 (Sept. 1915), 26; 28; "Unemployment in the United States," in U.S. Bureau of Labor Statistics, *Bulletin 195* (Washington: G.P.O., 1916), 6–7; 93; 98–99; 107–108.

62 Chicago. Municipal Markets Commission, *Report*, 11. For the problem of definition of the term "unemployed" see Clarence D. Long, *The Labor Force under Changing Income and Employment* (Princeton: Princeton University Press, 1958), 388–99; and Stanley Lebergott, "Unemployment: A Perspective," in idem, ed., *Men without Work: The Economics of Unemployment* (Englewood Cliffs, N.J.: Prentice-Hall, 1964), 3–8.

and even years of summarizing and tabulating severely restricted their use as a guidance aid for political decision-makers. What governmental measure introduced in 1904, when the results of the Twelfth Census were presented, could be based upon the latter's findings covering the period preceding 1 May 1900? From a practical standpoint "the whole investigation may be pronounced absolutely worthless," William F. Willoughby, at the time with the federal Department of Labor, noted in desperation when looking at the 1890 census.[63] He would have been justified in including other similar inquiries as well in this verdict.

It might thus be tempting to dismiss as irrelevant the direct efforts made during this period to learn the overall number of unemployed. But although no good results were obtained, at least the exigencies of the method were investigated, and the lessons learned could facilitate efforts in the future.

Testing the series

Counting attempts, at any rate, did not all belong to the census type. Much of the true value of unemployment data lay in their comparability with previous figures, and this consideration required the creation of data series. Gathering them was hampered by the lack of an adequate bureaucratic apparatus. It was conceivable, however, to attempt the exploitation of employment statistics assembled for other purposes or to enlist some union help.

Comparison of employment figures over time offered the possibility of a fair guess at the number of unemployed. The method had its drawbacks, as no guarantee existed that employers reported their figures reliably. The series was doubtful even as a trend indicator, because the figures from two subsequent months emanating from the same establishments could not confidently be compared. Moreover, statistics could not take care at all of "those unemployed who had been utterly displaced and consequently had no enrollment whatever on the books of manufacturing establishments," as an otherwise sympathetic observer correctly pointed out.[64]

---

63 Willoughby, "Measurement of Unemployment," 194.
64 For the hesitancy of some employers to reveal correct figures see H. H. Wheaton in "Reports of Official Delegates on the State of Employment," *ALLR* 4:2 (May 1914), 241. For the difficulty of comparing two subsequent months, consider that if in the first month establishment A employed ten workers and B two, and in the second month A

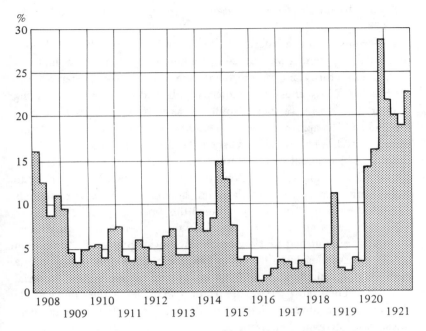

Figure 2-1. Percentage of unemployment among organized wage earners in Massachusetts, 1908–21, by quarters, as measured through trade
union returns. (Source: U.S. Dept. of Labor, *Bulletin 310*, Wash., 1922.)

Despite these fundamental deficiencies, employer statistics enjoyed a
good-deal of popularity. Massachusetts again acted as the ground breaker
(Figure 2–1). Wright succeeded in getting *Annual Statistics of Manufactures*
published from 1886. It offered, among other items, information on employment in the various industries on a monthly basis. The Dewey Board
used these figures in its 1894–95 study. Ohio assembled payroll data
annually from 1892 to 1906, and the New Jersey Bureau of Labor Sta-

employed two and B ten, the resulting unemployment figure would in either case have
been eight, indicating a 40% unemployment rate, although in reality all workers might
have been continuously employed. The example is Willoughby's. See his "Measurement
of Unemployment," 278. – Davis R. Dewey, "Irregularity of Employment," American
Economic Association. *Publications* 9:5–6 (1894), 59. Dewey was Professor of Economics
and Statistics at the Massachusetts Institute of Technology and Chairman of the state's
Board to Investigate the Unemployed.

tistics published similar information in its reports between 1894 and 1918.[65]

Depression also engendered the use of union data. Following British precedent, the New York Bureau of Labor Statistics gathered quarterly trade union returns on unemployment from March 1897. In March 1908, the Bureau's Massachussetts counterpart followed suit; although the filing of quarterly returns was not compulsory, as in New York, by the end of December 1913 approximately 73 percent of the total union membership were covered. The bureau published the results quarterly in its *Labor Bulletin* and its annual reports. Over time, however, the method met with considerable doubt. In 1915, New Hampshire made a brief attempt to gather union unemployment data, but abondoned the effort after six months. New York (State) discontinued the practice in 1916.[66]

Scott Nearing, an economics teacher at the University of Pennsylvania, in an article published in 1909 by the American Statistical Association (ASA), praised the union figures as "the most thoroughly compiled, the most ably presented, and the most up-to-date unemployment material available." Their most serviceable features were clearly their quick availability and their value as reliable trend indicators. But there were negative sides. Much depended upon the accuracy of the individual reports, which was in many cases open to doubt. More importantly, union figures could in no way be regarded as representative of the working population at large. In March 1900 the aggregate membership of all unions reporting in New York (State) was 221,917, whereas the nonagricultural working population may have numbered about 3 million. There was an unsub-

65 Massachusetts. Bureau of Statistics of Labor, *38th Annual Report, 1907*, xiii–xiv; Massachusetts. Bureau of Statistics of Labor, *Annual Statistics of Manufactures 1886/87* (Boston: Wright & Potter, 1889) and subsequent issues; Massachusetts. Bureau of Statistics of Labor, *24th Annual Report, 1894*, 121–25; Massachusetts. House Board to Investigate the Subject of the Unemployed, *Report* (Boston: Wright and Potter, 1895), vol. IV, 13–23; Bryce M. Stewart, *Unemployment Benefits in the United States* (New York: Industrial Relations Counsellors, 1930), 26; New Jersey. Bureau of Statistics of Labor and Industries, *17th Annual Report, 1894*, xvii; 24–69; and subsequent reports through 1918. An 1899 act gave the undertaking specific legislative sanction. New Jersey. Bureau of Industrial Statistics, *38th Annual Report*, 3.

66 New York (State). Bureau of Labor Statistics, *15th Annual Report, 1897*, 11–12; 420–430, and the corresponding tables in subsequent reports; *Massachusetts Labor Bulletin* 13:4 (May 1908), 177 and subsequent issues of the *Labor Bulletin*; Massachusetts. Bureau of Statistics, *39th Annual Report, 1908*, 182–84; 205; 206, and subsequent reports; New Hampshire. Bureau of Labor, *11th Biennial Report, 1915–16*, 7; 25–36.

stantiated assumption, acknowledged by the United States Industrial Commission, that unorganized workers suffered worse unemployment.[67] But nobody seriously proposed to assess the shape and size of the difference. Remarkably, the AFL itself decided that such figures were not worth the expense. In 1899 it had begun to collect voluntary monthly unemployment reports from its member unions and had published them, from December 1899 on, in its official organ. The chief value of this effort obviously lay in its nationwide character. The returns were meager and of uncertain value, however, and the *American Federationist* discontinued publishing them in 1909 because of the great variation over time in the number of unions reporting.[68]

Thus, almost four decades after the first governmental counting efforts had been made, no means to achieve satisfactory results had yet been worked out. It has to be acknowledged, on the other hand, that these endeavors helped to clarify the requirements of an adequate counting procedure and to demonstrate the shortcomings of the one-shot survey and the periodic report. The data obtained over the years made it sufficiently clear that more substantial governmental involvement was necessary to achieve acceptable returns. Still another remarkable development could be registered. If governmental readiness for action was to be achieved, it was essential to alert the public to the need for counting the unemployed and to the implications of the problem. In this respect, and this was not the least accomplishment of the period, considerable progress was visible. The *ALLR* recognized this in 1915 by stating that the investigations had served "a valuable purpose in awakening the public conscience."[68a]

67 Scott Nearing, "The Extent of Unemployment in the United States," American Statistical Association. *Publications* n.s. 11:87 (Sept. 1909), 528; New York (State). Bureau of Labor Statistics, *20th Annual Report, 1902*, 387; Sargent, "Statistics of Unemployment," 14–18; 24; Ernest S. Bradford, "Methods Used in Measuring Unemployment," American Statistical Association, *Quarterly Publication* n.s. 17:136 (Dec. 1921), 985; *Historical Statistics of the United States, Part 1*, 130; *Final Report of the Industrial Commission*, XIX, 754.

68 The first chart appeared in the November 1899 edition of the *American Federationist* with the data of the previous September; the last chart was published in December 1909, with the previous October data.

68ª John B. Andrews, "Introductory Note," *ALLR* 4:2 (May 1914), 211; Meeker in "General Discussion," ibid., 338; Frances A. Kellor, ibid., 333; idem, "The Way Out of the Unemployment Situation," *Survey* 31:21 (21 Feb. 1914), 638; "The Unemployment Crisis of 1914–1915," 483.

III   Search for tools: Labor exchanges

Aspects of the labor market

Attempts at assessing the size of the unemployment problem were certainly meritorious, but the real quest had to be for true remedies. Among the curative means under discussion before World War I, government-run labor exchanges caught the imagination of the reformers more than any other device. The First National Conference on Unemployment noticed "general agreement that the first step toward a solution of the problem is the organization of a connected network of free public employment exchanges." The Commission on Industrial Relations equally affirmed that "the first step must be the organization of the labor market on a systematic businesslike and efficient basis. Labor exchanges can . . . provide the information and administrative machinery which is essential to every other step in dealing with the problem."[69]

Public exchanges commended themselves for several reasons. They were inexpensive by comparison with public works or unemployment insurance. In addition, their mission to help the jobless to help themselves appealed to those who still felt a commitment to laissez-faire principles. To the progressive mind, furthermore, the potential of the exchanges to reduce human waste and enhance productivity had considerable allure. As a result of the combined efforts undertaken over two decades by reformers, various labor functionaries, and interested bureaucrats, half the states of the union had state-run employment exchanges by the time of the American entry into World War I. Whatever their practical value during this period, their creation was as important a step on the road to the welfare state as were the parallel endeavors to bring about minimum wage standards and workmen's compensation.[70] Not surprisingly in an age in which labor had begun to move in considerable numbers over state lines, there was even a drive for national legislation; although its success

---

69 "Resolutions," *ALLR* 4:2 (May 1914), 353. See similarly John B. Andrews, "Unemployment Survey 1914–1915," *ALLR* 5:3 (Nov. 1915), 543. – U.S. Congress. Senate, *Industrial Relations: Final Report and Testimony*, I, 108.

70 Edward Berkowitz and Kim McQuaid, *Creating the Welfare State: The Political Economy of Twentieth-Century Reform* (New York: Praeger, 1980), 26–41, esp. 26 single out minimum wage and worker's compensation laws as lying "at the heart" of governmental welfare concerns in the Progressive Era.

remained limited for the time being, it prepared the way for future developments.

In the decades before and after the turn of the century the American labor market was in a chaotic state. Normally, employers could count on a "labor reserve" of unemployed jobseekers in the industrial centers, fed by migration and immigration. Its size varied locally and with the economic situation, but it was usually substantial enough to allow easy hiring and firing, all the more so because the advance of industrialization increased the number of jobs for unskilled workers enormously. Rapid labor turnover did not beget any efficient machinery to bring employer and worker together, as plant owners generally found it easy to secure the hands they needed at the factory gate. In most cases the jobseeking individual had to tramp the streets, relying upon his own experience or tips from others for direction.[71]

Over time, some exchange facilities developed nevertheless. Employers, trade unions, charitable bodies, and (most significantly) private entrepreneurs opened agencies "designed to bring employee and employer together for the purpose of furnishing employment to the former and help to the latter," as Jacob E. Conner, an investigator for the federal Department of Labor, defined the institution in 1907. Employers' agencies as a rule sought to obtain workers without trade union links and thus acted as anti-union and open-shop organizations. Trade unions for their part were primarily or exclusively interested in securing work for their members. Although some union exchanges occasionally indicated employment possibilities to non-union workers, the better-led unions frowned upon such latitude. Trade unions still generally organized only skilled workers. Rare efforts toward extending unionism to unskilled laborers remained largely ineffective. In 1912, Gompers proposed the formation of a Department of Migratory Labor in the AFL and the creation of a system of employment agencies under its jurisdiction, but very little, if anything, seems to have come of this initiative.[72]

71 Don D. Lescohier, *The Labor Market* (New York: Macmillan, 1919), 9–13; 141–63; Daniel Nelson, *Managers and Workers: Origins of the New Factory System in the United States 1880–1920* (Madison: University of Wisconsin Press, 1975), 79–90; Keyssar, *Out of Work*, 69–76; 109; Jacoby, *Employing Bureaucracy*, 17–19.

72 J. E. Conner, "Free Public Employment Offices in the United States," in U.S. Bureau of Labor Statistics, *Bulletin 68* (Washington: G.P.O., 1907), 1; E. H. Sutherland, "Unemployment and Public Employment Agencies," in [Chicago.] Mayor's Commission on Unemployment, *Report* (Chicago, 1914), 121; U.S. Congress. Senate, *Industrial Relations:*

It was the plight of the unskilled workers in particular that attracted the attention of various philanthropic organizations. Their concern sprang from the recognition that unemployment had obviously become a task for society to solve. An early example of an exchange founded for this reason was the United Hebrew Charities office that opened in Chicago in 1870. Other religious or humanitarian organizations like the Associated Charities, the Young Men's Christian Association, or the Salvation Army soon emulated this endeavor. On occasion, even self-help exchanges sprang up. The idea was to provide broker services free, on the one hand to attract the employer and on the other to be easy on the destitute job seeker. Philanthropic agencies remained a part of the labor exchange scene for the next few decades, although their life spans were usually limited and it proved difficult for them to mediate in a depressed labor market. Even in good times they were of very circumscribed usefulness. Employers did not ordinarily care to hire workers registered there, because good workers tended to stay away from such offices.[73]

Exchanges organized by employers, unions, or charities thus handled only a very limited clientele. By far the largest amount of labor exchange activity occurred in the commercial agencies that secured jobs for a fee. Such private offices had been known for decades. Their number proliferated with expanding industrialization, and reached a peak in the years between the turn of the century and World War I. Most of these agencies concerned themselves exclusively with the local labor market, but the more enterprising sent their clients into neighboring cities, over state lines, and even thousands of miles across the continent. Some specialized in specific occupations, notably domestic service. The biggest business, however, was done with the unskilled workers needed in railway construction, highway building, and the growing industries. "The great de-

Final Report and Testimony, I, 26; Nelson, *Managers and Workers,* 88; Sargent, "Statistics of Unemployment," 61; 78; Thomas Sewall Adams and Helen L. Sumner, *Labor Problems: A Textbook* (New York: Macmillan, 1905), 282–83; E. E. Pratt, "Trade Unions as Employment Agencies," in Edward T. Devine, *Report on the Desirability of Establishing an Employment Bureau in the City of New York* (New York: Charities Publication Committee, 1909), 162; *American Federationist* 19 (Jan. 1912), 43–44.

73 Bogart, "Public Employment Offices," 347–48; Conner, "Free Public Employment Bureaus," 1; Sargent, "Statistics of Unemployment," 37; H. Roger Grant, *Self-help in the 1890s Depression* (Ames: Iowa State University Press, 1983), 41–58; Pennsylvania. Commissioner of Labor and Industry, *1st Annual Report, 1913,* 278; Devine, *Report on the Desirability,* 13–15; 112–28; [Chicago.] Mayor's Commission on Unemployment, *Report,* 55–60; New York (State). Commission to Inquire [etc.], *Third Report,* 57–58.

velopment," Edwin H. Sutherland, a young sociologist, noted about this in a treatise published by the Chicago Mayor's Commission in 1914, "has been in the field of unskilled labor and temporary employment."[74]

Among these profit-oriented exchanges, competition was usually fierce, and because most of them had no reputation to lose, they felt, as one observer put it, "a constant temptation to over-charge, to misrepresent, and to encourage frequent changes [of the working place] for the sake of the fee." There were a myriad ways to defraud the naive jobseeker. After the gullible worker had paid his registration fee, he could be put on endless hold; the fee could be exorbitantly high; if no receipt had been given out, the jobseeker could be charged again; hosts of workers could be sent to establishments seeking but a few laborers or that had no openings at all, or that offered worse conditions than announced, or were too distant for the workers. A favored method was fraudulent replacement, usually practiced in connivance with the employer or his foremen. The worker paid his fee and was hired, only to be discharged within a few days; if he wished to be rehired, he had to pay again. Sharp minds had countless opportunities, and the surplus of labor, often largely composed of inexperienced immigrants with language difficulties, made passive resistance difficult. "The employment agencies feasting upon the necessities of the army of unemployed," the Ohio commissioner of labor wrote in 1889, "filled up the ranks [of the labor gangs] as fast as the sad experience of the victims thinned them out."[75]

It was, of course, possible to counteract obviously fraudulent practices of this kind through legislative action. As early as 1885, Minnesota passed a law aiming at curbing the abuses, and in 1888, New York followed suit. By 1910, twenty-five states had enacted such legislation. Lack of enforcement, though, rendered the results disappointing. Moreover, many of the more important private agents did interstate work that would have

---

74 Sutherland, "Unemployment," 110; 112. Sutherland mentions a private exchange that opened in Baltimore in 1823. His report is contained in [Chicago.] Mayor's Commission on Unemployment, *Report*, 95–175.

75 Devine, *Report on the Desirability*, 12; Ohio. Bureau of the Statistics of Labor, *12th Annual Report, 1889*, 263. For descriptions of the private agents' fraudulent practices see Bogart, "Public Employment Offices," 345–47; Frances A. Kellor, *Out of Work: A Study of Employment Agencies: Their Treatment of the Unemployed, and Their Influence upon Homes and Business* (New York: Putnam's, 1904), 42–103; Sargent, "Statistics of Unemployment," 36; Sutherland, "Unemployment," 113–16; Grace Abbott, *The Immigrant and the Community* (New York: Century, 1917), 26–55.

required federal control; for the time being, nothing could be hoped for in this respect.[76]

Advocacy of public exchanges

The inadequacy of the existing institutions gave rise to the idea that governmental exchanges could offer more competent or permanent services. Such exchanges, which were known to exist in Europe, could not only match the jobless man with the manless job, but also rescue the unemployed from the fraudulent policies of the private agents. Among the advocates of state agencies were a substantial number of officials affiliated with governmental labor bureaus. These people were generally eager to enhance the size and importance of their own activities, and their pleas blended with those of reformers motivated by humanitarian concerns, an aversion to waste, or not infrequently even a fear of social disarrangement.

Humanitarian pleadings were often heard. If the state disapproved of idleness to the point of punishing vagrancy and mendicancy, Colorado Commissioner of Labor Statistics James Rice, a union man, wondered in 1888, was "it not wise for the State to go beyond mere penal measures ... and extend a helping hand to every person who desires to secure employment? Would not the manner of doing so be the establishment of employment bureaus ... under State authority?" "The State certainly can not undertake a more charitable or a more honorable and praiseworthy act," the Ohio Commissioner of Labor Statistics similarly advised his legislature in 1890, "than that of securing employment for her willing yet needy citizen laborers."[77]

---

76 Conner, "Free Public Employment Offices," 58; 83. Frances A. Kellor, "Interstate Immigration, Land and Labor Problems," *Survey* 29:11 (14 Dec. 1912), 326 reported that the New York (State) Bureau of Industries and Immigration had hundreds of cases which would have required federal intervention. See also U.S. Dept. of Labor, *1st Annual Report, 1913*, 44. For a general assessment of the situation see Mabelle Moses, "The Regulation of Private Employment Agencies in the United States," in Susan M. Kingsbury, ed., *Labor Laws and Their Enforcement, with Special Reference to Massachusetts* (New York: Longmans, Green, 1911), 362; 366.

77 Colorado. Bureau of Labor Statistics, *1st Biennial Report, 1887–1888*, 368; Ohio. Bureau of Labor Statistics, *14th Annual Report, 1890*, 21. For similar argumentation see Iowa. Bureau of Labor Statistics. *4th Biennial Report, 1890–91*, 240; Nebraska. Bureau of Labor and Industrial Statistics, *8th Biennial Report, 1901–1902*, xx; New York (State). Dept. of Labor, *1st Annual Report, 1902*, 85; Indiana. Bureau of Statistics, *13th Biennial Report, 1909 and 1910*, 18–19.

Humane concerns, in particular, demanded that the corrupt private agencies be reined in. If legislative efforts to regulate them did not succeed, Rice thought, the appropriate measure was to "supplant them."[78] It can certainly not be maintained, as has been done repeatedly, that the public employment agencies were established "primarily and almost entirely for the purpose of protecting the unemployed against the private employment agencies."[79] But this intention nevertheless played a significant role in the proponents' pleading. Governmental agencies offering free services, the Kansas Commissioner of Labor and Industry affirmed, would "automatically drive out the dishonest private agencies that thrive by imposing on the needy." Officials in many other states shared this hope.[80]

Demands for charity, however, were likely to evoke in many minds unwelcome associations with handouts, pauperism, and dead-end characters. Thus, advocates of governmental exchanges soon began to change the basis of their advocacy. Adapting old-fashioned enlightened ideas to modern exigencies, they implicitly argued from concepts characteristic of the social welfare state. Care should be taken, the Kansas commissioner advised, to avoid classifying public exchanges as charitable in their nature; an unemployed person should be able to profit from the service "as a citizen using of right a public agency provided for the benefit of all citizens, and in the spirit that the citizen seeks the advice or assistance of any other arm of the state." The ultimate task of government agencies, his New York colleague asserted, was to preserve in the worker "that self-respect, that dignity which proclaims nobility of character without which life would not be worth living."[81]

---

78 Colorado. Bureau of Labor Statistics, *1st Biennial Report, 1887–1888*, 368.
79 Sutherland, "Unemployment," 150. See also the corresponding statement of David W. Cook, "A History of Public Employment Offices in the United States" (New York University Ph.D., 1935), 46. Cook, who was apparently not acquainted with Sutherland's report, seems to have relied upon Conner, "Free Public Employment Offices," 82, for this assertion.
80 Kansas. Dept. of Labor and Industry, *13th Annual Report, 1914*, 240; Ohio. Bureau of Labor Statistics, *14th Annual Report, 1890*, 21; New Jersey. Bureau of Statistics of Labor and Industries, *16th Annual Report, 1893*, 73; Connecticut. Bureau of Labor Statistics, *15th Annual Report, 1899*, 13; Missouri. Bureau of Labor Statistics and Inspection, *19th Annual Report, 1897*, 486; Illinois. Bureau of Labor Statistics. Free Employment Offices, *10th Annual Report, 1908*, 2; Conner, "Free Public Employment Offices", 31; 73; 77; 83. See also Carroll D. Wright, "The Value and Influence of Labor Statistics," *Engineering Magazine* 6:2 (Nov. 1893), 140.
81 Kansas. Dept. of Labor and Industry, *13th Annual Report, 1914*, 240. Similarly Con-

The invocation of lofty ideals could be supplemented through an insistence upon the social value of public exchanges. There was above all the increase in efficiency in the use of society's resources. In 1902 the United States Industrial Commission pointed to the necessity of rectifying "the unscientific distribution of population," meaning the congestion of labor in certain places. Labor agencies could also help in selecting the right kind of worker. As for the jobseeker, he no longer needed to walk from one factory gate to the next in an exhausting search for employment. Gettemy perhaps said it best. "The enormous waste, both human and material, due to irregular and unsystematic employment – for which the worker is in no wise to blame and of which the employer is too often the victim, while society as a whole pays the penalty in times of industrial depression – has created a problem with which the State alone can successfully cope."[82]

There was one further reason not to leave the out-of-work merely to their own devices. As the Ohio secretary of state noted in 1890, "idle hands are prone to mischief, and the disturbances possible from unemployed labor . . . are historical in their danger." The concern for social peace thus joined the humanitarian and economic motivations. At the turn of the century the Connecticut commissioner of labor approvingly quoted the *New York Sun*, which felt that "inability to find work breeds discouragement, despair, pauperism, crime, and death." The depression before the first World War renewed these concerns for the chief of the Colorado Bureau of Statistics. Jobless men, he feared, "might lose respect for our written laws and assume to take unlawfully that which every man and woman is entitled to . . . an opportunity to provide for those dependent on them."[83]

necticut. Bureau of Labor Statistics, *15th Annual Report, 1899*, 13; Missouri. Bureau of Labor Statistics and Inspection, *19th Annual Report, 1897*, 222; New York (State). Dept. of Labor, *1st Annual Report, 1902*, 85.

82 Connecticut. Bureau of Labor Statistics, *17th Annual Report, 1901*, 188; 192; *Final Report of the Industrial Commission*, XIX, 758; New York (State). Industrial Commission, *Annual Report, 1915*, 274; Charles B. Barnes, "Some Problems in Organizing a State System of Employment Offices," AAPEO, Proceedings 1915, in U.S. Bureau of Labor Statistics, *Bulletin 192*, 107; Massachusetts. Public Employment Offices, *10th Annual Report, 1916*, 5.

83 Ohio. Bureau of Labor Statistics, *14th Annual Report, 1890*, 25–26. See also Ohio. Bureau der Arbeitsstatistik, *16ter Jahresbericht, 1892*, 11 (German Language edition); Connecticut. Bureau of Labor Statistics, *16th Annual Report, 1900*, 186. Similarly Indiana, Bureau of Statistics, *13th Biennial Report, 1909 and 1910*, 18; Colorado. Bureau

The idea of creating public offices ran counter to the tenet that government should keep out of the social sphere. Refuting this principle, the Iowa commissioner of labor statistics J. R. Sovereign, a man with strong union connections, asserted during the depression of the 1890s that a charge of paternalism could be made against public employment offices "with no more force than can be made against the State library." His Michigan counterpart added a more rational consideration. He recognized a "superiority of the services rendered by the state institution as compared with similar institutions operated by private parties." Some might claim, he admitted, that private enterprise worked more efficiently; but government should at least try its hand, because "the modern trend of governments seems to be toward extension of functions."[84] Time-honored laissez-faire principles were thus readily abandoned by many a labor department official.[85] But what did the prospective beneficiaries think of the institution in question?

Labor had difficulties reaching a clear verdict on public exchanges. Unorganized wage earners were naturally too inarticulate to be heard from, and the amount of their approval can only be guessed from the extent to which they patronized the public offices created over time. This will be attempted later. Skilled workers increasingly organized in trade unions, however, and these bodies not infrequently took a stand. Doubtless many unions were at first – into the first decade of the twentieth century – quite favorably disposed toward the creation of governmental exchanges. The Ohio offices, the first agencies to be opened by any state, were established on the initiative of the Municipal Labor Congress of Cincinnati. In 1892 the Knights of Labor, gathered in general assembly in St. Louis, Missouri, also strongly endorsed the cause. A similar pledge of support came from the Iowa State Federation of Labor in 1893. Unions seem to have backed the public agencies movement also in several other

of Labor Statistics, *Biennial Report, 1915–1916*, 189; Massachusetts. Public Employment Offices, *10th Annual Report, 1916*, 6.

84 Iowa. Bureau of Labor Statistics, *5th Biennial Report, 1892–93*, 12. Sovereign was at the time State Master Workman of the Knights of Labor and had published a labor journal for seven years. On him see Sutherland, "Unemployment," 154. – Michigan. Bureau of Labor and Industrial Statistics, *10th Annual Report, 1893*, xx; xxiii.

85 In 1891 the National Convention of Commissioners of Labor Statistics at Denver, Colorado, even passed an official resolution stating "That the Commissioners of Labor of the different States recommend to the legislatures of their different States the consideration of the advisability of creating free public employment offices, under State control and supervision." Iowa. Bureau of Labor Statistics, *5th Biennial Report, 1892–93*, 11–12.

states, notably Colorado, Missouri, Massachusetts, Indiana, Connecticut, Wisconsin, Rhode Island, and Illinois. Looking over the scene at the turn of the century, one observer thought that organized labor was "on the whole, in favor of free public employment offices."[86]

One may wonder, of course, why any unions would plead and lobby for the creation of a state service that few of its members needed or would ever use. A partial explanation is perhaps found in the fact that reportedly as many as 75 percent of the superintendents of the public employment offices were union men. Bogart thought that the offices in Montana and Nebraska, and perhaps the one in New York, were established "to win or conciliate the labor vote." The offices provided a regular salary and possibly social advancement for union functionaries. There may have been even more powerful incentives at work. "The presence of the unemployed person in the labor market," Sutherland noticed while studying the Chicago scene, "is regarded as a great hindrance to the securing of the demands of the unions." Any method of decreasing the number of job-seekers therefore meant the reduction of potential competition and could serve to advance organized labor's goals.[87]

Unions, however, had an interest in obtaining control of those exchanges that were created. If the employer side directed the offices, the president of the Illinois Federation of Labor cautioned, it would "break down the things that the organized workers in our country have already established by fighting for them hard and long." This fear was voiced as early as the 1890s, and because of it the first exchange laws of Illinois and Wisconsin contained clauses that prohibited state employment offices from sending prospective employees to work sites afflicted by labor dis-

86 Ohio. Bureau of Labor Statistics, *14th Annual Report, 1890*, 20; Iowa. Bureau of Labor Statistics, *5th Biennial Report, 1892–93*, 12; Missouri. Bureau of Labor Statistics and Inspection, *20th Annual Report, 1898*, 221; Massachusetts. State Free Employment Offices, *1st Annual Report, 1907*, 12; Colorado. Bureau of Labor Statistics, *12th Biennial Report, 1909–1910*, 194; Indiana. Bureau of Statistics, *13th Biennial Report, 1909 and 1910*, 17. For Connecticut and Wisconsin see Conner, "Free Public Employment Offices," 11; 78; for Rhode Island see Sargent, "Statistics of Unemployment," 119; for Illinois see Sutherland, "Unemployment," 151. – Bogart, "Public Employment Offices," 365.

87 Conner, "Free Public Employment Offices," 90; Bogart, "Public Employment Offices," 341; 364. The New York (State) Federation of Labor was apparently also "largely instrumental in securing the passage of the bill that established the State Employment Bureau" in 1914. A. J. Portenar, "Labour Unions and Public Employment Offices," IAPES, *Proceedings 1920* (Ottawa: King's Printer, 1921), 65. - Sutherland, "Unemployment," 153.

putes. Court decisions that declared these stipulations unconstitutional added to union apprehensions.[88]

Logic could, of course, also dictate the opposite. Public employment offices could suffer a "perversion into an immigrant distribution agency," offering the opportunity to break down wage standards. Because of this consideration, some unions showed outright hostility.[89] The attitude of the AFL revealed labor's ambiguity in this respect. In 1910, Gompers wrote in the *American Federationist* that "before trade unions can devote much time to the promotion of labor exchanges, they want better factory and mine inspection, better methods of protection against accidents, a better system of compensation for accidents, better child labor laws – yea, a heap of better conditions for the wage earners at work." In marked contrast, however, the AFL convention that met in the depressed fall of 1914 stated that it "endorses and urges" the establishment of state bureaus "for the purposes of aiding the unemployed in securing positions."[90]

If labor were divided, the employer side was equally unable to agree on a common philosophy. Overall, hesitation rather than enthusiasm seems to have prevailed. In the 1890s the Massachusetts Bureau of Labor Statistics found that employers did "not generally believe that such offices would be of any value to them or to the working classes." Subsequently, such indifference not infrequently gave way to utter antagonism, spawned by the fear that public exchanges could become union tools. Conner thought that the active opponents of public agencies were "such antiunion organizations as the Citizens' Industrial Association, the Employers' Association, the Manufacturers' Association." These forces succeeded in blocking the passage of a pertinent bill in Iowa in 1906. Employers were

---

88 John H. Walker, in "Public Responsibility – Discussion," *ALLR* 4:2 (May 1914), 271; Massachusetts. House. Board to Investigate [etc.], *Report*, vol. V, lx. See also Bogart, "Public Employment Offices," 365–66; 1899 *Illinois Laws*, p. 270; 1901 *Wisconsin Laws*, ch. 420, s. 8; Conner, "Free Public Employment Offices," 15; 90. The Wisconsin statute was closely modeled on that of Illinois.

89 Henry Bruère, "America's Unemployment Problem," *Annals* 61 (Sept. 1915), 18. See also Terrence V. Powderly's pertinent statement in U.S. Congress. Senate. *Industrial Relations: Final Report and Testimony*, II, 1308–09. Powderly was at the time Chief of the Division of Information of the federal Bureau of Immigration. – Conner, "Free Public Employment Offices," 34; 35; 52. For union hostility in Michigan see also Bogart, "Public Employment Offices," 364; for the same in Chicago see [Chicago.] Mayor's Commission on Unemployment, *Report*, 42. See also Sutherland, "Unemployment," 153.

90 Samuel Gompers, "Government Labor Exchanges," *American Federationist* 17 (Nov. 1910), 995; AFL. 34th Annual Convention, *Proceedings 1914*, 283.

also instrumental in testing the constitutionality of the Illinois law mentioned earlier, thereby scuttling it. Management's opposition was not
unanimous, though. In 1903 the Baltimore Merchants' and Manufacturers' Association good-naturedly notified its members of the opening
of the public exchange in that city, and in Indiana many members of
employers' associations used the public employment service to obtain
unskilled labor. But these were fairly infrequent occurrences. Don D.
Lescohier, who for a time had been superintendent of the Minnesota
public employment office, later recalled that before the war "a majority
of the employers of the country have been either hostile, indifferent, or
contemptuous."[91]

Increasing public awareness

A remarkably diversified discussion, carried on in the open since the
1890s, both contributed to and reflected the advance of the exchange cause
in the public consciousness. At first the voices were sparse, as the concept
was too novel to catch much attention. In the midst of the depression the
Forum and the *Journal of Political Economy* ran articles reviewing methods
of help for the unemployed that did not even mention public – or any
other – employment agencies. But the subject slowly began to attract
interest. One writer in the *Annals* who knew about employment information centers in Berlin, Germany, thought that in American cities the
police stations could render a similar service. The well-informed Massachusetts Dewey Board concluded that there was no immediate need
for a public exchange, but it provided a draft bill to enable the Bureau
of Labor Statistics to establish offices "in times of emergency."[92]

Around the turn of the century, the first serious, if brief, studies of the
matter appeared. In 1900, Bogart published his comparative article on
German and American public exchanges in the *Quarterly Journal of Eco-*

91 Massachusetts. Bureau of Labor Statistics, *24th Annual Report, 1894*, 263; Conner,
   "Free Public Employment Offices," 20; 88; 92–93; Sutherland, "Unemployment," 154.
   See also Indiana. Bureau of Statistics, *14th Biennial Report, 1911 and 1912*, 69. –
   Maryland. Bureau of Statistics and Information, *12th Annual Report, 1903*, 95; Sargent,
   "Statistics of Unemployment," 42; Lescohier, *Labor Market*, 164–65.
92 Josephine Shaw Lowell, "Methods of Relief for the Unemployed," *Forum* 16 (Feb.
   1894), 655–62; Carlos C. Closson, "Notes on the History of 'Unemployment' and
   Relief Measures in the United States," *Journal of Political Economy* 3 (Dec. 1895), 461–
   69; Brooks, "The Future Problem of Charity and the Unemployed," 21; Massachusetts.
   House. Board to Investigate [etc.], *Report*, vol. V, lx-lxiii.

nomics. He felt that the few agencies in existence in the United States did not perform satisfactorily, as they dealt mostly with unskilled labor. Somewhat more enthusiastic was William F. Willoughby, who thought that the state offices could in addition to their job mediation function collect "sociological data...for studying the causes and extent of unemployment."[93]

These treatises probably reached only a limited readership. The attention of a larger audience was assured with two publications resulting from thorough field investigations. In 1904, Frances A. Kellor, a young sociologist, came out with a book entitled *Out of Work: A Study of Employment Agencies.* Financed by the College Settlements Association, a staff of nine researchers under her guidance had visited over 700 private, charitable, and public exchanges in New York, Boston, Philadelphia, and Chicago in 1902–03. Her book had a muckraking quality to it in its impassioned denunciation of the methods of the private agents. As for public offices, she noted that poor management and political mongering caused the offices to "fall short of reaching their highest possibilities." Conner, who stressed the labor market function from the employers' point of view, came to a similar conclusion in 1907. At the behest of the federal Department of Labor he had visited the fifteen states that then had public employment offices, and he argued that the institution "must be regarded thus far as an experiment with some failures, many mistakes, and several successes."[94]

From the second half of 1907 on, the need to alleviate widespread unemployment manifested itself for the first time since the mid-1890s. The economic downturn proved to be short, but the experience stimulated further exploration of the potential of the institution. From this time on, the debate never fully subsided again; over the years it rather swelled to considerable proportions, and by about 1914, through the medium of the daily press, had even spilled over into the general public consciousness.

The most immediate consequence of the 1907–08 depression experience was an initiative by the New York philanthropist Jacob H. Schiff, who in October 1908 suggested the establishment, under the auspices of

93 Bogart, "Public Employment Offices," 341–77; William Franklin Willoughby, *Employment Bureaus in the United States* (Boston: Wright & Potter, 1900). Quotations pp. 10; 14. This pamphlet was reprinted in idem, *State Activities in Relation to Labor in the United States* (Baltimore: Johns Hopkins University Press, 1901), 18–32.
94 Kellor, *Out of Work* (1904), 245–57; Conner, "Free Public Employment Offices," 5; 104.

the COS, of an employment bureau with a substantial working fund. The COS decided first to examine the rationale for such an agency, and the Russell Sage Foundation, founded a year earlier with the goal of promoting the improvement of social conditions in the United States, agreed to meet the cost of the inquiry. Devine was charged with undertaking the task, and consulted thirty experts, most of them American academics but including British reformer Sidney Webb. After visiting state employment bureaus in Boston and the Midwest, he concluded that there existed a need at all times, "and in periods of even slight depression a very urgent need," of an efficient exchange system. He therefore unequivocally advocated the creation of the bureau in question. His report was published under the auspices of the Russell Sage Foundation, which assured its impact on interested reform circles. In the same year, 1909, Devine repeated his recommendation in his book, *Misery and Its Causes*. When his Columbia colleague Seager came out with his elementary study on social insurance the next year, he referred to the latter publication. As the principal reasons for the establishment of public exchanges, Seager discerned the reduction of human waste, the advantage to employers who obtained the kind of labor they desired, the collection of valuable social data, and the elimination of loafers.[95]

During his unemployment investigation for the Wainright Commission at about this time, Seager's pupil Leiserson, following Beveridge's lead, equally pleaded for public agencies. He proposed separate departments for juveniles and, moreover, stressed the offices' information gathering potential, which might prove useful especially with regard to future unemployment insurance plans. The Wainwright Commission, although hedging on the insurance aspect, practically adopted the other parts of his argumentation and even complemented it with a draft bill.[96]

At least in the restricted circle of people caring for a cure for unemployment, interest in public employment offices gathered further momentum around the beginning of the century's second decade. The New

---

95 Jacob H. Schiff to Charity Organization Society (New York), 27 October 1908, printed in Devine, *Report on the Desirability*, 3. On the Russell Sage Foundation see Joan M. Glenn, Lillian Brandt, and F. Eleanor Andrews, *The Russell Sage Foundation* (New York: Russell Sage Foundation, 1947). – Devine, *Report on the Desirability*, 3–11; idem, *Misery and Its Causes*, 139–43; Seager, *Social Insurance*, 96–102. Nelson, *Unemployment Insurance*, 11 rates Seager's book as "the first important work on unemployment to appear in the United States."

96 Beveridge, *Unemployment: A Problem of Industry*, 198–218; New York (State). Commission to Inquire [etc.], *Third Report*, 13–21; 60; 66; 67. Quotation p. 14.

York legislature's readiness to finance Voss's and Leiserson's fact-finding tour to Europe was a visible sign. So were hints of emerging attention in Congress, the federal Department of Labor's decision in 1912 to conduct and publish yet another survey of the American exchanges, the City of Chicago's noteworthy examination of the matter, a call for federal action by the National Conference of Immigration, Land and Labor Officials, and the founding of the AAPEO.

Perhaps prompted by the activities of the Wainwright Commission, in November 1910 the *New York Times* published an interview with Congressman-elect Martin W. Littleton (D-New York), a lawyer. On two pages Littleton argued that the absence of an "intelligent system" of labor distribution drove the jobseeker into the arms of the socialists; exchanges similar to those in Great Britain and Germany in each state of the union could remedy this. When a *New York Times* editorial called his proposal "a sound one," Littleton requested in the House an investigation of the practicability of his scheme (H.J.Res. 203). Nothing came of it, but the Socialist Party took up the idea at its 1912 national convention in Indianapolis, where it inserted a demand for governmental employment bureaus in its electoral platform.[97]

The failure of the National Employment Exchange in particular increased the willingness to discuss governmental involvement. The exchange had been founded under the auspices of the COS as a result of Devine's report mentioned earlier. Incorporated with great fanfare in New York (City) in April 1909 and equipped with a capital fund of $100,000, it was by far the most ambitious project of private charity in this field. Unfortunately, it neither spread across state lines as expected, nor did it handle the masses of unskilled workers that had been envisaged. Its capital dwindled rapidly, and its decision after two years of operation to charge a fee of two dollars to jobseekers and employers alike diminished its business volume without increasing its viability.[98]

Where private charity failed, public offices might still have a chance. Five years after publishing the results of Conner's investigation, the De-

---

97 Charles Willis Thompson, "To Bring Jobless Man and Manless Job Together: Congressman-elect Martin W. Littleton Will Urge Plan to Found Labor Exchanges for This Purpose All Over the Country," *New York Times*, 20 Nov. 1910, V, pp. 1–2; "An Employment Clearing House," *New York Times*, 21 Nov. 1910, p. 8; Donald Bruce Johnson, ed., *National Party Platforms*. 2 Vols. (Urbana: University of Illinois Press, rev. ed. 1978), vol. I, 190.
98 Ringenbach, *Tramps and Reformers*, 147–48.

partment of Labor had another researcher, Frank B. Sargent, prepare a follow-up study. Sargent visited exchanges in Boston, Providence, Indianapolis, Detroit, Minneapolis, and Chicago and researched material on the state offices elsewhere. He showed himself well disposed toward public exchanges, feeling that they had "great opportunity for usefulness" in reducing unemployment.[99]

Doubtless the most thorough examination of the subject before World War I was a study sponsored by the Chicago Mayor's Commission on Unemployment. The commission in May 1912 recommended that the legislature provide for the exchange of workers throughout the state. When in fall 1913 unemployment threatened again, the commission reconstituted itself and decided to publish Sutherland's research paper on public employment agencies that had reached it in the meantime. Henderson subsequently ensured that the writer, following Leiserson's example at Columbia, could successfully submit this report as a Ph.D. dissertation to the University of Chicago.[100] Although Sutherland did not undertake any field trips, his treatise provided as good a foundation for his conclusions as could probably be had at this time. He argued that the potential of state exchanges was not yet fully understood, and that their desirability depended "partly on the extent to which harmful reactions on the society can be prevented." Shifting workers from one locality to another, he felt, could cause a "decrease in the regularity of industrial operations, the reduction of emigration in times of depression, the destruction of the present trade union principle of trade exclusiveness, the partial dissipation of small group control, the promotion of the drift to the city, the increase in the class of shiftless workers, the fostering of parasitic industries." Sutherland was careful, however, not to sound altogether negative. He thought that employment agencies of some kind were probably a necessity, and the state seemed to be best equipped to manage them efficiently. Altogether the principal underlying problem of understanding society's structure had to be kept in mind. If unemployment was inherent in the modern industrial organization, "the broader problem of the modification of that organization is presented."[101]

The doubts expressed in Sutherland's study did not severely dampen

---

99 Sargent, "Statistics of Unemployment," 34.
100 [Chicago]. Mayor's Commission on Unemployment. *Report*, 6; 8–10; 12–13; 48–60.
Sutherland's contribution was also published separately with the title "Unemployment and Public Employment Agencies" (University of Chicago Ph.D., 1913).
101 Sutherland, "Unemployment," 171–72.

the reformers' eagerness, as the creation of a special organization demonstrated. In November 1912 the National Conference of Immigration, Land and Labor Officials requested the new federal Department of Labor to take steps to coordinate the work of the state employment agencies. As the conference was too busy with other matters, it was felt that a separate body was desirable. Leiserson, who in the meantime had been appointed superintendent of the Wisconsin employment offices, and Walter L. Sears of the state office in Boston convened a conference in Chicago, 29–30 December 1913, where the AAPEO was founded. Leiserson emerged as secretary-treasurer, to which post he was reelected during the next few years.[102]

While the AAPEO grouped the immediate circle of exchange officials, the AALL remained the standard bearer of the movement. At the First National Conference the issue of public employment agencies attracted the greatest attention by far. Shortly before the meeting, Kellor had called for further development of the institution. The conference itself, Seager confided to a correspondent, was mainly organized "to push for free public employment offices." On the floor, delegates from various states described the experiences of their offices. Seager, who chaired several sessions, gave an instructive and favorable paper on the English exchange system. Howe's contribution on the German system has already been mentioned. A researcher with the *ALLR*, Solon De Leon, surveyed the performance of the existing American state agencies. The most impressive presentation was made by Leiserson, who advocated government involvement, because the organization of the labor market had to be centralized and impartial.[103] The conference subsequently urged the creation of a federal Bureau of Distribution that could act as a clearing house; the establishment "or reconstruction," by the various states, of free employment agencies; the inspection

---

102 "Call for Conference," AAPEO, Proceedings, 1913, in U.S. Bureau of Labor Statistics, *Bulletin 192*, 8–9; W. M. Leiserson, "Public Employment Offices in the United States," ibid., 14; Walter L. Sears, "Distribution of Alien and Citizen Labor," ibid., 37.
103 Frances A. Kellor, "The Crying Need for Connecting up the Man and the Job," *Survey* 31:19 (7 Feb. 1914), 541–42; Seager to Leo Arnstein, 10 Feb. 1914, microfilm, reel 11, Andrews Papers; Henry R. Seager, "The English Method of Dealing with the Unemployed," *ALLR* 4:2 (May 1914), 281–93, esp. 282–84. For Howe, see page 32. – Solon De Leon, "Operation of Public Employment Exchanges in the United States," *ALLR* 4:2 (May 1914), 359–71; William M. Leiserson, "Public Employment Offices in Theory and Practice," ibid., 314–31. Leiserson also thought that government should organize the labor market for the same reasons for which it ran schools. He seems to have gotten this argument from Commons. Commons to Leiserson, 23 March 1912, Box 9, Leiserson Papers.

and control of private agencies through the federal government; and the further investigation through the AALL of aspects of the unemployment problem. Encouraged by the extensive coverage that the proceedings received in the press, notably the *New York Times*, the AALL began to lobby in New York, Massachusetts, and Pennsylvania for employment office legislation. The interdenominational Unemployment Committee of the Churches of New York joined in this effort.[104]

The growing public importance of the issue was clearly evident during the following months. The federal Commission on Industrial Relations gave the matter much attention. As indicated, Leiserson, on leave of absence from his position in Wisconsin, together with his staff held hearings in various cities between April and June 1914. The commission proclaimed itself persuaded that efficient public labor exchanges would eliminate unvoluntary idleness and moreover provide necessary information.[105] That Andrews' *Practical Program*, which came out almost simultaneously with the commission's report, considered the establishment of public employment exchanges "an essential step toward a solution of the problem of unemployment," has already been mentioned. At the AALL's second unemployment conference, public employment offices again figured prominently. But the discussion of the usefulness of the institution during these years was not just confined to the theoretical level. Considerable effort had already been expended in various states to try out the instrument in practice.[106]

Creating state labor exchanges

As the discussion about the merits of governmental exchanges gained momentum, a substantial number of such offices were already being

104 "Resolutions," *ALLR* 4:2 (May 1914), 353–54; *New York Times*, 1 March 1914, II, p. 3; Irene Osgood-Andrews to Leonard W. Hatch, 21 March 1914, microfilm, reel 11, Andrews Papers; Hatch to Osgood-Andrews, 22 March 1914, ibid.; Andrews to Mary K. Hale, 17 April 1915, microfilm, reel 14, ibid.; John Price Jackson to Andrews, 15 March 1915, ibid.; Andrews to T. Henry Walnut, 6 Feb. 1915, microfilm, reel 13, ibid.; *New York Times*, 7 March 1914, p. 5; ibid., 21 March 1914, p. 5.
105 Leiserson to Industrial Commission [of Wisconsin], 9 March 1914, Box 45, Leiserson Papers; U.S. Congress. Senate. Commission on Industrial Relations, *1st Annual Report* (Washington: G.P.O., 1914), 42–43. See in this context "Public Work: Suggestions in Re a Plan to Use Public Work as a Regulator of the Labor Market," memorandum, 16 Jan. 1915, Box 3, Commission on Industrial Relations Papers.
106 Andrews, "Practical Program," 176; Charles B. Barnes, "Public Employment Bureaus—Organization and Operation," *ALLR* 5:2 (June 1915), 200.

created and maintained. During an initial period of experimentation a few dead-end routes were traveled, but states establishing offices after the turn of the century profited from the experience gained elsewhere and mostly followed the route that had been found viable.

The first attempt to create a state office occurred before the depression of the 1890s. The Colorado Bureau of Labor Statistics began operations in 1887, and the commissioner managed to get an employment bureau bill introduced in the legislature in 1889. The proposal was defeated, however, and an 1891 law to regulate the private employment offices was all the legislators enacted for the time being.[107] Parallel endeavors by the Ohio commissioner proved more successful. When visiting Paris at the occasion of the international exposition in 1889, he learned about the work of the French *bourses de travail*. Back in Ohio he won the support of the Municipal Labor Congress of Cincinnati. After a bill was introduced in the legislature, an amendment placed some of the financial burden upon the respective cities before the measure passed in April 1890. The act stipulated the creation of a public employment office in each of the larger cities of the state and made some provisions for administrative procedure and the collection of data. Accordingly, the first public employment offices in the United States opened in Columbus, Cleveland, Cincinnati, Dayton, and Toledo in the same year. The Ohio experiment was widely noticed. Requests for information came from nearly all the states of the union and even from abroad. When the commissioners of labor were assembled in national convention in Denver in 1892, they recommended to their states "the consideration of the advisability of creating free employment offices, under State control and supervision."[108]

Fortunately for the movement the Ohio institution proved to be of durable quality, as in the depression decade various attempts in other states ended in failure. Usually the lack of financial appropriations doomed the endeavors, as was the case in 1892 in Iowa, Nebraska, and California. In the following year the Iowa commissioner launched a replacement bill that charged the county auditors with the task of performing employment agent functions. When this attempt also failed, the commissioner unsuc-

---

107 Colorado. Bureau of Labor Statistics, *1st Biennial Report, 1887–1888*, 368; idem, *3d Biennial Report, 1891–1892*, 162–63; 165–66.

108 Ohio. Bureau of Labor Statistics, *14th Annual Report, 1890*, 11–12; 20; idem, *16ter Jahresbericht, 1892*, 13 (German language edition); idem, *17th Annual Report, 1893*, 874; Willoughby, *Employment Bureaus in the United States*, 6–7; 1890 *Ohio Acts*, pp. 340–42; Iowa. Bureau of Labor Statistics, *5th Biennial Report, 1892–93*, 12.

cessfully tried to secure the help of the county auditors without legal sanction. The course of events in Nebraska and California was similar.[109]

In two more states, good will alone did not prove sufficient for success. During the depression year of 1895, Montana trade unionists demanded the establishment of public exchanges. The framers of the resulting bill despaired of obtaining an appropriation and modeled their proposal upon the second Iowa bill. It was enacted, but like the "mail order" versions elsewhere, it proved impracticable and was replaced in 1897. The new act dispensed with all state involvement and merely allowed municipalities to open their own labor exchanges. Equally ineffective was legislation in Kansas in 1901 that provided for a salaried "director of employment" and charged the city clerks with carrying out the functions of employment agents.[110]

Although the lack of funds was the most pervasive cause of failure, sheer ineptitude also played a role. A state labor exchange office that opened in New York (City) in July 1896 with much publicity could not maintain its initial success. An investigative commission found that the office filled mostly domestic help positions, and the legislature closed the agency in April 1906.[111]

With the exception of the Ohio offices, none of the early exchanges survived. These creations still served a useful function for the movement in general, however, as their very failure helped to narrow the options available. It was obviously difficult, if not impossible, to obtain valuable services without adequate financial arrangements. Indirect schemes of the mail order type in particular did not appear to be viable propositions. Developments over the next decade and a half showed that these two insights were largely taken to heart. Ultimately, the Ohio method, or

109 Iowa. Bureau of Labor Statistics, *5th Biennnial Report, 1892–93*, 8–10; idem, *6th Biennial Report, 1894–95*, 15; Nebraska. Bureau of Labor and Industrial Statistics, *3d Biennial Report, 1891 and 1892*, 579; idem, *4th Biennial Report, 1893 and 1894*, 155; idem, *7th Biennial Report, 1899 and 1900*, 437; idem, *11th Biennial Report, 1907–1908*, 17; 1897 *Nebraska Laws*, c. 39, sec. 2071; Conner, "Free Public Employment Offices," 6; California. Bureau of Labor Statistics, *7th Biennial Report, 1895–1896*, 18–19; table I, ibid. (after p. 32).
110 Montana. Bureau of Agriculture, Labor and Industry, *3d Annual Report 1895*, 18–20; Conner, "Free Public Employment Offices," 29–30; 50; Kansas, *General Statutes of 1901*, secs. 3833; 3838.
111 1896 *New York (State) Statutes*, c. 982, sec. 1; New York (State). Bureau of Statistics of Labor, *14th Annual Report, 1897*, 1024–26; New York (State). Dept. of Labor, *1st Annual Report, 1902*, 25; idem, *5th Annual Report, 1905*, I.15–17; idem, *6th Annual Report, 1906*, I.108.

modifications of it, prevailed. From before the turn of the century a string of office openings, which can roughly be grouped into two series, spanned the beginning of World War I. Few of these establishments, if any, became roaring successes. But they showed enough permanency for the proponents of the cause to feel vindicated and to continue the quest for the improvement and extension of the institution.

The offices that were started in the years from the turn of the century mostly resulted from the unemployment experience of the 1890s that lingered in the minds of promoters and legislators. The Missouri commissioner opened an agency in St. Louis in 1897, and two years later his legislature sanctioned this creation and allowed further offices. Similarly in 1900 his West Virginia colleague began exchange activities in Wheeling without specific authorization. Within a year the legislature passed an employment bureau act with an appropriation which set the agency on a permanent footing.[112]

By this time, several other states were already taking steps in the same direction. An Illinois act of 1899 provided for employment offices in cities of over 50,000 population. Because the act forbade the furnishing of labor to strikebound establishments, the employer side kept it from being implemented, and in 1903 the state's supreme court declared it unconstitutional. The legislature immediately passed a substitute bill without the contentious section, and by 1909 five offices had been opened. The Wisconsin development was closely related. An act, modeled on the Illinois example, was passed in 1901. When Illinois changed its law, Wisconsin followed suit, and by 1904 the state ran four agencies.[112a] Connecticut joined the movement in 1901, Maryland in 1902, Michigan and Minnesota in 1905, Massachusetts in 1906, Colorado in 1907, Rhode Island and Oklahoma in 1908, and Indiana in 1909.[113]

112 Missouri. Bureau of Labor Statistics and Inspection, *19th Annual Report, 1897*, 488–89; idem, *20th Annual Report 1898*, 212; 214; Nebraska. Bureau of Labor and Industrial Statistics, *3d Biennial Report, 1891 and 1892*, 568; 1899 *Missouri Laws*, pp. 272–73 (S.B. 307); Conner, "Free Public Employment Offices," 73; 1901 *West Virginia Acts*, c. 15.

112ª Conner, "Free Public Employment Offices," 15; 76; 1899 *Illinois Laws*, pp. 268–71; 1903 *Illinois Laws*, pp. 194–96; Illinois. Bureau of Labor Statistics. Free Employment Offices, *10th Annual Report, 1908*, 3; Sutherland, "Unemployment," 125; 1901 *Wisconsin Laws*, c. 420; 1903 *Wisconsin Laws*, c. 434.

113 Connecticut. Bureau of Labor Statistics, *15th Annual Report, 1899*, 13–14; 137–70; idem, *16th Annual Report, 1900*, 163–93; idem, *17th Annual Report, 1901*, 185–202; 1901 *Connecticut Acts*, c. 100; Conner, "Free Public Employment Offices," 10–11; 31–32; 1902 *Maryland Laws*, c. 365, sec. 6A; 1905 *Michigan Acts*, Act no. 37; 1905

During the years of relative prosperity following the economic downturn of 1907–08, little incentive existed to combat unemployment, and Indiana remained for some time the last state to inaugurate labor exchange offices. But the deterioration of the economy from 1913 on engendered further efforts. The new wave got off to a bad start with the passage of an ill-conceived law in South Dakota; as the legislature did not provide an appropriation, the act remained a dead letter. Two years later New Jersey indulged in similar tokenism, even though the biggest city in the state, Newark, had opened a municipal labor agency as early as 1909. But exchange proponents could take heart from the fact that in 1914 the New York legislature, under pressure from the State Federation of Labor, passed another act. It provided for five offices throughout the state and allocated close to $50,000, about ten times as much as the former office had obtained. The act clearly signaled the state's readiness to give the undertaking a new dimension. In January 1915, offices opened in Brooklyn and Syracuse, in the next month in Rochester and Buffalo, and in April in Albany.[114] Similar confidence was displayed by the Pennsylvania, California, and, to a lesser degree, Iowa governments, all of which created offices in 1915 or early 1916.[115]

Not only did new states enter the public employment exchange field, but additions of more offices by various states that already had exchanges working, notably Michigan, Oklahoma, and Illinois, further increased the scope of activity. By the last year before the American entry into World War I a total of ninety-six offices were in operation in twenty-four states. They differed very widely as to size, location, the amounts of working

Minnesota Laws, c. 316; 1906 *Massachusetts Acts*, c. 435; 1907 *Colorado Laws*, c. 129; 1908 *Rhode Island Statutes*, c. 1528; 1908 *Oklahoma Laws*, c. 53, art. III; 1909 *Indiana Laws*, c. 155.

114 1913 *South Dakota Laws*, c. 117; Cook, "A History of Public Employment Offices," 111; 1915 *New Jersey Acts*, c. 47; John G. Herndon, "Public Employment Offices in the United States," in U.S. Bureau of Labor Statistics, *Bulletin 241* (Washington: G.P.O., 1918), 15; 1914 *New York (State) Laws*, c. 529; New York (State). Industrial Commission, *Annual Report, 1916*, 257. The actual allocation was $49,440. The former New York office had received $5,000. See 1896 *New York (State) Statutes*, c. 982, sec. 10. For the State Federation of Labor involvement see Portenar, "Labour Unions and Public Employment Offices," 65.

115 Pennsylvania. Dept. of Labor and Industry, *1st Annual Report, 1913*, 282; idem, *2d Annual Report, 1915*, 518; idem, *3d Annual Report, 1916*, 187–88; 1915 *Pennsylvania Session Laws*, Act no. 373; California. Bureau of Labor Statistics, *17th Biennial Report, 1915–1916*, 21; 1915 *California Statutes*, c. 302, sec. 3; 1915 *Iowa Laws, 1915*, c. 212; Iowa. Bureau of Labor Statistics, *Biennial Report, 1916*, 169–74.

funds at their disposal, the quality of people running them, and thus their performance. But there could be no denying the fact that on the eve of the war state employment offices had become an accepted institution, even more so because for some time the problem of interoffice cooperation had arisen.

The network idea

The idea to coordinate the efforts of several employment exchanges was not far-fetched. During the period under consideration, labor in many instances moved quite freely over local and even regional boundaries, most notably in connection with the various enormous construction projects (railroads, highways, dams, harbors) of the age. As mentioned, private employment agencies were heavily involved in supplying the necessary hands for such ventures. Interlocal and interregional distribution of labor also constituted a field of great potential for governmental exchange services. Not only would such activities supplement the local efforts of duplicating the work of the privates, thus eliminating their abuses; more importantly, shifting labor from centers of heavy unemployment to places where workers were in demand would go a long way toward fulfilling the mandate of public offices as construed by many of their advocates. Three basic methods of such interoffice cooperation were conceivable. Exchanges inside a given state, governed by the same legislation, could organize an interconnecting service; there could be interaction between two or more states; and a nationwide network could be organized, preferably under federal guidance. Each of these possibilities was tried out before the United States entered World War I.

Although interoffice action inside a given state might have been looked upon as the easiest form of cooperation, it got nowhere beyond some hesitant initial steps. There were various reasons to account for this failure. Financial means were usually in short supply and were needed for the basic local services; the latter's expansion thus often appeared to be an unaffordable luxury. Furthermore, interoffice cooperation had to mean that manpower could be shifted from one employment scene to another. This demanded transportation arrangements, again largely a matter of cost. Finally, it is probably not unfair to surmise that any organizational set-up larger than individual offices would have required a sort of administrative know-how and personal initiative that was not easily found in most states in the ranks of those concerned with the running of

employment services. Competent administrators were few and far between, and the development of an interacting network of agencies would
in most cases have overtaxed the capabilities of the people in charge.

Whatever the causes, the sole form of cooperation that was occasionally
tried out was the periodic publication of employment opportunities. The
employment office acts of various states stipulated that office superintendents had to submit regular reports to their administrative centers,
usually the state bureaus of labor statistics, indicating the number of open
positions and workers available. Weekly statements were expected in Ohio,
Illinois, Wisconsin, Colorado, Indiana, and Massachusetts; Kansas agents
were to report as often as the state director required so.[116] Such reports,
however, proved to be of little practical value. Monthly lists, as required
in Missouri and Minnesota, were from the outset without obvious benefit.
It appears that Pennsylvania alone attempted to establish a central clearing
house. But the activities of the agency at Harrisburg, which was officially
assigned this role, fell short of the task. No effective and regular statewide
exchange of labor took place.[117]

If in-state cooperation proved difficult, combined action between different states was impeded by even greater obstacles. It testifies to the
enthusiasm that motivated some of the early pioneers that a number of
attempts were made nevertheless, even though success generally eluded
them. As early as 1901, representatives of the state services of Connecticut, Illinois, Missouri, and New York, joined by an emissary from
the Canadian province of Ontario, congregated at Niagara Falls to found
a "National Association of Free Employment Bureaus of America." Concrete aims were not yet formulated. A call "for the expression of ideas
as to the work in various States and the best way to advance the same"
betrayed the tentativeness of the venture. The conferees reconvened in
the following year, their number augmented by delegates from Minnesota

116 1890 *Ohio Acts*, sec. 308; 1899 *Illinois Laws*, p. 269; 1901 *Wisconsin Laws*, c. 420, sec.
4; 1907 *Colorado Laws*, c. 129, sec. 4; 1911 *Indiana Laws*, c. 274, sec. 4. Originally
quarterly reports had been asked for. 1909 *Indiana Laws*, c. 155, sec. 6. – 1901 *Kansas
Statutes*, sec. 3836.
117 Ohio. Bureau of Labor Statistics, *20th Annual Report, 1895*, 399; Sutherland, "Unemployment," 139–40; Missouri, *Revised Statutes, 1899*, sec. 10086; 1905 *Minnesota
Laws*, c. 316, sec. 2; Pennsylvania. Dept. of Labor and Industry, *2d Annual Report,
1915*, 519; 529–32; idem, *3d Annual Report, 1916*, 1088. Massachusetts asked for
semi-weekly reports from 1906, for weekly ones from 1909, but gave up the practice
shortly thereafter. 1906 *Massachusetts Acts*, c. 435, sec. 6; 1909 *Massachusetts Acts*, c.
514, secs. 6 and 8; Sargent, "Statistics of Unemployment," 68.

and Wisconsin. But they decided to merge with the National Association of Commissioners of Labor Statistics, thus ending this early endeavor at staking out common ground.[118]

The first appreciable interaction between state services took place around 1903. In that year, New York, Connecticut, Illinois, and Missouri supplied harvesters to Kansas. Typical for the haphazard character of this undertaking was the way the New York activity came about. The New York office superintendent had read press reports that Kansas needed harvest hands, and after contacting the Kansas state office he ended up sending 4,000 workers. Seeking a more reliable source of labor supply, representatives from seven mid-western states in 1905 founded the "Western Association of State Free Employment Bureaus." The office at Kansas City (Missouri) was selected to function as a clearinghouse, and each state was expected to report weekly the manpower available and required. But the enthusiasm quickly evaporated, and no evidence of further activities of the association has survived. Apart from a repetition of this endeavor a decade later, no noteworthy further attempts at interstate cooperation were made before the war. The task at hand seemingly exceeded the administrative possibilities or the political will in the states at the time.[119]

Governmental labor exchange across state borders could of course be regarded as primarily a task for the federal government, especially if the fight against unemployment was the principal objective. No state, Murdock declared on the House floor, could adequately cope with unemployment, because it had neither the authority nor the mechanism to disseminate information about labor and trade conditions beyond its boundaries; on the other hand, "many of the most serious conditions" were interstate in their very nature, and the state could not control them "any more than it creates its own weather"; help could come only through

---

118 New York (State). Dept. of Labor, *1st Annual Report, 1902*, 92–34. Quotation p. 93. The conference began on 24 Sept. 1901 in Niagara Falls (New York) and after adjournment met again two days later in Buffalo. – New York (State). Dept. of Labor, *2d Annual Report, 1902*, II.10–II.11.

119 Sutherland, "Unemployment," 141; New York (State). Dept. of Labor, *3d Annual Report, 1903*, 187–92. The association president's report of 1904 is in New York Public Library (C/F p.v. 1582, no. 13), but is inaccessible. Quoted from Cook, "A History of Public Employment Offices," 45; Conner, "Free Public Employment Offices," 52–53. – Sutherland, "Unemployment," 140. The founding states were Iowa, Kansas, Missouri, Nebraska and South Dakota, later joined by Minnesota and the Oklahoma Territory.

the establishment of a federal system of exchange bureaus.[120] Such federal involvement was not new. The establishment of the Interstate Commerce Commission in 1887 was one example, the creation of the Federal Reserve Board in 1913 was another. But although both measures were in their own ways responses to the increasing integration of American life as a result of advancing industrialization, they could be understood mainly to pertain to the economic sphere. This was an area in which, through tariff and currency legislation in particular, the federal government had traditionally played an accepted role. The creation of a federal labor distribution system, by contrast, constituted an inroad into the social domain. To downplay this fact and to emphasize the commodity character of labor would have belied the humanitarian argumentation of a full generation. To stress a social obligation of the federal government, on the other hand, meant occupying a constitutional position that could not yet hope to find widespread and sufficient popular support. Advocates of a federal exchange service thus had to tread cautiously so as not to arouse counterarguments too obnoxious to overcome, and any actual buildup had better be circumspect and guarded. In reality, though, for many years discussion of the matter was chiefly hampered by a patent lack of public interest, and a persistent shortage of funds served as a natural barrier to any precipitate actions of the federal authorities.

In the early period of the state employment agency movement, demands for federal involvement were seldom heard. The creation of individual offices used up the available energy, and the feeling prevailed that further steps could be taken later on. Before the war, most state offices did not get beyond the stage of experimentation, at least not in the eyes of legislators who had to approve of allocations for an expansion of services. Efforts to ensure the survival of the fledgling institution in its most primitive form thus remained the principal task, and more far-reaching proposals appeared untimely. A call like that of the New York office superintendent, who held in 1897 that labor distribution to alleviate the distress of the jobless was "a matter worthy [of] the consideration of our lawmakers, both in State and in nation," was bound to remain without echo. Similarly, Conner did not receive any noteworthy public response when he demanded the "national organization of the unskilled labor market." Even as reform-minded a promoter of public employment offices as Devine thought that federal involvement in large-scale labor exchange work was

120 *CR*, 63 Cong., 2 sess., Appendix, 1 May 1914, p. 413.

"impractical," as he could not see it to be the government's task to assess the quality of employers or jobseekers, a necessary function if workers were to take themselves to distant places.[121]

But there were people, especially in the federal government, who found virtue in the idea of an extended network. Hoping that public insight would grow, officials concerned in 1907 with labor matters embarked upon a scheme that they intended to expand into a nationwide system. In time they were able to combine their efforts with those of various reformers and lawmakers, especially when the depression of 1914–15 rendered the unemployment question urgent again. The structure they created did not satisfy even modest expectations, but a good deal of thinking and experimentation went into the effort, and later endeavors could build upon the experience thus gained.

The original federal decision to enter the exchange field did not spring from unemployment considerations. The creation of the "Western Association" had already shown that governmental employment services would embrace any task that would justify their existence. In that instance it had been the desire to accommodate the needs of Western farmers. Another intention – the wish to unclog the port cities by dispersing lingering immigrants – appears to have been behind the origin of a section of the Immigration Act of 1907. This section authorized the establishment of a Division of Information as a branch of the Bureau of Immigration and Naturalization in the Department of Commerce and Labor.[122] Shelby M. Harrison of the Russell Sage Foundation later implied in his handbook of public employment offices that the division, created "in the year of the panic, 1907," had as its primary purpose the alleviation of the suffering of the unemployed immigrants. But the Immigration Act was enacted on 20 February 1907, and the division began functioning on 1 July 1907, whereas the panic struck only in the fall. The real reason for the establishment of the division came to the fore in the congressional debate before passage of the bill, when Representative Anthony Michalek (R-Illinois), a native of Bohemia elected in a Chicago district, denounced the "stubborn mental antipathy toward a white person not born in this country" which many native Americans displayed, and hoped that the

---

121 New York (State). Bureau of Statistics of Labor, *14th Annual Report, 1897*, 1029; Conner, "Free Public Employment Offices," 102–03; Devine, *Report on the Desirability*, 16–17.
122 34 Stat. 1139 (1907), sec. 40.

Division of Information, to be established "for the special purpose of dealing with this [problem]," would live up to its mandate.[123]

Although the desire to dissipate nativist resentment caused the division's creation, the alleviation of unemployment soon became its professed purpose. It had barely begun its work when the recession set in and brought widespread joblessness. To demonstrate the serviceability of the division, a loose construction of the text of the law recommended itself. According to the Immigration Act, the task was "to promote a beneficial distribution of aliens" and to gather "useful information regarding the resources, products, and physical characteristics of each State and Territory"; the division was to publish this information in different languages for distribution to aliens coming to the United States "and to such other persons as may desire the same." When Secretary of Commerce and Labor Oscar S. Straus wrote his first report on the performance of the division, though, he stated that he considered it "a subject of great interest in all commercial countries how to provide work, especially in periods of industrial depression, for the unemployed," and he interpreted the act's wording to mean that the division should serve "all of our workers, whether native, foreign born or alien, so that they may be constantly advised in respect to every part of the country as to what kind of labor may be in demand." In other words, he construed the act as a mandate to create a federal employment service to deal with unemployment, foreseeing for it "a great and substantial extension."[124]

The secretary's wishful thinking, however, ran into several obstacles. One arose from constitutional concerns about his administrative latitude. Devine, for one, thought it difficult to see how the Bureau of Immigration "would equally be at the service of citizens and aliens." More important was a lack of adequate funds. The means that the Department of Commerce and Labor was subsequently able to dedicate to the purpose proved sufficient only for a small-scale operation. In 1907 a branch office was established in New York, and two more were opened in the following year in Baltimore and Galveston respectively. The principal activity of

---

123 Shelby M. Harrison, *Public Employment Offices: Their Purpose, Structure and Methods* (New York: Russell Sage Foundation, 1924), 127–28; *CR*, 59 Cong., 2 sess., 18 Feb. 1907, p. 3229; Darrell Hevenor Smith, *The United States Employment Service: Its History, Activities and Organization* (Baltimore: Johns Hopkins University Press, 1923), 2.

124 34 Stat. 1139 (1907), sec. 40; U.S. Dept. of Commerce and Labor, *Annual Report, 1908*, 23.

these offices consisted of contacting farmers through the township cor-
respondents of the federal Department of Agriculture, with the aim of
placing farm hands and domestics. The numbers handled remained min-
iscule, hovering annually around the 5,000 mark[124a](Table 2–1).

There were still other reasons that hindered a blossoming of the institution. Immigrants often proved to be reluctant clients, fearing deportation if they stayed too long in contact with the federal government.
Furthermore, the division's activities met with staunch opposition from
the trade union side. At a labor conference called by Straus in February
1909, Gompers bitterly complained that the division "was being turned
into a labor bureau to help tear down existing standards of life," because
it acted abroad as a recruitment tool for immigrant labor. A few years
later, unionists still argued that the federal offices might direct "cheap
alien labor" to already well-supplied labor markets and thus contribute
to a lowering of wages.[125]

Thus no significant developments occurred for several years. Endeavoring to upgrade the performance, in fall 1911 the department invited
representatives from states and territories to a conference "for the purpose
of securing cooperation between the various States and the Division."
Delegates from twenty-five states and one territory met in Washington
on 16–17 November, but the only tangible result was an appeal to Congress for more funds.[126] Nothing practical came of this, nor did the
separation of the Department of Labor from the Department of Commerce on 4 March 1913 materially enhance the work of the division in
a notable way.

124[a] Devine, *Report on the Desirability*, 16; Smith, *United States Employment Service*, 4; U.S.
Dept. of Commerce and Labor, *Annual Report, 1909*, 21; U.S. Dept. of Labor, *1st
Annual Report, 1913*, 44.

125 U.S. Dept. of Commerce and Labor, *Annual Report, 1909*, 22; Harrison, *Public Employment Offices*, 128; *Labor Conference: Proceedings of the Conference with the Representatives of Labor, Held in the Office of the Secretary of Commerce and Labor, February 10
and 11, 1909* (Washington: G.P.O., 1909), 26; U.S. Dept. of Labor, *Annual Report,
1913*, 43; Frances A. Kellor, *Out of Work: A Study of Unemployment* (New York:
Putnam's, 1915), 303–04.

126 U.S. Dept. of Commerce and Labor. Bureau of Immigration and Naturalization.
Division of Information, *Distribution of Admitted Aliens and Other Residents: Proceedings
of the Conference of State Immigration, Land, and Labor Officials with Representatives of
the Division of Information, Bureau of Immigration and Naturalization, Department of
Commerce and Labor: Held in Washington, D.C., November 16 and 17, 1911* (Washington:
G.P.O., 1912), 7–8; U.S. Dept. of Commerce and Labor, *Annual Report, 1912*, 61.

Table 2-1. *Federal labor exchange activities*

Fiscal year	Applications	Placements	Percentage	Fiscal year	Applications	Placements	Percentage
1909	26,477	5,008	18.9	1912	26,213	5,807	22.2
1910	18,239	4,283	23.5	1913	19,891	5,025	25.3
1911	30,657	5,176	16.7	1914	10,393	3,368	32.4

Source: Darrell Hevenor Smith, *The United States Employment Service: Its History, Activities and Organization* (Baltimore: Johns Hopkins University Press, 1923), 12.

Growing federal interest

The experience of the depression of 1914–15 engendered renewed efforts to strengthen the federal role in the labor market. Discussion about the need for such involvement increased, and led to several legislative attempts. Parallel to these endeavors the Department of Labor, under its Democratic leadership, took further administrative initiatives that aimed at augmenting its activities and even perhaps forcing the hands of the legislators. More voices than before could now be heard in public advocating an integrated labor distribution system covering a number of states, or even the entire nation.

The founding of the AAPEO in December 1913 indicated that public employment bureaus had now reached a stage of maturity that allowed a glance beyond regional boundaries. It was only logical that AAPEO's constitution stated as one of its objectives "the proper distribution of labor throughout the country by the cooperation of municipal, State, and Federal governments.[127] Supporters quickly took up the cause. Kellor perceived "a great need of co-ordination and of a clearing-house for prompt and reliable information on unemployment, and opportunities for work to be furnished throughout the country." At the First National Conference Henderson called for the existing offices in the United States to be bound together "in a national enterprise." As noted, one of the resolutions subsequently passed reflected this sentiment, urging the creation, in the federal Department of Labor, of a Bureau of Distribution "with power to establish employment exchanges throughout the country to supplement the work of state and municipal bureaus."[128]

The first legislative proposals to create a national exchange system went before Congress as a direct follow-up to the conference. Murdock, who suggested the creation of a "system of free labor exchanges" (H.R. 16130), specifically credited "the social service workers of the Progressive Party" with having prompted him. Kellor, for one, was probably among these workers, as he quoted from her writings. His bill was intended as a trial balloon, as was obvious from the lack of pertinent detail.[129] A few weeks

---

127 "Constitution of the Association," AAPEO, Proceedings 1913, in U.S. Bureau of Labor Statistics, *Bulletin 192*, 10.
128 Frances A. Kellor, "The Way Out of the Unemployment Situation," *Survey* 31:21 (21 Feb. 1914), 639; "Reports of Official Delegates on the State of Employment," *ALLR* 4:2 (May 1914), 226; "Resolutions," ibid., 353.
129 Hearings on H.R. 16130, p. 7. See also *CR*, 63 Cong., 2 sess., 1 May 1914, p. 416.

later, another bill (H.R. 17017), introduced by Progressive Congressman William J. MacDonald (R-Michigan), attempted to revive the postal scheme in a national set-up. The proposal divided the country into zones; one post office in each was to be designated as a "central labor exchange," with jurisdiction over the other post offices. These would serve as "labor exchanges," taking in applications from employers and jobseekers and listing them daily. It was a sign of the importance that the employment office question had gained by then that the House Committee on Labor held hearings in June and July 1914. Little criticism was aired. Andrews, Kellor, Leiserson, and a few others spoke strongly in favor of the Murdock scheme.[130] The Committee on Labor itself, though, saw virtue in the post office idea, because it used existing facilities. The committee consequently combined the salient features of both proposals. In handing the new bill (H.R. 19015) to the House in February 1915, it "earnestly urge[d] the immediate attention of Congress thereto." A few other bills with similar intent were introduced at about the same time, providing support from the flank. But despite vigorous demand on the House floor for consideration, the Sixty-third Congress soon adjourned, and the matter was left in abeyance. Andrews later stated that action was deferred to permit the Commission on Industrial Relations to come forward with a bill of its own, but the body failed to live up to this expectation.[131]

The advocates of a national system who were grouped in the AALL pursued the matter further. In December 1914, Andrews had already published an article in the *New Republic* offering a blueprint for the

Murdock was chairman of the Progressive National Committee. – *CR*, 63 Cong., 2 sess., Appendix, 1 May 1914, p. 414. Murdock's bill may have been the one which the North American Civic League for Immigrants had prepared, or a derivative of it. See Frances A. Kellor, "Three Bills to Distribute Labor and Reduce Unemployment," *Survey* 31:23 (7 March 1914), 694. Kellor was very actively involved in the organization of the Progressive Party in 1912 and later. Allen F. Davis, "The Social Workers and the Progressive Party, 1912–1916," *American Historical Review* 69:3 (April 1964), 679; 684–87. H.R. 16130 is reprinted in U.S. Congress. House. Committee on Labor, *National Employment Bureau.* H.Rept. 1429, 63 Cong., 3 sess. (to accompany H.R. 19015; 20 Feb. 1915), 2–3.

130 H.R. 17017 is reprinted in H.Rept. 1429, 4–5. It followed in intent the abortive S. 5180. – "Proposed Plan for a National System of Labor Exchanges to Cooperate with State and Local Public Employment Offices and to Regulate Private Employment Agencies in Interstate Business," Hearings on H.R. 17017, pp. 94–100.

131 H.Rept. 1429, 4; 8. H.R. 19015 is reprinted on pp. 2–3. – H.R. 21386; S. 7725; H.R. 21331. See the remarks of Rep. H. Robert Fowler (Illinois) in *CR*, 63 Cong., 3 sess., Appendix, 4 March 1915, p. 833. – John B. Andrews, "A National System of Labor Exchanges in Its Relation to Industrial Efficiency," *Annals* 61 (Sept. 1915), 145.

organization of a national service along the Murdock line. While the Murdock and MacDonald proposals were still pending in the House, Representative Richard W. Austin (R-Tennessee) inserted into the *Congressional Record* a "Petition to Congress for the Unemployed of America," signed by forty-one persons, that asked for a national exchange system. Andrews, for his part, succeeded in persuading Senator John W. Kern (D-Indiana) to take his article to the Senate floor in an effort to widen the campaign. At Kern's suggestion it was printed as an official Senate document in February 1915. The same article also appeared in slightly shortened form in the *Annals* issue of September 1915, supported by a strong statement of the chamberlain of the city of New York, Henry Bruère. Kellor, for her part, republished her book in a thoroughly revised and augmented edition. She took the MacDonald proposal to task as unrealistic and extravagant and appended a draft bill similar to Murdock's for the benefit of her readers.[132]

These initiatives were intended to keep the issue alive. For the same reason, bills abandoned earlier were reintroduced when Congress met again in December 1915. Senator Moses E. Clapp (R-Minnesota) warmed up the post office proposal (S. 679). Shortly afterward, Congressman John I. Nolan (R-California), a San Francisco union man and member of the House Committee on Labor, took up the bill that had resulted from merging the Murdock and MacDonald drafts, and resubmitted it with the blessing of Secretary of Labor William B. Wilson (H.R. 5783). Hearings produced only favorable statements. Secretary Wilson and Meeker stressed the advantages of transferring the Division of Information to the prospective national employment bureau. The committee, impressed by their arguments, amended the bill accordingly and in March 1916 reported it out favorably, but nothing further happened.[133]

In an apparent effort to help matters along, Leiserson, now a professor

---

132 John B. Andrews, "A National System of Labor Exchanges," *New Republic* 1:8 (Dec. 1914), 1–8; *CR*, 63 Cong., 3 sess., 20 Feb. 1915, p. 4236; "Labor Exchanges: An Article Suggesting 'A National System of Labor Exchanges,'" S. Doc. 956, 63 Cong., 3 sess. (19 Feb. 1915); Andrews, "A National System of Labor Exchanges," (*Annals*), 138–45; Bruère, "America's Unemployment Problem," 17–18; 23–24. Bruère was an AALL member. See also Andrews, "Unemployment Survey," 562–63. – Kellor, *Out of Work* (1915), 304–12; 488; 500; 511–17.

133 H.R. 5783; Hearings on H.R. 5783, pp. 12–13; 32–33; U.S. Congress. House. Committee on Labor, *National Employment Bureau*. H.Rept. 424, 64 Cong., 1 sess. (to accompany H.R. 5783, 24 March 1916), 2; U.S. Dept. of Labor, *5th Annual Report, 1917*, 88.

of political and social science at Toledo University, took a step of his own two months later. Elaborating on his recommendations to the Commission on Industrial Relations, he outlined the structure and organization of a "National Labor Reserve Board" in a paper given at the annual meeting of the NCCC. This proposal was basically the same as Andrews' earlier sketch, the difference lying mainly in Leiserson's effort to provide more of a theoretical foundation. The problems of the labor market, he claimed, were similar to those of the money market. In the latter, the Federal Reserve Board tried to regularize the employment of capital, to remove fluctuations and to make it more steady. Similarly, labor was "bought and sold in a market" that was subject to fluctuations. Leiserson accepted in principle the idea propounded "from Marx to Beveridge" that the unemployed constituted a necessary labor reserve. Labor might be "essentially different from capital," but the fluctuations in the labor market had to be fought with tools corresponding to those used in the capital market. He therefore advocated the creation of a Federal Labor Reserve Board with control over a system of clearing houses and local offices. Just as the Federal Reserve Board did not constitute a pervasive federal system but preserved the local banks, the Labor Reserve Board would function as a kind of umbrella organization that would allow the local offices "much freedom to develop in their own ways." But it would insist upon the standardization of business methods and records, and management had to be made uniform. The main task of the system would be to exchange employment information, probably by way of a regular labor bulletin. Leiserson also foresaw further possible functions, notably a role in the apportioning of public work to regularize the labor market, the administration of unemployment insurance, and vocational guidance of juveniles.[134]

Leiserson's plan was the best-considered proposal of its kind yet, even if he clearly still struggled with the dilemma of having to put the unemployment problem in economic terms while striving to maintain its fundamentally different character. In any event, his sophisticated justi-

---

134 After ending his stint with the U.S. Commission on Industrial Relations in March 1915, Leiserson had first unsuccessfully tried to obtain a position as an economics professor at Columbia. Leiserson to Seager, 12 March 1915, Box 36, Leiserson Papers; Leiserson to Frank P. Walsh, 17 March 1915, Box 42, ibid. – U.S. Congress. Senate, *Industrial Relations: Final Report and Testimony*, I, 114; William M. Leiserson, "A Federal Labor Reserve Board: Outlines of a Plan for Administering the Remedies for Unemployment," NCCC, *Proceedings 1916* (Chicago: Hildmann, 1916), 161–76.

fication and his informed attention to the structural detail easily proved him to be the best informed advocate of the institution. His plan constituted a summary of the thought and experiences of the preceding generation, and it was certainly appropriate that he had it also published in the *Annals*, a more widely read medium than the conference's proceedings.[135]

When the *Annals* article appeared in January 1917, unemployment had already considerably subsided as a result of war production. This improvement did not stop congressional attempts at exchange legislation. Aware that joblessness would reappear in the future, Nolan, with the approval of Secretary Wilson, reintroduced his bill in the House on 2 April (H.R. 153). Four days later, Senator James D. Phelan (D-California), a former San Francisco mayor who had already supported Nolan during the previous congressional session (S. 6205), followed with an identical step in the Senate (S. 842). By this time, though, President Woodrow Wilson had already given his war message to Congress, and attention was diverted to more urgent matters.[136]

Whereas discussions in public and activities in Congress aimed at providing a solid legal foundation for a nationwide exchange service, the federal Department of Labor undertook its own practical steps to create an interstate or even nationwide office system. One of them was renewed involvement in the harvest work in the Midwest, another the attempt to use the facilities of the post offices as envisaged by the MacDonald bill; endeavors were also made to beef up the immigration service and to enter into some cooperation with the existing state services.

The difficulties of the harvest in the depression year of 1914, when thousands of workers more than were needed flocked to the grain belt, made it appear imperative that the supply of labor be organized in a more rational way. Repeating the effort that had led to the creation of the shortlived Western Association, representatives of Kansas, Nebraska, Oklahoma, and the two Dakotas met at Kansas City in December 1914 and again at Omaha in February 1915. The federal Departments of Labor

135 William M. Leiserson, "A Federal Labor Reserve Board for the Unemployed: Outlines of a Plan for Administering the Remedies for Unemployment," *Annals* 69 (Jan. 1917), 103–17.

136 U.S. Dept. of Labor, *5th Annual Report, 1917*, 88. Phelan had apparently no immediate interest in the matter and used it to gather political capital. Robert E. Hennings, *James D. Phelan and the Wilson Progressives of California* (New York: Garland, 1985), 109; 158.

and of Agriculture sent delegates and assisted in the founding of the "National Farm Labor Exchange." All agreed to cooperate during the subsequent harvest seasons, and the Department of Labor undertook to assume a leading role by positioning agents in strategic locations. The organization seems to have worked reasonably well during the following years, in 1915 placing over 16,000 workers in Oklahoma and almost 28,000 in Kansas alone.[137]

The depression, furthermore, led to an attempt to marshall the postal resources. Secretary Wilson persuaded the Post Office Department to deposit blank application forms in its 60,000 offices, to be filled out by employers or jobseekers and mailed free of postage. Post Office officials at various levels were supposed to match employees' and jobseekers' forms and to notify the applicants accordingly. The results, however, were hardly more gratifying than those of similar attempts made on the state level in earlier years. Although Secretary Wilson still boasted in 1916 that "a ramifying network of communication ... has been spread all over the United States," the undertaking appears to have been a dismal failure. A knowledgeable insider later stated before a congressional committee that the experiment fell "absolutely flat ... utterly flat," and he strongly counseled against its repetition.[138]

If the post office scheme did not have much of a future, the Department of Labor's own resources still offered opportunities. In late 1913 the Bureau of Immigration, of which the Division of Information was a part, had begun to supplement its coastal stations by placing immigration agents at various points in the interior. Although it was the primary duty of the stations to take care of the needs of new immigrants, according to the Department of Labor's interpretation of the Immigration Act it seemed possible also to engage in more general employment exchange work. As a first step in this direction, Secretary Wilson had the entire country

---

137 U.S. Dept. of Labor, *Annual Report, 1915*, 39; idem, *Annual Report, 1916*, 68–69; Charles M'Caffree, "National Farm Labor Exchange," in AAPEO, Proceedings 1914, in U.S. Bureau of Labor Statistics, *Bulletin 192*, 117–18; Andrews, "Unemployment Survey," 552; Harrison, *Public Employment Offices*, 540.

138 U.S. Dept. of Labor, *Annual Report, 1914*, 38–39; 52–53; idem, *Annual Report, 1915*, 38–39; idem, *Annual Report, 1916*, 54–55; Kellor, *Out of Work* (1915), 306–12; Hearings on H.R. 5783, p. 43; 45. Statement of R. Meeker. – W. G. Ashton to Andrews, 27 Feb. 1915, microfilm, reel 13, Andrews Papers. Ashton was commissioner of labor of Oklahoma. – Hearings on S. 688 and 1442, and H.R. 4305, p. 89. Statement of Nathan A. Smyth, former assistant director general of the United States Employment Service.

subdivided into eighteen "employment zones," each headed by an immigration station doubling as a "public employment branch station."[139] This, of course, was plain window dressing. Although the scheme was further developed over the next few years and was given the imposing title of "United States Employment Service" (USES), nothing much practical was achieved, as jobseekers and employers alike refused to avail themselves of the institution's assistance. "A popular impression seemed fixed and irremovable," the secretary of labor lamented in 1917, "that only immigrant workers and employers wanting immigrant workers were being served."[140] Building up its own employment service was apparently a losing proposition for the federal Department of Labor as long as it did not have sufficient funds.

There was, of course, the possibility of the department's joining forces with the state services, most of which were in equal financial straits. Wilson explored this avenue as well. Because the states were supposed to be touchy regarding their own jurisdictions, he chose to advance by "friendly consultation." In April 1915 he sent out a formal call for a national conference of federal, state, and municipal officials engaged in labor distribution. Specific areas of discussion were to be unemployment in its various aspects, private agencies doing interstate business, and his own department's recent exchange activities.[141] At the meeting in San Francisco, 2–6 August 1915, the unemployment question dominated the debates. Wilson remained mindful of the sensitivities of the states. Although he later frankly admitted that he thought that a centralized federal service constituted the best solution, he pleaded for a federated system. But even this goal proved hard to attain.[142] The only tangible result of the conference was the creation of a twelve-member advisory board composed of delegates from all three levels of government. After this body submitted its first report in November 1915, nothing further was heard of it, the

---

139 U.S. Dept. of Labor, *1st Annual Report, 1913*, 42–43; idem, *2d Annual Report, 1914*, 56. A list of the zones is also found in "Federal Employment Work of the Department of Labor," *MLR* 1:1 (July 1915), 9.

140 The designation "USES" appears for the first time in U.S. Dept. of Labor, *4th Annual Report, 1916*, 54. Later the Department claimed that the USES "was established" in 1914. U.S. Dept. of Labor, *5th Annual Report, 1917*, 82; 88.

141 U.S. Dept. of Labor, *3d Annual Report, 1915*, 34; idem, *4th Annual Report, 1916*, 57–58.

142 For the department's expectations see Louis F. Post to [Anthony] Caminetti, 16 July 1915, Box 44, Chief Clerk's Files, General Records of the Department of Labor, Department of Labor Papers. Post was assistant secretary of labor, Caminetti was commissioner general of immigration.

geographical separation of its members being one reason for its ineffectiveness. A subsequent meeting, more regional in character, was held 16–17 December 1915 in Charleston, South Carolina, without any interesting results. A second national conference, contemplated for the following year, did not materialize, as in the meantime the European war had substantially changed the employment situation.[143]

Although the depression offered a powerful incentive, the federal Department of Labor therefore did not succeed in organizing an exchange network worthy of this name. This failure showed the financial and administrative limitations that even at the height of the Progressive Age constrained governmental efforts in the social sphere. It is not a surprise that under these circumstances the accomplishments of the existing services, on the state as well as on the federal levels, remained rather limited.

Achievements

It is difficult to gauge the impact that the twenty-four state employment services and the federal Bureau of Immigration had on the American labor market. Figures, where available, are not only unreliable, but also frequently incompatible with each other, and any assessment is therefore of dubious merit. The effort seems nevertheless worth making, because a few insights of a general nature may be gained.

With regard to the volume of the exchange work undertaken, some statistical material can be gleaned from the annual reports of the individual state offices. Table 2–2 shows a compilation of such figures for the years 1899, 1902, 1910, and 1912. They should be viewed with caution, however, because it was virtually impossible for any bureau to keep a truthful record of the number of job applicants. The coming and going in the offices, where people might look only at notices on the blackboard or be told about job opportunities by friends without bothering to register, rendered any attempt at strict accounting hopeless. Moreover, all officials had an interest in presenting as rosy a picture of the scope of their activities as possible. As early as 1907 the head of the Massachusetts office in Boston pointed out that during his first year 5,129 persons registered

---

143 "Department of Labor Conference on Employment, Held at San Francisco, Cal., August 2 to 6, 1915," *MLR* 1:4 (Oct. 1915), 5–13. Quotation p. 5; U.S. Dept. of Labor, *4th Annual Report, 1916*, 59; "Department of Labor Conference on Employment, Held at Charleston, S.C., December 16–17, 1915," *MLR* 2:2 (Feb. 1916), 111–16.

Table 2-2. *Work performance of state employment bureaus*

Year:	1899			1902			1910			1912		
	Applications	Placements	Percent	Applications	Placements	Percent	Applications	Placements	Percent	Applications	Placements	Percent
Colorado							30,102	18,865	62.7	25,465	15,392	60.4
Connecticut	24,984	14,851	59.4	14,198	7,679	54.1	13,003	8,126	62.5	14,615	8,725	59.7
Illinois				44,900	40,181	89.5	68,730	62,564	91.0	73,356	69,883	95.3
Indiana							5,058	2,387	47.2	18,723	14,434	77.1
Kansas				1,588	1,281	80.7	6,692	5,766	86.2	2,321[a]	833[a]	35.9
Maryland				734	205	27.9	151	32	21.2			
Massachusetts							47,377	12,292	25.9	28,951[a]	29,117[a]	100.6
Michigan							53,295	44,939	84.3	48,974[a]	42,423[a]	86.6
Minnesota					5,175	61.4	51,760	51,713	99.9	53,438[b]	63,339[b]	118.5
Missouri	4,849	2,318	47.8	11,836	7,263		14,713	10,664	72.5	16,063[a]	14,439[a]	83.9
New York	5,289	2,401	45.4	3,247	3,388	104.3						
Ohio	26,145	14,989	57.3	26,968	21,428	79.5	51,650	46,512	90.1	114,603[a]	67,425[a]	58.8
Oklahoma							14,306	12,852	89.8	23,159[a]	13,294[a]	57.4
Rhode Island							3,627	2,152	59.3	3,029[a]	2,386[a]	78.8
West Virginia				1,208	1,044	86.4	4,670	3,546	75.9	2,205	1,936	87.8
Wisconsin				22,077[c]	20,772[c]	94.1	(24,000)	23,852	(99.4)	50,548[a]	26,837[a]	53.1

[a] For year 1913.

[b] Eleven months.

[c] 124 weeks.

Sources: E. L. Bogart, "Public Employment Offices in the United States and Germany," *Quarterly Journal of Economics* 14 (May 1900), 351; William Franklin Willoughby, "Employment Bureaus," in idem, *State Activities in Relation to Labor in the United States* (Baltimore: Johns Hopkins University Press, 1901), 27–29; Massachusetts Bureau of Labor Statistics, *34th Annual Report 1904*, 152–77; Frank B. Sargent, "Statistics of Unemployment and the Work of Employment Offices," U.S. Bureau of Labor Statistics, *Bulletin 109* (Washington: G.P.O., 1912), *passim*; Solon de Leon, "Operation of Public Employment Exchanges in the United States," *American Labor Legislation Review* 4:2 (May 1914), 364–67; reports of individual state bureaus.

more than once – 15,089 times in the aggregate – and he gave as the reason his clerks' "undue enthusiasm to make a record and to have the work of the office loom large in the returns." On the other hand, Leiserson, when superintendent of the Wisconsin state employment offices, denounced the opposite practice of registering only those jobseekers who could readily be placed, a procedure that allowed the office to present a high success rate. AALL researcher De Leon deplored the "serious laxity" practiced regarding the placement figures, as some offices recorded referrals as actual placements, whereas others made it a point to obtain the employer's confirmation[144](Table 2–2).

Another problem was pointed to by the Ohio commissioner of labor in 1905. He allowed that "the greatest portion of [placed persons] was only procured odd jobs or temporary positions." He nevertheless thought that his service was "as good an employment office system as that in vogue in any of the states."[145] But even if one takes the existing figures at their face value, the emerging picture is not very favorable. Judgment can be passed by comparing the volume of activities of the public employment services with that of the private sector, and also by measuring the former's impact upon the existing unemployment, as the reduction of the latter was the often proclaimed goal of the public services.

It is impossible to find aggregate figures concerning the work of the private agencies, as their diverse and basically unregulated activities left usable records only in rare instances. But some notion of the dimensions of their work can nevertheless be gained from the extant information. The licensed offices alone must have dealt with several million clients.[146]

144 Hearings on H.R. 16130, p. 53. Statement of Walter L. Sears. Sears gave a comprehensive description of his work in U.S. Congress. Senate, *Industrial Relations: Final Report and Testimony*, II, 1275–90. – Massachusetts. State Free Employment Offices, *1st Annual Report, 1907*, 14–15; Leiserson, "Public Employment Offices in the United States," 15; De Leon, "Operation of Public Employment Exchanges," 360–61. See also Barnes, "Public Employment Bureaus," 197.

145 Ohio. Bureau of Labor Statistics, *29th Annual Report, 1905*, 8. See similarly [W. M. Leiserson], "Report of the Secretary-Treasurer," AAPEO, Proceedings 1915, in U.S. Bureau of Labor Statistics, *Bulletin 192*, 102–03.

146 In 1893 Boston had 119 commercial exchanges, eighty-seven of which registered 600,934 applicants, of whom 128,912 or 21 percent obtained jobs. Massachusetts. Bureau of Statistics of Labor, *24th Annual Report, 1894*, 107; 111. The 119 exchanges in Chicago handled over one million applicants in 1896. Bogart, "Public Employment Offices," 344. In 1907 Baltimore had 150 commercial agencies; in 1911 Chicago had 280 and New York had 828. Sargent, "Statistics of Unemployment," 55; 128; Sutherland, "Unemployment," 111. In Iowa the commercial agencies counted well over

Moreover there were a considerable number of unlicensed ones almost everywhere, and also any number of exchanges run by employers, trade unions, and charitable organizations. Boston had at least fourteen philanthropic agencies in 1893 that registered more than 30,000 jobseekers and may have found positions for half of them. Chicago counted over 100 exchanges of the charitable kind in 1916.[147] In view of these numbers it appears quite obvious that the operations of the state employment offices can have constituted but a small fraction of the entire labor market activities, and that there could be no claim to any controlling function as yet. Adding the official figures of the federal Division of Information (Table 2–1) to those produced by the state services does not change this verdict in any material way.

If their inroads into the labor market were small and basically insignificant, the value of the public offices as arms in the fight against unemployment cannot have been great. This conclusion would certainly be an easy one to corroborate if any reliable figures as to the extent of unemployment before World War I were available. As this is not the case, some guesses can confirm the obvious assumption. Hornell Hart, a research fellow at the Helen Trounstine Foundation in Cincinnati, once reconciled the available unemployment data. He thought that there may have been 2.7 million nonagricultural unemployed persons in 1902, 1.7 million in 1910, and 4.5 million in 1914.[148] These figures applied to the entire United States, and the number for the states under discussion must therefore have been smaller. The placements made by the public exchanges can in any case not be seen as having effectively coped with the task at hand. Reflecting upon the performance of the state offices around the turn of the century, Bogart thought that "not even the most ardent advocate of their extension would contend that they have been attended with striking success." This judgment certainly still applied during the following decade and a half.

The fact that for the most part only unskilled workers, often of the

40,000 applicants in 1914, half of whom they may have placed. Iowa. Bureau of Labor Statistics, *Annual Report, 1916*, 176.

147 Ohio. Bureau of Labor Statistics, *23d Annual Report, 1899*, 313; Bogart, "Public Employment Offices," 347–49; Massachusetts. Bureau of Statistics of Labor, *24th Annual Report, 1894*, 81–105; Charles J. Boyd, "Suboffices of Public Employment Bureaus," AAPEO, Proceedings 1916, in U.S. Bureau of Labor Statistics, *Bulletin 220* (Washington: G.P.O., 1917), 86.

148 Hornell Hart, "Fluctuation in Unemployment in Cities of the United States, 1902 to 1917," *Studies from the Helen S. Trounstine Foundation* 1:2 (1918), 48.

worse sort, sought to avail themselves of the services offered constituted a major worry. "One of our great difficulties," a Michigan official stated at the AAPEO meeting in 1913, "is the 'cheap lodging-house crowd' that keeps hanging around the offices." A colleague in New York complained to the Philadelphia unemployment conference that social workers regarded public employment agencies "as a convenient dumping ground for all the unemployable and near-unemployable people with whom they are compelled to deal."[149] Bad workers naturally did not attract good job offers, and the "indifference of the employing public," which the Connecticut commissioner of labor statistics perceived, contributed much to the inefficiency of the public bureaus. It appears that many employers thought of them only as a last resort, as was the case with the philanthropic agencies. "The free agencies," an insider regretfully observed, "get the refuse after all the best has been picked out in the private agency."[150]

There were other problems. Inadequate record-taking, as already mentioned, and lack of good administrative procedures in general were common impediments. Bad locations and poor office facilities also often hampered the growth of business activities. The head of the New York office deplored the fact that the employment offices were considered as "political plums" given to persons who had little or no administrative experience. Other observers concurred, and the First National Conference on Unemployment therefore passed a resolution "that appointments and tenure of office be governed by the merit system and be placed beyond control of political parties." Other public bodies, notably the Commission on Industrial Relations and the National Civil Service Reform League, took up this point in similar suggestions.[151] But political influence alone

149 Bogart, "Public Employment Offices," 364; "What Is the Matter with Our Free Employment Offices?", AAPEO, Proceedings 1913, in U.S. Bureau of Labor Statistics, *Bulletin 192*, 23; Barnes, "Public Employment Bureaus," 197.
150 Connecticut. Bureau of Labor Statistics, *17th Annual Report, 1901*, 191; "What Is the Matter with Our Free Employment Offices?", 24. For similar statements see also Bogart, "Public Employment Offices," 365; New York (State). Commission to Inquire [etc.], *Third Report*, Appendix III, 61; Sargent, "Statistics of Unemployment," 50; 53; Kellor, *Out of Work* (1915), 325; 334; Sutherland, "Unemployment," 137.
151 Charles B. Barnes, "A Report of the Condition and Management of Public Employment Offices in the United States, Together with Some Account of the Private Employment Agencies of the Country," AAPEO, Proceedings, 1914, in U.S. Bureau of Labor Statistics, *Bulletin 192*, 68; Leiserson to Frank A. White, 24 June 1915, microfilm, reel 14, Andrews Papers. Leiserson commented on the federal office in Baltimore. – U.S. Congress. Senate, *Industrial Relations: Final Report and Testimony*, I, 113–14; Barnes, "Report of the Condition," 68. For similar statements see Conner, "Free

could only partially explain the shortcomings of the public agencies. The pervasive lack of funds rendered it impossible to hire capable personnel. According to Henry G. Hodges, a research fellow at the Wharton School of Finance and Commerce of the University of Philadelphia, a superintendent should understand the technical principles involved in his business, be able to train his staff, supervise the work to be done, and develop administrative procedures. "Can such a man," he asked rhetorically, "be had for $1,000 or $1,200?" He could not, and as a result, Leiserson sighed, the officials at hand "have either mismanaged the offices... or else they performed their duties perfunctorily and in a wholly ineffective manner."[152]

Because it was so sweeping, Leiserson's complaint was not fully justified, even if it described the general situation well enough. There were states whose services obtained quite generous allocations. In 1914 the New York employment service disposed of $62,631.66, in Illinois the sum was $44,145, in Massachusetts $36,350, as opposed to $9,000 each in Indiana and Connecticut. And Massachusetts, Wisconsin, Ohio, and New York had by then placed their employment officials under civil service. But these were modest advances that could not yet substantially change the picture of an assortment of public employment services in much need of improvement. In late 1912, Leiserson confidentially expressed the opinion "that it will be many a year before reliable information about the labor market will be distributed by our national and state governments through labor exchanges or free employment offices." He would still stand by that statement several years later.[153]

Although even well-meaning contemporaries were dissatisfied with government-run exchanges, it appears appropriate to view the situation in a different perspective. For all their shortcomings, the employment services constituted the first attempts American governments had ever

Public Employment Offices," 94; Devine, *Report on the Desirability*, 25; Henry G. Hodges, "Statutory Provisions and Achievements of Public Employment Bureaus," *Annals* 59 (May 1915), 176; 184; Charles B. Barnes, "Public Bureaus of Employment," ibid., 186; "Resolutions," *ALLR* 4:2 (May 1914), 353; George T. Keyes to Andrews, 16 Jan. 1915, microfilm, reel 13, Andrews Papers. Keyes was secretary of the National Civil Service Reform League.

152 Hodges, "Statutory Provisions," 176; Leiserson, "Public Employment Offices in Theory and Practice," 314. See also "Resolutions," *ALLR* 4:2 (May 1914), 353.

153 See the table in Hodges, "Statutory Provisions," 182–83. – Barnes, "Public Employment Bureaus," 197; [Leiserson] to Fitch, n.d. [around 6 Nov. 1912] Box 14, Leiserson Papers.

made to help the jobless. No doubt, this aid was generally given hesitatingly, and as a consequence it almost necessarily remained ineffective.
It has to be kept in mind, however, that these governments, still very
much informed by the laissez-faire attitude of the day, were confronted
with an unaccustomed problem – unemployment alleviation – for whose
solution the institution in question was yet of unproven value. Under the
circumstances, some of them showed commendable enterprise. It was on
the whole probably unrealistic to expect them to endorse the experiment
with greater enthusiasm than they actually did. Their ventures into the
labor-exchange field belonged to the attempts by which fledgling bureaucracies sought to come to grips with the exigencies presented by large-
scale industrialization. The instruments were as untried as the task was
new.

The remarkable fact in our context is that ultimately those who followed
the urging of the reformers to establish and maintain exchange offices
through their actions recognized the existence of a governmental responsibility for unemployment care. Moreover, the very insufficiency of
the various efforts served a useful purpose. It demonstrated the need for
greater financial support if governmental exchanges were to have a chance
of success, and it also suggested directions for administrative and organizational improvement. The subsequent war expansion of exchange activities was perhaps, for particular reasons, not the most suitable
application of the knowledge gained in the preceding period. It, and the
developments of the following years, nevertheless ran in a straight line
from the prewar beginnings of the institution.

IV   Search for tools: Public works

Emergency measures

Although not glamorous in appearance or performance, public employment offices constituted the major instrument that American governments
used before World War I to combat unemployment; but it was not the
only tool at their disposal. The provision of public works shared with the
exchange idea the closeness to traditional tenets, as both referred to the
individual's capacity to earn his living through his own exertion. Such
works, on the other hand, were of necessity a far larger burden on the
public treasuries. In addition, obvious constitutional, administrative, and
technical difficulties rendered their use as a remedy for joblessness con-

siderably less attractive. During the decades under consideration, governments therefore approached this tool with even greater reluctance than the creation of exchanges.

It seems possible to differentiate between public works undertaken for relief purposes and work relief in its more narrow sense. According to one definition, the former term would designate "needed public improvements, which may have been advanced to give work in times of unusual unemployment, but which must have been undertaken in the near future regardless of the depression." Work relief, by contrast, would consist of "operations definitely undertaken to provide employment for those whose need of relief has been established." But in actual practice, the two methods appear to have overlapped in many instances so as to render any attempt at differentiation artificial. "The distinction between regular public works and work relief," a knowledgeable observer wrote in the 1930s, "is primarily a matter of emphasis." In our context it seems advisable, therefore, to understand "public works" and "work relief" to be identical in meaning, both designating projects intended to provide relief in work form at public expense.[154]

A more useful distinction has to be made between the provision of emergency work, designed to render immediate relief and usually arranged under the pressure of actual need, and the advance planning of public works, intended to counteract the detrimental effects of the business cycle by advancing or postponing necessary projects. During the decades before the outbreak of the war, both methods had their advocates, although practical application on the state and federal levels remained infrequent.

American attempts at using public works to alleviate unemployment can be traced back at least as far as the mid-nineteenth century. Because poor relief was the domain of the local authorities, public works were for this purpose first undertaken by municipalities. There is evidence that

154 Feder, *Unemployment Relief*, 31–32, note. See also Joanna Colcord, *Cash Relief* (New York: Russell Sage Foundation, 1936), 13; Vernor Arthur Mund, "Prosperity Reserves of Public Works," *Annals* 149 (May 1930), 3–4; and for an older opinion Amos G. Warner, "Some Experiments on Behalf of the Unemployed," *Quarterly Journal of Economics* 5:1 (Oct. 1890), 1–23. – Arthur E. Burns, "Work Relief Wage Policies, 1930–1936," in Federal Emergency Relief Administration, *Monthly Report* (June 1936), 22, note 2. Regarding the distinction of public work and work relief see also Joanna C. Colcord, *Emergency Work Relief as Carried Out in Twenty-six American Communities, 1930–1931, with Suggestions for Setting up a Program* (New York: Russell Sage Foundation, 1932), 11–17.

during the economic downturn of 1857, New York, Philadelphia, and Newton, Massachusetts, initiated work projects to help the unemployed, and that other cities emulated these examples in the 1870s. More extensive use of work relief was made by civic authorities during the depression of the 1890s.[155] The endeavor rarely gave full satisfaction to either side. The attempts were "so desultory, so short-lived, and usually so unsuccessful," as a writer in the bulletin series of the federal Bureau of Labor put it,[156] that improvement seemed mandatory. Solutions to the arising problems did not readily offer themselves, however, and a similar sort of difficulty soon harassed work projects on the state and federal levels as well.

The first question, of course, was whether any relief works should be undertaken at all. As such measures would take the government into spheres of life where in traditional understanding it did not belong, conservative circles were prone to regard them, according to settlement worker Stanton Coit, as "the entering wedge of socialism – the beginning of the downfall of the middle-class republic." Others, however, could feel, as did a writer in the *Survey*, that one "may be very far from accepting the Socialist program" and yet believe that government, by undertaking public works, should assume "the responsibility for assuring to every man the means of making a living somehow."[157] But even if one accepted the soundness of relief projects in principle, a host of other questions had still to be answered. The municipal bureaucracies usually lacked the expertise and apparatus to handle large works programs that involved job registration, handling of funds, and conducting the actual work under

155 Benjamin J. Klebaner, "Poor Relief and Public Work during the Depression of 1857," *Historian* 22:3 (May 1960), 264–79; Closson, "Notes on the History of 'Unemployment' and Relief Measures in the United States," 468–69; Feder, *Unemployment Relief*, 31–34; 67–70; 169–89; David M. Schneider and Albert Deutsch, *The History of Public Welfare in New York State 1867–1940* (Montclair, New Jersey: Patterson Smith, 1969), 40–44; 53–56. A detailed description of work relief measures in Boston is given in Massachusetts. Bureau of Statistics of Labor, *24th Annual Report, 1894*, 135–224. In 1894–1895, 21 out of 30 Massachusetts cities provided relief work. Massachusetts. House. Board to Investigate [etc.], *Report*, vol. I, xxv; 58–107.

156 Bliss, "What Is Done for the Unemployed in European Countries," 844.

157 Stanton Coit, "Necessity of State Aid to the Unemployed," *Forum* 17 (May 1894), 278; Otis H. Moore, "The Right of a Man to a Job: The States' Opportunity," *Survey* 34:2 (10 April 1915), 54. For a contemporary discussion of the 'right-to-work' idea from a moderate viewpoint see Charles Richmond Henderson, *Introduction to the Study of the Dependent, Defective, and Delinquent Classes and of Their Social Treatment* (Boston: Heath, 1908), 87–89.

extraordinary circumstances. Moreover, politics all too often entered the process, with politicians trying to use the situation to reward their own supporters. One way out might have been the transfer of the project execution to private agencies, but actual practice showed that this tended to create as many new problems as it solved.

There were other considerations. Eligibility of applicants posed a special dilemma. Should need be the yardstick, or ability to do the job? The former criterion brought inferior workers and consequently inferior products; the latter partially negated the relief idea. Closely related was the question of wages. To pay substandard wages meant that the public body entered into unfair competition with the private sector; wage rates at market level, however, were hard on the treasury. There was also the practical question of what kind of works should be undertaken. Traditionally, the bulk of public expenditures was spent on construction jobs, which had the advantage of being labor-intensive and thus relatively well suited to relief projects. But in many parts of the country, and especially in the densely populated Northeast, construction usually ceased with the arrival of winter weather, when unemployment tended to be at its highest. Furthermore, work on the building site demanded a sturdy physical condition; what about laid-off indoor workers unfit for such activity?[158]

While during the depressed 1890s the cities struggled with these difficulties, many observers came to the conclusion that the very nature and size of the existing unemployment transcended the ability of municipal authorities. A city's endeavor to provide relief work, humanitarian Josephine Shaw Lowell maintained in the *Forum*, did not diminish the trouble but aggravated it; by drawing jobseekers from afar, this supposedly beneficiary employment created "distress and vagrancy and begging in the locality where it is given."[159]

One possible means to overcome this problem on the municipal stage was to engage the state and federal governments in its solution. Scattered proposals aimed in this direction from the depression of the 1870s on. Radical demands for state public works programs could be heard as early as 1873. Philanthropist Peter Cooper, the presidential candidate of the Independent (Greenback) party in 1876, advised President Rutherford

---

158 For a contemporaneous discussion of these problems see Massachusetts. House. Board to Investigate [etc.], *Report*, III, 4–118. See also Philip Klein, *The Burden of Unemployment* (New York: Russell Sage Foundation, 1923), 73–87.
159 Josephine Shaw Lowell, "Methods of Relief for the Unemployed," *Forum* 16 (Feb. 1894), 658.

B. Hayes that the federal government could put unemployed workers on public improvements such as railroad building. Another Greenbacker, William A. Carsey, suggested to a House committee in 1878 that a public works program in the West might be financed through the issuance of greenbacks. There were also proposals that the federal administration establish farm colonies to employ the jobless.[160]

Such ideas were controversial by nature, as they begged the question of the advisability and even the constitutionality of welfare measures beyond the local sphere. As a consequence, in the unemployment crisis of the mid-1890s, as Samuel Rezneck has noted, "the public works controversy was...raised to a new level of political agitation and demonstration." Articulate resistance from the conservative side voiced its concerns. In May 1894 a writer in the *Forum* denounced public works undertaken by the state in aid of the jobless as "the compulsory waste of capital that would be productively employed under conditions of freedom." Governor Flower refused to contemplate a public works program. When urged by a conference of trade unionists in August 1893 to devise one, he answered with the standard conservative adage that "in America the people support the government; it is not the province of the government to support the people."[161]

Others saw virtue in the scheme. The governor's namesake Benjamin O. Flower, visionary editor of the *Arena*, believed that federal projects such as road-building and construction of Mississippi levees could be of substantial help and that such work moreover would "add vastly to the nation's wealth in increasing by untold millions the annual product of real wealth."[162] California Assemblyman Robert A. Dague proposed state legislation obliging the counties to engage the unemployed on public work

---

160 Herbert C. Gutman, "The Failure of the Movement by the Unemployed for Public Works in 1873," *Political Science Quarterly* 80:2 (June 1965), 259; 263; Sidney Fine, *Laissez Faire and the General-Welfare State: A Study of Conflict in American Thought 1865–1901* (Ann Arbor: University of Michigan Press, 1956), 307; 322–23. Regarding farm colonies, see pages 104–6.

161 Rezneck, "Unemployment, Unrest, and Relief," 332; D. McG. Means, "The Dangerous Absurdity of State Aid," *Forum* 17 (May 1894), 292; Bernard Mandel, *Samuel Gompers: A Biography* (Yellow Springs: Antioch Press, 1963), 122. It was Gompers who transmitted the demand to Flower.

162 B.O. Flower, "Emergency Measures Which Would Have Maintained Self-respecting Manhood," *Arena* 9 (May 1894), 822–26; idem, "How to Increase National Wealth by the Employment of Paralyzed Industry," *Arena* 18 (Aug. 1897), 209. See also the similar proposal by "razor King" King C. Gillette. Gilbert, *Designing the Industrial State*, 170–171.

projects. His bill passed the legislature in March 1897, but was not signed by the governor. To overcome the argument that no money was available, some advocates of action recommended inflationary schemes. In December 1893, Gompers told the AFL in convention that American workers had a right to expect "a guarantee that employment... is accorded to all," and the delegates adopted a resolution that in somewhat Keynesian fashion called for the issue of $500 million in paper currency for public works expenditure.[163] The most spectacular demand came from the "industrial armies," of which the best known was "General" Jacob S. Coxey's, marching on Washington in spring 1894. Coxey's call for road construction and other improvements, again to be financed by an issue of $500 million in legal tender notes, was echoed by similar requests from other quarters.[164] Somewhat later, Gladden reiterated the social gospel's approval of the idea. If traditional means of finding employment for the idle proved insufficient, he exclaimed before the NCCC, "then let the state organize for them employments by which they may eat their own bread."[165] Notwithstanding such appeals, however, the dreadful misery of the 1890s passed without any state or federal authorities trying out the public works tool.

During the following decade or so, little further discussion of work relief occurred. When mounting unemployment revived the debate, the latter's inconclusiveness showed that many observers had not lost their memory of the mixed experiences of the cities. This is not to say that enthusiastic supporters of the idea could not be found. In the depression winter of 1908, three years after the Unemployed Workmen Act had been adopted in Great Britain, the *Philadelphia Enquirer* editorialized that "it is the duty of the Government, both national and municipal, to throw as

---

163 Rezneck, "Unemployment, Unrest, and Relief," 333; Raphael Margolin, "Public Works as a Remedy for Unemployment in the United States" (Columbia M.A., 1928), 47–48; AFL. 13th Annual Convention, *Proceedings 1893*, 11; 47–48.

164 H.R. 7438; H.R. 7463. Carlos A. Schwantes, *Coxey's Army: An American Odyssey* (Lincoln: University of Nebraska Press, 1985), 37. See also Donald L. McMurry, *Coxey's Army: A Study of the Industrial Army of 1894* (Boston: Little, Brown, 1929), 25–33; Dorfman, *The Economic Mind*, III, 222. A more general predecessor to the House bills was S. 1050, introduced in October 1893. Its sponsor, Populist William A. Peffer (Kansas), personally had grave doubts about the practicality of his demand, stating in the Senate that he introduced the measure only "by request." *CR*, 53 Congress, 1 sess., 6 Oct. 1893, p. 2184. Another demand for greenback financing of public improvements was voiced by *Arena* editor Flower, "How to Increase National Wealth," 208–10.

165 Gladden, "What to Do with the Workless Man," 151.

much employment in the way of laborers as possible." In November of that year, the AFL again urged "that municipal, state and federal governments at once take steps to furnish work by constructing schools and other government buildings." There were two crying needs in the country – the employment of the unemployed and the building of good roads, Darwin J. Meserole, a concerned attorney from Brooklyn with socialist convictions, told the AALL at its annual meeting in 1911. "Is it too much to ask, to demand," he inquired of his audience, "that this necessary public work be started at once...?" The Socialist Party of America gave his request a plank in its election platform of 1912, and party member Victor L. Berger (Wisconsin) introduced a bill in the House providing for the employment "of all willing workers" (H.R. 25680).[166]

The thought was not alien even to the federal administration. Experiencing the progressive urges of the first weeks of his administration, President Woodrow Wilson suggested to Treasury Secretary William G. McAdoo that federal building be advanced so as to reduce unemployment. Little seems to have resulted, apparently, as Commerce Secretary William C. Redfield expressed it, because "the chairmen of the two appropriation committees...control the situation."[167] But the very fact that the thought was ventilated showed its progress in the general consciousness.

A somewhat more fanciful idea whose time would come only in the 1930s was also presented in Congress at various occasions. In June 1913, Senator Miles Poindexter (R-Washington), a former Superior Court judge, proposed to organize the unemployed into an industrial army, complete with oath and hierarchical structure, to be put to work "on any or all public works owned or controlled by the United States" (S. 2587). He repeated his proposal in 1915 (S. 1790) and 1917 (S. 301), but angry protests from the labor side kept the scheme from making headway. New York Democratic Representative George W. Loft's bill H.R. 21332 con-

---

166 The Unemployed Workmen Act of 1905 provided, in part, that regular workers out of work should be given temporary employment of actual and substantial utility at a wage below the customary wage rate for such labor. The act is described in U.S. Bureau of Labor Statistics, *Bulletin 76*, 847–51. *Philadelphia Enquirer* editorial in *CR*, 60 Cong., 1 sess., 22 Feb. 1908, p. 2335. The editorial was published on 22 Feb. 1908. – AFL. 28th Annual Convention, *Proceedings 1908*, 258–59; "General Discussion," *ALLR* 2:1 (Feb. 1912), 114–15. On Meserole see his obituary in the *New York Times*, 22 May 1952, p. 27. – Johnson, ed., *National Party Platforms*, I, 190.

167 Secretary [of Commerce William C. Redfield] to President [Wilson], 7 May 1913, Box 28, Chief Clerk's Files, General Records of the Department of Labor, Department of Labor Papers.

tained, besides its census section, a similar provision that combined some labor service features with a sort of militia concept. The bill authorized the president of the United States to "enlist" volunteering unemployed persons for employment on federal public works and to select from among them all able-bodied males between the ages of eighteen and thirty-five "and detail them for training in military service for four hours each day, the remaining four hours each day to be employed on public works." After a term of service of four months, those persons would be "maintained on the rolls of the Government as a special military reserve force" and would have to report for two weeks' military training each year. The sale of Panama bonds would be used to defray the expenses.[168]

If the labor unions were against what looked like governmental coercion, they were not opposed to the remedial use of public works as such. Their positive stand during the 1890s has already been mentioned. At its 1913 convention the AFL once more agreed that public construction, in particular road building, would be an adequate means to eliminate unemployment. A few weeks later, John H. Walker, president of the Illinois Federation of Labor, similarly demanded that "the government itself should endeavor to employ in the federal, state and municipal undertakings every man and woman who is unemployed."[169]

During the depression of 1914–15 the campaign gained momentum. Andrews asserted in his journal that it was "a much wiser policy" to start large projects for public works than to support the unemployed through private charity or public relief, and he advised a correspondent at Harvard that it might be "decidedly economical for the community as a whole" to undertake emergency public work "even though it is an additional cost in dollars."[170] At the Second National Conference on Unemployment, states and municipalities were challenged "to undertake contemplated

---

168 The idea seems to have originated with Dague. See Dague to [Secretary of Labor] Wilson, [?] May 1913, Box 29, Chief Clerk's Files, General Records of the Department of Labor, Department of Labor Papers. The text of the bill is printed in *The Miners Magazine* 205 (9 Jan. 1913), 11–12. For labor's indignation, see for instance the protest of Local No. 2, I.B.W.A. (Chicago). Nicholas Annes to [Department of Labor], [July 1913], Box 37, Chief Clerk's Files, General Records of the Department of Labor, Department of Labor Papers. Text of H.R. 21332 in *CR*, 63 Cong., 3 sess., Appendix, 4 March 1915, pp. 833–34.
169 AFL. 33d Annual Convention, *Proceedings 1913*, 89–90. See also ibid., 350; "Public Responsibility," *ALLR* 4:2 (May 1914), 273.
170 "The Prevention of Unemployment," *ALLR* 5:2 (June 1915), 183; Andrews to F. Ernest Richter, 16 March 1915, microfilm, reel 14, Andrews Papers.

public works and to project new ones."[171] The petition that Austin in February 1915 inserted into the *Congressional Record* asked that the federal government extend "every possible line of public works" and that it make loans to states and municipalities for public works of their own. In the second edition of her book, Frances Kellor contributed her share of encouragement, and in October 1916 a member of the Massachusetts Commission on Social Insurance declared that it was the state's task to "make provision for the conservation of the surplus of labor by furnishing employment to the worthy unemployed."[172]

Intensified governmental construction thus looked to many as a handy weapon. But still by far not all voices, even on the reform side, were supportive. Seager, drawing upon his knowledge of British and American experiences, could not remember one case of relief work "where the demoralizing consequences have not largely neutralized the expected benefits," and he felt it would be better to train the unemployed to do the work for which there was a demand than to put them on make-work projects. Others, notably Devine, Leiserson, and Henderson, concurred. Aware of such objections, the California Commission on Immigration and Housing, although desperate to find means to alleviate the prevailing distress, felt disinclined to go any farther regarding public works than recommending that an investigation into their possible use might be undertaken.[173]

In view of the lack of a consensus, it cannot be a surprise that administrations beyond the local level hesitated to commit themselves to any

---

171 "General Discussion," *ALLR* 5:2 (June 1915), 452. The requester was Mrs. James P. Warbasse, a member of the Brooklyn Committee on Unemployment. See also in similar vein Meserole to Andrews, 9 July 1915, microfilm, reel 14, Andrews Papers. Meserole was a member of the same committee.

172 *CR*, 63 Cong., 3 sess., 20 Feb. 1915, p. 4236. For the petition see also page 83. – Kellor, *Out of Work* (1915), 518–24; Roswell F. Phelps, "Memorandum in Re Unemployment Relief," 3 Oct. 1916, in Massachusetts. House. Special Commission on Social Insurance, *Report* (Boston: Wright & Potter, 1917), 297.

173 Henry Rogers Seager, *Social Insurance: A Program of Social Reform* (New York: Macmillan, 1910), 112–13; Edward T. Devine, *Report on the Desirability of Establishing an Employment Bureau in the City of New York* (New York: Charities Publication Committee, 1909), 27; New York (State). Commission to Inquire [etc.], *Third Report*, 68. Leiserson at the time actually thought that "it would be a real danger if the State were to create work for the unemployed." Leiserson to Commons, 23 March 1912, Box 9, Leiserson Papers. – Charles R. Henderson, "Recent Advances in the Struggle against Unemployment," *ALLR* 2:1 (Feb. 1912), 106. See also I. M. Rubinow, "The Problem of Unemployment," *Journal of Political Economy* 21:4 (April 1913), 330–31. – California. Commission of Immigration and Housing, *Report on Unemployment*, 7.

substantial measures. But some exploratory steps were taken nevertheless that engaged American government on the road that ultimately led to the momentous programs of the New Deal. Characteristic of the tentativeness of the early initiatives were attempts to encourage municipal activities. The first state to move in this direction appears to have been Illinois, where in 1909, as a consequence of the preceding economic downturn, a resolution was introduced in the House providing that cities with excessive unemployment must furnish work for "living wages" upon the roads, waterways, and at similar public projects. This resolution died in committee, but the idea was not lost out of sight. When the depression struck in winter 1914–15, a similar bill was adopted in New Jersey. It gave municipalities the right to employ workers on the unskilled laborer level on public projects and pay them according to a payment roster approved by the state's Civil Service Commission. There was also agitation in several states, notably New York and California, for the recall of constitutional sections forbidding the direct hiring of labor by municipalities.[174]

A few states moved beyond such tokenism. Republican maneuvering thwarted some efforts in the winter of 1913–14 by the Democratic governor of Oregon to provide state relief work on the roads. But the Idaho legislature became a pioneer in American public works legislation when it passed a bill in March 1915 that allowed counties providing relief work to deduct half the cost from future taxes that the state levied upon them. The act was remarkable not only because of its unprecedented provision of state funds for emergency employment. It also established in unequivocal terms a right to work, stipulating that every United States citizen who had been resident in the state for six months was entitled to "emergency employment." This approach was certainly imaginative and may have been worth a try. The state's judiciary, however, declared the act unconstitutional because of its general nature.[175] The distinction of being first in granting financial assistance to the jobless thus fell to Massachu-

---

174 Earl R. Beckner, *A History of Labor Legislation in Illinois* (Chicago: University of Chicago Press, 1929), 386. The resolution was H.J.R. 18. – 1915 *New Jersey Laws*, c. 43; "Memorandum to Dr. John B. Andrews . . . in re data on Relief through Public Work" [c. July 1915], microfilm, reel 14, Andrews Papers.

175 "Reports of Official Delegates on the State of Employment," *ALLR* 4:2 (May 1914), 243; 1915 *Idaho Session Laws*, c. 27. This act was probably the first legal recognition of the right to work in the United States. See John R. Commons and John B. Andrews, *Principles of Labor Legislation* (New York: Harper, 1916), 288. – Epperson v. Howell *et al.* (8 Jan. 1916), 154 Pac., 1st ser., 621.

setts. After looking in vain for executable work projects in winter 1914, the commonwealth in 1915 appropriated $100,000 for this purpose and expended the money for forest work such as moth control and fire protection. No other state emulated this example for the time being, although in Colorado a gubernatorial Committee on Unemployment Relief was instrumental in securing $100,000 from the Rockefeller Foundation that was spent on road building.[176]

During this period there was also some discussion of the possibility of rendering work relief in farm colonies. As governmental institutions of this kind were generally understood to have a function akin to that of the poor house, they are only of marginal concern in our context. Their special feature was the compulsion that they would exert, administering a sort of work test while giving material aid to the individual. The idea of moving the jobless back to the land found expression on the federal level as early as the late 1870s when three pertinent bills (H.R. 20, H.R. 110, H.R. 5141) were introduced in the forty-fifth Congress by representatives of industrial centers hit hard by the depression. In an 1894 *Annals* article, Brooks characteristically demanded that farm colonies and workshops be opened to teach discipline and provide training. After a thorough investigation of colony experiments abroad by the Massachusetts Bureau of Labor Statistics, the Dewey Board agreed with him by recommending the creation of a state labor colony in which tramps and vagrants under thirty years of age should be taught farming and industrial arts and "be compelled to work." The board even drafted a bill for this purpose, but no further action was taken. A similar proposal went a step further in California. The Dague bill, mentioned earlier, provided for lodging and three meals per day as well as thirty-five cents in wages for every day worked on highway construction or in a country farm.[177] A variation on the farm colony scheme, without the work test ingredient, was the state

176 President's Conference on Unemployment, *Report* (Washington: G.P.O., 1921), 106; Massachusetts. House. Special Commission on Social Insurance, *Report* (Boston: Wright & Potter, 1917), 297; Feder, *Unemployment Relief,* 234.

177 Albert V. House, Jr., "Proposals of Government Aid to Agricultural Settlement during the Depression of 1873–1879," *Agricultural History* 12:1 (Jan. 1938), 46–66; Brooks, "The Future Problem," 26. Similarly B. O. Flower, "A Problem for True Statesmanship," *Arena* 27:1 (Jan. 1902), 87–93; Massachusetts. Bureau of Labor Statistics, *24th Annual Report, 1894,* 23–53; Massachusetts. House. Board to Investigate [etc.] *Report,* vol. II, xix–xxiii. See also the approving descriptions of Bodelschwingh's Arbeiterkolonien in Germany by Josiah Flynt, "A Colony of the Unemployed," *Atlantic Monthly* 78 (Dec. 1896), 793–803; and Warner, "Some Experiments on Behalf of the Unemployed," 6–17. – Margolin, "Public Works as a Remedy," 47–48.

factory idea advocated by Edward Bellamy, utopian author of *Looking Backward*. In a submission to the Dewey Board he outlined a system of self-supporting settlements, each containing a farm, factories, dwellings, and a store.

Over the next two decades the more sober concept of constraint and forceful guidance prevailed. Around the turn of the century, Gladden advocated the creation of workhouses and farm colonies, which should "not be regarded primarily as penal institutions, but rather as educational institutions."[178] Seager, Henderson, and various others understood the necessity of founding such colonies in the same way. S. Thruston Ballard, a member of the Commission on Industrial Relations from Kentucky, even recommended the establishment of "Government concentration camps where work with a small wage would be provided, supplemented by agricultural and industrial training."[179]

Discussing the colony idea was one thing, implementing it quite another. One rare attempt in this direction was made in New York. There, several bills failed to be adopted until 1911, when the legislature passed an act establishing a "state industrial farm colony" whose purpose was the "detention, humane discipline, instruction and reformation of male adults." The bill made it clear that "reputable workmen, temporarily out

---

178 Massachusetts. House. Board to Investigate [etc.], *Report*, III, 109–11; Gladden, "What to Do," 147–48. See also Washington Gladden, *Social Salvation* (Boston: Houghton, Mifflin, 1902), 83–87.

179 Henry R. Seager, "Outline of a Program of Social Legislation with Special Reference to Wage-Earners," AALL, *Proceedings, 1907* (Madison, 1908), 87; idem, *Social Insurance*, 102–07; Henderson, "Recent Advances," 107; Orlando F. Lewis, "Vagrancy in the United States," NCCC, *Proceedings, 1907* (Indianapolis: Burford, n.d.), 64–65; Edmond Kelly, *The Elimination of the Tramp by the Introduction into America of the Labor Colony System Already Proved Effective in Holland, Belgium, and Switzerland, with the Modifications Thereof Necessary to Adapt This System to American Conditions* (New York: Putnam's, 1908), 51–86; Edward D. Carpenter, "The Experience of the National Employment Exchange," *ALLR* 2:1 (Feb. 1912), 103; Charles B. Barnes, "The Function of Public Employment Offices," NCCC, *Proceedings 1915* (Chicago: Hildmann, 1915), 506–07; Elizabeth S. Kite in "General Discussion," *ALLR* 5:2 (June 1915), 455–56. In 1903 the federal Department of Labor took note of the more liberally conducted settlement experiment of the Salvation Army in the United States and related governmental efforts in New Zealand and Canada. "Farm Colonies of the Salvation Army," in U.S. Bureau of Labor Statistics, *Bulletin 48* (Washington: G.P.O., 1903), 983–1105. Ballard's recommendation is in U.S. Congress. Senate, *Industrial Relations: Final Report and Testimony Submitted to Congress by the Commission on Industrial Relations*. S.Doc. 415, 64 Cong., 1 sess. (1916), vol. I, 250. That farm colonies would not reduce unemployment in winter when the need was greatest was pointed out by the California commissioner of labor, John P. McLaughlin, ibid., V, 5056.

of work and seeking employment," should not be committed. In the following year an appropriation of $100,000 allowed the purchase of a site. But in 1913, scared by new and higher cost estimates, the new administration recommended abandonment of the plan, which was subsequently shelved.[180]

Emergency works thus saw little practical application in the states as a remedy for joblessness before World War I, and the colony idea remained fully untried. Although reformers regretted this governmental hesitation, most admitted that both measures were still beset with flaws and could not be considered fully satisfactory approaches to the unemployment problem. Many as a consequence set much store by the development of the related tool of advance planning.

Advance planning

Emergency work might have its "virtue and necessity," Andrews explained to Meserole, but the principal endeavor should go toward "the constructive measures of prevention." The latter, he went on to explain, must constitute "a broader, more fundamental policy in the arrangement of public undertakings." What he had in mind was the advance planning of public works. The *Practical Program* was more explicit. "A program of the amount of public work contemplated for several years in advance should be laid out and then carefully planned," it postulated, so that construction could "be pushed ahead in the lean years which experience has shown to recur periodically, and in the months when private employment is at a low ebb."[181]

This idea of using public works in a countercyclical sense to fight unemployment had some early advocates before the turn of the century, but it took strong hold of reform-oriented minds only in the last years before the outbreak of the war. Herbert J. Davenport, one of the first respectable economists to give serious attention to unemployment, suggested in his *Outlines of Economic Theory* (1897) that the best ameliorative device was to be found "in the postponement of all works of national or municipal improvement to seasons of labor stagnation." Despite his sug-

180 1911 *New York (State) Laws*, c. 812; 1912 *New York (State) Laws*, c. 530; Charles K. Blatchly, "A State Farm for Tramps and Vagrants," *Survey* 24 (9 April 1910), 87–89; Schneider and Deutsch, *The History of Public Welfare in New York State*, 203–04.
181 Andrews to Meserole, 14 July 1915, microfilm, reel 14, Andrews Papers; Andrews, "Practical Program," 182.

gestion the concept was still widely unknown in the United States around the turn of the century. In 1904, Henderson thought that he was acquainting the American public with a very novel measure when he reported that two years earlier the German Society of Relief and Charity had recommended making a distinction between emergency work in the proper sense and the reservation of needed public work for slack times.[182]

It was only several years later that the idea began to be discussed in other than a fleeting manner. The reason for its surfacing may have been the developing concern with the business cycle. Theorists in the first half of the nineteenth century had attempted to explain economic recessions through analyses of particular incidents of the time, and had even denied the possibility that general explanations could be formulated. Later, some efforts were made to understand the nature of the periodical swings in business activity, but it was only in the years before the outbreak of the war that this matter aroused wider interest.[183] The most important American contribution in this field was Wesley C. Mitchell's book *Business Cycles* (1913). The author, who had studied at the newly opened University of Chicago in the 1890s under economists Laughlin and Thorsten Veblen as well as philosopher John Dewey, argued essentially, confirming Beveridge's contention, that unemployment was a problem of industry.[184]

Clearly, if the slack of business caused unemployment, the revival of business activity took it away. The proponents of advanced planning of public works thus maintained that a government intent upon alleviating unemployment should endeavor to smooth out the business cycle. By reducing its own expenditures in boom times and increasing them in

182 Herbert Joseph Davenport, *Outlines of Economic Theory* (New York: Macmillan, 1896), 358. See also Dorfman, *Economic Mind*, III, 375–90, in particular p. 380; Charles Richmond Henderson, *Modern Methods of Charity: An Account of the Systems of Relief, Public and Private, in the Principal Countries Having Modern Methods* (New York: Macmillan, 1904), 47–48.

183 Harry E. Miller, "Earlier Theories of Crises and Cycles in the United States," *Quarterly Journal of Economics* 38:2 (Feb. 1924), 295; Garraty, *Unemployment in History*, 143–44. For an example of the awakening attention to cycle causes see Francis A. Walker, *The Wages Question: A Treatise on Wages and the Wages Class* (London: Macmillan, 1882), 29–30.

184 Wesley Clair Mitchell, *Business Cycles and Their Causes* (Berkeley: University of California Press, 1959. Reprint of Part III of 1913 ed.), 131–34; 172–75. On Mitchell's background see Dorfman, *Economic Mind*, III, 455–73. Notable other contemporary works were Geo. H. Hull, *Industrial Depressions: Their Causes Analysed and Classified with a Practical Remedy for Such as Result from Industrial Derangements: Or, Iron the Barometer of Trade* (New York: Stokes, 1911); and Henry Ludwell Moore, *Economic Cycles: Their Law and Cause* (New York: Macmillan, 1914).

periods of depression, it could influence the economy's behavior. As most other governmental expenditures were quite inflexible, public construction was the one area where such contraction and expansion of spending could successfully be practised. The concept was strikingly persuasive in its simplicity. Once depression conditions rendered it timely, it found much enthusiastic endorsement, and little concern appears to have been directed at the many technical obstacles that implementation might have encountered.

The planning proposal began seriously to be aired in North America in the wake of the 1907–08 recession. In 1909, Beveridge mentioned the idea of "getting as much public work as possible done when private work is slack," and Leiserson in his report to the Wainwright Commission duly recommended that public work should "be postponed, as far as possible, to those times of the year and to those years when private industry is least active." The commission itself, while not yet ready to endorse such a policy unequivocally, at least admitted that "if intelligently and conservatively pursued," it might have its advantages. Hard as well as Henderson took the cue at the 1911 annual meeting of the AALL and proposed an active role for the association in the advocacy of the measure.[185]

Thereafter, the idea received continuous consideration. The IAU discussed the potential of public works at its meeting in Ghent in September 1913. Soon thereafter a pertinent article appeared in its bulletin.[186] The *Practical Program*'s concern with public works may have been partially prompted by this awakening of interest on the international scene. Many Americans now took it upon themselves to publicize its virtues.[187] Some

185 Beveridge, *Unemployment: A Problem of Industry*, 230; New York (State). Commission to Inquire [etc.], *Third Report*, 13; 67. Hard contacted Leiserson and Henderson as early as March 1911 in this respect. Hard to Leiserson, 4 March 1911, Box 16, Leiserson Papers; Hard, "Unemployment as a Coming Issue," 99; Henderson, "Recent Advances," 106–07.

186 Association internationale pour la lutte contre le chômage, *Première assemblée générale, Gand, 3–6 septembre 1913: Invitation* (n.p., n.d.); M. W. F. Treub, "Rapports sur le chômage et le mode d'exécution des travaux publics," *Bulletin trimestriel de l'Association internationale pour la lutte contre le chômage* 4:1 (janvier-mars 1914), 243–89. The article was quoted by John R. Shillady, *Planning Public Expenditures to Compensate for Decreased Private Employment during Business Depressions* (New York: Mayor's Committee on Unemployment, 1916), 9, note; and by Commons and Andrews, *Principles of Labor Legislation*, 289.

187 Frank O'Hara, "Redistribution of Public Work in Oregon," *ALLR* 5:2 (June 1915), 238–44; F. Ernest Richter, "Seasonal Fluctuation in Public Works," ibid., 245–64. O'Hara was associated with the Catholic University of America, Richter with Harvard University. – Morris L. Cooke, "Responsibility and Opportunity of the City in the

even went as far as to elaborate in detail on the feasibility of the scheme on the national level. In *Everybody's Magazine*, Hard outlined the merits of various projects to be undertaken by the federal administration at the prompting of a "National Unemployment Crisis Commission." Almost simultaneously, John R. Shillady, social worker and secretary of the New York Mayor's Committee on Unemployment, explained the implications of national public works planning to the NCCC.[188]

If contemplating federal involvement was rather premature, experiments could be made on the state level. Massachusetts tried a step in this direction, and Pennsylvania actually put a planning act on the statute books. The Massachusetts bill was introduced in the legislature during the mild economic downturn of 1903–04 by Democrat George Schofield. Intending to permit cities and towns to establish reserve funds to be used for public works projects "in times of business depression," it was defeated in the House. Over a decade passed before the advocates of the scheme enjoyed their first success. The Pennsylvania act was the handiwork of Otto T. Mallery, a member of the Pennsylvania State Industrial Board and the AALL who was establishing himself as the foremost proponent of the cause for many years to come. The act, adopted on 25 July 1917, became a model for many subsequent bills at the state and federal levels. It provided for a statistical service in the Department of Labor to observe the employment situation; government departments were charged with preparing and keeping project plans; an emergency fund was created; and a powerful commission had the task of administering it all. The measure, the *Outlook* cheered before the legislature took the final vote, could provide

---

Prevention of Unemployment," *ALLR* 5:2 (June 1915), 435. Cooke was director of public works of Philadelphia at the time. – Jackson, "Relation of the State to Unemployment," 443; Chicago. Municipal Markets Commission, *Report to the Mayor and Aldermen on a Practical Plan for Relieving Destitution and Unemployment in the City of Chicago* (Chicago: Municipal Markets Commission, 1914), 32; 55; N. I. Stone, "A National Employment Reserve for Lean Years and Seasons," *Survey* 33:17 (23 Jan. 1915), 439–40. Stone was an industrial statistician in New York. See also his testimony in Hearings on H.J.Res. 159, pp. 110–15. – "Suggestions in Re Plan to Use Public Work as a Regulator of the Labor Market," memorandum, 16 Jan. 1915, Box 3, Commission on Industrial Relations Papers. The author was Noel T. Dowling. – U.S. Congress. Senate, *Industrial Relations: Final Report and Testimony*, I, 115.

188 William Hard, "Big Jobs for Bad Times: Get Ready Now to Fight and Conquer the Miseries of Unemployment during Our Next Great Business Depression," *Everybody's Magazine* 35:2 (Aug. 1916), 129–41. Quotation p. 141. – John R. Shillady, "Planning Public Expenditures to Compensate for Decreased Private Employment during Business Depressions," NCCC, *Proceedings, 1916*, 176–91. Quotation p. 190.

"a tremendous stabilizing force." As the act became operative upon passage, the commission began to gather information regarding possible project acceleration. The industrial boom of the war years intervened, however, and no further activity occurred before the end of the fighting.[189]

Emergency works and advance planning thus found only hesitant application or implementation in the United States before the country's entry into World War I. At least the debate on the merits of both tools, though, definitely got under way, and first tentative attempts at their use were made. Valid verdicts were unattainable as yet, but it was foreseeable that discussion and experimentation would continue, especially so because the remaining major remedial instrument, unemployment insurance, looked even less promising as a prospect for immediate implementation.

V   Search for tools: Unemployment insurance

The maintenance of governmental labor exchanges and the provision of public works were both to some degree reconcilable with the convictions of laissez-faire society. In the eyes of most contemporaries, the sponsorship of unemployment insurance through government was not; the principle of general social insurance as such, first officially introduced in the German Empire in the 1880s, seemed alien to the traditional American way of life. Potential implementation of unemployment insurance in particular raised still other concerns. Could involuntary idleness even be insured against? The necessary financial commitments appeared little less than mind-boggling, and the question remained unanswered even after the British government took the plunge in 1911. There was, moreover, the complication that action by individual states in a national market must present – would employers in a state that enforced contributions not price themselves out of interstate competition? In view of such problems, American reformers who before the war came out in favor of this untried device clearly put their credibility at stake. It is thus quite remarkable that the issue received the attention it did, and that in one state even a trial attempt was made at getting legislation passed.

---

189 Keyssar, *Out of Work,* 259; 1917 *Pennsylvania Laws,* c. 411. For Mallery's involvement with the Pennsylvania law see Hearings on S. Res. 382, pp. 71–72. On Mallery's career see Udo Sautter, "Otto Tod Mallery," in *Biographical Dictionary of Social Welfare in America* (Westport, Connecticut: Greenwood, 1986), 339–41. The *Outlook* is quoted in Helen M. Muller, *Government Fund for Unemployment* (New York: H. W. Wilson, 1929), 131.

In contrast to the remedial use of public works, governmental unemployment insurance was a relatively new concept that began to be discussed only toward the turn of the century. Some local trade unions had run their own out-of-work benefit plans for several decades, and two schemes – those of the Deutsch-Amerikanische Typographia (since 1884) and the Cigar Makers (since 1889) – had been established on a national basis; in 1912 the Diamond Workers Union followed suit.[190] But these were exclusive plans without any public input. It appears that the idea of widening the insurance basis came to the United States from Europe. In 1887, John M. Gregory, a Baptist minister and former president of Illinois Industrial University (later the University of Illinois) who had travelled overseas published an article in the *Independent* in which he denounced the idea of individual responsibility for joblessness and proposed "plans of cheap and safe insurance against nonemployment" financed by contributions of workers and employers. More general interest arose when the depression of the 1890s induced a desperate search for unemployment remedies. Municipal insurance schemes, notably the Swiss experiments in Berne (1893) and St. Gallen (1895), were duly noted. Typical of this curiosity was an article in 1897 in the *American Journal of Sociology*, written by an academic of the University of Chicago, which concluded with the statement that these pioneer efforts were "certainly deserving of great credit and appreciative consideration." That the idea of social insurance in general made inroads into the American consciousness could be observed when William F. Willoughby came out in 1898 with the first book to appear on the subject in the United States. His department published an article on trade union out-of-work benefits the next year.[191]

The discussion soon zeroed in on the principle of the matter, on the

---

190 D. P. Smelser, *Unemployment and Trade Unions* (Baltimore: Johns Hopkins University Press, 1919), 130–37. Regarding the basic ineffectiveness of such schemes see Keyssar, "Unemployment and the Labor Movement in Massachusetts, 1870–1916," 239–40; and idem, *Out of Work*, 151; 187–88.

191 Gregory quoted in Irwin Yellowitz, "The Origins of Unemployment Reform in the United States," *Labor History* 9:3 (Fall 1968), 340. – Paul Monroe, "Insurance against Non-employment," *American Journal of Sociology* 2:6 (May 1897), 771–85. Quotation p. 784. See also John Graham Brooks, "Insurance of the Unemployed," *Quarterly Journal of Economics* 10:3 (April 1896), 341–48. – William Franklin Willoughby, *Workingmen's Insurance* (New York: Crowell, 1898). See also idem, "Insurance against Unemployment," *Political Science Quarterly* 12:3 (Sept. 1897), 476–89; and idem, "Insurance for the Unemployed," *Municipal Affairs* 4 (June 1900), 410–12. – Edward W. Bemis, "Benefit Features of American Trade Unions," in U.S. Bureau of Labor Statistics, *Bulletin 22* (Washington: G.P.O., 1899), 361–400.

question of what form public involvement might take, and on the opportuneness of such a commitment. Characteristic was an exchange that took place at the annual meeting of the American Economic Association in 1901. Charles A. Tuttle, a professor of political economy at Wabash College with a doctorate from Heidelberg, held that workers had a "fundamental industrial right" to "indemnification for loss of position through economic progress." But convention participants found various flaws in this proposition. One discussant pointed out that a worker's right to indemnification implied society's right to assign work to him. Others felt that joblessness benefits would hinder the endeavors of employers to keep a stable work force; that they would encourage loafing; that administrative costs would be too great; that businessmen bore risks equal to those of workmen; that such schemes ran counter to American tradition. Commons, though, endorsed Tuttle's idea and suggested a corporate income tax for the purpose.[192]

Among those reformers who approved of the concept in principle, ideas concerning its form and implementation only slowly gained shape. A case in point was Seager's ambiguous stand. Rather than being "critical of the Ghent system," as has been asserted, he originally favored it. In the Ghent model, implemented in 1900 in that Belgian city, trade unions provided the administrative structure as well as the necessary disciplining of their members who received unemployment benefits; municipal subsidies helped to keep the system viable. In 1907, Seager told his coreformers at the first convention of the AALL that all jobless benefit programs he knew about did more harm than good, "except those operated by trade unions," and he thought that "under suitable governmental regulation and control, they could undertake this . . . [function] for the common benefit." He therefore advocated "subsidizing them, as has been done by some Belgian cities." In his book, *Social Insurance*, published three years later, he showed himself somewhat more hesitant, thinking it to be "premature to commend the plan of subsidizing trade unions," for which he perceived "weighty objections." But he still felt that the state might well encourage unions to run their own benefit programs by providing them with information and possibly regulation. Still a few years later, however,

192 Charles A. Tuttle, "The Workman's Position in the Light of Economic Progress," *American Economic Association, Publications*, 3d series, 3:1 (Feb. 1902), 207–10. On Tuttle see Dorfman, *Economic Mind*, III, 303–05; "Discussion," American Economic Association, *Publications*, 3d series, 3:1 (Feb. 1902), 218; 221; 223; 225; 228; 230; 232–33.

he found great virtue with a comprehensive system of the British kind, seeing in it "a measure that will go far to substitute for the chaos of industrial relations." Leiserson, equally undecided, in his report published by the Wainwright Commission maintained that unemployment insurance could not be considered until much more accurate information regarding the amount and duration of idleness in various trades was obtained. The commission itself adopted his stance, declaring itself "not prepared to recommend legislation" for the time being.[193]

When he was writing his book, Seager believed that the Liberal government in the United Kingdom would implement a program similar to the Ghent plan. But at the insistence of Winston Churchill, president of the Board of Trade, the British unemployment insurance plan of 1911 created a government-run system that was financed by contributions from employers, employees, and the state. The passage of the act thus not only provided an important stimulus for American reformers to continue their deliberations concerning the principle of a governmental insurance measure; it also offered a further model that might be usable, after proper adaptation, for the American scene.[194]

Immediate reactions to the British plan varied. At the 1911 annual AALL meeting, Hard cautiously called for an examination of "the unemployment insurance devices developed in Europe," whereas Miles M. Dawson, a consulting actuary from New York, unhesitatingly demanded "a good, nationwide system of unemployment insurance" based on a compulsory plan. Also in favor of the British approach was attorney Louis D. Brandeis, who before acquiring nationwide fame in *Muller v. Oregon* had already distinguished himself in several insurance cases, notably by securing in Massachusetts the enactment of low-cost life insurance through savings banks in 1907. Although basically of the opinion that employment irregularity was largely remediable if business were "scientifically managed," he recommended that for any remaining joblessness "society and industry and the individual" should pay the cost through regular insurance premiums. The Progressive Party platform of 1912

---

193 Nelson, *Unemployment Insurance*, 11; Seager, "Outline of a Program of Social Legislation," 99–100; idem, *Social Insurance*; 111–12; idem, "Sharing the Load of Unemployment by Means of Insurance," *Survey* 33:21 (20 Feb. 1915), 554; New York (State). Commission to Inquire [etc.], *Third Report*, 13; 66.

194 Seager, *Social Insurance*, 100; Mary Barnett Gilson, *Unemployment Insurance in Great Britain: The National System and Additional Benefit Plans* (New York: Industrial Relations Counselors, 1931), 43; 61.

demanded protection against irregular employment "through the adoption of a system of social insurance adapted to American use," echoing in its vagueness the call made at the NCCC convention of the same year for the creation of unemployment insurance programs under state, municipal, or private auspices.[195]

One installment of the examination Hard had desired was presented to the public at the Social Insurance Conference in 1913, when Henderson described the main types of insurance programs in effect or proposed in Europe. Like Seager, he had earlier been inclined to back a trade union scheme, but now felt disposed to try out the British idea. Objecting to the introduction of the Ghent plan with the argument that American employers would not tolerate a further strengthening of unionism and that it made no provision for unorganized labor, he wondered whether it would not be better for Americans "to unite on a policy resembling in its main principles the British system?" In September he expressed the same thought at the annual meeting of the IAU in Ghent.[196]

The task at hand was obviously to keep the matter in the public consciousness and wait for it to mature in its own way. This was the approach the AALL took when at the First National Conference it proved difficult to work out an American governmental program, even though much advocacy of the idea in general was offered.[197] To get things going, Andrews commissioned Olga Halsey, an expert on the British act, to write a thorough description of the British system and published it in the *ALLR*. He also inserted unemployment insurance into the *Practical Program* as the fourth main device to deal with unemployment. He avoided, though,

195 Hard, "Unemployment as a Coming Issue," 99; "General Discussion," *ALLR* 2:1 (Feb. 1912), 116; Louis D. Brandeis, "Workingmen's Insurance – The Road to Social Efficiency," NCCC, *Proceedings 1911* (Fort Wayne: Fort Wayne Printing Co., 1911), 161–62; Johnson, ed., *National Party Platforms*, I, 177; NCCC, *Proceedings 1912* (Fort Wayne: Fort Wayne Printing Co., 1912), 394.

196 Henderson, "Recent Advances," 107–08; Charles Richmond Henderson, "Insurance against Unemployment," *ALLR* 3:2 (June 1913), 172–82. Quotation p. 182. The paper was also published as part of the Chicago commission's report. [Chicago.] Mayor's Commission on Unemployment, *Report*, 87–92. – Charles Richmond Henderson, "Insurance against Unemployment," *Quarterly Journal of the International Association on Unemployment* 4:1 (Jan.-March 1914), 110.

197 John B. Andrews, "Introductory Note," *ALLR* 4:2 (May 1914), 214; "Public Responsibility," ibid., 273; Henry R. Seager, "Introductory Address," ibid., 313; "General Discussion," ibid., 336–37; 339–41; 354; "Present Status of Unemployment Insurance," ibid., 373–87. See also Kellor, "The Way Out," 639; and *CR*, 63 Cong., 2 sess., Appendix, 1 May 1914, p. 416 (V. Murdock).

choosing among the principal methods (pure trade union plans; Ghent system; British program), unless his detailed account of the British procedure could be taken as a hidden endorsement.[198]

Immediate introduction of a national system along the lines of the British example was most fervently advocated by left-wing extremists. After harboring doubts for several years regarding the potential of governmental plans, Rubinow published a book on social insurance in 1913 in which he came to the conclusion that the American situation warranted "compulsory, subsidized unemployment insurance." His sophisticated analysis, radical as it was, remained the most elaborate statement on the issue before World War I. Rubinow's strength was the theoretical argument, but his approach soon found a dedicated supporter on the political scene. London, barely elected to the House, soon made a strong plea for the introduction of the British system in the United States. In his view, a national compulsory program was the only viable proposition, as municipalities and states were too limited in their reach. Employer plans, he felt, were impractical, because they punished "the good employer who has the instincts of humanity and follows them." Interestingly, Rubinow and London were not able to persuade their own party comrades to adopt their view. In 1912 the Socialist Party of America remained mute on the issue; in its 1916 platform it advocated that government "contribute money to unemployment funds of labor unions and other organizations of workers," which meant that it endorsed the Ghent system, not the British model.[199]

Andrews, who was not a socialist, began to see the merits of a national compulsory scheme. It would be impossible to force employers to regularize their own business, he advised a correspondent in March 1915, "unless we use the devise of insurance to bring about cooperative pressure of a financial nature." In his "Unemployment Survey" he recommended that concerned persons should work toward the establishment of a system of compulsory unemployment insurance, supported by contributions from

---

198 Andrews to Olga S. Halsey, 8 Jan. 1915; 27 Jan. 1915, microfilm, reel 13, Andrews Papers; Olga S. Halsey, "Compulsory Unemployment Insurance in Great Britain," *ALLR* 5:2 (June 1915), 265–78; Andrews, "Practical Program," 189–91.

199 I. M. Rubinow, "Compulsory State Insurance of Workingmen," *Annals* 24 (Sept. 1904), 341–42; idem, *Social Insurance with Special Reference to American Conditions* (New York: Holt, 1913), 439–79. Quotation p. 455. See also for the same conclusion idem, "The Problem of Unemployment," 331. – Meyer London, "The Nation and the Problem of Unemployment," *ALLR* 5:2 (June 1915), 446–49. Quotation p. 449; Johnson, ed., *National Party Platforms*, I, 211.

employers, employees and the state, "as the most just and economical method for the proper maintenance of the necessary labor reserves." He also thought that such a plan would provide incentives to employers to regularize their production by rewarding with reimbursements those who kept their workers on the payroll. As the misery of the depression had in the meantime considerably broadened the range of advocates of the measure, Andrews could now point to endorsements by trade unionists, academics, and social workers.[200]

On the whole, the enthusiasts remained few in number. The general public was still indifferent to the social insurance cause, and even recognized reformers stayed unconvinced. In 1913, Leiserson assured a member of the *Survey* staff that he saw the insurance matter "from an entirely different standpoint from that adopted by Rubinow." To the Commission on Industrial Relations he merely suggested an examination of the issue, and the commission concurred. Commons, who wrote the commission's minority report after consulting with Andrews, similarly warned that unemployment insurance required "a large amount of investigation" before it could be recommended. The California Commission of Immigration and Housing was of the same opinion. Other members of the public remained equally uncertain. The Chicago Commissioner of Health pronounced himself impressed with most that was contained in the *Practical Program*, but could not see virtue in its proposition to support unemployment insurance benefits with public subsidies. Frances Kellor had not yet mentioned such benefits in the 1904 edition of *Out of Work*. In the 1915 edition she devoted forty pages to the issue, but refrained from taking a definite stand.[201]

In view of the limited value of the trade-union schemes, the novelty

---

200 Andrews to Raymond Robins, 10 March 1915, microfilm, reel 14, Andrews Papers; "Standard Recommendations," 595; "Unemployment Insurance," *ALLR* 5:3 (Nov. 1915), 589–92. For another strong endorsement see Rufus M. Potts, "Welfare (Social) Insurance: To What Extent Is It Desirable and Feasible in the United States and by What Means Can It Be Accomplished," National Convention of Insurance Commissioners, *Proceedings 1916*, 1–13. Potts was Illinois insurance superintendent. Another positive voice was that of Johns Hopkins professor of political economy Jacob H. Hollander. See his *The Abolition of Poverty* (Boston: Houghton, Mifflin, 1914), 90–91.

201 Leiserson to Fitch, 15 Dec. 1913, Box 14, Leiserson Papers; U.S. Congress. Senate, *Industrial Relations: Final Report and Testimony*, I, 115; 200; David J. Sofoss to Andrews, 12 July 1915, microfilm, reel 14, Andrews Papers; Andrews to Commons, 15 July 1915, ibid.; California. Commission of Immigration and Housing, *Report*, 7; G. B. Young to Andrews, 13 Jan. 1915, microfilm, reel 13, Andrews Papers; Kellor, *Out of Work* (1915), 444–84.

of the British program, the lack of in-depth studies of the American situation, and the indecision or indifference of the public, it is understandable that American lawmakers hesitated to approach the problem. Although several initiatives were taken at both the state and federal levels, these steps were clearly of an exploratory nature, and the fact that they remained without palpable results surprised nobody.

The first attempt at securing apposite legislation was made in Massachusetts, where in early 1915 a trade unionist, Juliet Stuart Poyntz, became instrumental in forming a Massachusetts Committee on Unemployment as a branch of the American Association on Unemployment. The committee was headed by Robert G. Valentine, an industrial consultant from Boston and outspoken advocate of unemployment insurance. The subcommittee on unemployment insurance included Felix Frankfurter, who had just begun teaching law at Harvard, and Olga Halsey. After a public committee meeting favored drafting a measure consonant with the British precedent, the subcommittee agreed to get such a bill before the 1916 Massachusetts legislature. Joseph L. Cohen of Columbia University, together with Halsey and other experts, all profiting from the advice of the AALL, designed a draft that covered workers in a number of industries. Its main feature was the provision that employers and employees each pay 25 percent of the premiums, with the state contributing the other half. Endorsed by the Massachusetts Republican Party, the Massachusetts State Federation of Labor, and various progressive employers, the bill was introduced in the legislature on 4 January 1916. Opposition from the employers' side kept it from making progress, but a resolution calling for an investigative commission was passed in June. It was characteristic of the lack of public consensus that this commission in its report, submitted in February 1917, declared itself to be "in general accord with the ideas of Mr. John B. Andrews," but declined to recommend a compulsory program.[202]

---

202 Robert G. Valentine, "What the Awakened Employer Is Thinking on Unemployment," *ALLR* 5:2 (June 1915), 426; Mary Kee Hale to Andrews, 11 April 1915; 26 April 1915, microfilm, reel 14, Andrews Papers; Andrews to Hale, 17 April 1915, ibid.; Robert G. Valentine to Andrews, 12 July 1915, ibid.; "Outline of the Subject Matter to Be Incorporated into a Bill to Provide for Workmen Who Are Temporarily Unemployed in Certain Trades in the State of Massachusetts," [1915], microfilm, reel 67, Andrews Papers; "Draft for Unemployment Insurance Act," 1 May 1915, microfilm, reel 66, Andrews Papers; Andrews, "Unemployment Insurance," *ALLR* 5:3 (Nov. 1915), 591; Nelson, *Unemployment Insurance*, 17–18. For labor's support of the bill see

Other sporadic efforts were made across the country. A Michigan statute of 1915 permitted the formation of private insurance companies to pay unemployment benefits to railroad employees. In the same year the California legislature, following the Massachusetts example, created a commission to investigate "the various systems of social insurance now in use." A similar bill was introduced in Ohio but failed to pass. In Illinois a movement to introduce an insurance bill began in early 1915. Henderson had overcome his initial hesitation, and in February he announced to Andrews that he felt that "the public mind here is ripening for unemployment insurance." He began to work on a draft, but his death put an end to these endeavors.[203]

If insurance bills stood little chance of adoption on the state level, it would have been ludicrous to have made a serious attempt to obtain federal legislation. An occasional probing foray was made, nevertheless. In February 1915, when the depression reached its nadir, the petition that Austin had inserted in the *Congressional Record* demanded that Congress "proceed at once to develop and put in operation a national system of unemployment insurance." Even London felt it more fruitful, though, to try a cautious approach. In early 1916 he merely asked for the appointment of a commission to prepare a plan for a national insurance fund (H.J.Res. 159). The Committee on Labor, of which he was a member, held hearings in April. Rubinow and Poyntz eloquently pleaded for governmental unemployment insurance. Meeker thought it feasible. Andrews, although favoring social insurance in general, was mute on unemployment, possibly because he felt the case to be too hopeless for the moment. The most forceful presentation was made by Gompers; but he roundly refuted "the whole scheme, the whole fault, the whole philosophy" of the socialists. At best an investigation might be made, he told the committee, but only "with the understanding that the rights of the workers and the freedom secured by the workers shall not be frittered away by a patch upon our social system." Unemployment should be fought by reducing immigration. Compulsory insurance, he feared, would bring

Keyssar, *Out of Work*, 214. – Massachusetts. Special Commission on Social Insurance, *Report*, 107–09.
203 1915 *Michigan Acts*, c. 37; 1915 *California Statutes*, c. 275; Andrews, "Unemployment Insurance," 592; Henderson to Andrews, 6 Feb. 1915, microfilm, reel 13, Andrews Papers; Andrews to Henderson, 12 March 1915, microfilm, reel 14, Andrews Papers; "C. R. Henderson: Letter 2/23/15", microfilm, reel 66, Andrews Papers; Nelson, *Unemployment Insurance*, 19. Henderson died on 29 March 1915.

governmental regulation of industry and of the trade unions. The AFL president was apprehensive that such insurance would result "in every Government agent going into the homes and the lives of the workers as a spy." He could imagine a voluntary plan, but wanted to safeguard for the workers "the right to decide our course."[204] Gompers' diatribe, adding organized labor's voice to the arguments of the various foes of unemployment insurance, did not augur well for the measure itself. London consequently modified his suggestion and emphasized the investigative feature (H.J.Res. 250). This time the Committee on Labor reported the resolution without amendment, but no further action occurred.

Even the few ardent supporters of government-sponsored unemployment insurance must have felt that their idea had no realistic chance of implementation yet. But they were aware that their advocacy served the purpose of clarifying the options and probing the legislative ground. It was through their discussions, testimony, and lobbying that the issue was brought and kept before an increasing public. Further progress could come from the point reached by about 1916.

As a result of the reformist activities described in this chapter, a considerable part of the nation thus understood on the eve of the American entry into the war that involuntary idleness was a concomitant of industrialized society and that it was government that ultimately would have to find some means for the alleviation of the resulting distress. The spread of this insight was arguably the most significant achievement of the unemployment reform movement that had begun in the late 1870s. In this respect it did not matter too much that the various ways in which governments tentatively involved themselves did not yet yield satisfactory results. The very fact that these attempts were undertaken amounted to de facto recognition of governmental responsibility. A precedent was thereby set. In a larger sense, this recognition offered the prospect that the unstructured condition of the labor market with its attendant waste, both human and material, would ultimately yield to an organizational concept of more rational character.

In this regard it was significant – and this represented another important achievement – that virtually all the major tools that later found application in governmental unemployment action were designed and discussed dur-

---

204 *CR*, 63 Cong., 3 sess., 20 Feb. 1915 p. 4236. See page 28. – Hearings on H.J.Res. 159, pp. 16–17; 36–106; 118–21; 122–88. Quotations pp. 137; 151; 158; 188. For a suggestion that Gompers was guided by ulterior motives see Louis S. Reed, *The Labor Philosophy of Samuel Gompers* (New York: Columbia University Press, 1930), 116–17.

ing our period. Counting procedures, labor exchanges, and public works even underwent testing. In subsequent years, reformers and governments were to make use of the knowledge and experience accumulated in the prewar decades. Refinement and correction would prove necessary, but no essentially new concepts would surface anymore. These were indeed accomplishments fitting the aspirations of the Progressive era. To apply Otis L. Graham, Jr.'s, general comment on the age, "The truth was out, social evil was unmasked, and the appropriate remedies [were] formulated for the next generation that would finish the work."[205] For unemployment reform, the seedtime was clearly over before the nation entered World War I.

205 Otis L. Graham, Jr., *An Encore for Reform: The Old Progressives and the New Deal* (New York: Oxford University Press, 1967), 13.

3. Nascence and growth of the USES: World War I

World War I influenced unemployment reform in contradictory ways. The downturn of the American economy caused by the outbreak of the war in Europe stimulated an intensified quest for alleviative means, as described in the previous chapter. The entry of the United States into the war in April 1917, on the other hand, interrupted what might be called the natural development of reform. Unemployment ceased to be a generally noticeable problem, and further exploration into the potential of remedies such as the use of public works or unemployment insurance essentially came to a standstill. But the partial abandonment of the time-honored principles of laissez-faire that characterized much of the war effort brought unexpected prominence and growth to the favorite remedial instrument of the prewar period, the labor exchange. The USES, spurred on by the need to overcome the labor shortages caused by wartime production, developed into an imposing, nationwide organization. The growth of the USES constituted in many ways the fulfillment of the most ardent dream of the reformers, because it offered the chance to effect the intercity and interstate exchange of workers that many considered to be a necessary step in fighting unemployment. Unfortunately for the reformers' expectations, the haste of the wartime buildup produced shortcomings in the structure and performance of the service that threatened to seriously impede its further acceptance.

The beginning of hostilities in Europe in August 1914 immediately caused a disturbance in the American labor market. Lack of imported raw materials and semifinished goods, the congestion of seaports, and general uncertainty put millions of workers out of production. Soon, some recovery set in, but first it was only felt in certain lines of manufacturing such as gun powder production, the canning industry, and paper mills. The labor surplus took many months to dissipate. It is true that when the United States entered the war, thousands of employers panicked at the prospect of losing workers to the armed forces; however, even in 1917 major shortages occurred only in specific occupations, whereas the gross number of workers does not seem to have been inadequate. Much of the demand for employees, federal Secretary of Labor Wilson later stated, "was found to have been influenced more by eagerness for labor at wages relatively inadequate to the sharp rise in living expenses than by general labor shortage." Only from about May 1918 on did a definite overall need for more workers appear to have existed.[1]

The objective facts of the labor market were somewhat obscured by differing perceptions held in various quarters. Employers, worried by local or trade-specific difficulties to obtain workers, began as early as 1917 to engage in bidding wars, which caused the market to degenerate into veritable chaos. Production suffered because of high labor turnover, and the nation's war effort was the worse for it. "Human energies which might have been directed toward victory," USES Director General John B. Densmore wrote after the war, "were vainly expended."[2] As a result, the federal government undertook the buildup of its own labor exchange tool.

The task of organizing an orderly distribution system naturally fell to the Department of Labor. In April 1917 the USES had exchange stations located in ninety-three cities spread over thirty-seven states. Because the USES could serve as a departure point for expansion, Secretary Wilson submitted a request to Congress for $750,000 in fall 1917. The USES would absorb the personnel of the Division of Information, an arrangement that in a way constituted a reversal of the relationship between the two administrative entities. Congress, however, cut the sum to $250,000 and allotted it for spending "during the present emergency, in addition to existing facilities" only, thereby keeping the normal work of the Division of Information separate, a policy in line with the general intentions of the administration. War exigencies caused President Wilson to make another $825,000, taken from his national security and defense fund, available on 5 December 1917 to the USES. These monies gave the Department of Labor the opportunity to engage in the procurement of war production workers in grand style. The policy of isolating war-connected activities,

---

1 U.S. Dept. of Labor, *6th Annual Report, 1918*, 201. For similar argumentation see William M. Leiserson, "The Shortage of Labor and the Waste of Labor," *Survey* 39:26 (30 March 1918), 701–03; Charles B. Barnes, "Employment and the Labor Market," *American Economic Review* 8, Suppl. (March 1918), 171–78. – *MLR* (Sept. 1918), 300; *MLR* (Feb. 1919), 130–31; Don D. Lescohier, *The Labor Market* (New York: Macmillan, 1919), 177–82.

2 John B. Densmore, "Lessons of the War in Shifting Labor," *Annals* 81 (Jan. 1919), 32.

on the other hand, disappointed hopes that the national exigency would produce tangible and lasting benefits for the reform cause. There existed the distinct danger, Andrews wrote Edward Keating (D-Colorado), a railroad brotherhood journalist and member of the House Committee on Labor, that "the war emergency pass into history without providing for a *permanent* employment service on an adequate basis."[3]

Endeavors to give the USES a secure foothold had in fact started already. Keating and Senator Joseph T. Robinson (D-Arkansas), who as majority leader was later to support Roosevelt's New Deal programs, had introduced two identical bills providing generous operating funds on a permanent basis for the USES and enabling it to control the state level through a matching-fund scheme (S. 3078; H.R. 7222). The proposal was sponsored by the AAPEO, which at its annual meeting in Chicago on 6–7 June 1917 had demanded "the immediate establishment of a National Bureau of Employment Offices under the United States Department of Labor." Seager and his colleague Thomas I. Parkinson, who headed the legislative drafting department at Columbia, had subsequently written the bill and discussed it in detail with Department of Labor officials as well as with a legislative expert of the AFL. The latter organization's favorable involvement, which also manifested itself in a letter of support that Gompers wrote to Robinson in September 1917, may have been astonishing to outsiders who remembered Gompers' hands-off attitude before the war. It was, however, a reflection of a recent change of attitude whose reasons could be fully appreciated only during the postwar public debate regarding the future of the USES.[4]

Although the AALL made strenuous efforts to secure favorable congressional consideration of the Robinson–Keating measure, the initiative died in committee. The reasons are not fully clear. Nathan A. Smyth, assistant director general of the USES, could later not explain why the bill had not advanced. In view of the reluctant attitude of the

3 U.S. Dept. of Labor, *5th Annual Report, 1917*, 88–89; 40 Stat. 79 (1917), p. 376; U.S. Dept. of Labor, *6th Annual Report, 1918*, 208; Robert D. Cuff, "The Politics of Labor Administration during World War I," *Labor History* 21:4 (Fall 1980), 553; Andrews to Keating, 18 Jan. 1918, microfilm, reel 18, Andrews Papers.
4 Text of the bills in Hearings on S. 688, S. 1442 and H.R. 4305, pp. 477–79. – John C. Herndon, "Public Employment Offices in the United States", in U.S. Bureau of Labor Statistics, *Bulletin 241* (Washington: G.P.O., 1918), 71–72; Charles B. Barnes to Andrews, 22 Nov. 1917, microfilm, reel 18, Andrews Papers; Andrews to Miss McMakin, 15 Nov. 1918, ibid.; Gompers to Robinson, 23 Sept. 1917, U.S. Dept. of Labor, *5th Annual Report, 1917*, 91–92.

Joint Committees on Labor toward far milder postwar proposals concerning the USES, it stands to reason that the committee members doubted the wisdom of creating so strong an agency. In mid-February 1918, Andrews still thought that the bills, after revision in the Department of Labor, might be reintroduced "and pushed toward passage," and Commons tried to gain the American Economic Association's support for this cause, but their hopes proved vain.[5]

Meanwhile, the USES ventured upon an enormous buildup without specific legislative sanction. Charles B. Barnes, who as director of the state's Bureau of Employment in New York (City) had a first-rate observation post, soon confided to Andrews that an " 'after us, the deluge' feeling" spread in the service and that "the only idea seems to be to meet the emergency, without looking ahead to a permanent employment service on an adequate basis." The immediate trigger for this development was a directive issued on 3 January 1918 by Secretary Wilson that established the USES as a separate entity, independent of the Division of Information. Densmore, formerly solicitor of the Department of Labor, was appointed director general. Under his leadership the service now faced the twofold task of expanding, and at the same time exercising, its distribution function. This undertaking proved a formidable challenge that taxed the ingenuity and administrative gifts of those in charge to the utmost.[6]

It took considerable time to find an adequate form of organization. Three administrative shuffles produced a structure by mid-year in which direct relations between Washington and the federal directors of employment in the states replaced the zone system, an arrangement that at least superficially weakened the impression of a rigorously centralized operation. The director general's office ultimately contained five divisions, of which Field Organization and Clearance oversaw the actual exchange work. In addition to the offices derived from the immigration network since 1914 and to the bureaus hitherto under state administration, new offices were created "with such dispatch," as Secretary Wilson put it,

5 Henry R. Seager, "Coordination of Federal, State and City Systems of Employment Offices," *ALLR* 8:1 (March 1918), 22; Andrews to Owen R. Lovejoy, 28 Nov. 1917, microfilm, reel 18, Andrews Papers; Andrews to [Leon C.] Marshall, 6 Dec. 1917, ibid.; "Reasons for the Proposed Bill," memorandum, n.d., ibid.; Andrews to Robinson, 13 Feb. 1918, ibid.; Lucile Eaves to Commons, 4 March 1918, ibid.; Hearings on S. 688, S. 1442 and H.R. 4305, pp. 110; 475–80.
6 Charles B. Barnes to Andrews, 12 Jan. 1918, microfilm, reel 18, Andrews Papers; "United States Employment Service Organized by the Department of Labor," *MLR* 6:3 (March 1918), 568–70.

that by mid-1918 the USES had more than 400 employment exchanges. At that time, about 1,700 paid personnel staffed the USES field branches nationwide, with another 300 working in the Washington headquarters. These numbers increased to approximately 4,000 paid and 3,000 unpaid staff in about 500 offices by mid-February 1919. Specialized units (Women, Boys, Farm Work) looked after specific needs. A Public Service Reserve recruited skilled personnel for industries important to the war effort.[7]

The federal administration supported the USES activities. When the campaigns waged by employers for unskilled labor became intolerable, the War Labor Policies Board recommended that all exchange work in this regard should be conducted by the USES. President Wilson consequently issued a proclamation on 17 June 1918 in which he "solemnly urge[d] all employers engaged in war work" to refrain after 1 August 1918 from recruiting unskilled labor except through the USES. This directive generated a good amount of resentment, more so as restrictions on the hiring of skilled labor were also being contemplated. The USES, however, proved impervious to nascent criticism, and was proud of its accomplishments. Its placements, by its own reckoning, increased from 51,183 in January 1918 to 558,469 in November of that year. The total for the calendar year of 1918 was 2,698,887, when the civilian labor force may have numbered about 40 million.[8]

On 1 July 1918, Congress came through with a further appropriation of $5,500,000. Although these funds were again allotted for work "during

7 U.S. Dept. of Labor, *5th Annual Report, 1917*, 81; idem, *6th Annual Report, 1918*, 210; 218; idem, *7th Annual Report, 1919*, 276; 293; Cuff, "Politics of Labor Administration," 555. A glimpse at the pushing for offices in specific localities is provided in Thomas J. Walsh to Robert C. Elting, 23 April 1918, Box 191, Walsh Papers; Walsh to Densmore, 23 April 1928, ibid.; Elting to Walsh, 1 May 1918, ibid. For a detailed description of the administrative expansion in one state see Memorandum by Geo. P. Hambrecht, chairman of the Wisconsin Industrial Commission, 21 March 1919, Box 48, Leiserson Papers. For another state's war experience see Fred. C. Croxton, "War Employment Work in Ohio," *MLR* 4:6 (Dec. 1917), 995–1002. For an overall evaluation see William J. Breen, *Uncle Sam at Home: Civilian Mobilization, Wartime Federalism, and the Council of National Defense, 1917–1919* (Westport: Greenwood, 1984), 90–91.
8 U.S. Dept. of Labor, *6th Annual Report, 1918*, 700–01; 703; idem, *7th Annual Report, 1919*, 285; U.S. Employment Service, *Report of Proceedings of the National War Labor Conference, Washington, June 12–15, 1918* (Washington: G.P.O., 1918), 88; Densmore to Andrews, 20 July 1918, microfilm, reel 18, Andrews Papers. The *Historical Statistics* put the labor force at 40,023,000 for 1917 and 39,076,000 for 1918. U.S. Bureau of the Census, *Historical Statistics of the United States, Colonial Times to 1970: Bicentennial Edition, Part 1* (Washington: G.P.O., 1975), 126.

the present emergency" only, Secretary Wilson was confident that the situation would last. In August 1918, making an estimate for the fiscal year ending 30 June 1919, he envisaged an expansion to approximately 1,000 branch offices and decided that Congress should be asked for a further $14,801,382.[9]

The USES thus met the war situation with an outwardly impressive performance. This was made possible through the willingness of Congress and the presidential office to entrust the Department of Labor with an important role in recruiting the work force required for war production. The buildup of the necessary organization, on the other hand, did not occur without improvisation and waste, and the performance of the USES suffered accordingly. As early as January 1918, insider Barnes confided to Andrews that he was concerned that the service did "a lot of what is avowedly emergency work." The great question on the mind of USES officials was whether the hastily built structure would be capable of carrying on its labor exchange activities in peacetime. As far as this concern aimed at benefiting the jobless, it was shared by reformers interested in meeting future unemployment situations. In the latter regard, some hope could be gained from the fact that a federal umbrella organization had been erected for the first time, a precedent that might be pointed to later. Moreover, if the framework could be maintained, even if its fabric had to be tenuous for some years to come, it might serve as a structure to be filled out in time of need. Seen from this angle, unemployment reform had obviously profited from the war in the same way as various other reform causes were advanced during this period.[10]

9 40 Stat. 113 (1918), p. 696 (Sundry Civil Appropriation Act); U.S. Dept. of Labor, *7th Annual Report, 1919*, 287.

10 Charles B. Barnes to Andrews, 12 Jan. 1918, microfilm, reel 18, Andrews Papers. Allen F. Davis, "Welfare Reform and World War I," *American Quarterly* 19:3 (Fall 1967), 516–33, while pointing out the progress in labor standards, urban housing, etc., does not mention the unemployment cause.

4. Pondering the issues: Postwar to the mid-1920s

The decade following the end of hostilities did not witness the fulfillment of any high-flown reform expectations. This was not necessarily a result of the war experience, whose impact was mixed. By sharply reducing joblessness, the war diminished public support for intensified governmental action. But its regulatory and centralizing tendencies also increased public acceptance of governmental activity in general, and the very buildup of the USES seemed to bear promises for future reform. As it turned out, the incentives to continue or even increase governmental involvement in the social sphere were weaker than the countervailing forces. Demobilization and the depression of 1921 each briefly recalled the unemployment concerns of the prewar period, but they did not last long enough effectively to suppress the anti-interventionist sentiments that the war had engendered. The one outstanding event of these years, the President's Conference on Unemployment of fall 1921, in its caution epitomized this attitude.

I   Postwar and prosperity

Complacent normalcy

The lack of impressive signs of advancement was not evidence of the absence of any reform efforts altogether. The ranks of the reform proponents now included more professionals and more progressive businessmen. Convinced of the correctness of the scientific approach to social issues, they were eager to ensure that changes in the institutional frame of society kept up with technological development. As representatives of welfare capitalism, they not only strove to implement enlightened measures in their own firms; they also contributed in no small way to the continuing reflection on the correct means of fighting unemployment by financially sustaining institutions such as the National Bureau of Economic Research, the Industrial Relations Counselors, or the AALL. Although their goal probably was, as Berkowitz/McQuaid contend, industrial efficiency to be achieved through the enlightened selfishness of the market, their attitude and action helped to fertilize the soil for the growth of corrective-interventionist ideas. An increase in sophistication – concerning both the period's understanding of the political, economic, and technical obstacles that unemployment action had to surmount and the solutions sought – was the consequence.[1]

These aspirations have evidently to be grouped with the various attempts noticeable in the 1920s to overcome perceived deficiencies of the New Era through deliberate spending, planning, and market restoration activities. Whereas the businessmen just mentioned mostly sought to secure sustained growth and continued social progress through private action, theorists such as William T. Foster, Waddill Catchings, John Dewey, and Rexford G. Tugwell were beginning to assign the government an important role in this respect. With regard to unemployment policies, the clearest manifestation of this line of thinking was the endeavor, described later, to oblige state and federal administrations to institute advance planning of public works.[2]

Even though the reformers talked only to a sparse and largely uninterested audience, they were able to witness several significant developments. The most important was certainly the broadening recognition of the nationwide – and therewith federal – aspect of the matter. This became manifest when in 1921, by organizing the President's Conference on Unemployment, Harding's administration acknowledged an obligation to take unemployment into consideration. The years between the war and the onset of the Great Depression were characterized by a certain ambivalence. The states could not claim to be relieved of their ultimate responsibility; but a future sharing of the burden announced itself, in-

---

1 Edward Berkowitz and Kim McQuaid, *Creating the Welfare State: The Political Economy of Twentieth-Century Reform* (New York: Praeger, 1980), 79–80. For a discussion of the aims of welfare capitalists in the context of unemployment reform see Roy Lubove, *The Struggle for Social Security 1900–65* (Cambridge, Mass.: Harvard University Press, 1968), 160–64; Daniel Nelson, *Unemployment Insurance: The American Experience 1915–1935* (Madison: University of Wisconsin Press, 1969), 28–46. Stuart D. Brandes, *American Welfare Capitalism 1880–1940* (Chicago: University of Chicago Press, 1976) somewhat astonishingly does not consider the efforts at regularization or unemployment alleviation in any specific way.

2 For a summary of the various "visions of a new liberalism" see Ellis W. Hawley, *The Great War and the Search for a Modern Order: A History of the American People and Their Institutions, 1917–1933* (New York: St. Martin's Press, 1979), 119–23.

cluding the possibility that the federal government might assume the larger role. The fact that in the 1920s even those states with progressive traditions "slipped into the trough of conservatism," as James T. Patterson has remarked,[3] meant that unemployment reform would not receive much official endorsement from their side. The federal acknowledgment was all the more important, even if corroboration through active federal involvement remained slight.

More specific advances could be observed as well. The counting dilemma now enjoyed the attention of a growing group of experts who endeavored to define its inherent difficulties clearly. A barrage of efforts aiming at the achievement of federal labor exchange legislation refined the understanding of the technical and political implications and obstacles. The same held true, though on a smaller scale, regarding the curative use of public works. Finally, the problems of unemployment insurance, inchoatively examined before the war, were now more thoroughly sorted out, a process that added to the credibility of the proposed solutions. A student of the New York scene has written that the postwar period was remarkable "for its consideration – not its solution – of the problem of joblessness, which diminished with the return of prosperity."[4] This statement also applies to the country at large.

The speed of reform progress depended to a degree upon the amount of existing unemployment. Between the end of World War I and about 1927, the labor market situation underwent considerable changes, although during most of the period it favored the working population. Astonishingly, despite the fact that the manufacturing labor force had risen from 8.2 million in 1914 to 10.2 million in 1918 and over 4 million men had to be demobilized, the cessation of hostilities did not immediately bring the widespread unemployment many forecasters had anticipated.[5] Pent-up civilian demand and increasing purchases from abroad combined to take up the slack quickly and keep the momentum of the economy going. This certainly did not mean that the American nation would escape a slump entirely. Toward the end of 1920 the pace of production slowed down considerably, and a trough was reached in summer 1921, marking

3 James T. Patterson, *The New Deal and the States: Federalism in Transition* (Princeton, N.J.: Princeton University Press, 1969), 17.
4 Paula Eldot, *Governor Alfred E. Smith: Politician as Reformer* (New York: Garland, 1983), 201.
5 Peter Fearon, *War, Prosperity and Depression: The U.S. Economy 1917–45* (Lawrence: University Press of Kansas, 1987), 7; 15; 17.

a year of downright depression. The index of manufacturing production went from 100 in 1919 to 103.6 in 1920 and 79.4 in 1921. Accurate unemployment figures do not exist, but the best guess indicates that overall joblessness among nonfarm employees increased from 2.4 percent in 1919 to 8.6 percent and then 19.5 percent in the two following years, respectively. However, it is certainly wrong to claim, as distinguished social worker Frank J. Bruno has done, that unemployment "rose steadily from 1922 to 1929." There was a swift recovery, followed by prosperity during the subsequent period, with a slight dip in the curve for 1924. Nonfarm unemployment seems to have moved accordingly, falling to a nadir of 2.9 percent in 1926 and then rising slowly. "It can be stated at once," Secretary of Commerce Herbert C. Hoover complacently wrote to a correspondent in late 1925, "that there is no unemployment in this country in the sense of that existing in foreign countries." The combination of rapid economic expansion, price stability, and full employment, Peter Fearon has recently remarked, "was as close to economic paradise as seemed possible."[6]

Not surprisingly under these circumstances, many of the time-honored tenets of laissez-faire continued to mark the nation's political and economic leadership. The downturn of 1921 proved too short to raise other than quickly vanishing unemployment concerns and to instill lasting desires for decisive governmental action. Businessman and philanthropist Robert W. De Forest could be sure of widespread agreement when he asserted in September 1921 that the chief cause of the recession was "governmental interference with business." President Warren G. Harding saw fit to enjoin the delegates to his conference on unemployment to forgo any appeals to his government's largesse. "I would have little enthusiasm for any proposed relief," he admonished his listeners, "which seeks either palliation or tonic from the public treasury."[7]

6 Frank J. Bruno, *Trends in Social Work 1874–1956: A History Based on the Proceedings of the National Conference of Social Work* (New York: Columbia University Press, 1957), 298; Leo Wolman, "Labor," in President's Conference on Unemployment. Committee on Recent Economic Changes, *Recent Economic Changes in the United States* (New York: McGraw-Hill, 1929), 449; Gene Smiley, "Recent Unemployment Rate Estimates for the 1920s and 1930s," *Journal of Economic History* 43:2 (June 1983), 488. The nonfarm component of the labor force as such rose from 69% in 1910 to 74% in 1920 and 78% in 1930. U.S. Bureau of the Census, *Historical Statistics of the United States, Colonial Times to 1970: Bicentennial Edition, Part 1* (Washington: G.P.O., 1975), 139. See also Fearon, *War, Prosperity and Depression*, 25; 62–64. – Hoover to Allen B. Forsberg, 1 Dec. 1925, Box 615, Commerce Papers, Hoover Papers.

7 De Forest to Mary Van Kleeck, 22 Sept. 1921, Box 2, Van Kleeck Papers; President's Conference on Unemployment, *Report* (Washington: G.P.O., 1921), 27.

Harding basked in the certainty of being carried by the mainstream of public opinion. Government interference, warned the managing director of the National Industrial Conference Board, a business-oriented research institution founded in 1916, at about this time, would disturb "the working of certain economic laws," and he feared "the consequences if they are thwarted in their natural course." This was the general view. Much of the reform enthusiasm had vanished, smothered by the war experience and the fear of Bolshevik revolution. Organized labor's attitude conformed to this outlook. With its political clout weakening in the climate of the New Era, the movement sought to safeguard the interests of the unionized minority of the labor force. Unemployment reform thus held a very low ranking among its concerns. As prominent a social work exponent as *Survey* associate editor Bruno Lasker expressed doubts as to the social dangers of unemployment. "Any proposed change was suspect," Jane Addams later recalled, "even those efforts that had been considered praiseworthy before the war."[8]

This attitude was mirrored on the political scene. The president's own Republican party, when devising its 1920 election platform, kept silent about unemployment. Secretary of Labor James J. Davis took up the reserve army idea in September 1922 when he told the IAPES conferees that 3 million idle or part-time workers were "the normal condition in America."[9] The Democrats showed somewhat greater concern. In 1920 they offered the insight that labor was not a commodity, and in 1924 they went a step further by advocating the initiation of public works in periods of depression. But the matter was not a campaign issue, and the Democrats were soundly defeated in both elections.

The stand taken by the American government with regard to the efforts of the International Labour Organization (ILO), created by the Treaty of Versailles, reflected the general apathy. Immediately after the war some American enthusiasm manifested itself in anticipation of the first meeting of the International Labour Conference in October–November 1919. The

8 "Excerpts from Verbatim Stenographic Report of Meeting of National Conference Board, December 15, 1921," Box 672, Commerce Papers, Hoover Papers; Alexander Keyssar, "Unemployment and the Labor Movement in Massachusetts, 1870–1916," in Herbert G. Gutman and Donald H. Bell, eds., *The New England Working Class and the New Labor History* (Urbana: University of Illinois Press, 1987), 247; B[runo L[asker], "Unemployment and Immorality," *Survey* 45:21 (19 Feb. 1921), 735–36; Jane Addams, *The Second Twenty Years from Hull House* (New York: Macmillan, 1930), 154.

9 James J. Davis, "Address," IAPES, Proceedings 1922, in U.S. Bureau of Labor Statistics, *Bulletin 337* (Washington: G.P.O., 1923), 2–3. See also the indignant response " 'Normalcy' in Unemployment," *New Republic* 32:410 (11 Oct. 1922), 163–64.

very fact that Washington was to be the gathering place indicated a certain attentiveness on the part of Wilson's administration. There was also some public interest. In June the New York Academy of Political Science sponsored a symposium dealing with problems arising from any forthcoming international labor treaties. One of the participants, Joseph P. Chamberlain, a professor at Columbia University's law school, seized the opportunity to demonstrate that the federal government had the constitutional right to enter into such contracts. Andrews happily announced in his journal that the meeting would *inter alia* consider questions concerning unemployment.[10] But when the conference ended on 29 November 1919, American ratification of the peace treaty was already doomed. Although the United States could have joined the ILO without being a member of the League of Nations, the Republican administrations of the 1920s chose not to do so. As a consequence, the federal government could and mostly did disregard the various unemployment recommendations that emanated from the Washington conference and the subsequent ILO meetings. About the only venture that saw American participation during the 1920s was the reporting of employment data, described later, a one-horse undertaking that in its pitifulness expressed the basic lack of governmental interest.[11]

One specific measure that cost the government almost nothing should be mentioned here, though – the restriction of immigration. As had been the case before the war, foes of large-scale immigration exercised pressure to curb the influx of newcomers with the argument that the available amount of work should be reserved for those already in the country. Not only organized labor, but on occasion even state legislatures added their voices. Congress responded to these and differently motivated demands with the

10 J. P. Chamberlain, "The Power of the State under the Constitution to Enter Labor Treaties," Academy of Political Science in the City of New York, *Proceedings*, 8 (July 1919), 448–57. See also idem, "The United States and the International Labor Organization," *ALLR* 17:2 (June 1927), 171–75; "The International Labor Conference: Washington, October 29, 1919," *ALLR* 9:3 (Sept. 1919), 302.

11 Cf. in this context the pleading for international unemployment action by Ernest Greenwood, "International Aspects of Some of Our National Problems," IAPES, Proceedings 1922, 66. Greenwood was the American correspondent of the ILO. The general American abstinence did not pass unnoticed abroad. In the mid-twenties an English expert surveyed the unemployment situation in the United States for the Governing Body of the ILO. His report implied that he had not come across any particular endeavors worthy of note. J. R. Bellerby, *Stabilization of Employment in the United States* (Geneva: International Labour Office, 1926. Studies and Reports. Series C: Employment and Unemployment, no. 11), 2–3.

quota laws of 1921 and 1924, and immigration fell from over 800,000 in 1921 to less than 300,000 in 1925. Andrews articulated the hopes of many when he wrote that this development would "doubtless have some influence in the direction of stabilizing domestic employment."[12] But a panacea for unemployment the restrictive acts were certainly not, as became painfully clear a few years later when the depression struck and then persisted, despite the virtual end of immigration.

The prevailing general lethargy toward social questions affected even those active in social work. More professionalized and institutionally organized than before the war and captivated by the new developments in psychology, they reverted to casework with individuals, a move that resulted in "the retreat of social work from social reform," as John H. Ehrenreich has put it. Under the existing circumstances it evidently took some obstinacy to pursue the goal of unemployment reform during these years.[13]

One group that kept the faith and strove to propagate it was the AALL, which by late 1921 counted almost 3,000 members. It continued to lobby for various bills and distribute pamphlets. In its quarterly journal it published pertinent articles or reported on significant events. Most of the sessions at its annual meeting in December 1922 and various papers at subsequent conventions were dedicated to the problem. The association took particular pride in maintaining the connection with the IAU. Right after the war, some AALL members wondered whether the existence of the ILO would make activities of their own organization redundant, but they soon realized that there was room for the more aggressive work of voluntary associations. At the first postwar meeting of the IAU in Luxemburg, 9–11 September 1923, Andrews reported on the American sec-

---

12 "Recommendations of California Legislative Committee on Unemployment," *MLR* 8:4 (March 1919), 1091; "Labor Legislation of 1921," *ALLR* 11:4 (Dec. 1921), 326; "Gains of the Past Year in Combating Unemployment in the United States," *ALLR* 14:1 (March 1924), 166.

13 John H. Ehrenreich, *The Altruistic Imagination: A History of Social Work and Social Policy in the United States* (Ithaca: Cornell University Press, 1985), 83. Similar statements in Clarke A. Chambers, *Seedtime of Reform: American Social Service and Social Action 1918–1933* (Minneapolis: University of Minnesota Press, 1963), 93–96; idem, "Social Service and Social Reform: A Historical Essay," in Frank R. Breul and Steven J. Diner, eds., *Compassion and Responsibility: Readings in the History of Social Welfare Policy in the United States* (Chicago: University of Chicago Press, 1980), 19; Walter I. Trattner, *From Poor Law to Welfare State: A History of Social Welfare in America* (New York: Free Press, 1974), 213; 223; Michael B. Katz, *In the Shadow of the Poorhouse: A Social History of Welfare in America* (New York: Basic Books, 1986), 165–67.

tion. The major development of the next meeting, held in Prague, 2–6 October 1924, was the upsurge of a movement aimed at merging the International Association for Labor Legislation with the IAU. The fusion was accomplished in September 1925 at Berne, when the two organizations combined with the International Committee on Social Insurance to form the International Association for Social Progress. The AALL's international connection bestowed some prestige upon it and gave its members the feeling of swimming in the mainstream of comtemporary social thought, even though the immediate impact on the consciousness of the American public remained small.[14]

Of greater significance was the era's growing interest in the business cycle. The war had interrupted the natural course of economic development, but the 1921 depression at the latest signaled that periods of boom and downturn would still be very much the order of the coming years. Studies of the phenomenon proliferated accordingly. In 1919 the newly founded *Review of Economic Statistics* filled its entire first issue with reflections on the cycle by Harvard economist Warren M. Persons. His efforts to analyze time series were paralleled by those of other researchers such as Frederick C. Mills, Edmond E. Day, and Carl Snyder.[15]

Wesley C. Mitchell strengthened his position as the leading cycle theorist. In addition to holding his professorship at Columbia University, he now headed the staff of the National Bureau of Economic Research, a privately financed agency founded in 1920, that conducted quantitative investigations into public welfare subjects and displayed interest in the cycle discussion. Mitchell himself carried the factual investigation of business cycles far beyond earlier American efforts, attempting to clarify the interrelations of costs, prices, and profits. In revising his pioneering work

---

14 For the AALL strength see John B. Andrews, "Report of Work: American Association for Labor Legislation," *ALLR* 12:1 (March 1922), 80. The exact number was 2,978. – Henry R. Seager, "Progress of Labor Legislation, 1900–1925," *ALLR* 15:4 (Dec. 1925), 289–90; "International Labor Legislation," *ALLR* 13:4 (Dec. 1923), 265–66; Irene Osgood Andrews, "Report of Work: American Association for Labor Legislation," *ALLR* 14:1 (March 1924), 101; Congrès international de politique sociale tenu à Prague du 2 au 4 octobre 1924, *Compte rendu des séances et rapports* (Nancy: Berger-Lévrault, 1925), 411–12; "International Labor Legislation," *ALLR* 14:4 (Dec. 1924), 324.

15 Warren M. Persons, "Indices of Business Conditions," *Review of Economic Statistics* 1:1 (Jan. 1919), 1–107. See also idem, *The Index of General Business Conditions: A Nontechnical Explanation* (Cambridge, Mass.: Harvard University Committee on Economic Research, 1921); Frederick Cecil Mills, *Statistical Methods Applied to Economics and Business* (New York: Holt, 1924); Edmond E. Day, *Statistical Analysis* (New York: Macmillan, 1925); Carl Snyder, *Business Cycles and Business Measurements: Studies in Quantitative Economics* (New York: Macmillan, 1927).

of 1913, he came to the conclusion that the curves of general unemployment and of the production figures of large-scale enterprise were closely connected. Other investigators, notably Alvin H. Hansen, Henry L. Moore, Arthur B. Adams, and Simon Kuznets, similarly attempted to match the achievements of foreign leading cycle experts such as John A. Hobson and Arthur C. Pigou. These economists did not all agree in their conclusions, but the investigations left many of them, as Stephen W. Baskerville has written, "haunted by the spectre of unemployment and dissatisfied with the limited ability of neo-classical theory even to explain the cycle, much less to suggest ways of ameliorating its effects."[16]

Broad application of insights gained in this field depended on a willingness to act in a countercyclical way. Neither state nor federal administrations, however, betrayed as yet much readiness to explore these possibilities. There existed, nevertheless, a growing number of people, especially in business and academe, who felt that responsible action could produce socially desirable results. As for the avoidance of unemployment, it was above all conscious self-restraint that was asked for. "No matter what assistance the state may render," Harlow S. Person, managing director of the Taylor Society, asserted in 1920, "the effective effort to reduce unemployment will be made in the individual shop or office."[17] In periods of prosperity business might avoid over-expansion and build a cushion of demand that could smooth the eventual downturn.

This idea of voluntarily "regularizing" production, already bandied

---

16 Willard Long Thorp and Wesley C. Mitchell, *Business Annals: United States, England, France, Germany, Austria, Russia, Sweden, Netherlands, Italy, Argentina, Brazil, Canada, South Africa, Australia, India, Japan, China* (New York: National Bureau of Economic Research, 1926); Wesley C. Mitchell, *Business Cycles: The Problem and Its Setting* (New York: National Bureau of Economic Research, 1927), 86–87; 210–12; Alvin Harvey Hansen, *Cycles of Prosperity and Depression in the United States, Great Britain, and Germany: A Study of Monthly Data, 1902–1908* (Madison: [University of Wisconsin], 1921); idem, *Business Cycle Theory: Its Development and Present Status* (Boston: Ginn, 1927); Henry Ludwell Moore, *Generating Economic Cycles* (New York: Macmillan, 1923); Arthur B. Adams, *Economics of Business Cycles* (New York: McGraw-Hill, 1925); Simon Kuznets, *Cyclical Fluctuations: Retail and Wholesale Trade, United States, 1919–1925* (New York: Adelphi, 1926). See also Joseph Dorfman, *The Economic Mind in American Civilization.* 5 Vols. (New York: Viking, 1959), vol. IV, 546–52; and William E. Stoneman, *A History of the Economic Analysis of the Great Depression in America* (New York: Garland, 1979), 1–35; Stephen W. Baskerville, "Cutting Loose from Prejudice: Economists and the Great Depression," in Stephen W. Baskerville and Ralph Willet, eds., *Nothing Else to Fear: New Perspectives on America in the Thirties* (Manchester, Engld.: Manchester University Press, 1985), 262.
17 H. S. Person, "Scientific Management and the Reduction of Unemployment," IAPES, *Proceedings 1920* (Ottawa: King's Printer, 1921), 87.

about and experimented with in isolated instances before the war, enjoyed a considerable vogue in the 1920s.[18] It was germane to the economic thinking of the New Era, in which scientific management and the open shop, associationalism, and responsible corporate capitalism appeared to hold greater promise for the common welfare than governmental tinkering with the economic and social structures. "Regularity will obviate the thrill and excitement that come from booms and panics," the financial editor of the *New York Tribune* observed in 1921, "but will create the atmosphere for progressive prosperity and national economic development."[19]

Several books contemplated the question in some depth. Lionel D. Edie, an associate professor of political science at Indiana University, edited a volume entitled *The Stabilization of Business* in 1923. In the introduction, Hoover professed his confidence that in "this groping for stability...there are helpful solutions somewhere." Among the book's contributors were Wesley C. Mitchell, Yale economist Irving Fisher, Commons, Andrews, and Henry S. Dennison, the latter a progressive manufacturer of gift wrappings and shipping tags from Framingham, Massachusetts. The positive experiences of other American firms were described in a work published a year later under the auspices of the American Management Association (AMA) by Herman Feldman, an assistant professor of industrial relations at Dartmouth College. Sam A. Lewisohn, president of the AMA and himself an industrialist with interests in mining, presented his own compilation of essays entitled *Can Business Prevent Unemployment* (1925), including pieces by progressive New York businessman Ernest G. Draper as well as Commons and Lescohier. In summer 1929 the AMA even hoped to persuade the federal Department

18 One firm that tried out regularization after the 1908 depression was the Dennison Manufacturing Co. Evan B. Metcalf, "Secretary Hoover and the Emergence of Macroeconomic Management," *Business History Review* 49:1 (Spring 1975), 63–64.

19 Merryle Stanley Rukeyser, "Industrial Planning to Reduce Unemployment," *New York Tribune*, 3 April 1921, as quoted in *ALLR* 11:2 (June 1921), 124. For the general confidence in the ability of business to provide see David Brody, "The Rise and Decline of Welfare Capitalism," in John Braeman, Robert H. Bremner, and David Brody, eds., *Change and Continuity in Twentieth-Century America: The 1920's* ([Columbus:] Ohio State University Press, 1968), 147–78. For other voices advocating regularization, see Massachusetts. House. Special Commission on Unemployment, Unemployment Compensation, and the Minimum Wage, *Report* (Boston: Wright & Potter, 1923), 27; B. Seebohm Rowntree, "Some Necessary Steps toward a Solution of the Unemployment Problem," *Political Science Quarterly* 38:2 (June 1923), 195–96; Charles H. Chase, "Employment Stabilization through Consolidated National Industrial Budgeting," *American Federationist* 34:9 (Sept. 1927), 1072.

of Commerce to hold a major conference on regulation; but President
Hoover, preoccupied with farm and tariff questions, had, in Commerce
Secretary Robert P. Lamont's words, "the notion that the matter is not
sufficiently urgent at this time."[20]

The advocacy of business regulation for the sake of unemployment
prevention was part of the "New Emphasis," as Daniel Nelson has called
the movement, taking up a term of Feldman's. Underlying it was the idea
of efficiency and waste avoidance that had already governed much of the
progressive thinking before the war. The entire thought process did not
yet yield definite conclusions, however. As Nelson has pointed out, the
employers' approach to the unemployment problem raised almost as many
questions as it meant to answer, the general vagueness regarding the
target – seasonal, irregular, or casual joblessness – being a case in point.
There was also an occasional insight into some limitations of the measure
as such. "Private efforts," Lewisohn conceded in his book, "no matter
how significant or encouraging they may be, still remain individual as far
as a solution of the problem of unemployment in a large way is concerned."[21]

The problem of regularization was above all a psychological one. The
fear that business postponed would be business lost seemingly obviated
any general and effective implementation of the idea. "There is no widespread interest along these lines on the part of private citizens, and specifically employers," a *Baltimore Sun* editorial complained in January 1921.
And while the ALLR gamely published snippets of information about
some regularizing efforts here and there,[22] the picture on the whole was

20 Lionel D. Edie, ed., *The Stabilization of Business* (New York: Macmillan, 1923), vi-vii.
   Dennison's progressivism is considered in Berkowitz and McQuaid, *Creating the Welfare
   State*, 16–21. – H. Feldman, *The Regularization of Employment: A Study in the Prevention
   of Unemployment* (New York: Harper & Brothers, 1925); Sam A. Lewisohn et al., *Can
   Business Prevent Unemployment* (New York: Knopf, 1925); "Memorandum: Re: Proposed
   Conference on Industrial Leaders to Discuss the Problem of Seasonal Unemployment,"
   7 June 1929, Box 1, Draper Papers; Lamont to Draper, 9 July 1929, ibid.
21 Nelson, *Unemployment Insurance*, 28; 31. The idea to reduce unemployment through
   employer planning was already discussed before the turn of the century. Nathan Irvin
   Huggins, *Protestants against Poverty: Boston's Charities, 1870–1900* (Westport: Greenwood, 1971), 40. Note also the discussion of the problem in Bryce M. Stewart, *Unemployment Benefits in the United States* (New York: Industrial Relations Counsellors,
   1930), 61–68. – Lewisohn et al., *Can Business Prevent Unemployment*, 65.
22 "A Duty of Industrial Managers," *Baltimore Sun*, 18 Jan. 1921, as quoted in *ALLR* 11:1
   (March 1921), 4; "A Manufacturer Guarantees Steady Employment," *ALLR* 13:3 (Sept.
   1923), 199–200; Jean A. Flexner, "Stabilized Employment in a Garment Factory,"
   ALLR 14:1 (March 1924), 133–34; William J. Mack, "Improving Unemployment and

not encouraging. The general manager of the Hickey-Freeman Company, a Rochester clothing manufacturer, observed in 1924 with good reason that continuity of production and employment was the greatest problem challenging the ingenuity of the leaders of American industry. Despite the reformers' efforts, few of those leaders mustered the will to tackle the task seriously.[23]

Governmental involvement?

In view of the difficulties private enterprise experienced in its efforts to cope with the unemployment problem, governmental initiative would have been all the more important. But readiness to take action developed only hesitatingly. Gushers of interest welled up at the time of reconstruction and then during the 1921 depression, but the actual engagement remained small, with professions of concern being the most prominent result in either case. It should be recognized, on the other hand, that this attention and the discussion of possible involvement represented a decided advance over the standpat attitude prevalent during the prewar period. The federal government in particular, which before the war had scarcely acknowledged the existence of an unemployment question, now not only began to monitor the situation more watchfully, but significantly was also anxious to be perceived as doing so. The "Hamiltonianism" that according to William E. Leuchtenburg characterized the decade manifested itself.[24]

Because mobilization and war production had been the federal government's task, it could also be seen as Washington's duty to concern itself with labor market disturbances resulting from the end of hostilities. In November 1918, Howe, now Commissioner of Immigration at the Port of New York, expressed the widely held opinion in the *Annals* that rehabilitation "cannot be left to chance, to chaos, to private initiative." "Readjustment of domestic and national affairs," the Department of Labor's *Monthly Labor Review* equally acknowledged, "will demand the immediate and thoughtful attention of the government." This insight had

Improving Industrial Relations," ibid., 143–45; "Legislative Notes," *ALLR* 14:4 (Dec. 1924), 163.

23 "Legislative Notes," *ALLR* 14:1 (March 1924), 9. The potential of regularization is critically discussed in Paul H. Douglas and Aaron Director, *The Problem of Unemployment* (New York: Macmillan, 1931), 85–118.

24 William E. Leuchtenburg, *The Perils of Prosperity, 1914–32* (Chicago: University of Chicago Press, 1958), 103.

been slow in coming. Only a few legislative initiatives occurred before the actual end of the war. Some of them merely aimed at surveying the picture, although Socialist London went several steps further by demanding legislation "for the securing of employment to all" through nationalization of the basic industries, communications, and financial institutions (H.Con.Res. 54). But none of these quests received much attention for the time being.[25]

When the demobilization rush was on, the demands for governmental measures became more insistent.[26] Various congressional committees held hearings on unemployment related topics, often ranging over vast stretches of the social scene. The most extensive inquiry was conducted from 3 January to 24 January 1919 by the Senate Committee on Education and Labor pursuant to S.Res. 382. In its course, Leiserson, Mallery, Barnes, personnel management expert Ordway Tead, and progressive Boston businessman A. Lincoln Filene, co-owner of the huge Boston fashion retail store, spoke out in favor of governmental unemployment help. Gompers, on the other hand, asked for "just" wages that would stimulate consumption, rather than for public action.

The excitement soon abated, however. As early as December 1918, Secretary Wilson had advised the House Committee on Rules to play it calmly. The generally orderly absorption of discharged soldiers and the surprising lack of any pronounced unemployment difficulties during 1919 – the Red scare had different and more variegated causes[27] – proved him right. The smooth transition naturally took some wind out of the sails of the proponents of unemployment action, whether they advocated the customarily recommended remedies highlighted in Andrews' prewar *Practical Program* or pleaded for the implementation of hitherto somewhat less prominent schemes such as vocational training or land settlement.

25 Frederic C. Howe, "A Constructive Program for the Rehabilitation of the Returning Soldiers," *Annals* 80 (Nov. 1918), 150; "Reconstruction in Industry," *MLR* 7:5 (Nov. 1918), 1198. See also London in *CR*, 65 Cong., 2 sess., 18 Oct. 1918, p. 11377. Among the initiatives before the end of the war were H.R. 12139; S.Con.Res. 21; S.Con.Res. 22; H.Con.Res. 53; S. 4968.

26 Investigation was proposed in S.Con.Res. 25; H.R. 13592; H.Res. 452; H.Res. 463; H.Res. 525; H.Res. 529.

27 Hearings Pursuant to S.Res. 382, in particular p. 41. On Filene's progressivism Berkowitz and McQuaid, *Creating the Welfare State*, 11–16. Filene's firm employed over 3,000 people in 1931. Hearings Pursuant to S.Res. 483, p. 235. – Hearings on H.Res. 452 and H.Res. 463, p. 12; Leuchtenburg, *The Perils of Prosperity*, 66–83; John Milton Cooper, Jr., *Pivotal Decades: The United States 1900–1920* (New York: Norton, 1990), 325–33.

The possibilities of land colonization had earlier attracted some attention. In the years before the war, Secretary Wilson had shown warm sympathy for the concept, and in 1916 it had been the subject of a legislative proposal (H.R. 11329) and subsequent congressional hearings. Toward the end of hostilities, the idea surprisingly still enjoyed his support, perhaps because it could be viewed as a long-range undertaking relying for its success on the initiative and perseverance of the individual settlers. In his 1918 report, Wilson pleaded for the "early enactment" of legislation providing for "an orderly, properly planned scheme of colonization."[28] His department developed an elaborate plan for the settlement of agricultural, forest, and mineral lands. This program was incorporated in a bill that Representative M. Clyde Kelly (R-Pennsylvania) introduced in the House on 17 December 1918 (H.R. 13415). Lack of congressional interest quickly made it advisable to reduce the grandeur of the scheme, however, and even a new bill (H.R. 15672) fared no better than its predecessor. The same fate was suffered by a land reclamation plan (H.R. 15993) and various other reconstruction ideas.[29]

The flurry of initiatives taking aim at a possible unemployment threat was not confined to Congress. As, in principle, social questions fell mostly within the competency of the states, concern arose also at this level. Over twenty governors convened 16–18 December 1918 at Annapolis (Maryland) to discuss reconstruction problems. In some states, notably California, Massachusetts, New York, and Michigan, commissions were created to survey the situation and make recommendations. Some of these bodies made pertinent proposals – to be referred to later in more detail – but generally the enthusiasm died down rather quickly, and practical results were slim.[30]

Public heedfulness revived only toward the end of 1920, when the

---

28 U.S. Dept. of Labor, *4th Annual Report, 1916*, 71–73; idem, *6th Annual Report, 1918*, 223; Hearings on H.R. 11329. See also the somewhat sycophantic Roger W. Babson, *W. B. Wilson and the Department of Labor* (New York: Brentano's, 1919), 226–30.

29 U.S. Congress. Senate. Committee on Public Lands, *Work and Homes for Returning Soldiers, Sailors, and Marines*. S.Rept. 780, 65 Cong., 3 sess. (to accompany S. 5652, 27 Feb. 1919). Among the other reconstruction proposals were S.Con.Res. 25; H.R. 7009; H.Res. 452; H.Res. 463. See in this context Benton MacKaye, "Making New Opportunities for Employment," *MLR* 8:4 (April 1919), 121–39.

30 "Reconstruction Conference of Governors Held at Annapolis, MD., December 16–18, 1918," *MLR* 8:3 (March 1919), 669–71; "Appointment of State Reconstruction Committees," ibid., 671–72. The New York (State) body was Governor Smith's Reconstruction Commission on Business Readjustment and Unemployment.

economy began to seriously sag.[31] Governmental willingness to meet the emergency through tangible measures, however, was slow in developing. Andrews complained in his quarterly that of thirty-two gubernatorial messages in January 1921, only four or five had bothered to address the unemployment problem, usually by suggesting an increase in the volume of public works. But instead of fading away, the problem took on nationwide crisis proportions in the summer of 1921. It soon appeared that the lack of employment and the concomitant misery were greater than in 1914–15. Because in the meantime the federal government had marshalled the forces of the nation for the great war effort and had shown some readiness to accept responsibility for the needs arising out of reconstruction, federal involvement in dealing with the new situation seemed to many a logical step. Protection from unemployment distress, a former dean of the Harvard Graduate School of Business Administration wrote in June 1921, called for government intervention through legislation. Even inside the federal cabinet the understanding took root that the traditional hands-off attitude could no longer suffice. In a remarkable departure from its prewar behavior, the administration in Washington in summer 1921 therefore resolved to assume a leading role in the search for remedies.[32]

The man immediately responsible for this initiative was Hoover, in whose mind the progressive insight that the unrestricted capitalism of Adam Smith was dead combined with the engineer's aversion to waste and inefficiency.[33] In constrast to some of his Republican cabinet colleagues, most notably Secretary of the Treasury Andrew W. Mellon, he was not an exponent of old-fashioned laissez-faire capitalism. Members

---

31 Quests for investigation were contained in S.J.Res. 112; S.Res. 140; H.Con.Res. 20; H.Res. 25; H.Res. 608.

32 "Labor Legislation as Recommended in Governors' Messages," *ALLR* 11:1 (March 1921), 108; Andrews in "Unemployment Survey 1920–21 with Standard Recommendations," *ALLR* 11:3 (Sept. 1921), 194; Edwin F. Gay, "Is State Intervention Necessary to Prevent Unemployment?" *ALLR* 11:2 (June 1921), 159.

33 Carolyn Grin, "The Unemployment Conference of 1921: An Experiment in National Cooperative Planning," *Mid-America* 55 (April 1973), 83–84. See also Federated American Engineering Societies. Committee on Elimination of Waste in Industry, *Waste in Industry* (New York: McGraw-Hill, 1921). This study was initiated by Hoover who was president of the American Engineering Council. Regarding Hoover's progressive aversion to waste see also William R. Tanner, "Secretary of Commerce Hoover's War on Waste 1921–1928," in Carl E. Krog and William R. Tanner, eds., *Herbert Hoover and the Republican Era: A Reconsideration* (Lanham: University Press of America, 1984), 1–35.

of the "Old Guard" were grumbling during the Harding administration about the hold that "the liberal element" Hoover was gaining over the president.[34] The secretary of commerce believed that in the wake of the war a new economic system was emerging in the United States in which the excesses of competition would be mitigated through voluntary action by business and by cooperation between business and government. The latter's role was to provide information, coordination, and guidance, but to avoid coercion. Above all, it had to educate the public so as to awaken the associational impetus and foster the appearance of a "higher individualism."

An effective means to this end was the conference method. Well-publicized gatherings of key people, profiting from the advice of national experts, could bring the issues and possible solutions to the attention of the great mass of Americans. The intention was not to devise specific measures, but rather to instigate voluntary reform and possibly state and local legislation. The application of this method had to be combined with that other progressive endeavor, the spreading of scientific administrative and managerial techniques. In this way, malfunctions in the economy that caused the emergence of symptoms such as widespread joblessness could be corrected. Accordingly, a depression held nothing daunting. "The great *advantage* of a season of acute unemployment," Progressive engineer Morris L. Cooke remarked to Hoover's right-hand man Edward Eyre Hunt during the 1921 crisis, "is that only during such a time can we get that measure of public attention which is needed to effect ultimate solutions."[35]

In the existing crisis, Hoover envisaged a two-pronged effort along the lines of his thinking. "The first problem is relief," he told Hunt, "but what we are really going to do is tackle the fundamentals of unemployment." The commerce secretary suggested to the president that it would be wise to appoint "predominately [men] who can influence the action of employing forces and who can influence public opinion." Eventual meas-

---

34 Robert K. Murray, "Herbert Hoover and the Harding Cabinet," in Ellis W. Hawley, ed., *Herbert Hoover as Secretary of Commerce: Studies in New Era Thought and Practice* (Iowa City: University of Iowa Press, 1981), 34. See also Ellis W. Hawley, "Herbert Hoover and Economic Stabilization, 1921–22," ibid., 46–47; 51.

35 Joan Hoff Wilson, *Herbert Hoover: Forgotten Progressive* (Boston: Little Brown, 1975), 68–71; 82. For the belief in educating the public as constituting the quintessential progressive attitude see Otis L. Graham, Jr., *An Encore for Reform: The Old Progressives and the New Deal* (New York: Oxford University Press, 1967), 11–13; Berkowitz and McQuaid, *Creating the Welfare State*, 62; Robert H. Zieger, *Republicans and Labor 1919–1929* (Lexington: University of Kentucky Press, 1969), 90.

ures were to be taken by "employers and local authorities and civic bodies," as the invitations made clear.[36] A call for substantial federal action was definitely out of order. Lest anyone miss the point, Harding in his welcome address emphasized, as already mentioned, that the federal treasury would remain off-limits. With the guidelines thus firmly established, Hoover could even welcome a scattering of reformers and union men, among whom Andrews and Gompers were the most prominent. The great majority of the 102 conferees predictably belonged to the world of business or the administrative establishment.[37] (Figure 4–1).

The gathering did not deviate from its prescribed course. An eighteen-member Economic Advisory Committee, including Andrews and Seager, assembled on 7 September 1921 to prepare the proceedings. The conference itself, convening on 26 September, dealt with the emergency at hand and with long-range preventive measures. As for the former, "General Recommendations" were adopted on 30 September. Point 2 contained a pronouncement of the principle that was to guide all action – namely, that "the problem of meeting the emergency of unemployment is primarily a community problem. The responsibility for leadership is with the mayor." This meant that little action was to be expected from the government.

To deliberate on long-range proposals, the conference split up into various subcommittees, such as Statistics, Public Works, Employment Agencies, Agriculture, and Shipping. Reports, needing the unanimous agreement of the respective subcommittees, were subsequently adopted by the full conference. As the membership of the individual subcommittees had deliberately been kept mixed, no radical proposals received this blessing. Gompers later recalled that in the subcommittee on man-

36 Edward Eyre Hunt, "From 1921 Forward," *Survey* 62:1 (1 April 1929), 6; Hoover to Harding, 20 Aug. 1921, microfilm, reel 210, Harding Papers; President's Conference on Unemployment, *Report*, 16.

37 Gompers' participation caused Daniel J. Tobin to resign in protest from his position as AFL treasurer. "Mr. Hoover's Conference," *Survey* 46:20 (24 Sept. 1921), 697. Other reform-oriented conference participants were Dennison, Leiserson, Lewisohn, Samuel McCune Lindsay, Mallery, Seager, Van Kleeck, and Leo Wolman. When a correspondent complained to Hoover that Commons had been ignored, presumably because of his Democratic connections, Hoover emphatically stressed that only distance considerations had played a role in selecting conferees. James M. Lee to Hoover, 3 Nov. 1921, Box 615, Commerce Papers, Hoover Papers; Hoover to Lee, 9 Nov. 1921, ibid. Zieger, *Republicans and Labor 1919–1929*, 91–93 emphasizes the influence that the ideas of industrial engineering and scientific management had on Hoover at the time of the President's Conference.

Figure 4–1. President's Conference on Unemployment, Washington, D.C., 26 September 1921. Secretary of Commerce Herbert C. Hoover, organizer of the conference, is sixth from left in front row. (Source: *ALLR* 11:4 [Dec. 1921], after p. 306.)

ufacturing, on which he served, employer representatives "made it impossible for the conference to make recommendations embodying the most enlightened thought on industrial problems." The "General Recommendations for Permanent Recovery," formulated by the conference on 11 October 1921, reflected this intention. They did not go beyond pronouncements regarding the necessity of a "definite settlement of tariff legislation," the advisability of the "elimination of waste and more regular employment in seasonal and intermittent industries," and similar matters. The most remarkable action was perhaps the creation of a standing committee headed by Hoover that was to carry on any unfinished business of the conference and, through subcommittees, investigate the unemployment problem more thoroughly.[38]

The limited nature of the entire undertaking was decried by some dissatisfied onlookers. The *New York Globe* thought it inappropriate that the federal administration should "wash its hands of responsibility for the unemployed and piously ask the states and the cities to carry the full load." Others took issue with a perceived shortsightedness of the conferees. A writer in the *Survey* found them "interested in this particular unemployment period and in no others." The New York *Journal of Commerce* uttered similar criticism. Close scrutiny revealed that the immediate impact of the conference was very modest at best. A study of fifteen cities later showed that it had been private endeavor, rather than municipal action as advocated by Hoover's conferees, that had carried the burden of relief action.[39] (Figure 4–2).

It was probably significant that the conference had been organized by

38 Samuel Gompers, *Seventy Years of Life and Labor: An Autobiography.* 2 vols. (New York: Dutton, 1925), vol. II, 17. See also Bernard Mandel, *Samuel Gompers: A Biography* (Yellow Springs: Antioch Press, 1963), 489–91; President's Conference on Unemployment, *Report,* 16–23.

39 *Globe* and *Journal of Commerce* are quoted in *Literary Digest* 71:3 (15 Oct. 1921), 6. – William L. Chenery, "Mr. Hoover's Hand," *Survey* 47:4 (22 Oct. 1921), 107; Philip Klein, *The Burden of Unemployment: A Study of Unemployment Relief Measures in Fifteen American Cities, 1921–22* (New York: Russell Sage Foundation, 1923), 59. A few months later Hoover himself admitted a partial failure, stating that the cities of New York and Chicago "totally fell down on anything constructive" during the emergency. Hoover to President [Harding], 20 May 1922, microfilm, reel 210, Harding Papers. For a similar statement see "Resolutions by the Central Trades and Labor Council, Greater New York and Vicinity," 28 April 1922, microfilm, reel 210, Harding Papers. For labor's rather malcontented feelings see also "The Employers and the Press," *Survey* 47:12 (17 Dec. 1921), 438.

Figure 4-2. President's Conference on Unemployment as viewed by the *Chicago Tribune*. (Source: *ALLR* 11:4 [Dec. 1921], 310.)

the Department of Commerce rather than the Department of Labor.[40] Mary Van Kleeck, a sociologist with somewhat radical leanings who had from 1909 served as director of industrial relations at the Russell Sage Foundation, suspected in this "another sign that the new administration wishes to ignore the Department of Labor." Davis' involvement, at any rate, was so minimal that one observer felt compelled to state that "at the conference on unemployment, which was Mr. Hoover's, the best and only example of the unemployed present was the secretary of labor." The initiative had clearly been business-oriented, and it had thus been obvious from the start that nothing of a radical nature was in the offing. Nobody could have been surprised at the lack of substantial results. What the

40 Labor Secretary Davis dissociated himself from the undertaking. "I claim no part in this," he wrote to Hoover, "whatever has been accomplished has been entirely through your efforts, and you deserve all the credit." James J. Davis to Hoover, 22 Dec. 1921, Box 651, Commerce Papers, Hoover Papers.

conference essentially did, an article in the *International Labour Review* noted, "was to provide a forum where the business community could make its opinions heard."[41]

Hoover saw this in a more positive light. Although, or perhaps because, no lasting commitments were agreed upon, he declared the event to be "a milestone in the progress of public thought," because it emphasized the principle of voluntary organization, "consonant with the American spirit and American traditions." As Robert H. Zieger has remarked, in Hoover's view "the government had done what it properly should have, and no more.... It had simply identified a problem, mobilized available resources, coordinated private efforts." In spring 1922 the commerce secretary personally prevailed upon Van Kleeck to give a more optimistic assessment of the situation than she had intended in an article destined for publication in the *Survey*. Harding congratulated Hoover. The unemployment conference, he wrote his secretary, deserved "great credit for a work quietly and efficiently carried out."[42]

The most important merit of the meeting was probably not, as Martin L. Fausold has asserted, that Hoover applauded the idea of long-range planning on that occasion, but that the conference had taken place at all. As a contemporary observer put it, "for the first time intelligence of a very high order has been brought to bear upon the problem of unemployment in the United States."[43] The federal government had shown interest in the fate of the unemployed and had also taken a step that signified a certain readiness to get involved. Nothing of the sort had occurred during the depressions of 1907–08 and 1914–15. The intellectual climate had clearly undergone significant changes since the Roosevelt and first Wilson administrations, and government intervention in the social sphere was on its way to becoming thinkable even on the cabinet level.

---

41 Van Kleeck to [Shelby M.] Harrison, 10 Sept. 1921, Box 2, Van Kleeck Papers. Van Kleeck had during the war headed the Woman in Industry Service in the Department of Labor. – Hawley, ed., *Herbert Hoover as Secretary of Labor*, 27; William L. Chenery, "The President's Conference and Unemployment in the United States," *International Labour Review* 5:3 (March 1922), 365.

42 President's Conference on Unemployment, *Report*, 34; Zieger, *Republicans and Labor, 1919–1929*, 97; Van Kleeck to John M. Glenn, 5 June 1922, Box 4, Van Kleeck Papers; Harding to Hoover, 22 May 1922, Box 615, Commerce Papers, Hoover Papers. Similarly Harding to Secretary [Hoover], 4 Oct. 1921, microfilm, reel 210, Harding Papers.

43 Martin L. Fausold, *The Presidency of Herbert C. Hoover* ([Lawrence]: University Press of Kansas, 1985), 120; Chenery, "The President's Conference," 369.

The aftermath of the conference consisted of activities commenced or suggested during the proceedings. Attention to remedial matters remained shortlived, however, because the economy rebounded quickly. Only the standing committee produced a more tangible result. Heeding one of its points of reference, Hoover appointed a Committee on Unemployment and Business Cycles (CUBC) toward the end of 1921 with the mandate to investigate the unemployment problem further. To ensure that the right direction would be taken, Owen D. Young of the General Electric Company, who at the time was acquiring a reputation for open-mindedness in labor relations, was made chairman of the CUBC, propped up by two other representatives of big business. A vice-president of the AFL and Van Kleeck complemented the panel. Hunt, who had done relief work with Hoover in Belgium, was appointed secretary. After the Carnegie Foundation agreed in February 1922 to provide a grant of $50,000, the National Bureau of Economic Research was charged with conducting the actual investigation. Outside experts furnished additional help. The result was, in Wesley C. Mitchell's words, a "reconnaissance survey," put together "in the hope of enabling the social engineers to locate the most promising routes for the construction of new highways." Overall, the undertaking fitted well into the Hooverian concept of guidance without coercion, as the commerce secretary and his aides hoped that such studies could serve as key tools in the future management of economic prosperity.[44]

In its recommendations, based upon twenty-one individual contributions, the CUBC advocated better data collection by industry and governmental agencies; control of credit expansion by private banks and the Federal Reserve system; production regulation by private industry; regulation of private and public construction; caution with unemployment reserve funds; and the creation of a national system of employment bureaus. Although a governmental role was envisaged in some instances, especially data collection and exchange activities, the CUBC thus clearly stressed the primary importance of private initiatives.[45] Hoover publicly

44 Hoover was very concerned that no "European" remedies be recommended. Hoover to Edgar Rickard, 14 Nov. 1921, Box 615, Commerce Papers, Hoover Papers. – Hunt to Henry S. Pritchett, 11 Feb. 1922, Box 618, ibid.; Wesley C. Mitchell, "Introduction," President's Conference on Unemployment. Committee on Unemployment and Business Cycles, *Business Cycles and Unemployment: Report and Recommendations* (New York: McGraw-Hill, 1923), 1; Hawley, "Herbert Hoover and Economic Stabilization," 61.
45 "Report and Recommendations of the Committee on Unemployment and Business

praised these proposals as constituting "a definite advance in economic thought," and his acolyte Hunt claimed that the significance of the report for future greater security of employment "can hardly be overestimated." But not everybody was satisfied. In July 1922, Andrews had advised Hunt that "large numbers of people" were awaiting "a straight-out, constructive, far-reaching program." As these hopes were not realized, Andrews' associate editor at the *ALLR* denounced the committee's work. "Widespread social evils have never been solved by the good will and voluntary acts of scattering individual employers," he complained, asserting that "the vast majority have waited upon some uniform measure of social compulsion." Mitchell, who in his submission had asked for more time to complete his inquiry, was wrong; not time was lacking, "but greater social vision and more courage."[46]

This kind of courage was still in short supply. Of course, on occasion progressive industrialists thought along reform lines. The business men's group of the New York Society for Ethical Culture concluded in 1923 that "it has become necessary for the government to assume responsibility for providing employment when other agencies fail to cope with the problem." But theirs were rather isolated voices, and when another committee appointed by Hoover in the wake of his conference produced a more specialized study focusing on the construction industry, no great impact of any sort was felt. Progress in unemployment reform during this period was not a very spectacular affair, and it can only be discerned by reviewing particular endeavors in detail.[47]

II   Elusive Numbers

One area in which improvement was not readily perceptible in the decade following the war was counting. The extremely inconstant state of the

Cycles," in President's Conference on Unemployment. Committee on Business Cycles, *Business Cycles and Unemployment*, xxxi.

46 "Foreword," in ibid., v; Edward Eyre Hunt, "The Long Look Ahead," *Survey* 50:7 (1 July 1923), 401; Andrews to Hunt, 26 July 1922, Box 620, Commerce Papers, Hoover Papers; Frederick W. MacKenzie, "Stabilizing Employment: Official Findings," *ALLR* 13:2 (June 1923), 148.

47 "Ethical Culturists Produce Unemployment Program," *ALLR* 13:2 (June 1923), 157. See also similarly William Baum to O. E. Gram, 16 May 1923, Box 621, Commerce Papers, Hoover Papers. Baum was a Milwaukee entrepreneur. – President's Conference on Unemployment. Committee on Seasonal Operations in the Construction Industries, *Seasonal Operations in the Construction Industries, the Facts and Remedies: Report and Recommendations* (New York: McGraw-Hill, 1924).

labor market immediately after the end of hostilities made efforts at assessing the number of persons out of work rather pointless, and the subsequent boom period quenched the desire to know the volume of joblessness. The economic downturn of 1921–22 of course rekindled interest in the problem, but the authorities came up with only a few makeshift initiatives, and counting enthusiasm abated quickly as soon as prosperity returned. The environment thus hampered the emergence of innovative measures, and advance consisted in refinement resulting from reflection and experimentation rather than in revolutionary developments.

Some of the methods tested in the prewar period could not be employed any more. Mindful of the disappointing results that its former endeavors had yielded, the Bureau of the Census refrained from asking unemployment questions in the census of 1920. The kind of special investigation that the Bureau of Labor Statistics had conducted before the war was now equally out of the question. "An actual count upon a given date," Ethelbert Stewart, Meeker's successor in the Republican administration, sighed at the depth of the 1921 depression, "is, of course, prohibitive by the reason of its cost."[48]

This left for exploitation the few and incomplete data series available. But Massachusetts discontinued the collection of trade union returns in 1922, and thereafter employment records remained as the sole basis of interest. A small number of states and, in a rather unsatisfactory way, the federal government assembled this sort of data, but unfortunately the methods of collection were not uniform. New York had in June 1915 begun to collect employment data of representative establishments. In Wisconsin, similar reporting started in July 1920, and in Illinois in September 1921. Massachusetts, making up for its abandoned trade union information, commenced monthly collection and publication of employment statistics in September 1922 while continuing to compile its annual census of manufactures. Other states to embark upon the gathering of employment figures were Iowa (1922), Maryland (1923), California (1924), Oklahoma (1924), and New Jersey (1926). Ohio continued its annual collection of employment information regarding various industries.[49] The federal Bureau of Labor Statistics persisted in putting to-

48 CR, 67 Cong., 1 sess., 16 Aug. 1921, p. 5037.
49 Ernest S. Bradford, "Methods Used in Measuring Unemployment," *Quarterly Publication of the American Statistical Association* n.s. 17:135 (Sept. 1921), 985; Mary Van Kleeck, "Charting the Course of Employment," in President's Conference on Un-

gether the employment information published in each issue of the *Monthly Labor Review* since 1915. By early 1921, thirteen manufacturing industries were being covered, with reports from 700 establishments employing about 500,000 wage earners. After the depression experience the list was continuously expanded, so that by 1926 over 10,000 establishments in 54 industries with a total of about 3 million wage earners reported. Some other federal agencies also furnished information that could be utilized to assess the unemployment situation. From 1920 the Interstate Commerce Commission made monthly railroad figures available, and several of the Federal Reserve Banks published employment data in their monthly bulletins.[50]

The basic defects of all this employment information, if used for the purpose of learning the actual amount of unemployment, were of course still as evident as before the war. Nobody really knew the number of employable persons, and hence all calculations lacked a secure premise. Substantial segments of the workforce were not covered by the various surveys, among them agricultural and domestic help. Even in the federal surveys, wide areas of the United States received no – or at best, scant – attention. Most of the information was available only with a considerable time lag. It had also to be kept in mind that the data were supplied voluntarily by the employers, reporting was not always consistent, and the accuracy of the figures transmitted could not be verified by the gathering agency.

The lack of useful information became especially irksome during the depression of 1921–22. In early 1921 the USES surveyed employment in 182 cities and computed unemployment at 36.9 percent. On 5 August the Senate passed a resolution directing the secretary of labor to furnish an estimate of unemployment (S.Res. 126). By using as its basis the January USES figures, the Bureau of Labor Statistics consequently de-

employment. Committee on Unemployment and Business Cycles, *Business Cycles and Unemployment*, 347; 350; A. J. Altmeyer, "An All-Inclusive Employment Index for Wisconsin," American Statistical Association. *Journal* n.s. 18:138 (June 1922), 266–68. The data were published monthly in the *Wisconsin Labor Market*, issued by the Wisconsin Industrial Commission; Stewart, *Unemployment Benefits*, 26–27; "Committee on Governmental Labor Statistics of the American Statistical Association: Report for 1924," American Statistical Association. *Journal* n.s. 20:149 (March 1925), 95; Mary Van Kleeck, "Report of the Committee on Governmental Labor Statistics," ibid. 22:157 (March 1927), 96.

50 Van Kleeck, "Charting the Course of Employment," 357. The ICC covered about 90% of the railroads.

cided that in July 1921 a total of 5,735,000 fewer persons had been employed than at the peak of the 1920 employment season.[51] Eager to compete, the USES repeated its January endeavor, now covering 280 cities, finding an unemployment increase of 19 percent. A parallel inquiry that the Department of Commerce conducted by telegraph on 10 September, receiving responses from 139 firms, indicated a reduction of employment since January 1921 by 11.6 percent. When the President's Conference on Unemployment convened, the confusion about the actual situation was quite general. The conference's Committee on Unemployment Statistics added its share when it calculated, by extrapolating from the USES September data and incorporating some qualifying considerations, that unemployment among the nonagricultural working population in the United States at large was probably no more than 3.5 million.[52]

More important than the committee's guess was the fact that it also passed a series of recommendations, subsequently adopted by the conference, to improve knowledge of the unemployment situation in the future. It requested that the monthly employment series of the Bureau of Labor Statistics be extended to cover transportation, trade, and mining, and that the bureau collaborate for this purpose with the United States Geological Survey, which collected mining data, and the Interstate Commerce Commission. It suggested, moreover, that the bureau refrain from duplicating state activities, and proposed the creation of an interdepartmental exploratory committee.[53]

These were sensible recommendations. For the first time a group of experts, assembled in a semi-official body, had seriously deliberated on the American unemployment data dilemma and had come up with workable suggestions to enhance the dismal procedures in use. Hoover himself proposed to incorporate a statement in the committee's report that the Department of Labor "needs more substantial financial support" for its counting activities. The supply of such information was clearly consonant with his basic philosophy of governmental aid to substantial activities in

51 Hearings on H.R. 15422, p. 1754; *Industrial Employment Survey Bulletin* 1:1 (Jan. 1921), 1–2; *CR*, 67 Cong., 1 sess., 16 Aug. 1921, p. 5037.
52 This figure also received severe criticism. The National Metal Trades Association, Indianapolis Branch, for example, felt that while the USES had estimated the Indianapolis unemployed figure to be around 25,000, it was no higher than 10,000. A.J. Allan to Harding, 13 Sept. 1921, microfilm, reel 210, Harding Papers; President's Conference on Unemployment, *Report*, 28; 48–52.
53 President's Conference on Unemployment, *Report*, 38–39.

the private sector. AFL President Samuel Gompers, who viewed things for different reasons in a similar way, also applauded the idea.[54]

Confirmation of the new emphasis on methodicalness came in 1922 with the publication of a brief study of the problem by the Department of Labor. It was authored by Ernest S. Bradford, a statistician who as a member of the Economic Advisory Committee had had decisive input into the statistics recommendations of the conference. The fact that a federal department had sponsored this investigation gave authoritative weight to his conclusion that the "primary need" was for fuller and better data both on the state and federal levels.[55]

The depression produced some further pondering of the numbers question. In 1923 the CUBC published the result of its investigation and strongly emphasized the importance of employment statistics, recommending that state and federal gathering activities be expanded and standardized and that the results be promptly published under the aegis of the Department of Commerce. In the committee's opinion, private organizations were not in a position to assume this task. Useful statistics had to be uniform and continuous, and only government possessed the authority to secure the basic information without interruption. The committee's remark that the data "should be collected officially" suggested that it considered legislation as necessary.[56]

The contributions to the CUBC report were at least partially inspired by the work of another body, the American Statistical Association [ASA]'s Committee on the Measurement of Employment, which was chaired by Van Kleeck. Over the next few years this group worked purposefully at

54 President's Conference on Unemployment, *Report*, 39–40; 43–44; "The Unemployment Conference – A Picture," *American Federationist* 28:11 (Nov. 1921), 960; Chenery, "The President's Conference and Unemployment in the United States," 366.
55 Bradford, "Methods Used in Measuring Unemployment," 983–94; Ernest S. Bradford, *Industrial Unemployment: A Statistical Study of Its Extent and Causes*, in U.S. Bureau of Labor Statistics, *Bulletin 310* ((Washington: G.P.O., 1922), esp. pp. 22; 46.
56 W. A. Berridge, "Cycles of Employment and Unemployment in the United States, 1914–1921," American Statistical Association. *Journal* n.s. 18:137 (March 1922), 42–55; idem, "Cycles of Employment and Unemployment in the United States, 1903–1914," ibid. 18:138 (June 1922), 227–40. The substance of these articles was published in William A. Berridge, *Cycles of Unemployment in the United States 1903–1922* (Boston: Houghton Mifflin, 1923). See also idem, "Industrial Employment in the Present Business Cycle," *Review of Economic Statistics* 5:4 (Oct. 1923), 292–300; "Report and Recommendations of the Committee on Unemployment and Business Cycles," in President's Conference on Unemployment. Committee on Unemployment and Business Cycles, *Business Cycles and Unemployment*, xxi–xxiii.

the improvement of employment statistics by formulating recommendations and monitoring their implementation. In early 1926, ASA members William A. Berridge, an assistant professor of economics at Brown, and Ralph G. Hurlin, statistician at the Russell Sage Foundation, published a detailed compendium on the matter of employment data collection. The publication exemplified the association's hope that "carefully placed publicity in trade papers and elsewhere" would strengthen the existing endeavors, encourage appropriations by state legislatures, and stimulate dormant states into action.[57]

The advance achieved by about 1927 thus consisted in the fact that the problem had been thoroughly investigated several times and that the shortcomings of the material available had been clearly identified. A considerable number of experts had in the process honed their skills, with the result that the discussion was conducted on a level far above that of the prewar period. A most valuable byproduct of their endeavors was the insight, no longer seriously questioned by anybody, that government alone had the means to engage in worthwhile attempts to learn the extent of unemployment. More importantly still, the federal government had officially taken cognizance of the difficulties such attempts encountered. This recognition did not yet imply an immediate willingness to take adequate measures to overcome the obstacles. But it was a point of departure for future improvement.

III   The USES on hold

Demobilization and the USES

When hostilities ceased, nobody could realistically expect that unemployment counting procedures would make quick and sizable advances during the subsequent years; but the case was different with regard to the labor exchange instrument, as the generous build-up of the USES in 1917–18 apparently held much promise for future development. Of course there existed the danger that the decline in war production, and

---

57 Ralph G. Hurlin and William A. Berridge, eds., *Employment Statistics for the United States: A Plan for Their National Collection and a Handbook for Methods Recommended by the Committee on Governmental Labor Statistics of the American Statistical Association* (New York: Russell Sage Foundation, 1926); Mary Van Kleeck, "Report of Committee on Governmental Labor Statistics," American Statistical Association. *Journal* 21:153 (March 1926), 87.

with it the demand for labor, might spell a dramatic reduction in USES activities, to be followed by a concomitant shrinking of its organization. Officials in the Department of Labor were not unduly worried, however. They anticipated that the service had to fill an essential task in the demobilization and reconstruction process and hoped that from this activity a more permanent existence might somehow emanate.

The service's potential for fighting unemployment, which had been without importance to its wartime growth, was now the trump card that its proponents attempted to play to advantage. Department of Labor bureaucrats were backed up in this endeavor by reform-side lobbyists and even a growing number of legislators. Inevitably, though, their exertions occurred against the background of a general public desire to dismantle the war apparatus. As the USES' friends learned to their dismay, the most forbidding reaction originated in some business quarters. Not all of business looked askance at the USES, as a good number of firms, displaying some "corporate liberal spirit" in the sense Ellis W. Hawley has proposed to use the term, saw virtue in a continuation of its activity.[58] But pugnacious opposition nevertheless ultimately foiled the grand plans of the USES' supporters. They could find solace in the fact that the conservative triumph was not a complete one, as some service remnants survived that might eventually function as cadres for expansion in more propitious times. It was, moreover, not unimportant that the service's promoters gained a wealth of insights, technical as well as political, in the legislative struggles before their near-defeat; later initiatives could thus profit from the lessons learned in the postwar years.

When activities in Congress indicated concern regarding the problems of reconstruction, the USES' backers looked forward to exploiting the situation. The service had already engaged in placing discharged soldiers after some 50,000 men of the National Guard had returned from the Mexican border in early 1917. Toward the end of World War I, Densmore was eager to point out the usefulness of his organization in his 1918 report.[59] Now a two-pronged effort seemed indicated. A strong show during the demobilization period could establish the agency's potential, or perhaps even its indispensability for peacetime work. On the other hand, it appeared necessary to get this future role recognized through

---

58 Ellis W. Hawley, "The Discovery and Study of a 'Corporate Liberalism,'" *Business History Review* 52:3 (Autumn 1978), 314–15; 317.
59 U.S. Dept. of Labor, *5th Annual Report, 1917*, 84; idem, *6th Annual Report, 1918*, 709.

legislative provision so as to render the USES independent of the vagaries of the political scene.

The service tackled its postwar work immediately after the end of hostilities. One endeavor aimed at assessing the state of the labor market. USES officials in 122 industrial centers were instructed to report weekly by telegraph on employment conditions. Although this information had no perceptible influence upon the demobilization plans of the War Department or the War Industries Board, the USES continued the practice for several months. By handing the weekly statements over to the press, it obviously hoped to keep its name before the public in a positive way.[60]

Collecting information was conceivably useful, but more important was distributing the manpower that the end of the war set free. If this task had fallen to the USES alone, the service would in all certainty have been taxed beyond its capability. As a matter of fact, various other agencies also stood ready to take a hand. This carried the danger, of course, that their competition might deprive the USES of much of its chance. Labor Secretary Davis later recalled with misgivings the "conflict of interests" regarding job-finding activities that surfaced in the months after the armistice. USES officials sought to exploit the situation by assuming a leadership role, and called a conference that convened in Washington on 5 December 1918. Cooperation was arranged with the Council of National Defense as well as the War, Navy, and Agriculture Departments, the War Labor Policies Board, and assorted private organizations such as the American Red Cross and the Young Men's Christian Association. The participants agreed to create a Cooperative Central Board, to be chaired by Smyth. On 10 December 1918, the USES *Bulletin* carried extensive guidelines for the operation of emergency labor exchanges. In January and February, two-week training courses, in the planning of which the AALL gave some assistance, were held in Washington, and a thirty-four page training manual was designed for the upgrading of USES personnel.[61] Almost 3,000 special distribution bureaus opened throughout the

---

60 U.S. Dept. of Labor, *7th Annual Report, 1919*, 900; Edward T. Devine, "The Federal Employment Service: Analysis and Forecast," *Survey* 42:1 (5 April 1919), 12. A summary of the reports is found in Hearings on H.R. 6176, pp. 44–55.

61 James J. Davis to Hoover, 5 Oct. 1921, Box 651, Commerce Papers, Hoover Papers. The same letter is on microfilm, reel 210, Harding Papers. Operation guidelines also in "Federal Employment Service and Demobilization of the Army and of War Workers," *MLR* 8:1 (Jan. 1919), 122–25. See also the eight page memorandum "Bureaus for Returning Soldiers and Sailors," 5 Dec. 1918, Box 93, Chief Clerk's Files, General Records of the Dept. of Labor, Department of Labor Papers. For the cooperation with

country. The USES, moreover, placed representatives in seventy-six demobilization camps.[62]

Reintegration of the demobilized servicemen and dislodged production workers, however, went more smoothly than anticipated. Generally, employers took in their former employees, and the economy as a whole showed enough capacity during the following months to absorb even the peak demobilization rate of over 100,000 men per week. As beneficial as this development was for the nation at large, it did not augur too well for the USES, which pined for opportunities to prove its needfulness. The situation was not helped by the USES' ultimate failure to state in clear terms what its own share in the demobilization process had been. As few of the offices outside the USES jurisdiction reported usable figures, the USES' claim to have registered 758,474 jobseekers between 1 December 1918 and 27 September 1919, and to have placed 474,085 of them, lacked the benefit of neat comparison with the performance of others.[63]

With or without comparable data, there could be no denying the fact that the USES had not really borne the brunt of the placement activities. When it had to curtail its operations from March 1919 on, Colonel Arthur Woods, former police commissioner of New York (City) and at the time assistant to the secretary of war, had been appointed the War Department's liaison, with the mandate to stimulate the interest of the nation's chambers of commerce and other local agencies. Under his direction the

the Council of National Defense see Hearings on H.R. 13870, pp. 1288–90; 1476–77. Originally the designation of Smyth as liaison to the military by Frankfurter, then chairman of the War Labor Policies Board, created some displeasure in the Dept. of Labor. Frankfurter to Newton D. Baker, 14 Nov. 1918, Box 93, Chief Clerk's Files, General Records of the Dept. of Labor, Department of Labor Papers; Louis F. Post to Secretary of Labor, 17 Nov. 1918, ibid.

62 "Reconstruction Activities of the United States Employment Service," *MLR* 8:2 (Feb. 1919), 440; John B. Andrews, "Report of Work," *ALLR* 9:1 (March 1919), 167; Devine, "The Federal Employment Service," 15. Copy of the training manual in Box 42, Leiserson Papers. – "Review of the Activities of the United States Employment Service," *MLR* 8:4 (April 1919), 1089; U.S. Dept. of Labor, *7th Annual Report, 1919*, 286; 900. – Text of speech by Arthur Woods covering demobilization work, 26 March 1919, file "Unemployment Conference," Woods Papers.

63 Berridge, "Cycles of Employment and Unemployment," 49–50. Demobilization work of the USES is documented in U.S. Dept. of Labor, *7th Annual Report, 1919*, 899–901; idem, *8th Annual Report, 1920*, 151; 925–26; "Federal Employment Service and Demobilization of the Army and of War Workers," *MLR* 8:1 (Jan. 1919), 119–25; "Reconstruction Activities of the United States Employment Service," 435–41; "Review of the Activities of the United States Employment Service," 1086–91. See also "Demobilization: The Employment Service," *Survey* 42:1 (5 April 1919), 57.

Service and Information Department of the War Department had easily taken over leadership in the endeavor. During the first seven months after the armistice, altogether over two and a half million men had been discharged from military duty, and millions more had changed jobs because of production adjustment. The USES had handled only a fraction, and of the 2,594 Soldiers' and Sailors' Bureaus established in the country, only 300 had operated in its offices. Conceivably the demobilization process could have been led to a good conclusion without any USES participation.[64]

But even if the service's efforts would have been praiseworthy indeed, it would have been difficult to see how they would legitimize the continuing existence of the organization in its bloated form. Demobilization was of necessity a one-shot affair. By June 1919, discharged soldiers accounted for no more than 15 percent of the USES clientele. To secure the permanency of the service, Tead had told the AALL membership as early as December 1918, it was necessary "convincingly to justify it in the eyes of the taxpayers." Failing that, the USES faced the prospect that more people than just the editors of *Industry*, the newly founded organ of the NAM, considered its demobilization endeavors as little more than an attempt to use "the very soldiers . . . as stalking horses in a campaign for a large government appropriation."[65]

Essentially the USES battle was waged over two specific issues – the funding of current activities and a legal guarantee of future existence. Finding money was urgent, because the wartime appropriations were becoming exhausted. In the long run, however, the USES needed a clear concept and a sound legal base if it was to distinguish itself from the ineffective makeshift arrangements of the prewar period.

The search for funds quickly became frantic, as Secretary Wilson's request for almost $15 million received severe criticism because of its

---

64 "Provisions for Employment of Ex-servicemen," *MLR* 10:2 (Feb. 1920), 462–63; U.S. Dept. of War, *Annual Reports, 1919*, Vol I: *Report of the Secretary of War*, 17–18; Berridge, *Cycles of Unemployment*, 49; U.S. Dept. of Labor, *7th Annual Report, 1919*, 911. On the extent of cooperation between the USES and the Council of National Defense in demobilization work see William J. Breen, *Uncle Sam at Home: Civilian Mobilization, Wartime Federalism, and the Council of National Defense, 1917–1919* (Westport: Greenwood, 1984), 193–94.

65 Hearings on S. 688 and 1442, and H.R. 4305, p. 100; Ordway Tead, "The United States Employment Service and the Prevention of Unemployment," *ALLR* 9:1 (March 1919), 95; "Should Congress Perpetuate the United States Employment Service?", *Industry* 1:1 (1 April 1919), 8.

extravagance. The Department of Labor reduced its demand to $10,033,000 and then to $4,634,325.92. But even this sum met with stiff resistance, and the Committee on Appropriations scaled the request down to $1.8 million. The provision passed the House on 28 February 1919. The Senate failed to take the matter up before the end of the legislative session, however, and the money did not become available to the USES.[66] As a consequence of this conservative victory, the service, which in mid-February reached its manpower peak of 4,079 salaried employees, not counting 3,073 one-dollar appointees, found itself in dire pecuniary straits. Since demobilization was far from accomplished, the governors and mayors assembled in Washington, 3–5 March 1919, deplored the USES' impending demise. In a last ditch effort, Secretary Wilson appealed to the president. The latter, though, on his way back to the peace negotiations in Europe, did not offer any solace. His radiogram from the ocean liner *George Washington* claimed that the presidential fund was practically exhausted. Perhaps mindful of complaints he had received during the war about woefully inadequate USES work, and at any rate more disposed toward the voluntarist spirit of the New Freedom than the maintenance of powerful government institutions in peace time, Woodrow Wilson advised his secretary that he saw "no escape from disbandment." He nevertheless expressed his hope that it would be possible "to keep a skeleton organization."[67]

The president's decision ended the Department of Labor's dream of transforming its war employment service directly into a powerful peace-time labor market instrument. To dissolve the USES entirely, however, would have meant abandoning whatever prospects the prewar organization had offered. The departmental leadership therefore decided to maintain a bare bones structure, as suggested by the president, in the hope that at a later time some muscle might be added again. Densmore thus ordered the federal USES directors in the states to scale down their operations and to appeal to state and municipal authorities, welfare and labor organizations, chambers of commerce and similar bodies for funds to help

66 Hearings on H.R. 13870, pp. 1462; 1472–1501; U.S. Dept. of Labor, *7th Annual Report, 1919*, 287. On 22 Feb. 1919 Densmore actually asked only for $2,932,849.53. Hearings on H.R. 16187, pp. 412; 414–17. – *CR*, 65 Cong., 3 sess., 28 Feb. 1919, pp. 4652–64.
67 U.S. Dept. of Labor, *7th Annual Report, 1919*, 293. Text of Wilson's radiogramme (12 March 1919) ibid., 902. – *New York Times*, 6 March 1919, p. 3; Robert D. Cuff, "The Politics of Labor Administration during World War I," *Labor History* 21:4 (Fall 1980), 562.

defray the ongoing demobilization work. As a result, from 22 March 1919 on the USES financed only fifty-six offices. Outside contributions, prompted by the realization that placing demobilized soldiers was a public necessity, averaged about $168,000 a month, enough to sustain another 424 offices until mid-year.[68]

The quest for legislation

As funding was difficult to come by, it appeared ever more urgent to provide a statutory basis for the service. The assiduous and sustained effort of the friends of the USES, though, met with the growing resistance of strong segments of the employer side, whose determination and resourcefulness proved difficult to beat. It now appeared regrettable that passage of the Robinson/Keating bill had not been pressed with more insistence during the war. In this situation the Department of Labor first concentrated its hopes upon S.Res. 382, which *inter alia* mentioned the possibility of developing the USES into a national labor exchange. During the hearings the USES lobby proved well organized, but the investigation did not produce anything tangible. A more specific effort was obviously called for, and on 16 April Secretary Wilson invited the state governors "to discuss the subject of a National Employment Service ... and to project a program for legislation."[69]

The sixty conferees who met 23–25 April in the USES offices in Washington included delegates from twenty-eight states and one representative each of the AFL and the United States Chamber of Commerce. The presence of either of the latter had some special significance. The AFL's noncommittal stand before the war regarding the USES had apparently changed. The circumstance that many of the state delegates were union people obviously had to do with this turnabout. At least as interesting was the fact that a representative of the Chamber of Commerce spoke for the employer side. The Department of Labor had overlooked the NAM, which after all was the older and perhaps more powerful

---

68 U.S. Dept. of Labor, *7th Annual Report, 1919*, 902.
69 See in this context Margarett A. Hobbs, "A National Employment Service," *ALLR* 8:4 (Dec. 1918), 292. Hobbs' article was approved by the USES. Andrews to Division of Information, United States Employment Service, 2 Dec. 1918, microfilm, reel 18, Andrews Papers. - Hearings Pursuant to S.Res. 382, pp. 86; 100; 106; 144; "Minutes of the Conference on Employment Called by W. B. Wilson, Secretary of Labor, to Meet in Washington April 23, 24, and 25, 1919"; Hearings on S. 688 and 1442, and H.R. 4305, p. 71.

organization. Densmore later explained that during the war the NAM had been represented on the War Labor Policies Board; a feeling of justice suggested that now the Chamber should be given a chance, all the more so because it had collaborated with the USES. On further questioning he revealed his department's perception that the NAM was "more conservative and reactionary sometimes" than the Chamber, which could be claimed "to be made up of young people and the more progressive people."[70]

The specific objective of the conference, as described by Secretary Wilson, was "to define and establish the most effective form of relationship between national and state employment activities," in other words to come to an agreement regarding the service's future structure. Was a strongly centralized service preferable or rather a federated system? This was not a new problem. As early as 1915, at the San Francisco conference, Secretary Wilson had declared himself for a mixed arrangement. Later on he had reiterated this view, supported by experts like Leiserson and New Jersey State Director of Employment Joseph Spitz. Basically this plan called for federal-state-municipal cooperation, with federal subsidies providing the cohesion. The bills introduced in Congress by Nolan/Phelan and Robinson/Keating had essentially asked for such a scheme. When the wartime expansion of the USES was in full swing, Seager had also entered a strong plea for a federated structure.[71]

---

70 Delegates came from Alabama, California, Colorado, Delaware, Florida, Georgia, Illinois, Kansas, Kentucky, Maryland, Massachusetts, Nevada, New Jersey, New Mexico, New York, North Carolina, North Dakota, Ohio, Oklahoma, Oregon, South Carolina, South Dakota, Texas, Utah, Virginia, Washington, West Virginia, and Wyoming. "Conference on National Employment Service, Washington, D.C., April 23 to 25, 1919," *MLR* 8:5 (May 1919), 1404–06. – A list of the federal directors of the USES, indicating their union affiliations, is found in Hearings on S. 688, S. 1442 and H.R. 4305, pp. 113–14. – Hearings on S. 688, S. 1442 and H.R. 4305, p. 634. For the more cooperative attitude of the U.S. Chamber of Commerce towards governmental action see Richard Hume Werking, "Bureaucrats, Businessmen, and Foreign Trade: The Origin of the United States Chamber of Commerce," *Business History Review* 52:3 (Autumn 1978), 339–41.

71 U.S. Dept. of Labor, *7th Annual Report, 1919*, 903; William B. Wilson, "A National System of Employment Offices," AAPEO, Proceedings 1916, in U.S. Bureau of Labor Statistics, *Bulletin 220* (Washington: G.O.P. 1917), 23–27; William M. Leiserson, "A Federal Labor Reserve Board," ibid., 33–45; Joseph Spitz, "Federal-State-Municipal Offices," ibid., 30–32; Henry R. Seager, "Coordination of Federal, State, and Municipal Employment Bureaus," *American Economic Review* 8 (March 1918), Suppl., 114–46; idem, "Coordination of Federal, State and City Systems of Employment Offices," *ALLR* 8:1 (March 1918), 21–26.

Two important considerations favored such a system. For one, local responsibility allowed better catering to local situations; a decentralized system promised to be more flexible and responsive to specific needs. Moreover, centralization ran counter to states' rights feelings; a proposal that envisaged a straight command line originating in Washington would probably hurt itself against insurmountable political obstacles. The federal system, the National Catholic War Council observed, would have to act "in harmony" with the state employment bureaus.[72]

Against this concept, another school of thought stressed the advantages of a streamlined organization. As Johns Hopkins professor George E. Barnett explained at the 1918 meeting of the American Economic Association, the uniformity and efficiency of a centralized system would save an enormous amount of money to the taxpayer; moreover, more capable personnel could be hired, because the service would be more attractive and the danger of political appointments smaller; and last, but not least, the greater prestige of the federal government would inspire more confidence in the workers, therewith rendering the service more successful.[73] It was this kind of system that had practically been implemented during the period of wartime expansion. Circumstances permitting, it might be maintained and refined in the coming years.

At the Washington conference, practical considerations prevailed. Although few discussants doubted the technical advantages of a centralized structure, the insight quickly gained ground that politically it was an impossible proposition. The conferees therefore formulated guidelines for a federated structure in which the USES was reduced to the role of coordinating and supplementing state initiatives. A regular annual appropriation would allow the USES to allocate funds to those states that ran public employment systems of their own according to uniform USES standards; if a state chose not to organize its own system, the USES could establish federal exchange offices.[74]

This scheme did not exactly correspond to the tight organization Secretary Wilson had endeavored to create in 1918, but it was at least a

72 "Social Reconstruction Program of the National Catholic War Council," *MLR* 8:6 (June 1919), 45. See similarly Devine, "The Federal Employment Service," 17.

73 George E. Barnett in "Employment of Labor and the War – Discussion," *American Economic Review* 8 (March 1918), Suppl., 184–86.

74 "Conference on National Employment Service, Washington, D.C., April 23 to 25, 1919," *MLR* 8:5 (May 1919), 1404–07. See also Hearings on S. 688, S. 1442 and H.R. 4305, pp. 71–83.

proposal that might offer a chance of survival to the USES. Losing no time, the conferees selected a six-member subcommittee, including Meeker and George W. Kirchwey, New York (State) federal director of the USES and former dean of Columbia University, to write a pertinent bill. The Department of Labor approved the draft and passed it on to Nolan. President Wilson on 20 May 1919 urged the "developing and maintaining" of a federal employment service "on an adequate scale."[75] With hopes heightened by this pronouncement, Nolan introduced the bill in Congress on 31 May 1919 (H.R. 4305). A week later, William S. Kenyon (R-Iowa), a pro-labor progressive who had ties to the farm bloc and was chairman of the Senate Committee on Education and Labor, followed suit with a bill similar in intent, but containing an additional provision for an advisory council composed of representatives of employers and labor (S. 1442). This device, conceived to alleviate employer fears of union domination, had many advocates but had been stricken from the House bill by Secretary Wilson, perhaps for tactical reasons. Somewhat earlier, Robinson, following up on his wartime initiatives, had introduced still another bill of his own (S. 688). The Senate and House committees agreed to hold joint hearings in June and July on all three proposals.[76]

During these hearings the proponents and adversaries of the USES faced each other for the first time in full view of the public. Several novel and interesting points added fresh force to the dispute. The Department of Labor bureaucracy knew that it fought for the life of the USES. Densmore was backed up by Secretary Wilson, Meeker, and USES acting assistant director general William E. Hall, a lawyer with business connections. In advancing the familiar points in favor of a continuation of the service they found an able assistant in Lescohier. The latter had just finished writing his book on the labor market, concluding that a national service was a necessity and that the preferable structure was to be found

---

75 Meeker to Andrews, 26 April 1919, microfilm, reel 19, Andrews Papers. Kirchwey, a progressive who had been involved in the platform committee of the Progressive Party in 1912, served in the USES position only temporarily. Allen F. Davis, "The Social Workers and the Progressive Party, 1912–1916," *American Historical Review* 69:3 (April 1964), 675. From 1918 to 1932 Kirchwey taught criminology at the New York School of Social Work. – John B. Andrews, "A Federal-State Employment Service Advanced in Congress," *ALLR* 10:2 (June 1920), 122.

76 Hearings on S. 688, S. 1442 and H.R. 4305, pp. 53; 319. Secretary Wilson sent supporting letters to both congressional committees. U.S. Dept. of Labor, *7th Annual Report, 1919*, 938–40.

somewhere in between the two extreme forms under discussion. His help at the hearings had been solicited by the Department of Labor, and he strove to give a comprehensive endorsement to the pro-USES arguments presented. A disorderly labor market, he explained, was wasteful for employers and labor alike. Organization of the labor market was therefore essential. The economy transcended state lines, and so did the labor market. Only a national employment service could maintain the necessary information system, and through superior competition curb the ill practices of the private agencies. Furthermore, only a few states were capable of or willing to afford an adequate placement service. At any rate, dependency upon state offices made it impossible to attain uniformity in clearance and information gathering procedures. A federal service, functioning as a bracket, was therefore needed to bind state services together and supplement them where necessary.[77]

But this kind of theoretical argumentation failed to persuade a large number of interested observers. Their objections were not so much based on abstract conceptualization, but rather on past experiences with the USES. The service's lack of expertise and its behavior pattern emerged as prime areas of concern. That the USES, jerry-built and overexpanded, had not been a paragon of bureaucratic success was even admitted by its friends. In a *Survey* article, while endorsing the service's quest for statutory funding, Devine deplored its past inefficiency and wastefulness, its lack of a "strong, consistent directing policy," the top-heaviness and disorganization of its administration, the existing "friction between line and staff," and the fact that it had duplicated some operations conducted by the War Department. The *Nation* knew of "waste and red tape and a certain amount of political manipulation." Smyth conceded before the AALL membership that the USES had in some places "failed to realize a reasonable degree of success," and he demanded the weeding out of "incompetents."[78]

Wastefulness and indecision could probably be mended with the right kind of management effort. More important were sins of the mind, and

---

77 Hearings on H.R. 13870, p. 1488; Don D. Lescohier, *The Labor Market* (New York: Macmillan, 1919), 215–16. The book was published in December 1919. Lescohier to Andrews, 10 Dec. 1919, microfilm, reel 21, Andrews Papers. – Hearings on S. 688, S. 1442 and H.R. 4305, pp. 345–47.

78 Devine, "The Federal Employment Service," 9; 15. See also "General Discussion," *ALLR* 9:1 (March 1919), 101. – "The Employment Service," *Nation* 108:2798 (15 Feb. 1919), 245; Nathan A. Smyth, "Mustering Out the National Army," *ALLR* 9:1 (March 1919), 81.

in the eyes of powerful adversaries the USES had become guilty of quite an assortment of these as well. One case in point was its perceived arrogance. During the war, despite paying lip service to the cooperative idea, the USES had established what amounted to a centralized structure with little room for local decision making. Although a large percentage of the operating funds had come out of state and local treasuries, the USES, directed from Washington, had generally insisted on hanging out USES signs and imposing its own rules, claiming wartime necessity. As a result, much ill feeling had been created. New York Industrial Commissioner Henry D. Sayer, no foe of labor, remembered without pleasure the domineering attitude of the USES people and felt that state independence should now be safeguarded. For him the Nolan bill went far too far toward a nationally directed service. Kirchwey for the same reason even thought a federal body unnecessary for the time being.[79]

The relationship of the USES with the unions had equally aroused anger. Of considerable interest in this context was the attitude of the AFL. As noted earlier, on the eve of the American entry into the war the organization had endorsed the creation of state employment exchanges. In November 1917 it urged the establishment of such agencies "under federal control," and in June 1918 it demanded a $2 million appropriation for a full-fledged federal employment bureau in the Department of Labor. Gompers himself, who had earlier been indifferent toward public employment offices, had clearly changed his opinion. In early 1919 he went as far as assisting the USES in its lobbying efforts by sending a supportive cable from France. The participation of an AFL representative at the Washington conference in April, testifying to the same well-disposed attitude, has already been mentioned. At its annual convention in June 1919 the AFL officially and unanimously endorsed the Kenyon/Nolan bills. The reasons for this turnabout were not readily perceptible. AFL lobbyist Henry Sterling even pointed out in the hearings on S. 688 that union people did not need the public offices because the trade unions ran their own labor exchanges. If the AFL was now in favor of the Nolan bill, he asserted, it took its stand not for its own sake but "only for the general good of the laboring people of the country."[80]

---

79 Lescohier, *Labor Market*, 213; Hearings on S. 688, S. 1442 and H.R. 4305, pp. 358–61; 431.
80 *CR*, 65 Cong., 3 sess., 28 Feb. 1919, pp. 4624–25 (Thomas L. Blanton); AFL. 37th Annual Convention, *Proceedings 1917*, 141; idem, 38th Annual Convention, *Proceedings 1918*, 329; idem, 39th Annual Convention, *Proceedings 1919*, 375–76; "National-State

Altruism was doubtless a praiseworthy motivation. A remark of AFL secretary Frank Morrison, however, indicated that the organization may have had ulterior considerations. It had been the AFL, he claimed, that during the war "after a fight... got this employment service through, the President giving $800,000 out of his fund to do it." The Council of National Defense had wanted a separate bureau, but the AFL had prevailed, and the USES had been left in the Department of Labor. What Morrison did not say was that the AFL's engagement had not been gratuitous. The Department of Labor, as we have seen, had reciprocated by appointing many union people into USES positions, often apparently under considerable pressure from union side. The AFL, as a consequence, was able to influence, if not fully control, the service and could see advantage in its further development.[81] Morrison was well-advised not to emphasize the latter point. One of the principal arguments of the adversaries of the USES was exactly this union penetration. By 1920 at least thirty-seven employers' associations had passed resolutions disapproving of the service. According to the New Jersey Commissioner of Labor, Louis T. Bryant, this opposition arose "for the reason that [the employers] feel that domination by Washington, through the present organization, is going to build up the union machines."[82]

Much USES activity had obviously been carried on in collaboration with or directly through the good offices of labor organizations. At the April 1919 conference in Washington, Secretary Wilson, whose strong labor connections had brought him into office in 1913, even defended his department's friendliness toward the unions as justified. Of course,

Employment Service," *ALLR* 9:2 (June 1919), 197. See also similarly AFL. 40th Annual Convention, *Proceedings 1920*, 422; idem, 41st Annual Convention, *Proceedings 1921*, 113; 374; idem, 42d Annual Convention, *Proceedings 1922*, 107; 325. – Hearings on S. 688, S. 1442 and H.R. 4305, pp. 274–75.

81 Hearings on S. 688, S. 1442 and H.R. 4305, p. 453. Confirmation of Morrison's assertion is found in a "Memorandum for the Secretary (Through the Assistant Secretary)," signed by T. V. Powderly, 10 July 1917, reporting on a meeting in Washington between government officials and representatives of the Council of National Defense as well as of the AFL, including Morrison. Box 6, General Subject Files, Office of the Secretary, General Records of the Dept. of Labor, Department of Labor Papers. – Hearings on H.R. 13870, p. 1511. For an interesting look at feelings on the local union level see A. J. Portenar, "Labour Unions and Public Employment Offices," IAPES, *Proceedings 1920*, 65–69.

82 Daniel Nelson, *Managers and Workers: Origins of the New Factory System in the United States 1880–1920* (Madison: University of Wisconsin Press, 1975), 144; Hearings on S. 688 and 1442, and H.R. 4305, p. 307. See also Z. L. Potter to Andrews, 8 Feb. 1919, microfilm, reel 19, Andrews Papers.

nobody could prove that the trade unions had ultimately dominated the USES, but quite a few employers were convinced of it. In Muskegon County, Michigan, USES officials had participated in a union rally and given its resolutions their sanction. Elsewhere, sympathizers of the Industrial Workers of the World had been placed into jobs and had "demoralized" the other workers. Some employers felt that they had received bad USES service because they practiced the open shop. During the hearings on S. 688, Representative Thomas L. Blanton (D-Texas) even succeeded in establishing that union membership was a requirement for the advancement of officials in the USES. This caused him to wonder whether the United States should be governed for the benefit of 110 million Americans or "in the selfish interest of 3,000,000 members of the labor unions."[83]

But union penetration was only one of the faults of which the USES was accused by its opponents. Following an example set by the National Metal Trades Association, the NAM composed a special bulletin full of reasons why the USES should be denied statutory sanction. The basic argument was that any public employment services came under the jurisdiction of the states, not the federal government. The bulletin, moreover, denounced the USES for its general incompetence, inefficiency, and corruption, and offered examples galore for its accusations. One fact that particularly upset the association was the use of federal money for lobbying purposes in order "to create in the congressional mind sentiment favorable to the perpetuation of the service."[84]

The pamphlet still did not paint the full picture of the NAM's indignation. The association could only denounce in print behavior that was clearly illegal or detrimental to the common good. But its members saw

---

83 U.S. Dept of Labor, *6th Annual Report, 1918*, 699; Wilson had been a founding member of the United Mine Workers. *Dictionary of American Biography*, s.v. "Wilson, William Bauchop." See also William Bauchop Wilson, *Memories*. 2d ed. rev. (Washington: Trade Unionist, 1916). – "Secretary Wilson Answers Criticism That Department of Labor and United States Employment Service Have Been Pro-union...," press release, 25 April 1919, microfilm, reel 19, Andrews Papers; Hearings on S. 688, S. 1442 and H.R. 4305, pp. 107; 151–79; 285; 307; 387–415; 418; *CR*, 65 Cong., 3 sess., 28 Feb. 1919, p. 4626.

84 Hearings on H.R. 13870, pp. 1503–05; National Association of Manufacturers of the United States of America, *Special Washington Service Bulletin No. 26* (11 June 1919), printed in Hearings on S. 688, S. 1442, and H.R. 4305, pp. 554–62. – Hearings on S. 688, S. 1442 and H.R. 4305, pp. 554–56. The use of public funds by the USES for lobbying purposes had already aroused the ire of Blanton during the appropriation debate in the House. *CR*, 65 Cong., 3 sess., Appendix, 4 March 1919, pp. 234–39.

reason to be disgusted with at least two more USES sins. One was touched upon by Densmore when he stated during the hearings that the service had transferred about 65,000 skilled workers out of nonessential work into war work. The experience gave rise to the fear that the service could again enjoy similar authority "to the detriment of some of our manufacturing industries in the country." The other grievance was held by southern employers in particular. The war boom had lured black workers to better paying jobs in the North, and in order to safeguard wage levels, at least seven southern states had set towering license fees – reaching as high as $3,500 – for private employment agents doing interstate business. The USES, however, had freely attracted workers to the North. Furthermore, it had "induced thousands of Negroes to leave farms and [had] unionized them in the cities." The opponents of the USES thus feared above all a bureaucratic leviathan, directed from Washington and hostile to employers. Congressman Ira G. Hersey (R-Maine) tried to bring the antagonism into a formula by stating that "the one who is for the [Kenyon-Nolan] bill is the man who works. The man who employs the workman is against the bill"[84a] (Figure 4–3).

Hersey's view, though, was too simplistic. A substantial number of entrepreneurs had had good experiences with the USES during the war. Hall was able to produce a list of over 800 companies endorsing the work of the service. Similarly, the United States Chamber of Commerce, as has been shown, had no qualms about supporting the pending legislation. When it had polled its members concerning public employment offices in late 1918, they had declared themselves with a two-thirds majority in favor of establishing a national system.[85]

Obviously the adversaries of the USES were concentrated in the more conservative circles represented by the NAM, the National Industrial Conference Board, the Southern Metal Trades Association, and various farmers' unions. But if their support base was limited, their fighting fervor was not. Densmore described their exertions as "a definite and calculated

---

84a Hearings on S. 688, S. 1442, and H.R. 4305, pp. 275; 419–23; 492; 638; *CR*, 65 Cong., 3 sess., 28 Feb. 1919, p. 4626 (Thomas L. Blanton). The USES acknowledged its role in the migration of blacks. U.S. Dept. of Labor, *5th Annual Report, 1917*, 79–80. From 1918 the Urban League office in Chicago was in fact being run by the USES. Neil A. Wynn, *From Progressivism to Prosperity: World War I and American Society* (New York: Holmes & Meier, 1986), 182.

85 Hearings on S. 688, S. 1442, and H.R. 4305, pp. 534–47. The vote was 689.5 to 361.5. President's Conference on Unemployment. Committee on Unemployment and Business Cycles, *Business Cycles and Unemployment: Report and Recommendations*, 84.

—New Orleans Times-Picayune

The Mirage

—New York Call

Keeping the Negro in the South

Figure 4-3. Two views of the movement of black labor to the north initiated by World War I. (Source: *ALLR* 13:3 [Sept. 1923], 212.)

effort...to cripple this service." Congress members were inundated with information material, the hearings were vigorously used, and on the floors of Congress polemical indictments abounded. Additional efforts at persuasion were probably made in less visible form.[86]

The outcome of the controversy was gratifying to the opponents of a strong federal service. As early as February 1919, Kenyon had a premonition that the USES was doomed. Although subsequently some hope glimmered for over a year, his assessment ultimately proved correct. Neither the Robinson bill nor the proposals submitted by Kenyon and Nolan advanced beyond the hearings, "owing to the congressional situation in the months preceding the presidential campaign," as Densmore put it.[87] With this failure the matter was not yet fully disposed of, though. In May 1919, Nolan had introduced a similar bill (H.R. 544), and although it had not officially been an object of the hearings, the House Committee on Labor later used it to express its sentiments. And these were guided by the resolves of the Industrial Conference in the fall of 1919.

Before this conference got under way, the first International Labour Conference met in Washington. It adopted a draft convention stipulating that countries belonging to the ILO should "establish a system of free public employment agencies under the control of a central authority."[88] The supporters of the USES understandably hoped that this pronouncement would give their cause a powerful boost. But during those weeks, isolationists fought tooth and nail to keep the United States out of the League of Nations and its affiliated organizations, and as a result American ratification of the convention was problematic.

The Industrial Conference, composed of representatives from business, labor, and "public life," followed on the heels of the international meeting. The final conference report, published on 6 March 1920, urged "an immediate and thorough study of the problem [of unemployment] by individual industries" so that appropriate countermeasures could be de-

---

86 Hearings on S. 688, S. 1442, and H.R. 4305, pp. 285; 495; 562; Densmore to Thomas J. Walsh, 3 Feb. 1919, Box 191, Walsh Papers; *CR*, 65 Cong., 3 sess., 28 Feb. 1919, pp. 4624–26; 4652–66; ibid., 4 March 1919, 4988–5004; ibid., Appendix, 28 Feb. 1919, 234–38; 66 Cong., 1 sess., 27 May 1919, pp. 279–80; ibid., 29 May 1919, pp. 420–23; ibid., 1 July 1919, pp. 2154–79; ibid., 28 July 1919, pp. 8939–62.
87 *CR*, 65 Cong., 3 sess., 15 Feb. 1919, p. 3435; U.S. Dept. of Labor, *8th Annual Report, 1920*, 143.
88 League of Nations. International Labour Conference, *First Annual Meeting, October 29, 1919–November 29, 1919. Washington, D.C.* (Washington: G.P.O., 1920), 259.

vised. As one such measure it envisaged a system of public employment exchanges. But the resemblance of this recommendation to that of the international conference was only superficial. Whereas the latter had distinctly spoken of "the control of a central authority," the American conferees held that the employment problem was "in the first instance a local problem." The essential requisite was "to secure decentralized administration in the States under the supervision of its [sic] citizens [and] to avoid the establishment of a federal bureaucracy." The federal government should be restricted to establishing a clearinghouse. The distribution of a federal appropriation would follow the pattern of the cooperative relation between federal and state governments that existed "in other fields."[89]

The forces interested in keeping the USES powerless had clearly made their influence felt at the Industrial Conference. This was manifest if one looked at any of the "fields" in which the kind of cooperative relation contemplated by the conference existed. The best known among them, the construction of postal roads, was guided by the Post Roads Act of 1916, which left the initiative fully to the states and merely matched their expenditures with federal grants up to a certain ceiling.[90] The recommendation of the Industrial Conference thus agreed with the opinion of those who saw in the USES bills a danger to the decision-making power of the states.

It was this recommendation that the amended version of H.R. 544 embodied when the Committee on Labor reported it back on 18 May 1920. The committee did not indicate why it had taken so long to ponder the results of the hearings. Some criticism from women unionists had been voiced in the meantime, charging that the bill neglected specific women's interests. But it seems unlikely that such considerations had held up the committee. The fact that the report partially reprinted the recommendation passed by the Industrial Conference makes it probable that the committee had purposely waited for the outcome of the latter. There was no reason for the friends of the old USES, though, to get all worked up about these debilitating provisions. Despite Nolan's efforts "to do all I can to get immediate consideration" of the amended version

---

89 Report of Industrial Conference Called by the President," U.S. Dept. of Labor, *8th Annual Report, 1920*, 269–70. See also "Report of the President's Industrial Conference," *MLR* 10:4 (April 1920), 869–70.
90 39 Stat. 241 (1916), sec. 6.

and Andrews cheering on, Congress did not think even this innocuous proposal worthy of implementation and took no further action on it.[91]

The fact that after the war the Wilson administration failed to continue its active support for the USES has been explained as an attempt "to meet the labor problems of the postwar era with the repressive tactics of the Red scare rather than with the rational techniques of social engineering." But if the substantial segments of the business world that disliked the USES had decisive influence upon the administration's attitude, such a statement has probably to be qualified. Not abhorrence of rationality nor of social engineering as such guided their resolve, but rather the fear that the wrong kind of goal would be pursued. It is conceivable that if the USES had enjoyed a different reputation than it did, it might have been allowed, as was the case with the employment service in neighboring Canada, to play a more important role in the postwar era.[92]

Uncertain existence in the 1920s

The disappointments of the postwar period did not permanently discourage the advocates of an effective federal service. Over the following years they used the opportunities that came their way to keep the demand for an expansion of the existing public exchange facilities in the public consciousness. The most important efforts in this respect occurred during the unemployment crisis of 1921, although the occasional push was still made thereafter.

An upsurge of unemployment from 1920 on prompted various well-meant, if unsuccessful, exchange activities. Seager, who had served as executive secretary of the Industrial Conference, called in the *Survey* for a "rehabilitation and extension" of the USES. He argued that the criticism that the service had encountered during the war did not relate to its

---

91 Andrews to Ethel M. Smith, 19 Jan. 1920, microfilm, reel 19, Andrews Papers. The charge came from the National Women's Trade Union League of America, of which Smith was Secretary. – U.S. Congress. House. Committee on Labor, *To Establish a National Employment Bureau.* H. Rept. 999, 66 Cong., 2 sess. (to accompany H.R. 544; 18 May 1920); John J. Nolan to Andrews, 20 May 1920, microfilm, reel 22, Andrews Papers; John B. Andrews, "A Federal-State Employment Service Advanced in Congress," *ALLR* 10:2 (June 1920), 121–22.

92 John F. McClymer, *War and Welfare: Social Engineering in America, 1890–1925* (Westport, Conn.: Greenwood, 1980), 178. For the Canadian service see Udo Sautter, "The Origins of the Employment Service of Canada, 1900–1920," *Labour/Le Travailleur* 6 (Autumn 1980), 89–112, in particular 108–12.

principle but only to inefficient methods of execution. In March, not completely consistently, he came out in favor of passage of the still-pending Nolan bill (H.R. 544), as did representatives of the AFL and the railroad brotherhoods. Kenyon made a renewed effort in Congress in April 1921 for the establishment of an operable national service (S. 681), and a further proposal suggested the incorporation of the USES into a new Department of Social Welfare (S. 408). But nothing came of these initiatives.[93] When the AALL conducted a survey of unemployment conditions during the summer, many local administrations criticized the curtailment of the USES appropriation, as placement activities had been seriously crippled. In July 1921, even the Merchants' Association of New York (State) protested the discontinuance of the public employment bureaus. This prompted the *ALLR* to reprint the "Standard Recommendations" the AALL had formulated in 1915, thus again strongly advocating the passage of pertinent legislation.[94]

At the President's Conference on Unemployment in September the potential of employment agencies received considerable attention. The Economic Advisory Committee suggested that communities use the state employment bureaus for the registration of their unemployed and that all employers be urged to notify the bureaus of available jobs.[95] Leiserson was made executive secretary of the conference's subcommittee on Employment Agencies and Registration. During public hearings a spokesman of the AFL stated that organized labor favored "in the most emphatic way" the extension of public employment agencies. The lone opponent to such action, a representative of the Metropolitan Association of Employment Agencies, believed that private agencies could do a better job because their personnel were better qualified and motivated.

The conference itself, mindful of Hoover's emphasis on community action, recommended the creation of local agencies. Advice was given as to the advantages of keeping "in the closest possible contact" with neighboring cities "for the purpose of transferring labor from one community to another." Intercity exchange, of course, should have been a USES

---

93 Henry R. Seager, "The Present Industrial Situation in the United States," *Survey* 45:14 (1 Jan. 1921), 477–80; idem, "Passage of Employment Service Bill 'A Necessary First Step,'" *ALLR* 11:1 (March 1921), 24; "Legislative Notes," *ALLR* 11:2 (June 1921), 131.

94 "Unemployment Survey–1920–21 with Standard Recommendations," *ALLR* 11:3 (Sept. 1921), 192; 206; "Standard Recommendations for the Relief and Prevention of Unemployment," *ALLR* 11:3 (Sept. 1921), 219.

95 President's Conference on Unemployment, *Report*, 66–67.

task. The conferees, regretfully noting the service's impotence, drafted an "outline" of a permanent employment system. The state offices should coordinate the local units, and their number should be extended. The federal government should assume the task of coordinating the individual state systems. Its activity was to consist of collecting and making available statistical data and information to facilitate interstate placements, and of promoting the adoption of uniform procedures. A congressional appropriation of $400,000 was to finance the federal endeavor.[96]

These were moderate suggestions, although in the light of Harding's admonition to refrain from money demands a request of financial support was probably doomed to remain unsuccessful. For a moment, though, it seemed as if the proposal had a chance. The *American Federationist* proclaimed it to be "of a distinctly constructive character." Mallery, whose active participation in the conference afforded him a chance to gauge its mood, discerned "a praiseworthy willingness [on the part of the large employers] to forgive and forget the activities of the former United States Employment Service." Hoover considered the recommendation an aid to voluntarism and localism and endorsed it warmly. Conference enthusiasm, however, was not enough to translate the program into reality. On 21 November 1921, Hunt happily announced that "a large appropriation for the United States Employment Service is before Congress." But this proposal was not the original $400,000 request. Harding's new director of the budget, future vice-president Charles G. Dawes, had reduced it to $200,000. The House Appropriations Committee cut it out altogether. The Senate Appropriations Committee reinstated a $100,000 allocation, and even got it adopted on the Senate floor. But the bill did not get through the conference committee and was ultimately abandoned.[97]

After this failure the advocates of USES reform did not regain momentum quickly. Andrews, who had hailed the announcement of the President's Conference as marking "the end of the 'do nothing' attitude,"

---

96 President's Conference on Unemployment, *Report*, 19–20; 70–78; 84–87; 163.
97 "The Unemployment Conference – A Picture," 960; Otto T. Mallery, "The Unemployment Conference," *Survey* 47:7 (12 Nov. 1921), 255; Grin, "The Unemployment Conference of 1921," 97; "Postscript to the Report – Some Results of the Conference on Unemployment, by Edward Eyre Hunt, Secretary of the Conference," President's Conference on Unemployment, *Report*, 172; *CR*, 67 Cong., 2 sess., 14 Dec. 1921, p. 357; *CR*, 67 Cong., 1 sess., 22 Nov. 1921, p. 8128. The allocation was contained in H.R. 9237; U.S. Congress. Senate. Committee on Appropriations, *First Deficiency Appropriation Bill, 1922*. S.Rept. 341, 67 Cong., 2 sess. (to accompany H.R. 9237, 8 Dec. 1921), 2; *CR*, 67 Cong., 2 sess., 14 Dec. 1921, p. 356.

put on a brave face and urged Nolan to introduce still another exchange bill in the House. He also published in the *ALLR* the "Outline of Permanent Employment System" worked out by the conference subcommittee. But because unemployment decreased in 1922, the cause soon lost its prominence even with the reformers. As for organized private enterprise, it henceforth kept a watchful distance. If labor-placement facilities were to be considered necessary at all, the National Industrial Conference Board stated in 1922, then it might be the employers themselves who "could by agreement centralize the local labor market."[98]

Several events helped to keep the public employment office idea simmering during the mid-twenties. One of them was the publication of the CUBC's *Business Cycles and Unemployment* (1923). Harrison, who during the preceding few years had become strongly interested in the potential of public employment agencies, emphasized in it that public exchanges could cut the amount of time lost in job-getting, but also supply data to determine the best time for engaging in public works, and assist in the administration of unemployment insurance once it was set up. The CUBC made this view its own and gave "hearty approval" to the idea of a national system of employment bureaus.[99]

In October 1924, Harrison brought out his massive study of the public employment office question, written with four coauthors. It described the job-search procedures practised at the time, the administrative methods to be used in running an employment office, and the treatment of special groups like juniors, handicapped workers, and immigrants. Regarding the crucial question of structure, it squarely came out in favor of the Kenyon/Nolan bill with its strong decentralizing features, mainly because of "the opposition to federalism that has followed in the wake of the far-reaching control exercised by the federal government" during the war. Harrison's work certainly constituted "the most comprehensive collection of facts concerning the purpose,

98 John B. Andrews, "Introductory Note," *ALLR* 11:3 (Sept. 1921), 181–82; Andrews to John J. Nolan, 1 Sept. 1921, microfilm, reel 24, Andrews Papers; Andrews to Nolan, 14 Oct. 1921, ibid.; "Federal-State Employment Service: Outline of Permanent Employment System as Adopted by the President's Conference on Unemployment," *ALLR* 11:4 (Dec. 1921), 314; National Industrial Conference Board, *The Unemployment Problem* (New York: Century, 1922), 76.
99 Shelby M. Harrison, "A Study of Public Employment Service: A Statement of Scope and Status," IAPES, Proceedings 1920, 57–59; President's Conference on Unemployment. Committee on Unemployment and Business Cycles, *Business Cycles and Unemployment*, xxxi; 290–92.

structure and methods of public employment offices" that had yet been published in the United States, as Andrews approvingly noted. But its impact remained undeservedly small, as at the time of its appearance the issue no longer commanded much attention.[100]

Despite the prevailing indifference of the American public toward labor-exchange questions, an occasional foray occurred even in Congress. Thus in the spring of 1924, Representative Scott Leavitt (R-Montana), who had during the war served as a USES official in his state, proposed an inquiry into the need and form of a nationwide employment service (H.Res. 276). His initiative was prompted by the passage of the immigration quota law of 1924, which he feared might cause a labor shortage. His colleagues, though, did not act, and it seems that even the USES itself settled into complacent resignation. When interviewed by Andrews in January 1925, USES Director Francis I. Jones stated that he certainly would not need $1 million for the next year, as he "couldn't keep the [patronage-greedy] senators away with a shot gun," and that he would be quite happy with $500,000 for the budget year of 1927.[101] Under these circumstances nobody could be surprised that the prospects for the creation of a bureau system were not materially advanced by a bill introduced by Nolan's widow in February 1925 (H.R. 12443).[102]

While waiting for a statutory foundation, the USES had to survive financially as best it could. Congressional appropriations barely covered the absolute necessities. The third deficiency appropriation bill of 1919, enacted on 11 July 1919 (H.R. 16187), allotted $272,000 for the fiscal

100 Shelby M. Harrison et al., *Public Employment Offices: Their Purpose, Structure and Methods* (New York: Russell Sage Foundation, 1924), 163; 165–74. The publication date was 20 Oct. 1924. See press release of the Russell Sage Foundation in Box 35, Leiserson Papers. – J[ohn] B. A[ndrews], review of *Public Employment Offices*, by Shelby Harrison, in *ALLR* 14:4 (Dec. 1924), 327; Harrison to Andrews, 25 Sept. 1920, microfilm, reel 22, Andrews Papers.

101 *CR*, 68 Cong., 1 sess., 3 June 1924, p. 10377; "Memorandum from Talk with Francis I. Jones of the U.S. Employment Service January 24, 1925," microfilm, reel 66, Andrews Papers. Jones' statement reflected the attitude of Secretary of Labor Davis, who was complacent about the size and potential of the USES. "Memoranda for the President on the Activities of the Department of Labor, June 1, 1923," Book 4, Articles and Speeches, Davis Papers. Compare also the contented tone of the pertaining chapter in Roger W. Babson, *Recent Labor Progress* (New York: Revell, 1924), 69–77. Babson wrote his book with the blessing of the Dept. of Labor. See ibid., 7.

102 Rep. John J. Nolan had died on 18 Nov. 1922, and his widow Mae E. Nolan had been elected to his seat in the House on 23 Jan. 1923.

year that had ended on 30 June 1919. For the following year the Sundry Civil Appropriations Act (1919) (H.R. 6176) designated $400,000. The latter sum did not even constitute one-tenth of the $4.6 million the Department of Labor had asked for in December 1918. The states and civic bodies that in spring 1919 had so generously contributed to the maintenance of the service had done so because of demobilization worries. Their contributions soon dried up, and the USES was on its own. Over the following years it received about $225,000 per annum, and had to adjust its activities accordingly.[103]

Squeezed by administrative indifference and congressional parsimony, the service had little choice but to shrink. In the summer of 1919 a kind of hybrid arrangement prevailed, as the USES ran 62 offices in conjunction with 242 public offices maintained by other bodies. But on 10 October 1919 the USES offices were handed over to state or municipal authorities or were closed. For a few months some hope flickered that the USES could function as a clearance station for interstate labor exchanges, or at least as a national coordinator for regional clearance headquarters established by groups of states. But the lack of funds aborted these plans. Public placement in general was from now on conducted almost exclusively by those states and cities that maintained their own offices.[104]

The USES, reduced to its headquarters in Washington, henceforth led only a rudimentary existence. It cut its staff from thirty-one in April 1920 to fifteen by June 1924. The quality of its work was not enhanced by the fact that in spring 1921 it had to take on a number of political appointees who had been rejected by other departments but could enter the USES, because it did not operate under civil service rules. During the 1920s the service engaged only in a few activities. A Farm Labor Division maintained employment offices in Kansas City (Missouri), Sioux City (Indiana), and Fort Worth (Texas), and temporary offices at several other places during the harvest season. The division recruited agricultural workers in various states and distributed them as the need arose. A Junior Division endeavored, in co-

---

103 41 Stat. 6 (1919), p. 55; 41 Stat. 24 (1919), p. 225; Hearings on H.R. 13870, pp. 1473; 1519; 2168; 2188; Hearings on H.R. 15422, p. 1752; Hearings on H.R. 13316, pp. 281–305. Detail about USES revenues and expenditures for the years 1918 to 1924 is given in Darell Hevenor Smith, *The United States Employment Service: Its History, Activities and Organization* (Baltimore: Johns Hopkins Press, 1923), 122–23.
104 U.S. Dept. of Labor, *8th Annual Report, 1920*, 148–51.

operation with school boards, to provide vocational guidance and to place juveniles in appropriate positions. The Service's performance was not impressive, especially if one keeps in mind that many of the jobs were temporary in nature, often lasting only a few days. B. Seebohm Rowntree, a progressive British businessman, passed the appropriate verdict. No country, he wrote in the *International Labour Review*, "should adopt a national scheme of employment exchanges unless it is prepared to spend a good deal of money."[105]

The bulk of the public placement work during the 1920s was thus done by the surviving state services. With these the USES concluded socalled "cooperative" arrangements. The official head of a state employment service became the federal director of the USES in that state at the nominal salary of one dollar per year. The major benefit of this appointment, apart from maintaining appearances, was the continuation of the franking privilege on the state level. In March 1920, cooperative arrangements were in effect with forty states including the District of Columbia, of whom seventeen maintained at least one public employment office. The depression experience of 1921 induced several more states to create or reinstate offices, so that by 1924 twenty-eight states ran active exchanges.[106] The USES granted to the states small amounts of money that could be applied to the salaries of the federal director or other employees. In 1924 the sums ranged from $4,320 (New Jersey, New

105 Hearings on H.R. 13870, p. 2169; U.S. Dept. of Labor, *12th Annual Report, 1924*, 37; Anna Y. Reed, *Occupational Placement: Its History, Philosophies, Procedures, and Educational Implications* (Ithaca: Cornell University Press, 1946), 67. According to its own reports, the Farm Labor Division placed 106,743 field hands in 1922 and 559,571 in 1928. Smith, *United States Employment Service*, 64; "Public Employment Services," *MLR* 32:1 (Jan. 1931), 27. The Junior Division reported 18,260 placements in 1924. U.S. Dept. of Labor, *12th Annual Report, 1924*, 41. Regarding the unreliability of such figures see Benjamin M. Squires, "British Labor Exchanges and United States Employment Offices," *MLR* 9:2 (Aug. 1919), 452. – B. Seebohm Rowntree, "Prevention and Compensation of Unemployment," *International Labour Review* 4:3 (Dec. 1921), 459.

106 "Present Scope and Activities of the Federal Employment Service," *MLR* 10:5 (May 1920), 130–31; Hearings on H.R. 13870, pp. 2171–78. "Employment," *ALLR* 11:4 (Dec. 1921), 334–35; U.S. Dept. of Labor, *12th Annual Report, 1924*, 37. In 1924 there were state offices in Arizona, Arkansas, California, Connecticut, District of Columbia, Illinois, Indiana, Iowa, Kansas, Louisiana, Massachusetts, Michigan, Minnesota, Missouri, Montana, Nevada, New Hampshire, New Jersey, New York, North Carolina, North Dakota, Ohio, Oklahoma, Pennsylvania, Rhode Island, Virginia, West Virginia, and Wisconsin. Twelve states with cooperative arrangements did not run offices, namely Alabama, Colorado, Georgia, Kentucky, Maryland, Nebraska, Oregon, South Dakota, Tennessee, Texas, Washington, and Wyoming.

York, Pennsylvania) to $710 (Maryland). The state services were in return required to send in weekly reports on their placement work. Moreover, the USES had special agents in sixty-four industrial centers that reported monthly on employment conditions.[107]

At first glance the state-run employment exchanges in the 1920s thus differed little from their predecessors before the war. The upsurge and expansion of the USES during 1918 had been an interlude that barely left a lasting mark upon the existing system, or rather non-system. But some limited development could be perceived nevertheless. The cooperative arrangements constituted ties that bound the several services together, if ever so loosely; they could possibly be strengthened and used as channels for another build-up once the time came. The ready availability of these links had certainly to be considered an improvement over the chaotic prewar situation. Because almost everybody who gave the fight against unemployment his active support now thought that some sort of integrated public exchange system would be advantageous, the USES connections could be a point from which a future, better service might be launched.

This advance had been paid for dearly, of course. Of lesser importance in this context was the fact that the general federal exchange offices that the Division of Information had run before the war had had to be aban-

---

107 Hearings on H.R. 13316, p. 291. It is difficult to ascertain the volume of the work done. From 1921 to 1928, according to the calculations of the USES, the offices of the state employment services placed between 1.5 and 2 million jobseekers annually. (The low was 1,397,738 in 1921, the high 2,156,466 in 1923. See Table 5–1.) While these figures have to be taken with a large grain of salt, they indicate at least that despite the near-demise of the USES a good amount of governmental placement work was still carried on. Great differences continued to exist between the various services. The New York offices disposed of about $400,000 in operating expenses for the fiscal year of 1920, and in 1930 the service could still spend $166,280. New York (State). Governor Smith's Reconstruction Commission, *Report on a Permanent Unemployment Program, June 17, 1919*, 6; "Public Employment Services," *MLR* 32:1 (Jan. 1931), 22. By contrast, other state services like those of New Hampshire or Virginia had only a few thousand dollars at their disposal. See ibid. Only seven states (California, Illinois, Massachusetts, New Jersey, Ohio, New York, and Wisconsin) subjected their officials to civil service selection procedures. Ruth M. Kellogg, *The United States Employment Service* (Chicago: University of Chicago Press, 1933), 24. The performance results varied accordingly. While California, Illinois, New York, and Ohio could claim to have placed between 123,000 and 170,000 persons in the fiscal year of 1922, Arizona and Virginia each had found jobs for only about five thousand people, Rhode Island and Arkansas for even less. U.S. Congress. House. Committee on Appropriations, *Departments of Commerce and Labor, Appropriation Bill, 1924*. Hearings on H.R. 13316, p. 288.

doned; they or others could easily be reopened. Far greater significance had to be ascribed to the loss of innocence caused by the rise and fall of the USES. Before the war, public indifference or caution had been the main restraints hampering the creation of a large network. The war experience had changed this. Active and determined opposition had developed, and after the armistice, powerful interests had seen to it that the USES became – and remained – a skeleton. Anybody supposing that memories would be short and that the service could have an easy resurgence was being naive. It would take strong forces indeed to overcome the temporarily latent resistance.

Nevertheless, concerned people could at least find one certain bit of comfort in the USES experience. Even if no efficient exchange system was to be in place by the arrival of the next depression and the existing ties were tenuous, in the years after the war the fundamental merits of a nationwide service had been discussed at length. The available administrative options had been sorted out, constitutional questions had been debated, and the opponents had been located. Moreover, the potential of a public employment office network had been presented to a large segment of the public. As Lescohier expressed it, the USES debate "brought the idea, for the first time, to the attention of untold thousands of Americans."[108] If the adversaries of the USES were to recall their misgivings, the supporters of a federal network for their part could hope to build upon public knowledge about the intrinsic value of an employment office system for the fight against unemployment. They would, in this respect at any rate, not have to start entirely from the bottom again.

IV   Pondering public works

Federal public works: The postwar period

As a consequence of the war, the potential of public works as a tool in the fight against unemployment gained a new prominence. The discussion of the remedial value of public employment exchanges had already reached the governmental level years earlier, and not only a considerable number of states, but even the federal administration had made first

108 Don D. Lescohier, "The Unemployment Program of the International Labor Conference and Its Application to the United States," *ALLR* 10:1 (March 1920), 52.

attempts at their use. The debate about public works, on the other hand, had mostly remained confined to reform circles, and the few legislative initiatives of the period had been restricted to the state scene. As joblessness caused by demobilization and a possible postwar economic slump could be regarded as a federal responsibility, however, federal public works measures now appeared justifiable. In view of the paucity of effective governmental means for unemployment alleviation, they could even be seen as reasonable and advisable. Wilson's administration did not deny the validity of this contention. It might have acted accordingly, had not the economy behaved well enough to allow the government to get away without substantial action. In like manner the Harding administration managed to bide its time during the depression of 1921–22. But the discussion engendered by the President's Conference and the subsequent drive to implement the long-range planning idea made the possibility of future federal relief works in peacetime ever more thinkable. The fact that a parallel movement occurred on the state level aided and sustained this development.

As noted earlier, the armistice in November 1918 found the federal government without any definite reconstruction plans, although during the months and weeks before the end of hostilities many concerned voices had been raised. Representative was an article in the *New Republic* in August predicting "an enormous oversupply of labor," which the federal government should alleviate with public works to insure "that the entire labor force of the nation can be maintained at a fairly stationary level of employment." Several congressional initiatives envisaged the utilization of public works as a means to reduce coming unemployment.[109]

The federal government's arrangements in this field, however, were decidedly less than large-scale, and certainly not far advanced. At armistice time, Secretary of the Interior Franklin K. Lane hatched some plans to employ 100,000 men on reclamation and irrigation projects if Congress allocated the necessary funds, and he felt able to put to work another 500,000 men on similar undertakings in 1919. The Highway Transportation Committee of the Council of National Defense was preparing legislation for a $100 million highway appropriation. But nothing

109 "Stabilizing Demand for Labor," *New Republic* 16:200 (31 Aug. 1918), 126–27; Public works initiatives were proposed with S.Con.Res. 21; S.Con.Res. 22; and H.Con.Res. 54.

tangible resulted from these intentions. In November 1918, War Industries Board chairman Bernard M. Baruch was reported to be completing a "nonwar building construction program for the entire country far beyond the bounds of all precedent"; no further information was offered. About the only palpable action with regard to public works was the War Industries Board's removal of all wartime restrictions on building operations and other construction work.[110]

Although the federal executive was not moving toward rapid action, it was at least generous with encouragement for others. In November 1918 the War Labor Policies Board asked the major municipalities to take up work on public projects that the war had suspended. Secretary of War Newton D. Baker, with the backing of Labor Secretary Wilson, instructed all state and county councils of national defense to use their influence with local authorities to ensure that all public improvements be advanced. Secretary of Agriculture David F. Houston appealed to the states to get highway construction underway quickly. President Wilson, in his message to Congress on 2 December 1918, pronounced it important "that the development of public works of every sort should be promptly resumed in order that opportunities should be created for unskilled labor in particular."[111]

But neither the legislative branch of the federal government nor the administration moved speedily. Congressional inertia was not due to a want of suggestions. Various reconstruction bills were introduced during the third session of the Sixty-fifth Congress, most of them making no further headway. The outstanding example of an elaborate proposal not getting off the ground was Kelly's bill (H.R. 13415), mentioned earlier, which besides its land settlement features contained an interesting provision creating a National Emergency Board for Soldier Employment. This cabinet-level agency was to organize a "United States Construction

---

110 Frederic C. Howe, "A Constructive Program for the Rehabilitation of the Returning Soldiers," *Annals* 80 (Nov. 1918), 150–52; Otto T. Mallery, "A National Policy – Public Works to Stabilize Employment," *Annals* 81 (Jan. 1919), 59; *New York Times*, 18 Nov. 1918, p. 21; "Priorities Canceled and Restrictions Affecting Non-war Industries Removed by War Industries Board," *MLR* 8:1 (Jan. 1919), 38–39.

111 Circular of 20 Nov. 1918, as quoted in E. Jay Howenstine, Jr., "Public Works Program after World War I," *Journal of Political Economy* 51 (Dec. 1943), 524. See also circular of the Pennsylvania Emergency Public Works Commission to the mayors of the commonwealth's cities, December 1918, microfilm, reel 18, Andrews Papers; "Employment Service and Resumption of Public and Private Construction Work," *MLR* 8:2 (Feb. 1919), 437; *New York Times*, 1 Dec. 1918, II, p. 10; *CR*, 65 Cong., 3 sess., 2 Dec. 1918, p. 7.

Service" that would carry out various road projects and other public improvements. The revised bill (H.R. 15672) strengthened the emergency clauses by appropriating $100 million to the president. The proposal in a sense anticipated the New Deal's Civilian Conservation Corps, with a USES ingredient mixed in.[112] It may well be that it was the resemblance of this plan to the USES proposals under discussion at the time, as well as the sumptuousness of the reclamation and settlement provisions, that caused the demise of the bills.

The Department of Labor foresaw difficulties at any rate, and hoped to rescue at least the emergency public works provisions. It therefore prompted Kenyon to introduce S. 5397. This bill, some of whose features heralded provisions of the 1932 Emergency Relief and Construction Act (ERCA), was the only one of the various public works measures to make it beyond the committee stage, if barely so. It stipulated the creation of an Emergency Public Works Board that was to cooperate with federal, state, and municipal agencies so as to stimulate the execution of public works. An appropriation of $100 million could be used to construct authorized federal buildings; a further $300 million was to be advanced by the War Finance Corporation to states and municipalities for their public works. The bill received endorsements from various public bodies, but when the Committee on Education and Labor held hearings in January–February 1919, Secretary Wilson, apparently reflecting the cabinet's developing standpat attitude, showed himself far from keen on the proposal. The difficulties in the present economic situation were in his view only temporary. "It would be folly in my judgment to start work that is not needed," he advised the committee, "solely for the purpose of giving employment to anybody." Because the representatives of the construction industry who advocated passage of the bill could be suspected of having mainly their own interests in mind, the committee did not report the proposal out.[113]

---

112 For the U.S. Construction Service proposal see Benton MacKaye, "Making New Opportunities for Employment: Legislative Programs for Public Works and Land Development," *MLR* 8:4 (April 1919), 1076.

113 For various other bills see MacKaye, "Making New Opportunities for Employment," 1067–85. – O. T. Mallery, "Memorandum to a Group Interested in Stabilizing Labor and Industry during the Demobilization Period," n.d., microfilm, reel 21, Andrews Papers; Hearings on S. 5397, pp. 33; 81. For Secretary Wilson's resistance to action see also U.S. Congress. House. Committee on Rules, *Statement of Hon. W. B. Wilson, Secretary of Labor, on H.Res. 452 and H.Res. 463.* 65 Cong., 3 sess. (11 Dec. 1918), 6;

When the next Congress convened on 20 May 1919, demobilization worries had subsided. The odd action bill still received some consideration, though without making much headway. "General" Coxey succeeded in getting his old idea to increase the money supply reconsidered (H.R. 1473); the Committee on Banking and Currency held hearings but could not be convinced to advance the bill further. A proposal to investigate the potential of housing construction (S. 168) had the same fate. In July 1919, Representative Carl W. Riddick (R-Montana), once a homesteader himself, proposed to spend $50 million for the construction of irrigation projects (H.R. 7026). The bill reached the floor, where it withered away.[114]

Congressional inertia was matched by the unwillingness of the executive. The Department of Labor's activity record reflected its secretary's convictions. On 30 December 1918 a Division of Public Works and Construction Development was organized in the department under the direction of Felix Frankfurter, then assistant to the secretary of labor. The division's major undertaking was an investigation of the construction industry. Mallery, who was assigned to the division to stimulate public works in states and cities, lacked the means to do much more than exhort his clientele through circulars and addresses.[115]

This wait-and-see attitude very much reflected the chief executive's philosophy. "It will not be easy to direct [the process of reconstruction] any better than it will direct itself," President Wilson advised Congress. Given this line of thought, his call for a conference of governors and mayors in Washington on 3–5 March 1919 for the purpose of devising "a definite nationwide policy to stimulate public and private construction and industry in general" could not be understood to be much more than window-dressing. The conferees, at any rate, vociferously deplored the government's lack of action. "We believe that the trouble is not in our own localities but here in Washington," Mayor James Rolph, Jr., of San Francisco exclaimed in desperation. But the federal government felt otherwise. It had no plans for a comprehensive public works program, and

12. About the positive attitude of the social work profession during the period in question see Chambers, *Seedtime of Reform*, 170–74; 188–94.

114 Hearings on H.R. 1473. At the time, Frederick Law Olmsted, director of the National Housing Association, praised home building as "one of the most economic means of reducing unemployment." Hearings on S. 168, p. 16. – *CR*, 66 Cong., 1 sess., Appendix, 10 July 1919, pp. 8920–22.

115 Howenstine, "Public Works Program," 535; Hearings Pursuant to S.Res. 382, p. 70.

it clearly did not intend to devise any. It knew that it would be able to ride out the postwar disturbance.[116]

When the production index fell during 1921 by almost twenty percentage points, interest in the public works tool revived. On 28 July 1921, Hoover sent a letter to the state governors urging them to let contracts for road building in autumn instead of waiting until the following spring. A month later he prompted Harding to convene the President's Conference on Unemployment. The pressing concern was the emergency at hand. The "General Recommendations" stressed that municipalities ought to coordinate the activities of their private and civic relief agencies; governors ought to expedite state construction programs; a congressional appropriation for road building appeared advisable. On 4 October 1921, Harding announced that Woods had been put in charge of an agency in Washington to promote "appropriate coordination" on the lower levels. But Woods' Committee on Civic Emergency Measures, appended to the Department of Commerce, had no mandate to devise concrete aid. Embodying Hoover's arm's-length approach, its ultimate mandate was, as Hawley has expressed it, to act as "a model of how an associative state should function."[117]

The fact that the conference remained short on decisions for palpable action came under public criticism. "Nowhere did the conference indicate any realization," an observer in the *Survey* remonstrated, "that employment or unemployment in the building industry presented any problem to which the government should attend." Equally unsatisfied was the General Conference of Workers, a group of unemployed in California, which in September 1921 had asked that "an appropriation of $5 billion be made immediately" for highway construction, irrigation, and hydroelectric enterprises. Gompers took issue with the meagerness of the activities envisaged. As governmental public works would not directly intrude into labor relationships, he apparently could reconcile their advocacy with his rigid noninterventionist stance. "Why

---

116 *CR*, 65 Cong., 3 sess., 2 Dec. 1918, p. 7; *New York Times*, 26 Feb. 1919, p. 1; Governors of the States and Mayors of the Cities. Conference with the President of the United States and the Secretary of Labor, *Proceedings, Washington D.C., March 3, 4, and 5, 1919* (Washington: G.P.O., 1919), 214.
117 President's Conference on Unemployment. Committee on Recent Economic Changes, *Recent Economic Changes* 105; "Legislative Notes," *ALLR* 11:3 (Sept. 1921), 189; President's Conference on Unemployment, *Report*, 17–18; 20–21; Ellis W. Hawley, "Herbert Hoover, the Commerce Secretariat, and the Vision of an 'Associative State,' " *Journal of American History* 61:1 (June 1974), 135.

not expenditures on public works *not covered by existing appropriations?*,"
he queried in the *American Federationist*, and went on to outline a
sumptuous program of public improvements that the United States,
"where the public credit is excellent," could undertake in times of
need.[118]

Quasi-Keynesian pronouncements like Gompers', however, could
find no echo in Harding's administration. Woods busied himself for a
while with the production of cheerful circulars and press releases.
Commenting on increased sales of municipal bonds, his office hoped
that they would finance "highways, schools, sewers, filtration plants,
water works, hospitals, parks, forest preserves, bridges, lights, paving,
court houses, fire department and police department equipment,
streets, and sidewalks, beach improvements, and memorial play-
grounds." In January 1922, Harding requested the members of his
cabinet to advance the start of authorized works. This encouragement
produced no results, however, as the funds available were insignificant.[119] The enthusiasm in any event faded soon. Many cities did not
need Woods' admonitions, as they had already begun emergency public works before the President's Conference. It is true that municipal
public works gained somewhat in volume, but the increase owed probably more to such factors as the conservation of borrowing power during the war, rapid urbanization, and the booming automobile industry
than to the exhortations of the Woods agency. About the only tangible
measure taken at the federal level was a highway bill, pending since
April 1921, which was enacted on 9 November 1921 (S. 1072). It appropriated $75 million, to be matched by the states, but little work got
under way before the end of the winter.[120]

118 Chenery, "Mr. Hoover's Hand," 107; H. R. Wright to President [Harding], 30 Sept.
1921, microfilm, reel 210, Harding Papers; Samuel Gompers, "Abolish Unemployment: It Can and Must Be Done; Labor's Remedy," *American Federationist* 29:1 (Jan.
1922), 19; 21–25. Emphasis in the original. See also AFL. 42d Annual Convention,
Proceedings 1922, 72–78, in particular 77.
119 Press release, 8 Nov. 1921, Box 615, Commerce Papers, Hoover Papers; Harding to
Secretary of Commerce, 26 Jan. 1922, *CR*, 67 Cong., 2 sess., 15 Feb. 1922, p. 2593;
Harding to Secretary of War, 26 Jan. 1922, microfilm, reel 210, Harding Papers; Otto
T. Mallery, "The Long-range Planning of Public Works," in President's Conference
on Unemployment. Committee on Unemployment and Business Cycles, *Business Cycles
and Unemployment*, 244.
120 "Unemployment Survey – 1920–21 with Standard Recommendations," *ALLR* 11:3
(Sept. 1921), 207–10; E. Jay Howenstine, Jr., "Public Works Policy in the Twenties,"
Social Research 13:4 (Dec. 1946), 483–84; President's Conference on Unemployment.

Activities at the state level had much in common with the developments on the federal scene. After the war, several states made emergency moves, and advance-planning legislation was enacted here and there, before the prosperity of the mid-twenties put the matter into dormancy. In February 1919 a special reconstruction committee appointed by the Wisconsin legislature recommended that employment be furnished by means of road building, and similar proposals were made by legislative or other public bodies in California, Illinois, New York, Louisiana, and Oregon.[121] Little action resulted. During the economic downturn of 1921 a Massachusetts gubernatorial Committee to Promote Work succeeded in persuading the legislature to appropriate $100,000 for work relief. A like effort was undertaken in New York.[122]

Each time, the business slowdown was too shortlived to test the effectiveness of emergency public works in a valid way. An observer of the Illinois situation remarked that "very little, if anything, was actually done." In Massachusetts, only $60,000 was ultimately expended. The New York resolution was buried in committee. The survey conducted

Committee on Recent Economic Changes, *Planning and Control of Public Works* (New York: National Bureau of Economic Research, 1931), 88; Eugene C. McKean and Harold C. Taylor, *Public Works and Employment from the Local Government Point of View* (Chicago: Public Administrative Service, 1955), 54. For a more detailed elaboration of this point see Udo Sautter, "Government and Unemployment: The Use of Public Works before the New Deal," *Journal of American History* 73:1 (June 1986), 68–69. – Grin, "The Unemployment Conference of 1921," 99; Mallery, "The Long-range Planning of Public Works," 243; [Miss] Sluski to Hunt, 3 June 1922, Box 4, Van Kleeck Papers.

121 "Appointment of State Reconstruction Committees," *MLR* 8:3 (March 1919), 671–72; "Recommendations of California Joint Legislative Committee on Unemployment," *MLR* 8:4 (April 1919), 1092; Earl R. Beckner, *A History of Labor Legislation in Illinois* (Chicago: University of Chicago Press, 1929), 386. The resolution (S.J.R. 11) was effective 6 March 1919; New York (State). Governor Smith's Reconstruction Commission on Business Readjustment and Unemployment, *Report, April 14, 1919* (Albany: J. B. Lyon, 1919), 3; 19–21; International Labour Office, *Unemployment and Public Works* (Geneva, 1931. Studies and Reports, Series C [Employment and Unemployment], no. 15), 61. The Louisiana act was Special Act no. 15. The date of the Oregon memorandum (H.J.M. 12) was 17 Feb. 1919. "Labor Legislation of 1919," *ALLR* 9:4 (Dec. 1919), 443.

122 Leah Hanna Feder, *Unemployment Relief in Periods of Depression: A Study of Measures Adopted in Certain American Cities, 1857 through 1922* (New York: Russell Sage Foundation, 1936), 321; "Labor Legislation of 1922," *ALLR* 12:4 (Dec. 1922), 240; Benjamin Antin to Andrews, 11 March 1921, microfilm, reel 24, Andrews Papers. Antin was the mover of the resolution (7 Feb. 1921). Text of the resolution ibid. – "Plan to Relieve Unemployment by Co-ordinating Public Works," *ALLR* 11:2 (June 1921), 173.

in February 1921 by the Ohio Council on Women and Children in Industry showed that of thirty-five state governments only eleven knew of public works programs undertaken, most of them by municipalities and counties. During the period under consideration, authorities at both the state and federal levels thus took cognizance of the availability of the emergency public works tool, but did not yet seriously examine its usefulness. The reform advance in this respect did not really consist in the advent of governmental action but rather in a change in governmental rhetoric. The latter now revealed, to use Keyssar's words, that "the creation of jobs was implicitly recognized as a legitimate goal of public policy during depressions."[123]

Advance planning

In the eyes of many unemployment reformers, emergency works constituted only a palliative. The ultimate usefulness of the public works tool had to come to the fore when it was utilized through long-range planning. The hubbub of the postwar period did not lend itself to a serious consideration of this idea, but the depression of 1921–22 provided renewed impetus for reflection. Progress was originally impeded by lack of administrative concern and business reluctance. In 1921, Hoover, Cooke knew, was "about ten times as much interested in getting some methods that will [a]ffect the immediate situation than he [was] in longtime procedures." The idea to plan public works in advance in order to execute them when unemployment rose on the other hand very much corresponded to the growing enthusiasm for planning that was developing in some quarters in the 1920s. The issue thus aroused enough attention to sustain the discussion over the following years, and one informed observer was justified in stating at the end of the decade that "much educational work is carried on in behalf of this proposal." By this time, most of the pertinent questions had been clearly identified, and answers had been suggested.[124]

123 Beckner, *Labor Legislation in Illinois*, 386; Klein, *Burden of Unemployment*, 57; "Plan to Relieve Unemployment," 173; Ohio Council on Women and Children in Industry, *Ohio and Unemployment in 1921* (Toledo, 1921), 6–9; Alexander Keyssar, *Out of Work: The First Century of Unemployment in Massachusetts* (Cambridge: Cambridge University Press, 1986), 278.

124 Cooke to Andrews, 12 Sept. 1921, microfilm, reel 24, Andrews Papers. For the growth of the planning idea see Patrick D. Reagan, "Creating the Organizational Nexus for New Deal Planning," in Jerold E. Brown and Patrick D. Reagan, eds., *Voluntarism,*

The advocates of long-range measures came from various quarters. Some were efficiency-minded executives like the Business Men's Group of the New York Society for Ethical Culture who in 1923 agreed upon an "Unemployment Program" containing the demand "that the state should plan long-range public improvements capable of immediate expansion or contraction as the conditions of employment make necessary." Others, like Vernon A. Mund or Frank G. Dickinson, economists at Princeton and the University of Illinois respectively, had their home in academia. Labor frequently also endorsed the idea, obviously understanding that such governmental action did not threaten its independence. The general approval that the building industry gave has already been mentioned earlier. And there were the prominent voices of such freelancers as Mallery or Foster and Catchings, the latter a pair of business-oriented authors advocating public spending to overcome a lack in consumer purchasing power. They all pointed out that public construction constituted a sizable proportion of the total building volume and was the most flexible public expenditure. Although they recognized that the lower levels of government spent far more on construction than the federal administration, they understood that the national government should supply leadership through good example[125] (Table 4–1).

The leverage provided by this tool was considered substantial, not only because of its own size, but even more so because of its impact on the economy at large. Mallery, who had a fondness for expressive similes, thought that public work "is like a pebble dropped into the industrial pond. The waves spread outward in all directions to the farthest shores." The wages earned through the increase of public works in depression times, he asserted at another occasion, would be "sufficient to buy enough blue overalls and black socks to call idle

Planning, and the State: The American Planning Experience, 1914–1946 (New York: Greenwood, 1988), 85–104, in particular 87–95. – William Haber, *Industrial Relations in the Building Industry* (Cambridge, Mass.: Harvard University Press, 1930), 125.
125 "Ethical Culturists Produce Unemployment Program," *ALLR* 13:2 (June 1923), 157; Keyssar, *Out of Work*, 213. On Foster and Catchings see Dorfman, *Economic Mind*, IV, 339–52. At the time employees in the construction industry constituted about 4% of the total work force. See Stanley Lebergott, "Labor Force and Employment, 1800–1960," in National Bureau of Economic Research, ed., *Output, Employment, and Productivity in the United States after 1800* (New York: Columbia University Press, 1966), 110. Lebergott's figures are 5.2% in 1880, 6.5% (1890), 5.7% (1900), 5.2% (1910), 3.0% (1920), 4.1% (1930), 3.3% (1940).

Table 4-1. *Estimated construction volume in the United States (in million $)*

Year	Cities and counties	Percent of total	States	Percent of total	Federal	Percent of total	Total public	Total U.S.	Public percent of total
1915					92		982	4,186	
1916					88		972	4,724	
1917					676		1,563	5,550	
1918					1,659		2,541	6,523	
1919					1,201		2,338	7,785	
1920					302		1,803	8,322	
1921					230		2,078	7,815	
1922					212		2,205	9,193	
1923					216		2,163	10,855	
1924					231		2,495	11,989	
1925	2,061	76	441	15	245	9	2,717	10,805	25
1926	1,978	76	404	16	230	9	2,612	10,912	24
1927	2,367	78	438	14	240	8	3,045	11,153	27
1928	2,251	74	502	17	270	9	3,023	11,339	27
1929	1,895	68	576	21	305	11	2,776	10,492	27
1930	2,204	67	706	21	390	12	3,300	9,250	35
1931	1,631	55	786	27	510	18	2,927	6,888	42
1932	934	45	551	27	580	28	2,065	4,064	51
1933	500	39	300	23	500	38	1,300	2,777	47

Source: U.S. Dept. of Commerce. Bureau of Foreign and Domestic Commerce, *Construction Activity in the United States 1915–37* (Washington: G.P.O., 1938), 24 (for the years 1915–24); Arthur D. Gayer, *Public Works in Prosperity and Depression* (New York: National Bureau of Economic Research, 1935), 298.

textile workers back to their looms and to liquify frozen credits in cotton and wool." Dickinson estimated that during 1919–25 "the volume of public construction was sufficient to have prevented the major portion of factory unemployment if this construction had been properly allocated."[126]

Another advantage frequently stressed was the possible savings to the public purse. Avoiding construction activity in boom periods when prices were high and making use of the cheap tenders obtainable during slow times must keep costs down. Applying the long-range policy would be sound economically, Kenyon opined in 1924, because it would "afford an opportunity for tax reduction." By 1926, Treasury Secretary Mellon thought likewise. Not only would advance planning save money for the taxpayers, he wrote Mallery, but "the wages paid would add to the purchasing power of the country, thus improving the general situation." The supporters of this idea believed that the theoretical questions were solved, and that the delay in implementation was due to political considerations. To Bryce M. Stewart, former director of the Employment Service of Canada, it seemed as early as 1923 that reserving public works for periods of depression was "mainly a question of overcoming budgetary regulations and the inertia of the legislatures." This view was on the whole confirmed in a study undertaken by the ILO pursuant to a resolution adopted at the 1926 International Labour Conference[127] (Figure 4–4).

It is noteworthy that others were more doubtful, however. They pointed to the unreliability of business forecasts, the slowness of public admin-

126 Otto T. Mallery, "Preventing Job Famines," *Survey* 45:15 (8 Jan. 1921), 530; idem, "Unemployment and Public Works," *ALLR* 13:1 (March 1923), 26; idem, "A National Policy," 56; F. G. Dickinson, "Public Construction and Cyclical Unemployment," *Annals* 139 (Sept. 1928), Suppl., pp. i–v; 175–209, esp. 208. The latter article is a reprint of Dickinson's 1927 University of Illinois Ph.D. dissertation (same title). – William Trufant Foster and Wassill Catchings, *The Road to Plenty* (Boston: Houghton Mifflin, 1928); Vernon Arthur Mund, "Prosperity Reserves of Public Works," *Annals* 149 (May 1930), i–iv; 1–49.

127 William S. Kenyon, "A Federal Public Works Policy," *ALLR* (14:2 June 1924), 155. Mellon is quoted in "Legislative Notes," *ALLR* 16:4 (Dec. 1926), 256. – Herbert Stein, *The Fiscal Revolution in America* (Chicago: University of Chicago Press, 1969), 10–12; William J. Barber, *From New Era to New Deal: Herbert Hoover, the Economists, and American Economic Policy, 1921–1933* (Cambridge: Cambridge University Press, 1985), 16–22; Bryce M. Stewart, "The Functions of Public Employment Services and Public Works," *ALLR* 13:1 (March 1923), 61; International Labour Office, *Unemployment and Public Works*, 173.

Figure 4-4. A reserve for a rainy day. (Source: *ALLR* 21:1 [March 1931], 98.)

istrations, financing difficulties, the impossibility of construction delay in many cases, and the danger that withdrawal of public expenditure might hasten a decline in business. To them, careful experimentation was essential before any larger steps could be taken. Only cooperation in a nationwide program could hope for success, as otherwise any area that undertook major works projects in a depression would be swamped by migrating workmen.[128]

The most important impediment, though, originated beyond the realm of economics. As the New York superintendent of public works put it on one occasion, the "pressure of politics is too great to permit holding back work in boom times." And it was not only public pressure that might make delays unadvisable. Office holders were "lukewarm about doing the work necessary to get authorization and funds for a public project," Lewisohn regretfully remarked, "and allow someone else to put it through at some future time." Wesley C. Mitchell, himself sympathetic to experimentation with advance planning, was certainly right in stating that its implementation was "no simple matter, which might be effected offhand by a glimmer of sense and a spice of good will.[129]

Notwithstanding the objections of the doubters, those convinced of the virtue of the planning idea labored hard to make gains on the political scene. Although they achieved no spectacular legislation, as a result of their endeavors significant strides were made in sifting the ground and testing its fertility. Less progress was noticeable in the states than on the federal scene, a reflection of the fact that the national viewpoint was now increasingly gaining acceptance and engendering reform efforts. But some remarkable activities occurred on the lower level as well. In December 1918, Mallery, representing the federal Department of Labor at the reconstruction conference in Annapolis, sounded the clarion call to advance

128 President's Conference on Unemployment. Committee on Recent Economic Changes, *Planning and Control of Public Works*, 159–81; Georg Bielschowsky, "Business Fluctuations and Public Works," *Quarterly Journal of Economics* 44 (Feb. 1930), 286–319; Ralph G. Hurlin, "Use of Public Work in the Treatment of Unemployment," National Conference of Social Work, *Proceedings 1931* (Chicago: University of Chicago Press, 1931), 265–70; Douglas and Director, *Problem of Unemployment*, 208–19. That planning public works has potential to reduce unemployment is clearly denied in Clay J. Anderson, "The Compensatory Theory of Public Works Expenditure," *Journal of Political Economy* 53:3 (Sept. 1945), 258–76. – Stewart, *Unemployment Benefits*, 60.
129 Frederick Stuart Greene during Unemployment Hearings, New York (State) Legislative Assembly, 5 Dec. 1931, microfilm, reel 66, Andrews Papers. See also for the same argument L. W. Wallace to Hunt, 23 May 1923, Box 621, Commerce Papers, Hoover Papers; and B. Seebohm Rowntree, "Some Necessary Steps toward a Solution of the Unemployment Problem," *Political Science Quarterly* 38:2 (June 1923), 197. – Sam A. Lewisohn et al., *Can Business Prevent Unemployment* (New York: Knopf, 1925), 145; Wesley C. Mitchell, "Unemployment and Business Fluctuations," *ALLR* 13:1 (March 1923), 20–21.

when he outlined to the governors the merits of planning legislation and presented to them a standard draft act that he had worked out.[130]

Success eluded Mallery for the time being, as the authorities preferred to deal with the emergency at hand. It did not help that his own creation, the Pennsylvania law of 1917, did not live up to expectations. In the beginning of 1919 he still noted that the state departments had begun "to study the expansion of their public works," but ultimately the law remained largely inoperative because of insufficient appropriations. Although in 1921 unemployment triggered a spending authorization, technical difficulties prevented the immediate expenditure of funds. When they were finally used for road improvements around the capitol in Harrisburg in summer 1922, the depression had subsided. In 1923, as a consequence, Mallery even had the disappointment of seeing the legislature repeal the act.[131]

The Pennsylvania experience, however, did not bar some new planning moves elsewhere. In May 1921 the California legislature, following a suggestion of its 1919 unemployment committee, adopted an act providing for the extension of public works "during periods of extraordinary unemployment caused by temporary industrial depression"; the necessary moneys were to be taken from the state's emergency fund for unforeseen contingencies. The *ALLR* was enthusiastic. "Here is a notable effort, in a year of general legislative reaction," it commented, "to make permanently effective a cardinal principle of unemployment prevention – prevision." Wisconsin followed suit when its legislature passed an almost identical law in 1923. Neither of these measures, though, was put into actual operation during the 1920s.[132]

An attempt at similar legislation was also made in Massachusetts. After the 1920 AFL state convention passed a resolution urging public works planning, the gubernatorial message to the legislature in January 1921 took up the idea. Nothing specific came of this suggestion, but after a

---

130 "Reconstruction Conference of Governors Held at Annapolis, MD., December 16–18, 1918," *MLR* 8:3 (March 1919), 670.
131 Mallery to Andrews, 29 Jan. 1919, microfilm, reel 19, Andrews Papers; Mallery to Andrews, 19 Sept. 1922, microfilm, reel 27, ibid.; "Legislative Notes," *ALLR* 12:3 (Sept. 1922), 144–45; Mund, "Prosperity Reserves of Public Works," 6.
132 "Recommendations of California Joint Legislative Committee on Unemployment," *MLR* 8:4 (April 1919), 1092; 1921 *California Statutes*, c. 246; Mund, "Prosperity Reserves of Public Works," 6; "State Legislation to Plan Public Works against Unemployment," *ALLR* 11:3 (Sept. 1921), 220; 1923 *Wisconsin Laws*, c. 76.

depression-induced unemployment commission reiterated it in early 1923, the AALL assisted in drafting a bill, which was introduced in the legislature in the following year. Andrews and Mallery appeared at the hearings to help it along, and in amended form it passed the lower house. The Senate, however, rejected it. In New York, corresponding efforts got even less far, because a 1919 Reconstruction Commission concluded that the idea of advance planning was of doubtful value. This left California and Wisconsin the only states for the time being to have planning laws on their statute books.[133]

Palpable legislation was not passed on the federal level either, but considerable discussion and legislative effort prepared the terrain for future action. As the war had shown that the federal government was capable of such involvement, and the integration of the economy asked for measures transcending state lines, much of the advocacy of planning legislation now focused on Washington. The President's Conference offered the first usable forum. Despite Hoover's aloofness, Mallery promoted the planning cause as best he could. His membership in the Economic Advisory Committee provided him, in Andrews' words, with "an excellent opportunity to present [the] facts and get good criticism and favorable attention." As a result, the committee recommended long-range public works planning; a central federal agency should advise the president and make corresponding proposals to the states, municipalities, and counties. When the conference's Committee on Public Works held hearings, strong endorsements came from virtually all witnesses, among them Woods, Dennison, and two representatives of the AFL. But the committee remained cautious. It genially acknowledged that federal long-range planning required "no great change from existing procedure" and that the corresponding laws in Pennsylvania and California were "examples of present tendencies," but could not persuade itself to go further than suggesting that the chairman of the conference "be requested to

133 Keyssar, *Out of Work*, 213; "Labor Legislation as Recommended in Governors' Messages," *ALLR* 11:1 (March 1921), 108; Massachusetts. House. Special Commission on Unemployment, Unemployment Compensation, and the Minimum Wage, *Report* (Boston: Wright & Potter, 1923), 34–35; "Unemployment in Massachussetts – Its Cause, Prevention, and Compensation," *MLR* 16:6 (June 1923), 189; "Progress in Public Works Program," *ALLR* 14:2 (June 1924), 159; International Labour Office, *Unemployment and Public Works*, 62; New York (State). Governor Smith's Reconstruction Commission, *Report on a Permanent Unemployment Program, June 17, 1919* (Albany: J. B. Lyon, 1919), 13–15.

consider the advisability of appointing a committee to study methods" of implementing the advance planning scheme.[134]

In this guarded form, the recommendations were adopted by the conference as a whole. Somewhat gratuitously the conferees even professed their conviction that long-range planning, if ever applied, "would not only greatly decrease the depth of depressions but would at the same time diminish the height of booms." Although it seems a trifle exaggerated to claim, as Arthur M. Schlesinger, Jr., has done, that with these suggestions the conference "ventured into new fields," the planning idea had at least been discussed in full view of the public and found potentially meritorious.[135]

Apparently the task was now to make use of what momentum the conference had provided. With the Treasury Department's consent, Mallery immediately prepared a bill that Kenyon introduced on 19 November 1921 (S. 2749). It stipulated that the heads of federal executive departments prepare plans for construction so that work could begin as soon as an appropriation was obtained; the Department of Commerce was instructed to publish monthly reports on business trends. Hunt worked hard behind the scene to get the necessary support during hearings held 21–22 December by the Committee on Education and Labor, of which Kenyon was chairman.[136] Mallery as well as John Mitchell and representatives of the AFL, the United States Chamber of Commerce, and the construction industry made appearances, and the committee reported the bill out favorably. But difficult obstacles remained. During the floor debate, liberal Senator George W. Norris (R-Nebraska) voiced the fear that announcing the start of postponed public works could trigger a depression that otherwise might not have occurred. The conservative side had objections of principle. Senator Thomas Sterling (R-South Dakota) cautioned that the time had not yet come "when we simply appropriate

---

134 Andrews to Mallery, 13 Sept. 1921, microfilm, reel 24, Andrews Papers; Otto T. Mallery, "Preventing Periods of Unemployment by Expanding Public Works," *ALLR* 11:1 (March 1921), 48; President's Conference on Unemployment, *Report*, 97–98; 106–10.

135 President's Conference on Unemployment, *Report*, 160; Arthur M. Schlesinger, Jr., *The Crisis of the Old Order 1919–1933* (Boston: Houghton Mifflin, 1956), 85.

136 Otto T. Mallery, "Memorandum for Secretary Hoover, Colonel [Arthur] Woods, and Mr. Hunt," 17 Nov. [1921], Box 615, Commerce Papers, Hoover Papers; "Memorandum of the Conversation with Under-Secretary of the Treasury Gilbert," 5 Dec. 1921, Box 653, ibid.; Hunt to Leiserson, 23 Nov. 1921, Box 17, Leiserson Papers; Hunt to All Members of the President's Conference on Unemployment, 4 Feb. 1922, microfilm, reel 25, Andrews Papers.

money for the support of the people." A few weeks later his colleague Duncan U. Fletcher (D-Florida) saw a constitutional dimension to the question. The discretion to postpone works, he asserted on the floor of the Senate, "is a very broad power to put into the hands of the Executive," and he declared himself not at all sure "whether it is a safe thing and a wise thing to do."[137]

More hidden considerations may have played a role as well. The Chicago Association of Commerce, it was claimed in Woods' circle, did not like the Kenyon bill, "because they think labor ought to be liquidated after every depression and everything the government does to prevent that is bad . . . they want to either starve or subjugate the unemployed." The principal concern was, however, that the executive branch might behave in a partisan way. To a writer in *Management Engineering* it appeared doubtful in March 1922 that governmental economic prognostics could "be kept free from the influence of politics." He was not alone. The Democrats killed the measure, Mallery complained to Progressive Senator James Couzens (R-Michigan), "apparently because they feared that public works in the Democratic South might be postponed by a Republican administration." Whatever the reasons were, a nullifying amendment was passed. The disappointed Kenyon had the bill sent back to his committee, where it died.[138]

Somewhat more tangible were the results of the investigative efforts in the wake of the conference. The section on public works in *Business Cycles and Unemployment* was written by Mallery, who presented the European and Canadian experiences as supportive of his own scheme. He proposed the setting up of federal highway aid for five-year periods and the advance authorization of a "contingent bond issue" to be sold only during a period of industrial depression. None of his ideas was really new, but their implementation would have spelled a significant departure from the conservative politics of the day. It could thus have not been a surprise that the CUBC in its formal recommendations did not follow him but merely

---

137 Hearings on S. 2749; U. S. Congress. Senate, *Journal*, 67 Cong., 2 sess., p. 34; *CR*, 67 Cong., 2 sess., 15 Feb. 1922, pp. 2587–97, esp. 2588; ibid., 16 Feb. 1922, pp. 2646–58.

138 "Minutes of Colonel Woods' Conference," 12 Dec. 1921, Box 654, Commerce Papers, Hoover Papers. The *Management Engineering* article is quoted in Helen M. Muller, *Government Fund for Unemployment* (New York: H. W. Wilson, 1929), 153. – Mallery to Couzens, 29 March 1922, Box 636, Commerce Papers, Hoover Papers; R. G. Tugwell and E. C. Banfield, "Governmental Planning at Mid-Century," *Journal of Politics* 13:2 (May 1951), 150.

endorsed advance planning in principle, discerning a "need for careful drafting" of any future act. Hoover praised the committee's "constructive suggestions."[139] But not everybody shared his view. "The report is a great disappointment to me," affirmed Meserole, now president of the National Unemployment League, a reform group created in 1922 that advocated the utilization of public works as an unemployment remedy, "it does not seem to deal ... with the suffering and plight of the unemployed.[140]

Those dissatisfied with the CUBC's noncommittal pronouncements had not much reason to be happier with the seasonality committee's submission, in the drafting of which the Division of Building and Housing in the Department of Commerce had played a leading role. The committee recommended extending the building season and stressed that "the efforts to encourage long-range planning of public works deserve the support of the public, legislators, and administrative officials." Further, it would not go. Hoover himself made clear the conceptual framework. "The service that the government can give in these matters," he advised the American Construction Council in May 1925, referring to the problem of seasonality, "lies only in the conduct of its own construction, in the service it can give in investigation of economic fact and provision of adequate statistical services. The problem must mostly be solved by the industries themselves." Government, in other words, should concentrate upon playing an auxiliary role.[141]

139 President's Conference on Unemployment. Committee on Unemployment and Business Cycles, *Business Cycles and Unemployment*, vi (Hoover's preface); xxvii–xxix; 231–61.
140 Meserole to Hunt, 24 April 1923, Box 621, Commerce Papers, Hoover Papers. For members of the executive of the National Unemployment League see U.S. Congress. House. Committee on Labor, *Investigation of Needs of Nation for Public Works to Be Carried on in Periods of Business Depression and Unemployment*. H.Rept. 1684, 67 Cong., 4 sess. (to accompany H.R. 14185; 22 Feb. 1923), 2. On its goals see "Discussion," Academy of Political Science in the City of New York, *Proceedings* 123 (July 1927), 134. – Hearings on H.J.Res. 679, pp. 226–29. Meserole became prominent in the Progressive Party, heading its Finance Committee in the 1924 presidential campaign. Kenneth Campbell MacKay, *The Progressive Movement of 1924* (New York: Octagon, 1966), 149.
141 President's Conference on Unemployment. Committee on Seasonal Operation in the Construction Industries, *Seasonal Operations in the Construction Industries*, 11; "Statement by Secretary Hoover for Meeting of American Construction Council on Elimination of Construction Peaks and Depressions, New York City, May 9, 1925," Box 618, Commerce Papers, Hoover Papers. The council included representatives of the construction industry, the banking and insurance interests, the railroads, labor, and civic authorities.

From 1921 to 1928, total construction volume in the United States more than doubled, increasing steadily.[142] Under these circumstances and given the prevailing intellectual climate, all attempts at pushing long-range public works legislation after the failure of Kenyon's measure had to be an uphill drive. Remarkably, some headway was nevertheless made on occasion. Even though in each case the obstacles proved ultimately too rough to be overcome, the efforts helped to rally interested forces and clarify their thinking.

A good example was provided by the two identical bills (H.R. 14185 and S. 4472) that the National Unemployment League succeeded in getting introduced in Congress in early February 1923. The bills created a commission on unemployment that would determine which roads, afforestation, drainage, and irrigation projects were suitable; it would prepare plans for federal action and obtain the cooperation of state and municipal officials in the planning of their public works. During hearings in mid-February the proposal received support from various labor representatives and Meserole. It was also backed by progressive business as well as AFL president Gompers, who wrote an endorsing letter to the bill's co-sponsor, Representative Frederick N. Zihlman (R-Maryland), himself a union man. But despite a pleading letter by Meserole to Harding, the bill was only half-heartedly supported by Hoover, and in the end failed to pass. So did a repeat bill (S. 2543) a year later. The AALL had intended to bring in a planning bill of its own during the Sixty-eighth Congress, and could have felt encouraged by the knowledge that in Britain "distinguished writers," as a friend put it, did think much of such a measure's potential,[143] but in view of the failure of the National Unemployment League's initiative it decided to bide its time.[144]

Legislation was obviously hard to come by. That there existed still

142 Arthur D. Gayer, *Public Works in Prosperity and Depression* (New York: National Bureau of Economic Research, 1935), 37.

143 The support came from the AFL, the Brotherhood of Railroad Trainmen, the Order of Railway Conductors, and the International Association of Machinists. Hearings on H.R. 14185, pp. 2–17. – Grant A. Scott to Hoover, telegram 10 Feb. 1923, Box 651, Commerce Papers, Hoover Papers. Scott was acting secretary of the Brooklyn Chamber of Commerce. See also Zihlman to Hoover, 26 Feb. 1923, Box 651, Commerce Papers, Hoover Papers. – Gompers to Zihlman, 15 Feb. 1923, in H.Rept. 1684.

144 *CR*, 72 Cong., 1 sess., 23 May 1932, p. 10919 (Sen. Bronson Cutting's statement); Hoover to Zihlman, 27 Feb. 1923, Box 651, Commerce Papers, Hoover Papers; Meserole to Harding, 28 Feb. 1923, microfilm, reel 210, Harding Papers; H.Rept. 1684; Mallery, "Unemployment and Public Works," 28; Rowntree, "Some Necessary Steps," 196.

active, if usually somewhat hidden, opposition came briefly to light in 1923. The promise of a booming economy caused Hoover in mid-March to write an open letter to Harding suggesting that federal departments take it easy with their building projects so as to alleviate the demand on the construction industry. In immediate response, the *Manufacturers' Record* made an emphatic protest against this suggestion on the ground that the secretary of commerce intended to bring down building prices at an inopportune moment.[145]

It is difficult to ascertain Mallery's claim that Hoover's initiative resulted in considerable postponement of public works during 1923 and 1924,[145a] but the idea as such apparently began to take hold of the executive. A partial reason may have been the fact that the Democratic platform in 1924 urged legislation authorizing that "public works be initiated in periods of acute unemployment." President Calvin Coolidge, at any rate, soon publicly professed to be a partisan of the concept. If implemented, he advised the Associated General Contractors of America in an address on 12 January 1925, "the result would be a stabilization and equalization which would moderate the alternations of employment and unemployment."[146]

Advocates of long-range planning legislation could gain much-needed encouragement from such pronouncements, and in 1926 many set their hopes upon a new initiative. When in January of that year a bill was introduced in Congress providing for an appropriation of $150 million for the construction of public buildings over the next six years (H.R. 6559), reformers and various construction interests joined forces in the attempt to have a planning provision incorporated in the act. The chairman of the House Committee on Public Buildings, Richard N. Elliott (R-Indiana), denied their request for a hearing, possibly because the bill as such already met heavy opposition from congressmen concerned that the

145 *New York Times*, 19 March 1923, p. 19; Lewisohn et al., *Can Business Prevent Unemployment*, 127.

145a Howenstine, "Public Works Policy in the Twenties," 488. A similar assertion was made by Edward Eyre Hunt, "Recent Industrial Investigations: Business Cycles and Unemployment," National Conference of Social Work, *Proceedings 1923* (Chicago: University of Chicago Press, 1924), 138.

146 Donald Bruce Johnson, ed., *National Party Platforms*. 2 Vols. (Urbana: University of Illinois Press, rev. ed. 1978), vol. I, 252. The Progressive Party did not mention public works in its 1924 platform, as maintained in Walter La Feber and Richard Polenberg, *The American Century: A History of the United States since the 1890s* (New York: Wiley, 1979), 148. – "President Coolidge Urges Planning of Public Works to Stabilize Employment," *ALLR* 15:1 (March 1925), 51.

long-time feature took authority away from Congress to the advantage of the executive. When the bill had passed the House, some planning advocates, actively supported by Hunt, as a consequence persuaded Senator George W. Pepper (R-Pennsylvania) to present a planning amendment in the Senate. Mallery later claimed that the amendment did not pass due to a misunderstanding on the floor, but the *ALLR* was probably more to the point when it stated that "despite its acceptance 'in principle' of advance planning, the present Administration . . . is not willing to support it in a specific measure."[147]

Pepper's intended amendment had been the first legislative proposal to spell out in concrete terms that a certain economic condition would trigger an immediate move toward executive action aiming at stabilization in the construction field. The thought seemed worth pursuing to the sponsors, and during the subsequent session of Congress they attempted to put a rider on the Department of Agriculture appropriation bill (H.R. 15008). The wording appeared innocuous enough, as it did not provide for any factual appropriation. But the drafters' reserve proved unsuccessful. Despite Mallery's active lobbying, the amendment made no headway.[148]

Tenaciously, Pepper tried a third time, taking the matter immediately to the Senate floor. In mid-February 1927 he introduced a resolution (S.Res. 354) creating a special committee to study the ways and means of utilizing federal construction projects as stabilizing forces. The Committee on Commerce held a hearing. Mallery, Hunt, Andrews, Donald H. Sawyer, executive secretary of the Associated General Contractors of America, and others pleaded in support, and the proposal was reported out favorably. The crowded condition of the calendar during the closing days of the session prevented a vote on it.[149] The fact that not only some

147 Otto T. Mallery, "Principle of Public Works Planning to Stabilize Employment Is Still Up to Congress," *ALLR* 16:3 (Sept. 1926), 237–38; *CR*, 69 Cong., 1 sess., 15 Feb. 1926, pp. 4023–27; 4090. The hearing was requested by the AALL, the American Engineering Council, the American Institute of Architects, and the Associated General Contractors. – Hunt to Leiserson, 20 Feb. 1926, Box 17, Leiserson Papers; Mallery, "Principle of Public Works Planning," 237–38; "Legislative Notes," *ALLR* 16:1 (March 1926), 6.

148 Mallery to Hoover, 16 Dec. 1926, Box 615, Commerce Papers, Hoover Papers. Pepper was not even allowed to submit a supporting brief. "Filibuster Postponed Senate Study of Advance Planning of Public Works to Stabilize Employment," *ALLR* 17:3 (Sept. 1927), 210.

149 "Legislative Notes," *ALLR* 17:1 (March 1927), 5–6; "Filibuster Postponed Senate Study," 210; Wesley L. Jones, "Federal Expenditures and the Construction Industry,"

reformers and a smattering of sympathetic legislators but also a strong business segment had shown interest in the matter, however, augured well for the passage of pertinent legislation at a future occasion.

By the mid-1920s the proponents of the use of public works in the fight against unemployment had not yet achieved the public recognition of their tool that they sought, but they had received enough encouragement to keep them en route. After casting a look at Canadian, British, and German experiences, Lewisohn and his coauthors assessed the situation well enough by declaring that there were "large possibilities in the wise use of public works to alleviate unemployment," but that constitutions needed to be amended, sinking funds to be accumulated, long-time plans to be worked out, and politics to be kept in check. "When this procedure is adopted," they confidently concluded, "effective results in easing of distress will undoubtedly accrue."[150] Their statement summed up the insights gained over the preceding two decades. At the same time, it represented a program.

V   Who needs unemployment insurance?

For and against unemployment insurance

During the war the unemployment insurance question had lain more or less dormant. Characteristic in this respect was the discussion of the subject contained in a book on social insurance published in 1918 by Gurdon R. Miller, a professor of sociology and economics at a Colorado teachers' college. Stating industry's responsibility to care for unemployed workers, he restricted himself to an explanation of the Ghent system.[151]

In the postwar decade it appeared to many reformers that the time for social insurance had come.[152] But unemployment insurance was not advocated with the same fervor as health or old age provision, and it also continued to hold an insignificant place among the proposals to remedy distress caused by lack of work. By definition a long-term measure which could not yield quick benefits after introduction, it looked unimportant

Academy of Political Science in the City of New York, *Proceedings*, 12 (July 1927), 90–91.

150 Lewisohn et al., *Can Business Prevent Unemployment*, 150–51.
151 Gurdon Ransom Miller, *Social Insurance in the United States* (Chicago: McClurg, 1918), 63–104.
152 Chambers, *Seedtime of Reform*, 23.

when reconstruction tasks were to be performed. The same held true in the 1921–22 depression, although this experience provided enough stimulation to keep attention alive in some quarters during the following years. Of special interest in this regard were the implementation of private insurance plans in the textile industry, the initiatives of some independent firms, and the quest for legislation in several states, most notably Wisconsin.

Interest in unemployment insurance was low in the years immediately after the end of hostilities. Kenyon's S.Res. 382 listed as one of ten tasks an inquiry into "the feasibility of a national insurance law against non-employment," but a few negative remarks by Gompers was all that was said of the matter during the ensuing Senate hearings. Another 1919 resolution proposing a similar investigation (H.J.Res. 144) was of no consequence at all. The extensive recommendations of a California legislative unemployment committee, submitted in March of that year, did not contain any reference to unemployment insurance. When New York Governor Smith's reconstruction commission looked for permanent measures against joblessness, it asked Andrews for help; but although it subsequently noted that government-sponsored insurance had been resorted to "in other countries," it saw no virtue in pursuing the matter further until other measures had been tried out.[153]

The reference to "other countries" meant primarily the United Kingdom. The British experience was characterized by an expansion of the workforce coverage and benefit periods beyond actuarial soundness, and from 1921 on, in answer to the resulting financial difficulties, by continuous governmental bailouts. Opponents of unemployment insurance in the United States found in the British development plenty of ammunition for their fight against a compulsory scheme. For advocates of an American measure, on the other hand, it proved disconcerting, because it weakened their public position and raised questions about the proper form of unemployment insurance. The advice offered in 1919 by the International Labour Conference was not much help in this regard. The conferees passed an official recommendation that ILO members establish unemployment insurance programs "either through a government system or through a system of government subventions to associations whose rules

153 Hearings Pursuant to S.Res. 382, p. 17; "Recommendations of California Joint Legislative Committee on Unemployment," 145–47; Robert Moses to Andrews, 10 Feb. 1919, microfilm, reel 19, Andrews Papers; New York (State). Governor Smith's Reconstruction Commission, *Report on a Permanent Unemployment Program*, 15.

provide for the payment of benefits to their unemployed members." This left the field wide open, and the United States was in any case not going to be a member.[154]

Only a few groups attempted to boost interest in insurance possibilities after the war. The *Survey* was first to come out with a proposal. But its unrealistic scheme, which intended to finance an unemployment insurance fund with government moneys originally designated for war production, had no chance to be taken seriously. Jobless insurance appealed also to some ecclesiastical circles. The National Catholic War Council, in its social reconstruction program of 1919, advocated a levy on industry as in the case of workmen's compensation, and the Catholic Bishops' Program endorsed the idea. The Committee on the War and the Religious Outlook, an interdenominational group formed by the Federal Council of the Churches of Christ and the General Wartime Commission of the Churches, went along in a press release of 30 August 1920.[155]

On the whole, however, leadership in the advocacy of governmental involvement was assumed by the AALL and its quarterly. Taking up from where the war interruption had left the campaign, the association, with Andrews at its center, strove to act as a rallying force, encouraging legislative efforts and other promotional work, providing publicity material as best it could, and publishing cheerful articles as well as informational tidbits on the subject. It found some enthusiastic allies in the ranks of various unions and also with a few progressive elements on the employer side. At least one major insurance firm, the Metropolitan Life Insurance Company of New York, also showed a certain attention to the matter. But the endeavor hurt itself against the inertia of the public at large and the dedicated opposition of assorted vested interests.

Even the AALL was slow in warming to the subject. A writer in the December 1918 issue of the *ALLR* thought she could note "a revived

154 Mary Barnett Gilson, *Unemployment Insurance in Great Britain: The National System and Additional Benefit Plans* (New York: Industrial Relations Conselors, 1931), 44–52; 366–68; League of Nations. International Labour Conference, *First Annual Meeting, October 29, 1919–November 29, 1919. Washington, D.C.* (Washington: G.P.O., 1920), 259.

155 N. I. Stone, "Buying Unemployment Insurance Cheap," *Survey* 41:3 (28 Dec. 1918), 399–400; "Social Reconstruction Program of the National Catholic War Council," *MLR* 8:6 (June 1919), 1598; John A. Ryan to Andrews, 16 Dec. 1919, appendix "Social Insurance," microfilm, reel 21, Andrews Papers; undated memo in microfilm, reel 66, ibid.; Joseph M. McShane, *"Sufficiently Radical": Catholicism, Progressivism, and the Bishop's Program of 1919* (Washington: Catholic University of America Press, 1986), 165. The Federal Council of the Churches of Christ had already in May 1919 asked for some form of unemployment insurance. Chambers, *Seedtime of Reform*, 22.

interest" in the issue, and the association's business meeting of that month demanded the "development of plans for social insurance against the contingencies of involuntary unemployment, invalidity and old age." But there seemed to be no urgency in this respect. AALL president and Columbia professor Samuel M. Lindsay, an expert on social legislation, addressed that same meeting on "Next Steps in Social Insurance in the United States" virtually without mentioning the unemployment contingency.[156] It was only when the depression year of 1921 announced itself that more specific consideration was given to the matter. At the meeting of the International Association of Public Employment Services (IAPES) in September 1920 in Ottawa (the former AAPEO then adopted this new name), Andrews drew the attention of his audience to the insurance part of the 1914 *Practical Program*. He happily related that he had "recently" received requests from a number of states for copies of the association's unemployment insurance bill prepared before the war. Over the next years his journal published informative articles and notes on the subject in almost every issue, several pieces being authored by noted experts like Rowntree, Commons, and Dennison. Andrews and Commons also inserted an approving section on unemployment insurance in the 1920 edition of their *Principles of Labor Legislation*.[157]

The going was rough, as the treatment of the insurance question at the President's Conference on Unemployment in fall of 1921 readily proved. The Economic Advisory Committee counted among its number assorted AALL members in addition to Mallery – notably, Andrews,

---

156 Margaret A. Hobbs, "A National Employment Service," *ALLR* 8:4 (Dec. 1918), 292; Samuel McCune Lindsay, "Next Steps in Social Insurance in the United States," *ALLR* 9:1 (March 1919), 107–14. For a progressive establishment voice outside the AALL advocating governmental unemployment insurance action (former New Hampshire governor Robert Bass) see James Wright, *The Progressive Yankees: Republican Reformers in New Hampshire, 1906–1916* (Hanover: University Press of New England, 1987), 159–60.

157 John B. Andrews, "Unemployment Prevention and Insurance," IAPES, *Proceedings 1920*, 96–100. See also Andrew' press statement in "Unemployment," *Survey* 45:7 (13 Nov. 1920), 245; "Report of Work, 1920," *ALLR* 11:1 (March 1921), 115; Dennison Manufacturing Company, Framingham, Massachusetts. Personnel Division, "Plan in Use by an American Industry for Combatting Unemployment," ibid., 53–58; B. Seebohm Rowntree, "Unemployment Compensation an Aid to Economic Security," *ALLR* 11:4 (Dec. 1921), 295–98; John R. Commons, "Unemployment Prevention," *ALLR* 12:1 (March 1922), 16–24; Henry S. Dennison, "Depression Insurance: A Suggestion to Corporations for Reducing Unemployment," ibid., 31–36; John R. Commons and John B. Andrews, *Principles of Labor Legislation* (New York: Harper, 1920), 442–48.

Dennison, Lindsay, Seager, and young economist Leo Wolman. It hedged, though, regarding compulsory insurance schemes; all the reformers were able to insert was a passage stating that "any forms of unemployment insurance which would create an economic motive to regularize employment is [sic] worthy of the most careful consideration." Such hesitancy was in line with the thought of the conference organizer. "In other countries," Hoover asserted with obvious reference to Great Britain, "solution has been had by direct doles to individuals by their government"; he expressed the hope that the conferees could rather find remedies that did not "come within the range of charity." On a less official occasion he would be even more straightforward. "Unemployment insurance in the hands of the government," he was to tell a group of insurers in early 1923, "would bring the disaster of incompetent and vicious encroachment of bureaucracy into the daily life of our people." The promoters of compulsory insurance could thus consider it almost a success that the Advisory Committee's noncommittal pronouncement did find its way into a conference recommendation. In it the future CUBC was requested to examine the potential of the Huber bill, then pending in the Wisconsin legislature, and also of employer insurance programs and trade union out-of-work benefits.[158]

It took much good will to interpret this deferment as a positive step toward the ultimate goal of governmental involvement. Mallery, for one, was willing to see things this way. A month after the conference he wondered whether a bill too hastily passed would not be "necessarily imperfect and resulting in maladministration, waste, and abuse, discredit[ing] unemployment insurance for a long time?" In his opinion it could not be the federal government's task to pioneer legislation in social matters. The example of workmen's compensation taught that states should test the ground. "The federal government must walk," he maintained, "before it can run."[159]

More people actually thought that the federal government should move at a snail's pace, as the recommendations of the CUBC soon revealed.

158 President's Conference on Unemployment, *Report*, 29; 161; 167; "Address of Secretary Hoover, Metropolitan Insurance Managers Banquet, January 27, 1923," Box 615, Commerce Papers, Hoover Papers.
159 Otto T. Mallery, "The Unemployment Conference," *Survey* 47:7 (12 Nov. 1921), 255. See also "Minutes of Colonel Wood's Conference, Dec. 12, 1921, at 10:30 a.m.," Box 654, Commerce Papers, Hoover Papers.

The National Bureau of Economic Research tackled its task gamely enough. Andrews, charged with examining the out-of-work benefits of trade unions, found them inadequate.[160] Wolman, who wrote the part on unemployment insurance, affirmed that the British system had not shown itself unworkable, and that the debate had shifted from cost considerations to criticism of particular features like administrative inefficiency or inadequate rates of contribution. The CUBC itself, however, mindful of Hoover's proctorship, did not honor Andrews' and Wolman's suggestions. In its carefully crafted Recommendation IX it avoided any reference to a governmental role for fear that "solutions which may prove to be fundamentally unsound will be attempted without the benefit of practical experience." All Wolman could do was argue in a postscript that only "the operation of general systems of insurance ... may be expected to furnish the data on which further and more intelligent preventive measures will be based." By this he meant that practical experience could not be obtained without taking the plunge. But the momentum that the 1921–22 depression had given the cause was lost by then and would not be regained for some time to come.[161]

Over the following years the advocacy of unemployment insurance was mainly connected with the campaigns for state legislation, which will briefly be considered later. Otherwise, promoters of the measure could only hope to keep the matter before the public through occasional thrusts. At the end of 1925 the American Economic Association, in conjunction with the AALL, held a roundtable conference in New York on the subject, attended by, among others, Rubinow, Wolman, and Feldman. They understood, as an observer from the Columbia School of Business reported, that unemployment insurance "had passed through the stage of propaganda and speculation, and that it was now pertinent to discuss ways and means, particulary the question of cost." To help this process

160 John B. Andrews, "Trade Union Out-of-Work Benefits," President's Conference on Unemployment. Committee on Unemployment and Business Cycles, *Business Cycles and Unemployment*, 293–301. See also Andrews to Hunt, 26 July 1922, Box 620, Commerce Papers, Hoover Papers; and Donald J. Murphy, "John B. Andrews, the American Association for Labor Legislation, and Unemployment Reform, 1914–1929," in Brown and Reagan, eds., *Voluntarism, Planning, and the State*, 13.

161 Leo Wolman, "Unemployment Insurance," President's Conference on Unemployment. Committee on Unemployment and Business Cycles, *Business Cycles and Unemployment*, 303–41. Recommendation IX in ibid., xxx–xxxi. – Idem, "The Future of Unemployment Insurance," *ALLR* 13:1 (March 1923), 45.

along, Allen B. Forsberg, a Commons student in Wisconsin, came out in 1926 with a collection of articles and bibliographic material in the Debaters' Handbook Series.[162]

The cause also received some faint boosts from a number of unions or employers. After the war, union schemes funded exclusively by workers' contributions did not expand in a significant way. David P. Smelser, a student of the subject, discerned as reasons the unwillingness of union members to pay sufficiently high dues and a lack of administrative expertise in the union offices. But the stagnation in the development of such plans was not indicative of an absolute absence of interest on the part of labor. It is true that quests for government involvement still ran counter to the considered policy of the AFL. When delegates from the International Association of Machinists at the Denver convention in June 1921 moved a resolution asking for federal public works and unemployment insurance legislation, the committee on resolutions struck out the insurance part. Gompers explained that this was done to ensure that "the working people of the country [do not] place themselves under the guardianship of the government." In September, William Green, then still secretary of the United Mine Workers of America, informed Andrews that pushing unemployment insurance would "divert from concentration upon the other two important social justice purposes" – health insurance and old age pensions.[163] The very fact, however, that employees' contributions alone could apparently not provide adequate funding led in some of the more radical unions to a quest for legislation or, as was the case in the textile industry, to experiments with employer participation.

Union demands for governmental involvement could be noted throughout the period. As early as 1919 the United Cloth, Hat, and Cap Makers of America sent a petition to the New York legislature and to Congress "that state and federal laws be enacted, extending the principles of accident insurance to the hazards of . . . unemployment." At the President's

---

162 Ralph H. Blanchard, "Rates for Unemployment Insurance: Report of a Round Table Conference," *ALLR* 16:1 (March 1926), 57; Allen Bennett Forsberg, ed., *Unemployment Insurance* (New York: H. W. Wilson, 1926).

163 Andrews, "Trade Union Out-of-Work Benefits," 295–98; Stewart, *Unemployment Benefits*, 85–94; National Industrial Conference Board, *Unemployment Insurance in Theory and Practice* (New York: Century, 1922), 18; D. P. Smelser, *Unemployment and Trade Unions* (Baltimore: Johns Hopkins University Press, 1919), 146; AFL. 41st Annual Convention, *Proceedings 1921*, 212–13; 375–78. Quotation p. 377. – Andrews to Green, 2 Sept. 1921, microfilm, reel 24, Andrews Papers; Green to Andrews, 9 Sept. 1921, ibid.

Conference in 1921, John L. Lewis, president of the Mine Workers, saw fit to call for federal legislation requiring individuals and corporations engaged in interstate commerce to build an unemployment reserve fund. "We are for unemployment insurance, payable by the employing class," applauded the *Illinois Miner*, "for the same reason that we do not suffer a horse owner to turn his animals out on the street the minute they are no longer needed." In early 1925 the Illinois State Federation of Labor's immediate legislative program demanded the passage of a bill for unemployment insurance. A mass meeting in Oakland in the spring of that year sent a petition for the enactment of unemployment insurance to the California legislature. In 1926 the Brotherhood of Locomotive Engineers investigated the possibilities of such insurance, and the Michigan State Federation of Labor considered pressing for corresponding legislation.[164]

A special kind of experiment was undertaken by several unions in the textile industry. By 1920, about 85 percent of the textile work force was controlled by the Amalgamated Clothing Workers of America (ACWA). Spurned on by the experience of the 1921 depression, the ACWA, under its president Sidney Hillman and with the expert guidance of Wolman, who headed its research department, developed the so-called Chicago Plan, which provided for a joint fund to be accumulated through equal employer and employee contributions. This plan was adopted by the Chicago textile industry in 1924, with fund chairman Commons, Leiserson, and Bryce M. Stewart, then head of the ACWA employment office, playing a major role during the initial phase. Benefit payments started in 1924, and the example was followed by ACWA locals elsewhere, notably in Rochester and New York. Other workers' organizations in the needle trades, such as the International Ladies' Garment Workers' Union and the International Fur Workers, also concluded joint agreements with their employers. The plans were not overly successful, but the publicity created by the various ventures served to keep the unemployment insurance issue in the public consciousness. The obvious insufficiency of the arrangements rendered it clear over time that little short of governmental intervention could bring improvement.[165]

164 M. Zuckerman to Andrews, 7 June 1919, microfilm, reel 20, Andrews Papers; Philip Murray, "Unemployment in the Coal Industry," *ALLR* 12:1 (March 1922), 40. *Illinois Miner* is quoted in "Legislative Notes," *ALLR* 14:4 (Dec. 1924), 266. – "Legislative Notes," *ALLR* 15:1 (March 1925), 8; "Legislative Notes," *ALLR* 15:2 (June 1925), 84; "Legislative Notes," *ALLR* 16:2 (June 1926), 126.
165 Commons to Leiserson, 20 Sept. 1923, Box 9, Leiserson Papers. It may be noted that

The same held true of several programs in which progressive employers provided the funding of unemployment benefits exclusively out of their own profits. The lead was taken by Dennison, whose company initiated the first such plan in North America in 1916. Payments between 1920 and 1922 amounted to $23,000, and over the next seven years $57,000 was disbursed. The Leeds and Northrup Company of Philadelphia showed that the scheme also fitted the metal trade. In 1922 the S. C. Johnson Company of Racine, Wisconsin, a wax manufacturer, started a plan that provided for company and employee contributions. Like the two others mentioned, it lasted into the depression of the 1930s, in contrast to scattered attempts elsewhere that were soon abandoned.[166]

Such programs, although they were not yet groundbreaking in any concrete sense, caused publicity that helped keep the interest in unemployment insurance alive. On the whole, however, the advocates of jobless benefits were certainly still a minority. The fact that legislation did not come easily was probably due in large measure to the general inertia of the public. During the prosperous years of the decade it did not see much reason to engage in the initiation of a little tried and potentially expensive welfare undertaking. Progress of the concept, moreover, hurt itself against the bitter opposition of most employers and the indifference of the AFL. The vast majority of businessmen were appalled at the cost and paternalism that they feared would come with the introduction of the British experiment on American soil. "The information is that [the] effect [of unemployment insurance abroad] has been to reduce industrial efficiency and promote idleness and fraud," a special committee composed of representatives of blue-ribbon companies concluded in March 1921. This concern was voiced as early as 1919 by President Wilson's Industrial Conference, which urged the development of methods "suitable to our industrial fabric and consonant with American institutions."[167]

Congressman Meyer London, who had introduced the first unemployment insurance bill in Congress in 1916 (H. J. Res. 159; see page 118), served as legal counsel of the ACWA at the time. – Matthew Josephson, *Sidney Hillman: Statesman of American Labor* (Garden City, N.Y.: Doubleday, 1952), 252–55; 300; 342; Nelson, *Unemployment Insurance*, 79–103.

166 Nelson, *Unemployment Insurance*, 50–56; Morris E. Leeds, "An Unemployment Insurance Fund for Skilled Employees," *ALLR* 14:1 (March 1924), 132–33. A summary description of the company plans existing up to 1933 is found in William Haber and Merrill G. Murray, *Unemployment Insurance in the American Economy: An Historical Review and Analysis* (Homewood, Ill.: Irwin, 1966), 63–65.

167 "Supplement to the Report of the Special Conference Committee," n.d. [March 1921], Box 665, Commerce Papers, Hoover Papers. Committee members represented Du

There also existed a specific apprehension. "The chief objection by employers to unemployment insurance," wrote Draper, personally in favor of such insurance, in the *New York Times* shortly before the President's Conference, "is that it adds one more burden to overhead expense." Robert J. Caldwell, a Connecticut cotton fabrics manufacturer and executive member of the AALL, got an inkling of this attitude when in early 1920 he "desperately" but unsuccessfully tried, as Andrews remembered later, to get some of the leaders of the Republican party, of which he was "a very active member," to interest themselves in unemployment insurance.[168] It was clearly this conservative reluctance that caused the President's Conference and its follow-up committees to bestow so little attention on the issue. When the National Industrial Conference Board, prompted by the 1921 depression, published a research report in June 1922, it gave vent to the same feelings. It pointed to the "enormous expense" that an actuarially sound insurance system would demand and the "gigantic" administrative problems presented by a nationwide operation, especially because of constitutional requirements for forty-eight separate kinds of legislation.[169]

Surprisingly enough – or perhaps not altogether so – in this instance the employers received solid support from the AFL. Even though some regional or local unions felt that compulsory unemployment insurance might offer advantages, AFL president Gompers adamantly opposed any governmental sponsorship. When asked by Kenyon in early 1919 what he thought of the insurance idea, he answered that he objected "to leaving it within the power of the government or its agent or agents to determine what was nonemployment." Louis S. Reed later observed that the AFL president's anti-political leaning in his last years became "a veritable obsession . . . a sort of governmental nihilism." In Gompers' view, at any rate, workers should be paid sufficiently well so as to allow provision for

Pont de Nemours, General Electric, Standard Oil, Westinghouse, Bethlehem Steel, International Harvester, General Motors, Goodyear, and Irving National Bank. – U.S. Dept. of Labor, *8th Annual Report, 1920*, 267.

168 Ernest G. Draper, "To Reduce Unemployment: Individuals, the State and Insurance Legislation Can Help," *New York Times*, 11 Sept. 1921, p. 9. See also Nelson, *Unemployment Insurance*, 30. – Andrews to Commons, 9 March 1921, microfilm, reel 24, Andrews Papers.

169 National Industrial Conference Board, *Unemployment Insurance*, 101–02. The force of the interstate competition argument as a time-honored device to obviate social legislation in other spheres such as factory inspection or child labor is treated in William Graebner, "Federalism in the Progressive Era: A Structural Interpretation of Reform," *Journal of American History* 64:2 (Sept. 1977), 331–57.

times of idleness. His stand against unemployment insurance was thus in line with the larger strategy of keeping out of the political arena, which dictated the AFL's behavior regarding workmen's compensation, old age pensions, or health insurance. "As I live, upon the honor of a man," Gompers at one time declared, "I would rather help...a revolution against compulsory insurance and regulation than submit."[170]

Implementation attempts in the states

In view of the circumstances described, it is almost astonishing that in the decade under consideration several efforts were made, one of them in a rather serious and sustained manner, to get unemployment insurance legislation on the statute books. Their failure was probably preordained, but the ground preparation that they furnished, especially in the Wisconsin case, facilitated later enactment. One attempt that followed the prewar Massachusetts precedent occurred in New York, where on 21 February 1921 Assemblyman Samuel Orr, a socialist from the Bronx, introduced a bill establishing a social insurance system benefiting workers. This proposal, which remained unsuccessful, could be termed traditional in the sense that it took up the British scheme as reflected in the 1916 Massachusetts bill.[171]

Of considerably greater significance for the debate in the 1920s was a bill different in intention as well as method that was introduced in the same month in the Wisconsin legislature. The driving force behind it was Commons, whose interest in workmen's compensation had already before the war led him to develop his theory of "prevention." The fundamental principle of the British unemployment insurance system was distress alleviation – employers' payments into the insurance fund were graded by industries, and employee contributions were mandatory. Commons, however, who saw this system as "philanthropic and paternalistic in character," believed that there existed a possibility of prevention by providing an

---

170 For the socialist or progressive opposition to the official stand in the unemployment insurance question see James O. Morris, *Conflict within the AFL: The Study of Craft versus Industrial Unionism, 1901–1938* (Ithaca, N.Y.: Cornell University Press, 1958), 43–44; 105. – Hearings Pursuant to S.Res. 382, p. 17; Louis S. Reed, *The Labor Philosophy of Samuel Gompers* (New York: Columbia University Press, 1930), 47. See also Philip Taft, *The A.F. of L. in the Time of Gompers* (New York: Harper, 1957), 365–66. Gompers is quoted in Harold C. Livesay, *Samuel Gompers and Organized Labor in America* (Boston: Little, Brown, 1978), 135.

171 *New York Times*, 22 Feb. 1921, p. 2; Stewart, *Unemployment Benefits*, 577.

inducement for employers to keep their payrolls intact. By adjusting the compulsory payments of employers according to their individual employment record, their interest in stable conditions could be kept alive. Commons thought that the same behavioral pattern as in the case of workmen's compensation would evolve. "Employers under a law of this kind will organize their employment and labor departments as effectively as they have their safety departments," he predicted, hoping moreover that the liability that employers incurred when laying men off would prevent them from overexpanding in busy periods.[172]

Even in reform circles, Commons' idea was not accepted all at once. Edwin E. Witte, at the time secretary of Wisconsin's industrial commission, strongly felt that prevention should not be considered the only motivation, but that unemployment insurance "is a proposal for a sharing of ... losses on a more equitable basis than the present system." Union leaders with whom Commons conferred in summer 1920, on the other hand, had no difficulties with the preventive idea, but objected to employees' contributions. In their opinion, a larger burden on the employers would strengthen the stabilizing intentions. Commons found this argument convincing, and subsequent legislative proposals in Wisconsin contained no provisions for payments by employees.[173]

State Senator Henry Allen Huber, a Progressive Republican, agreed to present a resulting bill in the legislature on 4 February 1921. The measure provided for unemployment benefits paid out of mutual insurance funds established by employers. Over the following months, Commons and various allies, including the *ALLR*, mounted an intensive publicity campaign. But the entire effort proved unrewarding. Resistance put up by the Wisconsin Manufacturers' Association (WMA) and likeminded circles kept the bill from being seriously acted upon. Some inroad on public opinion was made, however. In a post-mortem the conservative *Wisconsin State Journal* commented that the defeat of the Huber bill was "a bit of history that may be reviewed with regret at a later date," because the United States was "nearing a time in which society will discountenance

---

172 "Abstract of Address by Professor John R. Commons at Meeting of the Section on Economic and Industrial Problems, National Conference of Social Work, Milwaukee, June 25, 1921, 11 a.m.," microfilm, reel 66, Andrews Papers.

173 Witte to Commons, 2 July 1921, Box 1, Witte Papers; Andrews to J. J. Handley, 24 Sept. 1920, microfilm, reel 22, Andrews Papers. Handley was secretary-treasurer of the Wisconsin State Federation of Labor. – Charles A. Myers, "Employment Stabilization and the Wisconsin Act" (University of Chicago Ph.D., 1939), 20, note 2.

a system under which men willing and able to work must suffer with their families because of unemployment."[174]

The publicity surrounding the introduction of the Huber bill resulted in parallel efforts in two other states. The Pennsylvania State Federation of Labor, together with the Women's Trade Union League of Philadelphia, asked the AALL for help in drafting a bill. The Eastern Consumers' League added its backing. The resulting proposal narrowly followed the Wisconsin model except for the facilitating provision that insurance could be placed with any authorized carrier. Introduced in the House on 21 March 1921, it was immediately stalled, not to the surprise of its sponsors. "We have no chance to enact the bill into law at this session," the head of the Women's League had written to Andrews a few days before the bill's introduction, hoping that with the advent of "a more favorabl[e] legislature, we will have this sentiment to build on."[175] A similar proposal introduced in the Massachusetts General Court at the depth of the unemployment winter of 1922 was also submitted very much for the record only, as by the early 1920s the progressive mood noticeable in the legislature before the war had been replaced by more conservative attitudes favoring the "neutral state." At the instigation of Andrews, Republican assemblyman Henry L. Shattuck, a prominent Boston attorney and member of the AALL, offered a bill on 5 January drafted along the lines of the Wisconsin measure. It was referred to the Special Commission on Unemployment, but when the latter presented its report on 9 February 1923, the extraordinary unemployment of the depression had passed, and public interest had abated.[176]

---

174 Nelson, *Unemployment Insurance*, 110–11; Commons to Andrews, 16 March 1921, microfilm, reel 24, Andrews Papers; "American Legislation on Unemployment Compensation," *ALLR* 11:1 (March 1921), 59. Andrews worked actively to find support for the bill. Andrews to R. J. Caldwell, 7 March 1921, microfilm, reel 24, Andrews Papers; Andrews to Commons, 9 March 1921, ibid. – Stewart, *Unemployment Benefits*, 579–80; Andrews to Commons, 9 March 1921, microfilm, reel 24, Andrews Papers; Commons to Andrews, 16 March 1921, ibid.; *Wisconsin State Journal* is quoted in "Legislative Notes," *ALLR* 11:3 (Sept. 1921), 183.

175 Frieda S. Miller to Andrews, 9 March 1921, microfilm, reel 24, Andrews Papers; Andrews to Miller, 17 March 1921, ibid.; Stewart, *Unemployment Benefits*, 577; Nelson, *Unemployment Insurance*, 72.

176 J. Joseph Hutmacher, *Massachusetts People and Politics 1919–1933* (Cambridge, Mass.: Belknap Press, 1959), 60–61; Andrews to Meeker, 16 Feb. 1922, microfilm, reel 26, Andrews Papers. The bill was H. 278. See in this context Henry L. Shattuck, "Unemployment Insurance Legislation in Massachusetts," *ALLR* 12:1 (March 1922), 49; Keyssar, *Out of Work*, 214–15; Massachusetts. House. Special Commission on Un-

The first round of attempts at securing passage of unemployment insurance legislation thus ended without tangible results. The fact that even
the depression of 1921–22 with its widespread joblessness did not provide
the legislators sufficient incentive showed the strength of the opposing
forces and did not bode well for the ensuing years of greater prosperity.
The matter was not dead, however. After the failure of the Shattuck bill,
the *New Bedford Standard* optimistically commented that "legislation of
some kind, aimed at the prevention of unemployment, will appear year
after year until action is taken."[177] The paper was right, as in several
states reformers kept the subject under discussion, even though success
in legislative terms remained beyond hope for the time being.

Again the most sustained effort occurred in Wisconsin, where Huber
introduced a modified version of his bill on 25 January 1923. The adversaries stood solid, however. As Huber drearily wrote Leiserson, "businessmen of the 'proprietorship' school vehemently" opposed his bill. It
failed, as did a substitute measure calling for a study of unemployment
legislation.[178] Commons at least had the consolation of seeing his efforts
recognized abroad. In September 1923 at its meeting in Luxemburg the
IAU adopted a resolution drawing attention to his Wisconsin proposals.
But this was of no great value on the American scene. When the 1925
legislative session came around, Huber had quit his senate seat to become
lieutenant-governor. In his stead, State Senator Max Heck from Racine
presented a bill on 3 February that closely resembled that of 1923. The
constellation of supporters and opponents had not changed, and the senate
again voted for indefinite postponement. Undeterred, Assemblyman William Coleman, a Milwaukee socialist, introduced a similar proposal on 1
March 1927. Although organized labor endorsed it, its unenthusiastic
support was too weak to persuade the assembly. A repeat bill in 1929
suffered the same fate.[179]

employment, Unemployment Compensation, and the Minimum Wage, *Report*, 44–45;
Stewart, *Unemployment Benefits*, 575–77.
177 Quoted in "Legislative Notes," *ALLR* 12:2 (June 1922), 96.
178 Nelson, *Unemployment Insurance*, 113–14; National Industrial Conference Board, *Un-
employment Insurance*, 105–20; "Legislative Notes," *ALLR* 13:1 (March 1923), 7; 9;
Huber to Leiserson, 16 March 1923, Box 42, Leiserson Papers; Stewart, *Unemployment
Benefits*, 580; Witte to Andrews, 14 July 1923, microfilm, reel 26, Andrews Papers.
179 "International Labor Legislation," *ALLR* 13:4 (Dec. 1923), 265; Herbert F. Johnson,
"Unemployment Compensation Legislation to Check Over-Expansion," *ALLR* 15:3
(Sept. 1925), 223; "Legislative Notes," *ALLR* 15:2 (June 1925), 77; Stewart, *Unem-
ployment Benefits*, 580; Nelson, *Unemployment Insurance*, 118. The 1929 bill was introduced by Robert Nixon.

The Wisconsin bills, helped by Commons' strong presence especially in the early years, went farthest of any unemployment insurance proposals in the United States in the 1920s and gave the cause the most exposure, arousing interest well beyond the state borders. Attempts elsewhere helped to keep the debate going. In 1922, Democratic gubernatorial candidate John F. Fitzgerald promised to recommend unemployment insurance legislation in Massachusetts, but he was not elected. The matter went a step further in New York. In January 1923, Hoover suggested at a dinner of the Metropolitan, with whom Bruère served as a vice-president, that private insurers might consider underwriting unemployment insurance. In May, at the annual meeting of the Actuarial Society of America, the Metropolitan's actuary indicated his company's interest, and in the following year the insurer attempted to secure pertinent legislation. State Senator J. A. Hastings, a Democrat from Brooklyn, introduced the bill on 28 February 1924. But after a letter from Gompers was read at a public hearing in which he claimed that such insurance was a shrewd move to lower wages, no further action was taken. To keep the issue alive, on 30 December 1925 the AALL in conjunction with the American Economic Association organized the roundtable already mentioned, where a spokesman for the Metropolitan again stated his company's readiness to move. Democratic Assemblyman Louis A. Cuvillier consequently introduced several bills in 1926 and 1927, but all failed to pass.[180]

In Minnesota, unemployment insurance bills were introduced in the legislative sessions of 1923, 1925, and 1927. Virtual copies of the Huber proposal, they were endorsed by the State Federation of Labor and the AALL. The senate committee on workmen's compensation reported the

---

180 Fitzgerald is quoted in "Legislative Notes," *ALLR* 12:3 (Sept. 1922), 143. – *New York Times*, 23 Jan. 1923, p. 15; ibid., 18 May 1923, p. 33; ibid., 29 Feb. 1924, p. 19. Bruère had long been involved in social welfare causes. In 1918 he directed the New York (State) division of the USES. See on him the obituary in *New York Times*, 19 Feb. 1958, p. 27; and the editorial ibid., 20 Feb. 1958, p. 24. – "Gains of the Past Year in Combating Unemployment in the United States," *ALLR* 14:1 (March 1924), 165; Blanchard, "Rates for Unemployment Insurance," 57; Stewart, *Unemployment Benefits*, 577; "Legislative Notes," *ALLR* 16:1 (March 1926), 11. Vaughn Davis Bornet, "Herbert Hoover's Planning for Unemployment and Old Age Insurance Coverage, 1921–1933," in John N. Schacht, ed., *The Quest for Security: Papers on the Origins and the Future of the American Social Insurance System* (Iowa City: Center for the Study of the Recent History of the United States, 1982), 35–43, though somewhat spotty, provides further detail on the New York (State) experience.

bills back each time, but they did not make headway. A replica of the Wisconsin proposal, sponsored by the Socialist Party, was also introduced on 26 January 1927 in the Connecticut legislature. House and senate rejected the measure, as they did another bill in 1929.[181]

Superficially seen, the insurance cause on the eve of the Great Depression was thus barely further advanced than it had been a decade earlier. The discussion had mostly dealt with questions concerning the benefits to the individual, whereas the macroeconomic impact of insurance premiums and payments had seldom been touched upon as yet. But as later developments proved, some considerable terrain had been gained nonetheless, if only in an incremental way. The various legislative attempts in particular had not been undertaken fully in vain. The endeavors forced the insurance proponents to formulate their plans and to assess the technical requirements and possibilities of a viable program. This, moreover, instructed them regarding the arguments of the political opposition and the tactics it would use. Although subsequently the early phase of the Great Depression, asking for emergency measures, was not going to see an immediate and successful push profiting from the experience gained in the 1920s, it was to prove that the ultimate goal of unemployment reform had to be the institution of a nationwide insurance scheme. The knowledge accumulated in the period just considered came in handily when the implementation drive was seriously on.

An earlier chapter demonstrated that the decades up to World War I have to be viewed as the seedtime of unemployment reform. Staying with that image, the years between the war and the onset of the Great Depression may be called the period of germination or incubation. No new practical concepts came to the fore, but the ideas that had emerged before the war were further tested for their endurance and performance value. The adverse political climate of these years had its beneficial side in that it checked conceptual fancifulness, forcing reformers and sympathetic politicians constantly to reevaluate their proposals regarding technical realism and political viability. As a result, a degree of sophistication was reached in the understanding of counting procedures, of the establishment of a national exchange system, of the use of public works, and of the

---

181 "Legislative Notes," *ALLR* 13:1 (March 1923), 13; "Legislative Notes," *ALLR* 13:2 (June 1923), 103; Stewart, *Unemployment Benefits*, 574; 577; "Legislative Notes," *ALLR* 17:1 (March 1927), 8.

exigencies of unemployment insurance, by comparison with which the knowledge available by World War I could at best be seen as crude. On the eve of the depression, the advocates of reform knew what they had to ask for.

5. Accepting the task: 1928–1933

Pre-New Deal unemployment reform entered its last phase with the onset of the Great Depression. Increasing joblessness actually attracted the attention of labor scene observers already two years prior to the Wall Street disaster, and reformers attempted to respond accordingly. But it was the sharp rise in unemployment in the wake of the stock market crash that justified their exertions in the eyes of a growingly sympathetic public. State governments, their relief responsibility long-since established, now began seriously to grope for solutions. Their efforts to fight from the state house a catastrophe of at least national scope remained highly unrewarding. As a consequence the federal administration had ultimately to overcome its well-considered reluctance to move conspicuously and in a definite manner. It had implicitly recognized its essential responsibility as early as 1921 by organizing the President's Conference. Grudgingly, but step by step, it now followed through by translating this acknowledgment into deeds.

In the process, all remedial measures that had been conceived before World War I were now fully tested on the federal level. The first area to witness substantial federal commitment was counting. The extension of the Department of Labor's statistical services and the 1930 census inquiry were honest efforts; their inadequacy resulted from their technical limitations, not from a lack of federal good will. Somewhat less fervent, but still recognizable, was the Hoover administration's readiness to put a long-range planning bill on the statute books. The resulting Federal Employment Stabilization Act had with the counting ventures in common that neither required immediate follow-up action. The time for tokenism was running out, however. By spring 1931 the Department of Labor thus began to reorganize the USES. As this move did not produce satisfactory results, a year later the federal government took the ultimate step of providing funds for relief works and even for the dispensation of direct relief. The adoption of the ERCA set the precedent that opened the way for the larger measures of the New Deal.

I   From prosperity to depression

Rising unemployment

Signs that unemployment was again on the rise began to appear many months before the stock market crash of October 1929. In 1927 the AFL believed it timely to hold two unemployment conferences, and in September of that year it started among its members another nationwide monthly survey of the employment situation. The *ALLR*, ever alert to labor's difficulties, took care to warn in December 1927 that indications of a steady increase in unemployment were multiplying even though the federal administration would not admit it. In March 1928 the *American Federationist* resumed publishing monthly unemployment estimates. In the same month, Governor Smith ordered a study of unemployment in New York.[1] By February 1928 the daily press, notably the *New York Times*, the *New York World*, and the *Washington Star*, showed considerable concern, and periodicals like the *New Republic* and the *Survey* gave alarm.[2] Hiring rates in the manufacturing sector were conspicuously down in 1927 and

---

1 AFL. 48th Annual Convention, *Proceedings 1928*, 42; Spencer Miller, Jr., "The Unemployment Conference," *American Federationist* 34:9 (Sept. 1927), 1050; "Legislative Notes," *ALLR* 17:4 (Dec. 1927), 253. See also John B. Andrews, "Increasing Unemployment Calls for Adoption of Constructive Program of Relief and Prevention," *ALLR* 18:1 (March 1928), 65–75. For the method of compilation of these union statistics see "Unemployment Statistics," *American Federationist* 35:3 (March 1928), 329. – *Commercial and Financial Chronicle*, 3 March 1928, pp. 1268–69.

2 For various newspaper articles see *CR*, 70 Cong., 1 sess., 21 Feb. 1928, pp. 3321–23. – Sumner H. Slichter, "The Price of Industrial Progress," *New Republic* 53:688 (8 Feb. 1928), 316–18; Leo Wolman, "Shadows of Prosperity," *Survey* 59:11 (March 1928), 677–78; Beulah Amidon, "Is Unemployment Here?" ibid., 679–81; 721–22. See also "President Thomas F. McMahon's Address at Unemployment Conference at Passaic, New Jersey," memorandum, 5 Feb. 1928, Box 189, Chief Clerk's Files, General Records of the Dept. of Labor. McMahon was president of the United Textile Workers. In April 1928 the National Federation of Settlements sponsored an unemployment study headed by Helen Hall; it was published by Clinch Calkins, *Some Folks Won't Work* (New York: Harcourt Brace, 1930). See also Helen Hall, "Introducing Our Neighbors," in National Federation of Settlements. Unemployment Committee, *Case Studies in Unemployment* (Philadelphia: University of Pennsylvania Press, 1931), xxiii–1; and Elizabeth S. Magee, "Ohio Takes Stock," National Conference of Social Work, *Proceedings 1932*, 285. For a general assessment of the situation see Margaret D. Meyer, "What about Unemployment?" *ALLR* 18:2 (June 1928), 153–62.

1928 compared with the preceding years, whereas layoff rates were up. Zieger has thus been justified in remarking that Hoover's claim in August 1928 that "unemployment in the sense of distress is widely disappearing" was simply not true. In early 1929, on the contrary, relief agencies in thirty out of thirty-six communities polled by the *Survey* reported that the relief burden had markedly increased over the previous year because of swelling unemployment.[3]

Expert opinion differed as to the main cause of the deterioration, but there was a growing consensus that "technological" joblessness, due to the progress of labor-saving machinery, played an important role. Commons/Andrews had not yet shown any concern in this regard in their 1920 edition of *Principles of Labor Legislation*, and the problem had barely been mentioned at the President's Conference in 1921 and in the related publications. Over the subsequent years, however, discussion had increased. In 1926, Barnett published sample studies showing some effects of machine use upon the need for labor. In his reports for 1927 and 1928, USES Director General Jones noted "considerable unemployment," which he partially blamed on "the new methods and devices" in production. The federal Bureau of Labor Statistics thought the assumption not unreasonable that as much as half of the labor surplus was due to technological improvements.[4] The lack of pertinent data rendered any definite conclusions unattainable, but by the end of the decade observers were convinced that the problem had reached serious proportions[5] (Figure 5–1).

3 For hiring and layoff rates see chart 4, President's Conference on Unemployment. Committee on Recent Economic Changes, *Recent Economic Changes in the United States* (New York: McGraw-Hill, 1929), 465. – Robert H. Zieger, *Republicans and Labor 1919–1929* (Lexington: University of Kentucky Press, 1969), 250; Beulah Amidon, "Relief and Unemployment," *Survey* 63:8 (15 Jan. 1930), 456.

4 George E. Barnett, *Chapters on Machinery and Labor* (Cambridge, Mass.: Harvard University Press, 1926); U.S. Dept. of Labor, *15th Annual Report, 1927*, 31; idem, *16th Annual Report, 1928*, 125; "Unemployment in the United States: Report of the Secretary of Labor," *MLR* 26:4 (April 1928), 31.

5 B. M. Squires, "Unemployment—Discussion," *American Economic Review* 19:1 (March 1929), Suppl., 35; Isador Lubin, "Measuring the Labor Absorbing Power of American Industry," American Statistical Association, *Journal* 24 (1929), Suppl., 27–32. See also David Weintraub, "The Displacement of Workers through Increases in Efficiency and Their Absorption by Industry, 1920–1931," ibid., 27:180 (Dec. 1932), 383–400; Willford I. King, "The Relative Volume of Technological Unemployment," ibid. 28:181A (March 1933), Suppl., 33–39; Boris Stern, "Technological Displacement of Labor and Technological Unemployment," ibid., 42–47; Ewan Clague, "Memorandum on Technological Unemployment," in U.S. Bureau of Labor Statistics, *Report of the Advisory Committee on*

THIS CHART SHOWS THE OUTPUT OF AMERICAN MANUFACTURING
PLANTS (SOLID LINE) IN RELATION TO THE NUMBER OF WORKERS
EMPLOYED IN THEM (BROKEN LINE) SINCE 1914. THE GROWTH
OF THE POPULATION IS SHOWN BY THE DOT AND DASH LINE.
THE SHADED AREA SHOWS THE NUMBER OF PERSONS EMPLOYED
IN 1919 FOR WHOM THERE HAS SINCE BEEN NO NEED.

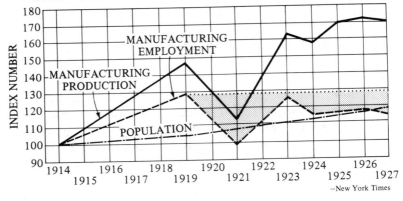

--New York Times

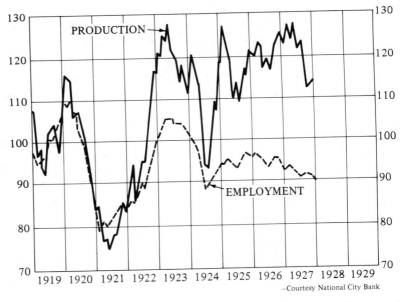

--Courtesy National City Bank

Figure 5-1. Concern about "technological unemployment" prompted
the publication of these two charts in 1928. (Source: *ALLR* 18:1 [March
1928], 68; 70.)

The general public, it is true, did not treat unemployment with any sense of urgency before the Wall Street crash. Complacency about the economic situation was common, and voices like Dickinson's, who warned in 1927 that "the present... era of great prosperity must terminate sometime in a more or less severe depression," were rare. Symptomatic was the report of the Committee on Recent Economic Changes, a body that Hoover had brought together in 1927 as a follow-up to the President's Conference of 1921. The report, published in May 1929, emphasized the high standard of living in the country and noted only in passing that the time had seemingly come to devote attention to cyclical unemployment and "also to this newer problem of 'technological' unemployment."[6]

In the crash's wake, however, awareness jumped. Unemployment figures, which according to one estimate averaged 1.5 million in 1929, seem to have tripled in 1930, almost doubled again during the next year, to reach by 1932 a plateau of some 12 million, or 24 percent of the civilian labor force. The number of employees on nonagricultural payrolls fell from 31.3 million in 1929 to 23.6 million in 1932. The impact on specific regions naturally differed according to prevailing industrial patterns, cli-

Employment Statistics (Washington: G.P.O., 1931), 16–31; Leo Wolman, "The New Unemployment," *ALLR* 18:1 (March 1928), 81–84; President's Conference on Unemployment. Committee on Recent Economic Changes, *Recent Economic Changes*, 514; Michael B. Scheler, "Technological Unemployment," *Annals* 154 (March 1931), 17–27; Paul H. Douglas and Aaron Director, *The Problem of Unemployment* (New York: Macmillan, 1931), 121–58. For differing opinions see Henri Fuss, "Rationalization and Unemployment," *International Labour Review* 17:6 (June 1928), 802–17 and, more poignantly, Magnus W. Alexander, "No Basis for Belief in Technological Unemployment," *ALLR* 19:1 (March 1929), 106–09. The problem has been discussed recently by Harry T. Oshima, "The Growth of U.S. Factor Productivity: The Significance of New Technologies in the Early Decades of the Twentieth Century," *Journal of Economic History* 44:1 (March 1984), 161–70. By 1927 the non-farm component of the labor force appears to have amounted to about 77% of the total. Stanley Lebergott, "Unemployment: A Perspective," in idem, ed., *Men without Work: The Economics of Unemployment* (Englewood Cliffs: Prentice-Hall, 1964), 27. For a recent discussion of the reasons for unemployment in the Great Depression and a new attempt at interpretation see Michael A. Bernstein, *The Great Depression: Delayed Recovery and Economic Change in America, 1929–1939* (Cambridge: Cambridge University Press, 1987), 18; 144–69. The relationship between unemployment and wages is dealt with in Ben Bernanke and Martin Parkinson, "Unemployment, Inflation, and Wages in the American Depression: Are There Lessons for Europe?" *American Economic Review* 79:2 (May 1989), 210–14.

6 F. G. Dickinson, "Public Construction and Cyclical Unemployment," *Annals* 139 (Sept. 1928), Suppl., iii; President's Conference on Unemployment. Committee on Recent Economic Changes, *Recent Economic Changes*, v; x; xxiii.

mate, and other variables, but over time the distress seemed to be all-pervasive. Better-off places magnetically attracted idle migratory workers, whose number was estimated at a congressional hearing in early 1933 to be in the neighborhood of 2 million. The worst hit of all economic sectors was probably construction, which showed a production decline, from its peak in the 1920s to the depression trough, of more than 70 percent. During the whole of 1932 only 34 percent of the industry's workforce was employed. At the end of the Hoover era no sign of abatement was visible as yet, and Americans could only hope that the incoming administration might have greater success in combating the evil than its predecessor.[7]

The depression caused public attitudes finally to undergo a profound change, although in many quarters the shift came hesitantly and substantial pockets of resistance lingered on. Business remained on the whole the principal bastion of individualism in the field of unemployment care, sticking to the tenet enunciated by *Law and Labor* well before the downturn that "the more relief you give to unemployed persons, the more certainly do you extend unemployment." Business's leading spokesmen did not see much reason even at the nadir of the depression to give up the values that had served it for generations. "Fundamentally ... the responsibility for providing against the unforeseen," National Industrial Conference Board president Magnus W. Alexander still believed in the second winter of misery, "rests in our democracy with the individual." Governmental spending on behalf of the unemployed was perceived as essentially wrong. A ballot of bank presidents taken in June 1932 showed that 2,509 were in favor of immediately balancing the budget, with only 694 thinking differently.[8]

This did not mean that industry should not get involved. What employment stabilization could be brought about through private efforts

7 U.S. Bureau of the Census, *Historical Statistics of the United States, Colonial Times to 1970: Bicentennial Edition, Part 1* (Washington: G.P.O., 1975), 135; "Employment and Earnings: United States, 1909–72," in U.S. Bureau of Labor Statistics, *Bulletin 1312–9* (Washington: G.P.O., n.d.), viii; Peter Fearon, *War, Prosperity and Depression: The U.S. Economy 1917–45* (Lawrence: University Press of Kansas, 1987), 100; Hearings on S. 5125, p. 5. Information on regional, professional, and age distribution of unemployment can be found in Lester V. Chandler, *America's Greatest Depression 1929–1941* (New York: Harper & Row, 1970), 33–47.

8 "Unemployment Plans," *Law and Labor* 10:5 (May 1928), 112; Magnus W. Alexander, "Factors That Contribute to Insecurity of Workers," *Annals* 154 (March 1931), 57; Edgar Eugene Robinson and Vaughn Davis Bornet, *Herbert Hoover: President of the United States* (Stanford: Hoover Institution Press, 1975), 224.

had to be undertaken. A conference of eight employer organizations in February 1930 saw the "need for heroic measures looking toward the stimulation of private industries and enterprises." Shortly thereafter, the National Industrial Conference Board, through the publication of a handbook entitled *Lay-off and Its Prevention*, equally recognized this obligation. Generally, the basic tenets of welfare capitalism still prevailed. The feeling dominated that they were valid ones and that their obvious failure, as David Brody has remarked, was not due to their lack of potential, but to an extraordinary turn in the business cycle.[9]

Here and there the understanding was growing, though, that regularization of production, the most obvious business instrument to keep unemployment at bay, was at best a limited tool. Paul H. Douglas of the University of Chicago, a left-leaning economist, asserted that "the great masses of business men" feared the additional cost, and that style changes and weather factors worked against the scheme. The New York Committee on Stabilization of Industry recognized that there were many industries in which the elimination of fluctuations in employment was "at present almost impossible."[10] Draper, a member of this committee, admitted that society could not rely on industry alone to solve the unemployment problem "because no agencies exist in industry that can compel all of industry to share the burden." Notwithstanding these doubts, how-

---

9 U.S. Senate, *Stabilization of Industry*, S.Doc. 109, 71 Cong., 2 sess., p. 1; National Industrial Conference Board, *Lay-off and Prevention* (New York: National Industrial Conference Board, 1930). See similarly Edwin S. Smith, ed., "What Employers Can Do to Prevent Unemployment," in Conference on Permanent Preventives of Unemployment, *Permanent Preventives of Unemployment* (Baltimore: Belvedere Press, [1931]), 7–17, in particular 9–13. – David Brody, "The Rise and Decline of Welfare Capitalism," in John Braeman, Robert H. Bremner, and David Brody, eds., *Change and Continuity in Twentieth-Century America: The 1920's* ([Columbus:] Ohio State University Press, 1968), 178.

10 Paul H. Douglas, "Can Management Prevent Unemployment?" *ALLR* 20:3 (Sept. 1930), 273–81. On Douglas see Joseph Dorfman, *The Economic Mind in American Civilization*. 5 Vols. (New York: Viking, 1959), vol. V, 526–34. In 1928 Douglas, together with John Dewey, Oswald G. Villard, and others was cofounder of the League for Independent Political Action which in 1932 supported the candidacies of Norman Thomas and James H. Maurer. Kenneth Campbell MacKay, *The Progressive Movement of 1924* (New York: Octagon, 1966), 255. – New York (State). Governor's Commission on Unemployment Problems, *Less Unemployment through Stabilization of Operations: A Report . . . by the Committee on Stabilization of Industry for the Prevention of Unemployment* (Albany: J. B. Lyon, 1930), 13. See also E[ugene] E. Agger, "What Answer to Unemployment?" *American Bankers Association Journal* (Nov. 1931), 349. Agger was an economist at Rutgers University.

ever, business on the whole fought tenaciously for continued adherence to the traditional principles. "The safeguarding of individual and voluntary action," a writer in *Barron's* warned, "is set against flabby dependence and compulsion."[11]

Less clear was the attitude of labor, of which the AFL still was the most articulate voice. Under the leadership of Green, president since December 1924, it continued for years to follow Gompers' original line, stressing self-reliance and distance from governmental intrusion. But as in former times, the stance was not a pure one. Even before the depression the AFL thought it advantageous to welcome the improvement of governmental statistics-gathering. This could still be construed as compatible with professed principles, but the AFL's active involvement with the USES reorganization in 1931 and its official advocacy of governmental unemployment insurance by 1932 clearly indicated a willingness to be pragmatic rather than consistent. In February 1932 the AFL leadership, over one hundred strong, marched more than a mile to the White House and then on to the Capitol to appeal for aid for the unemployed.[12] Many local bodies had already shown their receptiveness much earlier. Organized labor was thus altogether prepared to accept and even demand governmental unemployment action when Roosevelt came into office in March 1933.

A similar statement would probably be even more appropriate with regard to the mass of unorganized working people. They, of course, had few representative spokespersons; but it needs no elaboration to say that the despair generated by widespread unemployment welcomed help regardless of traditional principles. An assortment of self-appointed bodies, advocating governmental involvement with varying degrees of insistence, pushed themselves to the foreground. The People's Lobby, to whom the presidency of philosopher John Dewey and the advisory support of personalities like Columbia economics professor Tugwell and *Nation* editor Oswald G. Villard gave some respectability, urged the Democratic junior

11 Draper to John H. Finley, 30 July 1931, Box 1, Draper Papers. Draper was 1930–1932 president of the AALL. The smallness of the efforts to regularize is noted in Sanford M. Jacoby, *Employing Bureaucracy: Managers, Unions, and the Transformation of Work in American Industry, 1900–1945* (New York: Columbia University Press, 1985), 209–10. – *Barron's*, 6 July 1931, p. 5. See also Draper to Daniel B. Luten, 8 May 1931, Box 1, Draper Papers. Luten, a contractor from Indianapolis, Indiana, disputed the benefits of regularization.

12 *New York Times*, 10 Feb. 1932, pp. 1; 19.

senator from New York, Robert F. Wagner, as early as April 1930 to
fight for governmental unemployment insurance.[13] It and some fifteen
other organizations, among them Meserole's National Unemployment
League, the Social Service Commission of the Methodist Church, and
Abraham J. Muste's Conference for Progressive Labor Action, the latter
an association founded in 1929 out of factions of the non-Communist
left, soon formed the Joint Committee on Unemployment. Chaired by
Dewey, this body counted among its officers as diverse personalities as
Father Ryan and old-age pension advocate Abraham Epstein and saw its
primary role as a lobbying force for governmental action against unemployment distress. Specific proposals were understandably variegated and
characteristic of the conceptual uncertainty of the age. An article published by Father Ryan in November 1931 provided a significant example
in this respect, when he recommended in the same breath international
production and export allocations, back-to-the-land measures, big public
works programs, the payment of higher wages, and the shortening of
working hours.[14]

13 The reasons for the lack of significant active responses by the unemployed to their
    condition are pondered by Bernard Sternsher in his introduction to Bernard Sternsher,
    ed., *Hitting Home: The Great Depression in Town and Country* (Chicago: Quadrangle
    Books, 1970), 3–44, in particular 22–36. – Benjamin C. Marsh to Wagner, 4 April
    1930, Box 189, Legislative Files, Wagner Papers. The People's Lobby had been or-
    ganized in early 1921 under the name of People's Reconstruction League as a liberal
    pressure group, funded by the railway unions; Marsh had led it from its inception. See
    Benjamin C. Marsh, *Lobbyist for the People: A Record of Fifty Years* (Washington: Public
    Affairs Press, 1953), 69–70; and Eugene M. Tobin, *Organize or Perish: America's
    Independent Progressives, 1913–1933* (New York: Greenwood, 1986), 131–32; 217. A
    copy of the "National Unemployment Program of the People's Lobby" is in Box 9
    ("Addresses 1917–1932"), Huber Papers. According to a membership solicitation, dated
    2 March 1932, ibid., the Lobby "organize[d] hearings, before Committees of Congress,
    and meetings all over the country, prepare[d] briefs and [kept] the facts before the
    nation through publicity." The 71-year-old Dewey ended his teaching career at Co-
    lumbia in 1930. On his commitment to social causes see Robert M. Crunden, "Essay,"
    in John D. Buenker, John C. Burnham, and Robert M. Crunden, *Progressivism* (Cam-
    bridge, Mass.: Schenkman, 1977), 84–97; and James T. Kloppenberg, *Uncertain Victory:
    Social Democracy and Progressivism in European and American Thought* (New York: Oxford
    University Press, 1986), 350–52.
14 Hearings on H.R. 206, H.R. 6011, and H.R. 8088, 22–23; 83–85; Hearings Pursuant
    to S.Res. 483 (71st Cong.), 208–11. For examples of grass roots organizations, see Karl
    Broders, "They Speak Up in Chicago," *Survey* 67:12 (15 March 1932), 663–65; Hulet
    M. Well, "They Organize in Seattle," ibid., 665–67. In this context, see discussion on
    the Conference for Progressive Labor Action, Bernard Karsh and Phillips L. Garman,
    "The Impact of the Political Left," in Milton Derber and Edwin Young, eds., *Labor
    and the New Deal* (Madison: University of Wisconsin Press, 1961), 90–91. – John A.

Although some radical elements made themselves occasionally heard in the Joint Committee and outside, the vast majority of the proponents of unemployment reform did not intend, even with ever-deepening misery, to change the existing social system.[15] They readily concurred with Wagner's dictum that what was needed was "not a new economic order but greater precision and better organization in the existing order." The AALL and bodies such as the National Conference of Social Work still held the front rank in the fight for this goal. The expertise of the former and the enthusiasm of many of the social workers organized in the latter deserve more credit for the growing acceptance of an increased governmental role than any other discernible forces working in the same direction. The *ALLR* and the *Survey* were the most articulate voices of concern and the most readily available forums for the discussion during the early depression. In December 1928, unemployment was the main topic of the AALL's annual meeting, and in March 1929 the *ALLR* published the papers presented there. In April 1929 the *Survey* helped to bring the debate onto a serious level by running a full issue on unemployment questions, demanding in its editorial that President Hoover call an unemployment conference as Harding had done eight years earlier. Both organs in the long run suffered from an attrition of funds and had to cut back on space, but their fervor did not diminish for it.[16]

The social work profession underwent a conceptual transformation. The comparative prosperity of the 1920s had allowed a concentration on

Ryan, "International Aspects of Unemployment," *Catholic World* 134:800 (Nov. 1931), 129–36.

15 The essentially unsuccessful efforts of the radical left to organize the unemployed into a revolutionary instrument are described in Roy Rosenzweig, "Organizing the Unemployed: The Early Years of the Great Depression," *Radical America* 10:4 (July–Aug. 1976), 37–62. See also Karsh and Garman, "The Impact of the Political Left," 86–90; Roy Rosenzweig, "Radicals and the Jobless: The Musteites and the Unemployed Leagues, 1932–36," *Labor History* 16:1 (Winter 1975), 52–77; idem, " 'Socialism in Our Time': The Socialist Party and the Unemployed, 1929–1936," ibid. 20:4 (Fall 1979), 485–509; Daniel J. Leab, " 'United We Eat': The Creation and Organization of the Unemployed Councils in 1930," ibid. 8:3 (Fall 1967), 300–15; Frances Fox Piven and Richard A. Cloward, *Poor People's Movements: Why They Succeed, How They Fail* (New York: Pantheon Books, 1977), 41–72; William H. Mullins, "Self-Help in Seattle, 1931–1932: Herbert Hoover's Concept of Cooperative Individualism and the Unemployed Citizen's League," *Pacific Northwest Quarterly* 72:1 (Jan. 1981), 11–19.

16 Robert F. Wagner, "Unemployment – A National Issue," *ALLR* 21:1 (March 1931), 13; "Our Stake in Steady Jobs," *Survey* 62:1 (1 April 1929), 5.

case work, but methods devised to treat the customary clients were ill-suited for dealing with the new types of applicants that the 1930s produced. Persons who were habituated to regular work and who had hitherto planned and directed their own affairs did not need, and actually resented, detailed inquiry into their personal concerns. The transient class, which in normal times consisted of floaters and hoboes, was soon swelled by many bona fide migratory workers, single men as well as men with families, often skilled people who were uprooted by the circumstances. The sheer increase in numbers played its role. The ever-growing volume of need, the California State Unemployment Commission noted, produced for the social work profession "a change, not only in standards, but in aims." The objective was no longer specific treatment in individual cases, but maximum coverage with the funds available. The environmental viewpoint gained renewed prominence, and social workers again felt the urge to call for social action.[17]

As the distress grew, the debate widened to reach most parts of the nation. In academic circles the underconsumptionist theories of Hobson and John Maynard Keynes began to attract attention, and interest in planning and institutional reform widened.[18] Learned bodies con-

17 California. State Unemployment Commission, *Report and Recommendations* (San Francisco: California State Printing Office, 1932), 274; Clarke A. Chambers, *Seedtime of Reform: American Social Service and Social Action 1918–1933* (Minneapolis: University of Minnesota Press, 1963), 192; Walter I. Trattner, *From Poor Law to Welfare State: A History of Social Welfare in America* (New York: Free Press, 1974), 229–30; John H. Ehrenreich, *The Altruistic Imagination: A History of Social Work and Social Policy in the United States* (Ithaca: Cornell University Press, 1985), 84. See also Clarke A. Chambers, "Creative Effort in an Age of Normalcy, 1918–33," *Social Welfare Forum* (1961), 252–71; and idem, "An Historical Perspective on Political Action vs. Individualized Treatment," in Paul E. Weinberger, *Perspectives on Social Welfare: An Introductory Anthology* (Toronto: Macmillan, 1969), 89–106, in particular 96–99.

18 Arthur M. Schlesinger, Jr., *The Crisis of the Old Order 1919–1933* (Boston: Houghton Mifflin, 1956), 185–203; M. F. Bleany, *Underconsumptionist Theories: A History and Critical Analysis* (New York: International Publishers, 1976), 203–05; William E. Stoneman, *A History of the Economic Analysis of the Great Depression in America* (New York: Garland, 1979), 29–30; 37–47; 78–81; Stephen W. Baskerville, "Cutting Loose from Prejudice: Economists and the Great Depression," in Stephen W. Baskerville and Ralph Willett, *Nothing Else to Fear: New Perspectives on America in the Thirties* (Manchester, Engld.: Manchester University Press, 1985), 259–84, in particular 266–74; William J. Barber, *From New Era to New Deal: Herbert Hoover, the Economists, and American Economic Policy, 1921–1933* (Cambridge: Cambridge University Press, 1985), 54–58. For labor's interest in planning see Charles H. Chase, "Employment Stabilization through Consolidated National Industrial Budgeting," *American Federationist* 34:9 (Sept. 1927), 1068–77; and Edward Eyre Hunt, "National Planning for Avoidance of Unemployment," ibid., 1063–65.

centrated on the need for remedial action, as did the American Academy of Political and Social Science, which in December 1930 organized a special unemployment meeting, and the New York Academy of Political Science, which dedicated the better part of its annual gathering in November 1931 to the matter. The public at large proposed cures in any number and shape. A writer in *Social Science* felt that the unemployment could be remedied through tax reform, tariff adjustment, better employment agencies, production regulation, municipal ownership of utilities, national economic planning, and "wisdom and frugality" of wage-earners in prosperity periods. In winter 1930–31, the President's Emergency Committee for Employment (PECE) received nearly 2,100 suggestions for improvement measures, ranging from money circulation schemes to the deportation of aliens. Although much of this debate remained inconclusive or produced impractical concepts, it opened the public's mind to the more serious advocacy of unemployment reform advanced by those who were through training or experience closer to the cause.[19]

Government gropes for solutions

Ultimately it was the manifest inability of the traditional dispensers of relief to meet the challenge that forced state governments and finally Washington to come to the rescue. All intent to safeguard the individual's basic responsibility for his welfare must fade in the face of the jobseeker's obvious incapacity to make a living on his own. Humanitarian, economic, and social concerns ordained governmental rescue action, and the so-called American values lost their philosophical necessity as well as their mandatory character in the process. "The aid of dependent members of a community is a legal obligation upon the public," the California unemployment commission affirmed in 1932.[20] Following this insight, some state governments had already begun to bestir themselves, and more were following suit. At about the same time, the federal administration shifted from tokenism to the first substantial engagement, therewith in a clearly discernible way abandoning

19 *Annals* 154 (March 1931); Academy of Political Science in the City of New York, *Proceedings* 14 (Jan. 1932); E. W. Mounce, "The Unemployment Problem," *Social Science* 7:1 (Jan. 1932), 9–15; "Summary of Suggestions – 1930–31," Box 209, Series 6, POUR Papers. See also "Suggestions of a Less Serious Nature," Box 158, Series 4, ibid.
20 California. State Unemployment Commission, *Report and Recommendations*, 275–76.

the tenets of yore and setting the precedent for the interventionist exuberance of the Roosevelt era.

As in former depressions, one halfway step was the creation of unemployment commissions. Such bodies could investigate the problem, a necessity given the blatant need for hard information. Terms of reference might also ask for the coordination of local relief efforts or the stimulation of private initiatives.[21] The establishment of such commissions demonstrated the goodwill of the administrations without burdening treasuries, and one could hope that at reporting time the problem had shrunk or gone away. At the very least it was possible to appoint the right mix of people to ensure that the forthcoming recommendations did not aim at rocking the boat. The first state in which an unemployment committee was appointed after the beginning of the depression was New York, where Governor Franklin D. Roosevelt in March 1930 created the Committee on Stabilization of Industry for the Prevention of Unemployment, composed of business leaders and labor representatives and chaired by old hand Bruère, now of the Bowery Savings Bank. By the end of the year some eighteen more states had emulated this example in one form or another. Two months later, similar committees existed in thirty-one states[22] (Figures 5–2 and 5–3).

As a rule these bodies were composed of persons who appeared suitable

21 The work of these bodies is described in Mabel L. Walker, "The Urge to Organize," *ALLR* 21:2 (June 1931), 228–30; and in "Activities of Official Unemployment Committees," *ALLR* 21:2 (June 1931), 231–34. There was also hesitation about the creation of such bodies, as in Michigan, whose Governor Fred W. Green told President Hoover privately in October 1930 that "such a move would only emphasize the [unemployment] problem." His successor, however, appointed a State Unemployment Commission in August 1931. Richard T. Ortquist, "Unemployment and Relief: Michigan's Response to the Depression during the Hoover Years," *Michigan History* 57:3 (Fall 1973), 219; 221.

22 The Wisconsin legislature passed a joint resolution introduced by a socialist member in January 1928 to have the industrial commission conduct an inquiry into employment conditions. Bryce M. Stewart, *Unemployment Benefits in the United States* (New York: Industrial Relations Counsellors, 1930), 580; New York (State). Committee on Stabilization of Industry for the Prevention of Unemployment, *Report* (Albany, 1930), 3. – "Third Unemployment Survey," *ALLR* 20:4 (Dec. 1930), 395. Unemployment committees were also appointed in Arizona, California, Illinois, Indiana, Kentucky, Massachusetts, Michigan, Minnesota, Mississippi, New Jersey, New York, Ohio, Tennessee, Vermont, Virginia, West Virginia, and Wisconsin. The Pennsylvania committee appointed by Pinchot carried on after his election as governor in Nov. 1930. – Forrest A. Walker, *The Civil Works Administration: An Experiment in Federal Work Relief, 1933–1934* (New York: Garland, 1979), 15.

Figure 5-2. New York Joint Legislative Committee on Unemployment, 1931. Senator Arthur H. Wicks is seated, second from left; to his left, Assemblyman William L. Marcy, Jr., chairman. (Source: *ALLR* 22:3 [Dec. 1932], after p. 128.)

because of their political background, welfare administration experience, or professional habitat. Assessing the unemployment problem as best they could, the commissioners not infrequently arrived at a set of proposals that took a page out of Andrews' prewar *Practical Program*. Innovative thought was rare and restricted to detail. In most cases government response was slow, and often enough the appointment of yet another commission, as in Kentucky where an Unemployment Relief Agency was followed by a State Welfare Committee, to be superseded by a state Relief Commission, appeared as a convenient substitute for action, or at least as a supplement to it[23] (Figure 5–4).

States hesitated to take more effective measures for a variety of reasons. Fear of establishing uncomfortable precedents and shortage of funds figured prominently, but they were not the only impediments. Often, constitutional obstacles barred the way, or the lack of an adequate administrative apparatus had to be overcome. Many legislatures met only every second year, and action could not be taken unless a special session was called (Figure 5–5). The determination and tactical deftness of a state's leadership played a significant role, and so did political and administrative traditions. In New York, a resolute governor, Roosevelt, had

23 George T. Blakey, *Hard Times and New Deal in Kentucky 1929–1939* (Lexington: University Press of Kentucky, 1986), 17–22.

Figure 5-3. California State Unemployment Commission, 1931. Seated in the middle is Archbishop Edward J. Hanna, chairman. (Source: *ALLR* 22:3 [Dec. 1932], before title page.)

the good fortune of being supported by a comparatively well-developed administration that had been gathering some experience in unemployment questions in the previous decades; their cooperation resulted in the creation of the Temporary Emergency Relief Administration (TERA) in fall 1931, the first of its kind in the United States. The depression hit Chicago certainly as hard as it hit New York, but Illinois proved far less capable, or willing, to help itself; by July 1932 the federal government had to rescue the Chicago welfare administration from imminent collapse. In Pennsylvania, reform-minded and strong-willed Governor Gifford Pinchot clashed with an uncooperative legislature, and the relief effort was the worse for it.

The federal government could feel even more justified in standing aloof than the states. Few state administrations made direct appeals to Washington for help, fearing federal curtailment of their prerogatives. The federal government, at any rate, was one further step removed from the relief scene, and no clear precedent for involvement existed. Retreating on this high ground, the majority party on the whole struggled for much of the early depression to keep the distance. Symptomatic was Secretary Davis' pronouncement that in the fight against unemployment "something more than government action is needed," that the problem

—Louisville, (Ky.) Times

Figure 5-4. The unemployment commission and its possible findings, as seen by the *Louisville Times*. (Source: *ALLR* 20:3 [Sept. 1930], 256.)

Figure 5-5. Joint meeting of the Massachusetts Special Commission on the Stabilization of Employment and the Connecticut Unemployment Commission, around 1932. Seated, first and second from left are Governors Joseph B. Ely, Massachusetts and Wilbur L. Cross, Connecticut. (Source: *ALLR* 22:2 [June 1932], before title page.)

"must be studied and dealt with by those who own the industries of America."[24]

This attitude was nevertheless questioned with growing insistence in Congress. A loose group of insurgent Republican progressives such as Couzens (who had been appointed to the Senate in 1922 and elected in 1924), Hiram W. Johnson (California), and Robert M. La Follette, Jr. (Wisconsin), could in many instances ally itself with Democrats like Wagner, Thomas J. Walsh (Wisconsin), or Edward P. Costigan (Colorado), who either from conviction or political opportunism chose to challenge the administration's stance. The Democratic party stewards, though, avoided openly taking over the leadership in relief legislation, even after garnering the House majority in the Seventy-second Congress. They feared having to share the blame for the ongoing distress and thus jeopardizing their chances in the 1932 elections. As a consequence, partisan lines on budgetary and relief issues began to blur. The "depths of intellectual confusion among the parties" that Arthur M. Schlesinger, Jr., has noted were a sign that old concepts were los-

---

24 For the "do it ourselves" attitude in many states see James T. Patterson, *The New Deal and the States: Federalism in Transition* (Princeton, N.J.: Princeton University Press, 1969), 30–31. – "The Worker's Outlook, by Honorable James J. Davis, U.S. Secretary of Labor, for New York Herald Tribune Sunday Magazine, March 23, 1930," Book 17, Articles and Speeches, Davis Papers.

ing their validity. Their fading made it possible that reform ideas could gain ground.[25]

As early as February 1928, Wagner, in a widely publicized move in the Senate, demanded information concerning the extent of unemployment (S.Res. 147). As a state senator in Albany and then as a judge on his state's supreme court, Wagner had shown decided openness for social problems, but before becoming a senator in Washington he had not paid much attention to the unemployment question. He seems to have hit upon this specific issue somewhat fortuitously when readying himself to aid Al Smith in his presidential campaign. After having made unemployment the topic of his maiden speech in Congress on 5 March 1928, however, he did not abandon the cause any more, and quickly established himself among Washington legislators as the prime promoter of remedial action. A few weeks after his first initiative he came out with three bills, which in their advocacy of better statistics (S. 4158), more effective labor exchanges (S. 4157), and the judicious use of public works (S. 4307) contained a full action plan.[26]

Wagner's bills were buried in committee, but their introduction may have helped to advance La Follette's motion to investigate the unemployment problem, which passed on 19 May (S.Res. 219). Couzens, who headed the Senate Committee on Education and Labor that was to conduct the investigation, was looking forward to "some splendid information" to be submitted. He took the precaution, though, of having the hearings start only after the November elections, busying himself in the meantime with circularizing the employer organizations. For the time being, this left the theme to the political opposition. If there was one economic question more suitable than another for office candidates to get involved in, Tugwell wrote in May in the *New Republic*, "it will be this one of unemployment." Consequently the Democratic platform stated in June that "unemployment is present, widespread and increasing" and deplored the fact that no governmental program prevented "awful suffering and economic losses."[27]

25 Regarding the insurgents' attitude toward labor in general see Zieger, *Republicans and Labor 1919–1929*, 164–89. – Jordan A. Schwarz, *The Interregnum of Despair: Hoover, Congress, and the Depression* (Urbana: University of Illinois Press, 1970), 62–63; Schlesinger, Jr., *Crisis of the Old Order*, 229.

26 J. Joseph Huthmacher, *Senator Robert F. Wagner and the Rise of Urban Liberalism* (New York: Atheneum, 1971), 57–59; *CR*, 70 Cong., 1 sess., 5 March 1928, pp. 4067–75.

27 William Haber and Merrill G. Murray, *Unemployment Insurance in the American Economy: An Historical Review and Analysis* (Homewood, Ill.: Irwin, 1966), 71, mistakenly state that Couzens moved S. 219. – Couzens to John Carson, 8 Aug. 1928, Box 58, Couzens

Much depended, of course, on the president. During Coolidge's tenure, the unemployment question did not pose itself with sufficient urgency to elicit any pertinent responses from the administration. When Hoover moved into the White House, he could be expected to show greater concern. He had been the propelling force behind the 1921 conference, and he had since endeavored to present himself as open-minded and alert to the needs of the country.[28] But as became clear after the first months of his presidency, the Great Humanitarian could not be counted on for governmental handouts. A case in point was his administration's willingness to see the Sheppard-Towner Act lapse on 1 July 1929, ending federal grants-in-aid to the states for maternity care.

Hoover basically believed that any remedial action should originate with the people rather than their government. The latter should remain restricted to giving auxiliary support, as exemplified in the adoption of the protectionist Hawley-Smoot Tariff in June 1930. First consideration had to be given to the maintenance of governmental financial stability. In this the president did not stand alone. Majority opinion, as Fearon has put it, "favored the orthodoxy of balanced budgets," and a massive governmental spending spree would have been impossible to justify either intellectually or politically.[29] Hoover thus strove to salvage voluntarism and personal initiative, which to him constituted the essence of Americanness. When reality demonstrated the superannuation of this concept, he seems to have felt in almost Hegelian fashion that this was the fault of reality. Events ultimately forced his administration to take steps that were tantamount to an official abandonment of the voluntarist principle. The president appears to have endeavored to keep them small enough so as to hide their quantum leap quality.[30]

Papers. Carson was Couzens' right-hand man in Washington. – Couzens to Carson, 6 July 1928, Box 57, ibid.; Couzens to C. O. Hardy, 5 Sept. 1928, Box 58, ibid.; R. G. Tugwell, "Hunger, Cold and Candidates," *New Republic* 54:700 (2 May 1928), 324; Donald Bruce Johnson, ed., *National Party Platforms*. 2 Vols. (Urbana: University of Illinois Press, 1978), vol. I, 275.
28 For Hoover's public image at the eve of the depression see Kent Schofield, "The Public Image of Herbert Hoover in the 1928 Campaign," *Mid-America* 51:4 (Oct. 1969), 278–93.
29 Robinson and Bornet, *Herbert Hoover*, 211. On Hoover's attitude see also Robert S. McElvaine, *The Great Depression: America, 1929–1941* (New York: Times Books, 1984), 58–62; 78–82; Fearon, *War, Prosperity and Depression*, 123.
30 The interpretative literature on Hoover's handling of the depression is large and growing. Older opinions are summarized in Albert U. Romasco, "Hoover-Roosevelt and the

Hoover's aversion to the display of governmental generosity was seconded by his dislike of the lawmakers in Congress and the difficulties he experienced even within his own party. Restricting his dealings with the legislative meant that he could keep any "raids" on the treasury to a minimum. When it became impossible from December 1930 on to ignore the soon partially Democratic Congress, the president responded defensively. He thus did not listen to suggestions that he call a special session in 1931 but asserted that "we cannot legislate ourselves out of a world economic depression." Governmental aid, Jordan A. Schwarz has observed, was from early on to be "an executive function utilizing the existing federal machinery."[31]

When the business crisis after the stock market crash called for some government response, Hoover announced the acceleration of several construction projects, and in conjunction with the United States Chamber of Commerce convened a National Business Survey Conference in December. The effect of the new organization was slight at best, and by May 1930 it had vanished.[32]

In spite of Secretary of Agriculture Arthur M. Hyde's announcement on 5 June 1930 that unemployment proved to be "little more than seasonal," a business revival did not materialize over the summer. In some parts of the country the drought added its impact. As a

Great Depression: A Historiographic Inquiry into a Perennial Comparison," in John Braeman, Robert H. Bremner, and David Brody, eds., *The New Deal: The National Level* (Columbus: Ohio State University Press, 1975), 3–26. See also Martin L. Fausold and George T. Mazuzan, eds., *The Hoover Presidency: A Reappraisal* (Albany: State University of New York Press, 1974); Robert H. Zieger, "Herbert Hoover: A Reinterpretation," *American Historical Review* 81:4 (Oct. 1976), 800–10; and Martin L. Fausold, *The Presidency of Herbert C. Hoover*, (Lawrence: University Press of Kansas, 1985), in particular pp. 97–100; 132–37; 147–66. A case study that critically examines the chances of Hoover's voluntarist concept is Mullins, "Self-Help in Seattle." For the erosion of the voluntarist principle as guide in the Hoover administration's financial policies see George D. Green, "The Ideological Origins of the Revolution in American Financial Policies," in Karl Brunner, ed., *The Great Depression Revisited* (Boston: Martinus Nijhoff, 1981), 220–52.

31 William Starr Myers, ed., *The State Papers and Other Public Writings of Herbert Hoover.* 2 Vols. (Garden City: Doubleday, Doran, 1934), vol. I, 565; Schwarz, *Interregnum of Despair*, 12; 51–53; Albert U. Romasco, *The Poverty of Abundance: Hoover, the Nation, the Depression* (New York: Oxford University Press, 1965), 38. In the 72d Congress (1931–33) seat distribution was as follows: Senate, 48 Republicans, 47 Democrats, 1 Farmer-Laborite; House, 220 Democrats, 214 Republicans, 1 Farmer-Laborite.

32 Myers, ed., *State Papers*, I, 183; Romasco, *Poverty of Abundance*, 44–51; Julius H. Barnes, "The New Ebb and Flow of Industry," *Survey* 64:5 (1 June 1930), 233. Barnes, chairman of the U.S. Chamber of Commerce, headed the National Business Survey Conference.

consequence, on 17 October Hoover announced that he had requested his cabinet to submit plans for "strengthening the organization of Federal activities for employment during the winter." In his opinion the federal government could make efforts in conjunction with the states and local communities, through cooperation with national industries, and through the undertaking of public works. Harking back to the 1921 experience, on 21 October he charged Colonel Woods with developing an activity program (Figure 5–6). At Woods' instigation, Hoover established the PECE on 30 October with Woods as chairman. The membership, ultimately totaling thirty-three, included businessmen as well as experienced social welfare hands such as Hunt, who was appointed secretary, Fred C. Croxton, then of the Ohio Department of Industrial Relations, and Bryce M. Stewart, who in 1927 had joined Industrial Relations Counselors Inc., a nonprofit organization specializing in labor relations. A sprinkling of academics, notably Porter R. Lee, director of the New York School of Social Work, Wolman, now at Columbia, and Joseph H. Willits of the Wharton School of Finance and Commerce in Philadelphia, added further expertise.[33]

In addressing his committee, Hoover insisted that any "breach of the responsibilities" of the state and local governments, or any centralization or bureaucracy of relief, would be "disastrous." The dispensation of direct relief by Congress would "result in politics, graft and waste such as we had never witnessed." The federal government could at best play a subsidiary role, mainly through public construction. The committee's main mandate, resembling that of the President's Conference of 1921, was thus exhortation and coordination, rather than substantial action. In creating the PECE, Hoover, in Joan Hoff Wilson's words, attempted "to revitalize trade associationalism with a decentralized nation planning program."[34]

Woods consequently applied himself, as he had done a decade earlier, to admonishing state and municipal officials to show initiative and inventiveness. Radio pep talks and addresses to trade associations and

---

33 "Legislative Notes," *ALLR* 20:3 (Sept. 1930), 229; Myers, ed., *State Papers*, I, 401. For a full list of the PECE's members see E. P. Hayes, *Activities of the President's Emergency Committee for Employment (October 17, 1930—August 19, 1931)* (Concord, N.H.: Rumford Press, 1936), vii-viii.
34 William Starr Myers and Walter H. Newton, *The Hoover Administration: A Documented Narrative* (New York: Scribner's Sons, 1936), 53–54; Joan Hoff Wilson, *Herbert Hoover: Forgotten Progressive* (Boston: Little, Brown, 1975), 137.

Figure 5-6. Colonel Arthur Woods gets ready for action. (Source: *ALLR* 20:3 [Sept. 1930], 350.)

professional groups by committee members aimed at fostering the voluntarist spirit. Citzens were invited to contribute to community chests, to spruce up homes and backyards so as to provide work for idle hands, or if in need themselves, to plant subsistence gardens. Aware of the basic insufficiency of this kind of endeavor, Woods concluded in early 1931 that only large-scale federal public works could bring alleviation. As he also disagreed with Hoover's veto of the employment exchange bill (S. 3060), the president replaced him on 1 May with Croxton, who had hitherto served as regional advisor. Under Croxton's direction the committee, enfeebled by the departure of other members and renamed the President's Advisory Committee for Employment (PACE), lingered on for the next few months.[35]

The performance of the economy did not improve substantially over the summer, and in due time demands were heard, even from the Republican side, that preparatory action for the approaching winter get under way. Following a suggestion by Woods to entrust the matter to "new brooms," on 19 August Hoover replaced the ailing PACE with a 100-member body dominated by businessmen. Whereas in the former committee's name the word unemployment had studiously been avoided, the new President's Organization on Unemployment Relief (POUR) appeared to signify a change in philosophy. But the organization's task, as assigned by Hoover, was still "to cooperate with the public authorities and to mobilize the national, state and local agencies of every kind." As the *Survey* saw it, the creation of the POUR was essentially "a move to forestall 'a flood of socialist legislation' and a widespread demand for federal unemployment insurance when Congress meets."[36]

The new body's membership exuded conservative reliability. Walter S.

---

35 The gist of the PECE's philosophy may be gleaned from the ten radio addresses contained in U.S. Department of Commerce, *Unemployment: Industry Seeks a Solution: A Series of Radio Addresses Given Under the Auspices of the President's Emergency Committee for Employment* (Washington: G.O.P., 1931). – Fred C. Croxton, "The Federal Role in a Public Employment Service," *ALLR* 21:3 (Sept. 1931), 303. For an account of the PECE's activities see Hayes, *Activities*. Woods was the author of the book, using Hayes, executive assistant at the PECE, as a front. Hoover to Walter S. Gifford, 20 Nov. 1936, Box 336, Presidential Papers, Hoover Papers.

36 See, for instance, the calls for action by Sen. J. Couzens (*New York Times*, 5 Aug. 1931, p. 20); Sen. J. J. Blaine (ibid., 8 Aug. 1931, p. 1); Pennsylvania Gov. Gifford Pinchot (ibid., 14 Aug. 1931, p. 9). – Woods to Hoover, 7 Aug. 1931, Box 338, Presidential Papers, Hoover Papers; Myers, ed., *State Papers*, I, 609–10; "Unemployment Leadership," *Survey* 66:12 (15 Sept. 1931), 537.

Gifford, president of the American Telephone and Telegraph Company, president of the COS, and formerly wartime director of the Council of National Defense, was appointed chairman. Croxton and other former PACE members continued to serve, and the new committee also took over the clerical organization and files of the PACE. The number of economists and social workers had shrunk, however, and there was a more distinct slant toward business. *Fortune* interpreted this to mean that the POUR was "to symbolize solidity, to become a sort of national Rock of Gibraltar trademark, reassuring, soothing."[37]

Gifford soon clarified his understanding of his task. On 18 September he issued a statement announcing that his organization would act "in support of and not in place of existing agencies." Gifford appointed one representative in each state to act as liaison between the central organization and the various relief agencies in the state. But the major venture of the POUR was a publicity campaign in support of the Association of Community Chests and Councils' fundraising, an activity that Pinchot called "an attempt to get by without increasing income taxes, without letting the big fellows come in to carry their part of the load." Another effort was the publication of ten recommendations in October, exhorting the employed population to resume "normal buying," asking bankers to grant liberal credit, admonishing employers to spread the work among as many employees as possible, and inviting communities to consider "the possibility for transfer of surplus labor from cities to farms." In spring 1932, Congress declined to make a deficiency appropriation for the POUR, and it was disbanded on 30 June.[38]

During the winter of 1931–32 the insufficiency of traditional relief methods resulted in conditions of distress among parts of the population in over a dozen states, most of them industrial, that had to be considered unbearable by time-honored standards.[39] In December

---

37 "To Symbolize Solidity... Is the Mission of Mr. Hoover's Latest, Greatest Committee for Unemployment Relief," *Fortune* 4:5 (Nov. 1931), 55.

38 "The President's Organization on Unemployment Relief," *MLR* 33:5 (Nov. 1931), 1042–43; Gertrude Springer, "Where Is the Money Coming from?" *Survey* 67:2 (15 Oct. 1931), 71; Hearings on S. 174 and S. 262, p. 217; "Program for Promotion of Employment," *MLR* 33:6 (Dec. 1931), 1341–42. For a summary of the activities of the POUR see Edward Ainsworth Williams, *Federal Aid for Relief* (New York: Columbia University Press, 1939), 31–41.

39 Frank Bane, "Conditions Showing Possible Need for Federal Aid," *Survey* 67:9 (1 Feb. 1932), 465; "How the Cities Stand," *Survey* 68:2 (15 April 1932), 71–75; 92; H. L.

1931 the Communists staged a National Hunger March on Washington. The federal administration still experienced difficulties seeing a case for greater involvement, and took comfort from listening to voices such as that of a "Democrat who usually votes the Republican ticket," who felt that Hoover was not responsible for the existing problems because they were "not only national, but international." The "dominant national necessity," the president told the state governors assembled in conference in late April 1932, "is to reduce the expenditures of all our governments."[40]

However, the sheer weight of the need, translating itself into political pressure, began to have its impact. For some time there had actually been indications that a slowly evolving process was under way. One was Hoover's agreement to the creation of the Federal Employment Stabilization Board (FESB) in February 1931. Another was the large-scale reorganization of the USES with strong centralist features, undertaken from March 1931 on. Hoover followed up on these precedents when on 8 December of that year he proposed to Congress the formation of a government lending agency "of the nature of the former War Finance Corporation," with wide powers to extend credit "to established industries, railways, and financial institutions." With the concurrence of Congress, the Reconstruction Finance Cooperation (RFC) was created on 2 February 1932. This undertaking finally testified to the Republican administration's readiness, in Albert U. Romasco's words, "to use the power of the federal government in a direct manner when voluntary cooperative action proved insufficient to handle . . . a vital function." It was the first instance in which the federal government intervened directly in the economy in time of peace not for the promotion of development but for rescue from distress and support of macroeconomic stabilization.[41]

Lurie, " 'Spreading Relief Thin,' " *Social Service Review* 6:2 (June 1932), 223–34. Joanna C. Colcord, *Cash Relief* (New York: Russell Sage Foundation, 1936), 17–32, describes the search for new relief methods.
40 John Dos Passos, "Red Day on Capitol Hill," *New Republic* 69:890 (23 Dec. 1931), 153–55; J. B. to Walter Newton, 9 November 1931, printed in Robert S. McElvaine, ed., *Down and Out in the Great Depression: Letters from the "Forgotten Man"* (Chapel Hill: University of North Carolina Press, 1983), 40–41. Newton was Hoover's secretary. – Governors' Conference, *Proceedings, Twenty-fourth Annual Session, Held at Richmond, Virginia, April 25–27, 1932* (n.p., n.d.), 49.
41 Myers, ed., *State Papers*, II, 50; Romasco, *Poverty of Abundance*, 190; Green, "The Ideological Origins of the Revolution in American Financial Policies," 237.

Although the RFC authorized a total of $1.2 billion within the first six months of its existence, its impact on the American economy was not big enough to contribute visibly to a reduction of the unemployment misery. Realizing this, Hoover reluctantly inched toward an augmentation of its powers. Election-year considerations and the increased pressure from a depression-weary public influenced the administration's decision. The passage of the ERCA on 21 July consummated the development toward an interventionist role of the federal government in the alleviation of unemployment distress. It was the legislative consequence of a "radical and universal change in public temper" that Wolman noticed at the time.[42] However insufficient the actual provisions of the ERCA turned out to be, its very adoption negated the principle of exclusive lower-level self-help and voluntarism that had been the professed guide of federal policy over the previous decades. It constituted a new departure, and the New Deal could readily follow up on it.

II   Numbers beyond count

The development discussed in the last section was clearly perceptible in all the areas under consideration in this study. Counting was no exception. Despite the substantial amount of theoretical reflection spent during the 1920s on the unsolved problems, the onslaught of the depression found the states as ill-prepared to assess the volume of unemployment as they had been in the previous decades. The urge to heed other priorities, though, as well as the lack of time and administrative means, prevented most of them from now looking for more satisfactory solutions. This task devolved almost naturally upon the federal government.

Only two states continued the search. In New Jersey the relief authorities tried registration in 1931. Counties and municipalities were supplied with forms and asked to list the unemployed. Lack of uniformity made the venture less than a success, and the attempt was discontinued in January 1932. A more sophisticated approach was taken by the New York department of labor. It concentrated on two industrial cities, Buffalo and Syracuse, where it used a sampling method with which Columbus (Ohio) had experimented in the early 1920s. In Buffalo, nine districts,

---

42 Leo Wolman, "The Problem of Unemployment," Academy of Political Science in the City of New York, *Proceedings* 15 (Jan. 1933), 211.

with about 7 percent of the total population, were canvassed in November 1929, and the exercise was repeated in 1930, 1931, and 1932. As important as the global results – unemployment appeared to be at 6.2, 17.2, 24.3, and 32.6 percent, respectively, over the four years – were the detailed findings regarding part-time work, age and gender distribution of the jobless, industry groups affected, as well as causes and duration of unemployment. The department was so pleased that it started a similar study in November 1931 in Syracuse. These various surveys were not without merit, less so because of the specific data obtained than because of the experience they provided. But they were woefully unsuited to furnish guidance for policy decisions on the state level or beyond[43] (Figure 5–7).

Attention thus began to focus upon the federal government. Early attempts to improve federal statistical intelligence could be observed well before the depression struck. As early as February 1927, Senator David I. Walsh (D-Massachusetts), a friend of labor, demanded an investigation of the amount of unemployment (S.Res. 378). The issue resurfaced a year later. Possibly inspired by timely election considerations, Senator Wagner now repeated Walsh's request in more specific form. His resolution (S.Res. 147) directed the secretary of labor to investigate the extent of unemployment in the United States and also to seek out methods for periodic measuring. Probably unknown to him, at about the same time there was discussion in the Department of Commerce in favor of taking a sample unemployment census. His proposal found a majority, and over the next few weeks the Bureau of Labor Statistics busied itself with readying the desired information.[44]

The administration was not going to come out with any figures detrimental to the image of prevailing prosperity in the country. The bureau compared employment data of 1925 and January 1928 and

---

43 New Jersey. Emergency Relief Administration, *Unemployment and Relief Conditions in New Jersey: An Interim Report* (n.p., 1932), 23; "Methods Used in Unemployment Surveys of Baltimore, Philadelphia, and Buffalo," *MLR* 30:5 (May 1930), 962; "Employment in Cincinnati in May, 1931," *MLR* 33:1 (July 1931), 65–66. For the Columbus study see Frederick E. Croxton, "Unemployment in Columbus, Ohio, 1921 to 1925," in U.S. Bureau of Labor Statistics, *Bulletin 409* (Washington: G.P.O., 1926) (whole bulletin); "Unemployment in Buffalo, N.Y., November 1932," *MLR* 36:1 (Jan. 1933), 77–78; idem, "An Analysis of the Buffalo, N.Y., Unemployment Surveys, 1929 to 1932," *MLR* 36:2 (Feb. 1933), 283–94; Frederick E. Croxton and John Nye Webb, "Unemployment in Syracuse, N.Y., November 1931," *MLR* 34:4 (April 1932), 770–78.
44 Lawrence B. Mann to Julius Klein, 28 Feb. 1928, Box 615, Commerce Papers, Hoover Papers.

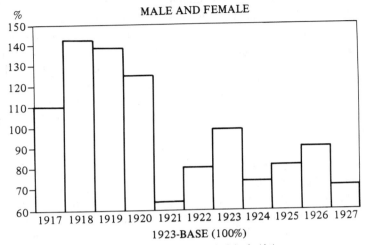

HELP WANTED ADS
N.Y. WORLD
MALE AND FEMALE

1923-BASE (100%)

Prepared by Margaret D. Meyer, American Association for Labor Legislation

Figure 5-7. "Help Wanted" advertisements in the *New York World*. (Source: *ALLR* 18:1 [March 1928], 67.)

found a shrinkage of 1,874,050, a figure that Davis presented to Congress as "the actual number now out of work." Wagner was understandably furious. On the Senate floor he pointed out that if Davis had taken into account unemployment existing in 1925, the farm-to-city movement, population growth, and immigration, he might well have arrived at about 4 million unemployed in January 1928. Rejecting, moreover, nonstatistical unemployment information published regularly by the USES as "poppycock" and "the most concentrated piffle that has ever been printed at the Government's expense," he proposed the expansion of the data gathering work of the Bureau of Labor Statistics (S. 4158).[45]

By and by, the lack of good information, together with general concern about unemployment, won stature as a political issue. Senator Walter E. Edge (R-New Jersey), a former governor with extensive business connections, warned Hoover as early as spring 1928 that many Republicans

45 James J. Davis to President of the Senate, 24 March 1928, *CR*, 70 Cong., 1 sess., 26 March 1928, pp. 5337–38; "Report on Unemployment in the United States," ibid., pp. 5338–40.

felt it "imperative that this unemployment argument be answered before the Senate adjourns." Congress responded by adopting a request by La Follette for a thorough investigation (S. Res. 219), and on 29 May it came up with a $100,000 increase in the Bureau of Labor Statistics' appropriation. As a result, from the beginning of July 1928 the bureau, conforming to Wagner's demand, could augment the number of manufacturing establishments from which it collected employment data and expand its coverage to various other industries.[46]

Further progress, even if it did not amount to a breakthrough, came in the following year. During the hearings pursuant to S.Res. 219, Labor Statistics Commissioner Ethelbert Stewart, Berridge, and USES Director General Jones testified regarding employment statistics. As a result, the Committee on Education and Labor recommended that unemployment questions be asked in the 1930 census. In the following weeks, advocacy of this idea gained momentum.[47] But considerable resistance had to be overcome. The director of the census feared that other items in his program might suffer, and the National Industrial Conference Board remained doubtful whether the census could provide unemployment information "commensurate with the expense involved." It took Wagner's political skills to implement the idea through an amendment to the census bill. The census was taken in April and May 1930. Preliminary data, published in August, indicated that an unemployment rate of 5 percent at census time could be assumed.[48]

---

46 Walter E. Edge to Hoover, 4 May 1928, Box 615, Commerce Papers, Hoover Papers; U.S. Dept. of Labor, *16th Annual Report, 1928*, 127.
47 Hearings Pursuant to S.Res. 219, pp. 182; 190–91; U.S. Congress. Senate, *Causes of Unemployment.* S.Rept. 2072, 70 Cong., 2 sess. (pursuant to S.Res. 219; 25 Feb. 1929), viii; Mary Van Kleeck and Ada M. Matthews, "Shall We Count the Unemployed?" *Survey* 62:1 (1 April 1929), 22; Walter Lippmann, "A Bench Mark of Unemployment," *New York World*, 14 April 1929; "An Unemployment Census," *American Federationist* 36:5 (May 1929), 532; William Green to Wagner, telegram, 22 Jan. 1929, Box 452, Wagner Papers. See also AFL. 49th Annual Convention, *Proceedings 1929*, 84–85. Other bills asking for an unemployment inquiry in the census were H.R. 1577; H.J.Res. 87.
48 "Memorandum: Recent Action by the Committee on Governmental Labor Statistics with Regard to Statistics of Employment and Unemployment," 22 Jan. 1929, Box SM 456, Wagner Papers; Stewart to W. M. Steuart, 28 Jan. 1929, ibid.; Stewart to Committee on Governmental Labor Statistics of the American Statistical Association, Memorandum, 20 Feb. 1929, ibid.; Magnus W. Alexander to Wagner, 25 Jan. 1929, ibid.; *CR*, 70 Cong., 2 sess., 16 Jan. 1929, p. 1755; U.S. Congress. Senate, *Census and Reapportionment*, S.Rept. 2, 71 Cong., 1 sess. (to accompany S. 312; 23 April 1929), 1; "Preliminary Returns from the United States Unemployment Census of 1930," *MLR* 31:4 (Oct. 1930), 884–85.

Critics were quick to point out the dubiousness of the results. Typical was Charles E. Persons, who had been the unemployment expert in the Bureau of the Census but had resigned his position, protesting the bureau's efforts to minimize the number of the jobless. He could not see much value in the figures gathered, because part-time workers were not included and the unemployment questionnaire might have discouraged many census takers. Equally skeptical was the *Pasadena Labor News*, which had found out that among a group of seventy-six persons enumerated, only eleven had been asked the unemployment question.[49] But even though the census results could not convince critical observers, the very fact that they existed indicated growing governmental attention to the problem of unemployment data. For the first time the attempt had been made to count all the unemployed in the United States in the same relatively short period of time, whereas the censuses from 1880 to 1910 had only tried to find out how many working people had been unemployed in a whole year.

Whatever their value, the census data constituted at best one-shot intelligence that could not satisfy the need for current information. Some advance came also in this respect. Wagner's 1928 statistics bill (S. 4158) had aimed at finding a solution, and its provisions had practically been implemented through the increase in the appropriation for the Bureau of Labor Statistics in summer 1928. The senator now sought to make this arrangement permanent. One of the three unemployment bills he introduced on 9 January (S. 3061) virtually repeated the earlier proposal. The economic downturn made for a better reception this time around, and the bill passed Congress easily. On 7 July 1930 it received presidential approval.[50]

Hoover even went a step further. On 12 August he appointed an Advisory Committee on Employment Statistics to look into the methods used by government agencies. In its report of 9 February 1931 this committee essentially recommended that the Bureau of the Census continue taking the decennial unemployment census and consider a quinquennial census of employment as well as an annual census of manufactures. The

---

49 "Unemployment Census," *ALLR* 20:3 (Sept. 1930), 308; Charles E. Persons, "Census Reports on Unemployment in April, 1930," *Annals* 154 (March 1931), 12–16. For a summary of pertinent criticism see Mary Van Kleeck, "The Federal Unemployment Census of 1930," American Statistical Association. *Journal* 26:173A (March 1931), Suppl., 191; *Pasadena Labor News*, 15 May 1930, p. 1.

50 46 Stat. 873 (1930).

committee, moreover, thought that the Bureau of Labor Statistics should be further strengthened through an allotment of $200,000, enabling it to widen its employment data-gathering activities and hasten their publication.[51]

Public perception of the administration's good faith hinged upon at least partial implementation of these recommendations, all the more so because the Wagner statistics act had remained inoperative due to the lack of an appropriation. At the New York senator's prompting, Congress came through on 4 March 1931 by voting $140,000 for the purpose. As a result, from 1932 the monthly tabulations of employment statistics published by the bureau were broken down by states, and from 1933 on the scope of coverage was enlarged to include real estate, banking, insurance, and canning and preserving industries. The value of the congressional allocation lay not only in the fact that it enabled the bureau to expand its activities, but also in the hope it nurtured, as a writer in *Social Forces* expressed it, that Congress might follow up the precedent with "at least a fairly substantial increase in the annual appropriations."[52]

Although these developments advanced the cause, they came too late for any insights to be gained in winter 1930–31. The severe distress of these months made it desirable, on the other hand, to assess the existing unemployment immediately. In January 1931 the Bureau of the Census therefore undertook a partial repetition of the April 1930 census, for cost reasons confined to nineteen leading industrial cities. By extrapolation it found that a total of 6,050,000 people were out of work in the United States, about 18 percent of the nonagricultural workforce. Another official effort at the national level appeared to vindicate this result. When the PECE got underway in October 1930, it had recourse to the Metropolitan, which still showed some interest in the possibility of underwriting unemployment insurance. In December 1930 the insurer's agents canvassed 213,787 policy-holding families in forty-six cities from coast to coast. They calculated that approximately 24 percent of the wage or salary

---

51 *Report of the Advisory Committee on Employment Statistics*, in U.S. Bureau of Labor Statistics, *Bulletin 542* (Washington: G.P.O., 1931), 4–15. See also "Report of Advisory Committee on Employment Statistics," *MLR* 32:4 (April 1931), 814–17.

52 "Better Employment Statistics," *ALLR* 21:1 (March 1931), 112; Social Security Board, Washington, D.C., *Social Security in America: The Factual Background of the Social Security Act as Summarized from Staff Reports to the Committee on Economic Security* (Washington: G.P.O., 1937), 58; Donald Anthony, "An Appraisal of the Wagner Unemployment Act," *Social Forces* 9:3 (March 1931), 425.

earning members were unemployed, a finding that a writer in the *ALLR* thought satisfactorily close to the January 1931 census figure in view of the fact that the Metropolitan number included the sick and the voluntary idle.[53]

The federal Department of Labor, eager to downplay the importance of these figures, insisted that the insurer's survey was biased in favor of wage earners and that a nationwide, all-inclusive estimate, using the Metropolitan data, might arrive at a rate of approximately 10 percent total unemployment, or between 4.5 and 5 million persons. As the January 1931 unemployment might well have been somewhat larger, the census bureau result thus seemed to have a realistic quality to it. Not everybody was convinced, however. A writer in the *ALLR* denounced the "devious series of hypotheses" that he felt underlay the bureau's calculations, and New York Industrial Commissioner Frances Perkins thought that her federal colleagues were playing games, as the number of jobless seemed to her to be rather close to 7 million.[54]

The dispute about the correctness of the available figures demonstrated that toward the end of the Hoover era the highly industrialized United States did not yet possess any valid current information regarding the number or distribution of its jobless. Most everybody who understood how unemployment figures were arrived at had to share Meeker's desperation that "the fatal defect in all these unemployment statistics, near statistics, and pseudo statistics is that we do not know exactly what they mean."[55] But the picture was perhaps not as gloomy as it presented itself

53 The Bureau of the Census did not receive special funds for this undertaking. Stewart to Arthur Woods, 28 Oct. 1930, Box 254, Series 12, POUR Papers; "Unemployment in the United States, 1930 and 1931," *MLR* 32:4 (April 1931), 809–13; Edwin M. Fitch, "Counting the Unemployed," *ALLR* 21:2 (June 1931), 206.

54 "Unemployment Survey of Metropolitan Life Insurance Co.," *MLR* 32:3 (March 1931), 572–79; Fitch, "Counting the Unemployed," 207; *New York Times*, 9 Feb. 1931, p. 18.

55 Royal Meeker, "The Dependability and Meaning of Unemployment and Employment Statistics in the United States," *Harvard Business Review* 8:4 (July 1930), 392. Meeker was with a private statistics institute at the time. For attempts to make do with the dubious basis see Robert R. Nathan, "Estimates of Unemployment in the United States, 1929–1935," *International Labour Review* 33:1 (Jan. 1936), 49–73; Social Security Board. Washington D.C., *Social Security in America*, 55–71; Russell A. Nixon and Paul A. Samuelson, "Estimates of Unemployment in the United States," *Review of Economic Statistics* 22:3 (Aug. 1940), 101–11. It should be noted that the unemployment rates given for 1890 to 1940 in U.S. Bureau of the Census, *Historical Statistics of the United States*, 135, basically rely upon the decennial censuses; intercensal figures were obtained by estimating the civilian labor force as well as employment and deducting one series from the other. See ibid., 122. For recent discussions of the technical problems involved

to contemporaries. Some change had certainly occurred over the decades. For one thing, almost every method statisticians could think of had been tried out by the early 1930s, and in the process valuable insights concerning the ultimate goal and the pitfalls to avoid had been gained. In addition, the gathering of employment statistics occurred now in a larger field, yielding more sophisticated and plausible results. Perhaps more important still was the fact that the political decision-makers were rapidly becoming fully aware of the need for proper unemployment statistics and the difficulties encountered in securing them. It was this experience, which helped to prepare the ground for the eventual introduction of unemployment insurance from 1935 on, that was ultimately to solve the disconcerting information problem.

The quest for unemployment remedies could of course not wait until reliable data regarding the extent of the evil became available. The search actually intensified again as soon as unemployment was on the rise. Interest now concentrated on the effective implementation of the devices designed in the preceding years.

III   Revival of the USES

Renewed quests for legislation

Government-run labor exchanges had been the instrument favored by the reformers before the war, and the potential of a good service was still very much on their minds when joblessness increased again toward the end of the 1920s. Efforts to obtain appropriate legislation immediately focused upon the federal level, taking up where the abortive attempts of the postwar period had left the movement. Resistance came from the same quarters as before, but this time environmental pressure was strong enough to bring about a breakthrough. The USES reorganization undertaken from 1931 did not occur in the form most reform-side strategists had hoped, but it nevertheless signaled the federal government's willingness finally to commit considerable resources to the labor distribution task in order to bring unemployment down.

As was the case with counting procedures, the spadework of reformers

in finding valid figures see Robert M. Coen, "Labor Force and Unemployment in the 1920's and 1930's: A Reexamination Based on Postwar Experience," *Review of Economics and Statistics* 55:1 (Feb. 1973), 46–55; Gene Smiley, "Recent Unemployment Rate Estimates for 1920s and 1930s," *Journal of Economic History* 43:2 (June 1983), 487–93.

and congenial legislators prepared the ground for palpable administrative action. The arguments used did not differ markedly from the reasoning during the first decades of the movement. The potential of public offices in fighting the corrupt private agencies still figured prominently, because inefficient state laws and weak enforcement had brought no substantial change in the private's behavior.[56] The demand for a federal network obtained a boost especially as a result of the United States Supreme Court decision in the Ribnik case (28 May 1928). The court, against the votes of liberal justices Harlan F. Stone, Oliver W. Holmes, Jr., and Louis D. Brandeis, declared unconstitutional a New Jersey measure that had put the fee-charging agencies under supervision. After Ribnik, some "healthy growth of the public employment service," as Andrews put it, appeared to be the most promising means for curbing the corrupt practices of the private sector. "The best protection against the evils accompanying private profit-making agencies will not be state legislation," Royal E. Montgomery of the University of Texas affirmed in December 1929, "but a system of federal aid contingent upon state appropriations and state maintenance of specific standards."[57]

Apart from weeding out the undesirable agencies, a good public employment agency system could fulfil other functions. It would, for instance, enable the authorities better to assess the general employment situation. "There can be no inclusive statistics showing the amount of unemployment," Montgomery held, "until we have operated an inclusive system of public employment offices." Moreover, any future unemployment insurance system would have to be backed up by an employment service, as no payments should be made if work was

---

56 In 1928 the California labor commissioner received 664 complaints against licensed employment agencies. "Private and Public Employment Agencies in California," *MLR* 30:2 (Feb. 1930), 260. The New York (State) Industrial Survey Commission found in 1929 that the fee-charging agencies were "still infested with unscrupulous characters who do not hesitate to mulct the helpless, and who find the jobless worker an easy victim." "Employment Agencies Officially Exposed: Sworn Testimony Shows Urgent Need of State Action," *ALLR* 20:1 (March 1930), 27.

57 *Ribnik v. McBride*, 48 Sup. Ct., 545–53. The provision required all fee schedules to be approved by the commissioner of labor. On the legal problem see Glenn A. Bowers, "Employment Service in the United States," *Law and Labor* 12:1 (Sept. 1930), 201; John B. Andrews, "Fee-charging Employment Agencies: Court Action Creates Emergency: New Legislation Now Needed," *ALLR* 18:4 (Dec. 1928), 399–403. Quotation p. 402. – Zella Wright Newcomb, "The Scylla and Charybdis of the Unemployed," *American Federationist* 36:11 (Nov. 1929), 1347–50, esp. 1349; Royal E. Montgomery, "Employment Exchanges Needed," *ALLR* 19:4 (Dec. 1929), 283.

available. "In any scheme of unemployment insurance," Commons advised the Senate Committee on Education and Labor in early 1929, pointing to European precedents, "the first requisite is a satisfactory system of employment offices for registration." But the most important task of the envisaged service was, of course, labor distribution. The labor market had to be organized like any other market, the *American Federationist* contended, in order "to prevent waste and conserve the best interests of all concerned." Municipal agencies alone would not do. There was to be "a state system in every state" in order to "reduce unemployment for many."[58]

Some movement aiming at an improvement of the exchange situation on the federal level could be perceived from 1928, when the need of the unemployed was greater than ever since 1920–21. On 25 February, Albert Johnson (R-Washington), chairman of the House Committee on Immigration and Naturalization, suggested that a Federal Bureau of Employment might be serviceable for a proper distribution of surplus labor. The idea was officially taken up in Congress by Wagner. The exchange bill he presented in April (S. 4157) was almost identical with the former Kenyon/Nolan proposal for a national employment system, a few minor adjustments having been made with Andrews' help. Spurned by the Democratic initiative, Secretary Davis considered framing a bill of his own. Election-year considerations made dwelling on the unemployment issue inopportune, though, and no further action was taken.[59]

The public-agencies issue was no longer out of sight. When Congress reconvened in December 1928, John J. Casey (D-Pennsylvania), who had a union background, introduced a bill similar to the Wagner proposal (H.R. 14454). Shortly thereafter, during the hearings pursuant to S.Res. 219, emphatic endorsement came especially from Bryce M. Stewart. He pointed out that a national system could reduce the so-called labor reserve to the smallest possible size. Another industrial relations expert, Whiting Williams of Cleveland, Ohio, de-

58 Montgomery, "Employment Exchanges Needed," 284. See also Hearings Pursuant to S. Res. 219, pp. xi; 226. – "Public Employment Service," *American Federationist* 37:11 (Nov. 1930), 1334; "Employment Exchanges," ibid. 37:12 (Dec. 1930), 1459.

59 *Commercial and Financial Chronicle* 126 (3 March 1928), 1270; Huthmacher, *Wagner*, 62. A parallel bill (H.R. 13901) was submitted in the House. – Francis I. Jones to Leiserson, 24 May 1928; 1 June 1928; 12 July 1928; 6 Sept. 1928, Box 42, Leiserson Papers; Leiserson to Jones, 26 May 1928, ibid. Jones was Director General of the USES.

scribed in a lengthy memorandum the exchange legislation in sixteen countries. The *ALLR* gave what support it could. As a result, the Committee on Education and Labor came out more strongly in favor of public exchanges than any congressional body ever before. "The burden of assisting the unemployed to find work," it declared, "should be borne by organized society." The committee had well absorbed the constitutional and corruption arguments of the preceding decade. It advised that the USES should concentrate upon coordinating the work of the states; to ensure competent performance, all USES employees should undergo "rigid" civil service examination before hiring. But Congress adjourned a few days after the report reached the Senate floor, and the next session (Summer 1929) was too busy with agricultural and tariff questions to deal with unemployment concerns.[60]

On 9 January 1930, Wagner reintroduced his employment service proposal as one of his three bills (S. 3060). Federal conditional grants, ensuring uniformity of service, were to be paid to the individual states. At his suggestion the bill went to the Committee on Commerce, whose sympathetic chairman Hiram W. Johnson arranged hearings in March. The AALL, AFL President Green, and New York Industrial Commissioner Frances Perkins argued in favor. This time the adversaries took the matter more seriously. The NAM in a lengthy brief and Hiram Bingham (R-Connecticut) on the Senate floor offered the constitutional argumentation that a federal monster had to be avoided. On 12 May 1930 the bill nevertheless passed by a vote of 34 to 27.[61]

Stiffer resistance loomed in the House, where the Judiciary Committee held hearings in June. The tone was again set by Bingham who attacked the proposal in a nationwide broadcast on 7 June, asserting that "it is not the business of Washington to look out for the general welfare of the people, but for the general welfare of the states." The NAM's general counsel, James A. Emery, and a representative from the National Employment Board, a national association of private employment agencies, took the same position before the committee.

60 Hearings Pursuant to S. Res. 219, pp. 149–68; "Financing Public Employment Service," *ALLR* 18:4 (Dec. 1928), 405–08; U.S. Congress. Senate. Committee on Education and Labor, *Causes of Unemployment*. S. Rept. 2072, 70 Cong., 2 sess. (pursuant to S. Res. 219, 25 Feb. 1929), viii–xi.
61 Hearings on S. 3059, S. 3060, S. 3061, pp. 48; 59–63; 104–09; *CR*, 71 Cong., 2 sess., 12 May 1930, pp. 8742–49.

However, Douglas, who at the time conducted an unemployment investigation sponsored by Swarthmore College, argued that the constitutional objections were only a screen, and that the NAM feared that "the employment services would be used to colonize manufacturing plants with union organizers." He also suspected that the employers thought a federal service might hasten the coming of compulsory unemployment insurance.[62]

The constitutional dispute prompted even Wagner to appear before the House committee. While pointing out that federal aid for road building or vocational training was not considered coercion, he left no doubt that in the final analysis a deeper issue was involved, that of industrialized society's task to provide for its needy citizens. He found a mandate for the assumption of this obligation in the general welfare provision of the constitution. At any rate, he declared, the constitution could be adjusted, since "[it] is what the judges say it is." In Wagner's view the interest of man came before adherence to the barren letter. "Men are starving, hungry, in a country of plenty," he exclaimed, "and someone will talk about some constitutional inhibition." His questioning of fundamentalist views of the constitution was representative of a new concept of the task of government. The fact that the committee reported the bill out favorably indicated that acceptance of his viewpoint was spreading. But two minority reports, one of them authored by seventy-nine-year-old committee chairman George S. Graham (R-Pennsylvania), took adversary positions, and the greater triumph was still the opponents', because the bill did not reach the House floor before the end of the session in July 1930[63] (Figure 5–8).

As the year advanced, the proponents of an expanded federal-state service strove to keep the issue in the public consciousness, because the employment picture offered no ground for optimism. Douglas proposed

---

62 National Broadcasting Company, press release for 8 June 1930, Box SM 485, Wagner Papers; Hearings on S. 3059, 3060, H.R. 8374, 8655, 9560, 11414, 12550, and 12551, pp. 22–50; 65–71; 74–92; 109–29; 142–53. The Swarthmore study was published by Douglas and Director, *Problem of Unemployment*. – Paul H. Douglas, "Connecting Men and Jobs," *Survey* 65:5 (1 Dec. 1930), 255–56.

63 Hearings on S. 3059, 3060, H.R. 8374, 8655, 9560, 11414, 12550, and 12551, pp. 19–20; 168–180; U.S. Congress. House. Committee on the Judiciary, *To Provide for the Establishment of a National Employment System and for Cooperation with the States in the Promotion of Such System, and for Other Purposes.* H.Rept. 2033, 71 Cong., 2 sess. (to accompany S. 3060; 26 June 1930).

Figure 5-8. Congressional resistance to Wagner's unemployment bills, as seen by the *New York Telegram*. (Source: *ALLR* 20:3 [Sept. 1930], 298.)

a concerted campaign for the three bills, making his own contribution with a strong article in the *Survey*.[64] During the fall, Samuel Joseph of the College of the City of New York organized meetings with Perkins, Paul U. Kellogg, and others to discuss strategies. Croxton pleaded the

64 Fred C. Croxton, "Development of a Federal Public Employment System in the United States," IAPES, Proceedings 1930, in U.S. Bureau of Labor Statistics, *Bulletin 538*

cause at the annual IAPES meeting in Toronto in September. Roosevelt's
Committee on Stabilization of Industry saw a need for "a vigorous and
effective federated system of state employment offices which will manage
inter-state clearances of labor and which will promote efficient employment work." Even PECE chairman Woods urged the president to ease
passage of Wagner's bill, as it was ultimately the attitude of the administration that would decide the issue.[65]

Doak's reorganization of the USES

Hoover, for his part, experienced some difficulty in making up his mind.
He was in no mood to help institute a measure advocated by left-wingers
and trade unions and would clearly have liked to block any strengthening
of the flaccid USES. But the difficult situation persuaded him to upgrade
the service. He endeavored to ensure, though, that the development
remained under control. The result was unsatisfactory in itself, but iron-
ically the very inadequacy of this attempt finally eliminated the arguments
against the creation of a structure that corresponded to the ideas of the
reformers.

When in late 1930 he felt unable to ignore the issue any longer, the
president decided to divert the push and charge his new secretary of labor
with preparing a proposal without the grant-in-aid feature. The appointment of a new head of the Labor Department had become necessary as
Davis had in the meantime been elected to the Senate. Rather than
listening to the social-work lobby and choosing Grace Abbott, the chief
of the department's Children's Bureau, the president had named William
N. Doak, formerly national legislative representative of the Brotherhood
of Railroad Trainmen. This latter organization, it is true, was on record
as endorsing the Wagner bill, as did the AFL; moreover, Doak himself-

(Washington: G.P.O., 1931), 162–66; Paul H. Douglas, "Toward Unemployment Relief: The Wagner Bill for Adequate Employment Service Provides the First Steps,"
Woman's Press (Oct. 1930), 699–700; idem, "Connecting Men and Jobs," 253–56; Henry
Raymond Mussey, "Fighting Unemployment: I. Organizing the Labor Market," *Nation*
131:3414 (10 Dec. 1930), 641–43; "Public Employment Service," *American Federationist*
37:11 (Nov. 1930), 1334; Douglas to Wagner, 14 June 1930, Box 188, Legislative Files,
Wagner Papers.
65 Samuel Joseph to Wagner, 11 Nov. 1930; 17 Dec. 1930, Box 188, Legislative Files,
Wagner Papers; Croxton, "Development of a Federal Public Employment System,"
162–68; New York (State). Governor's Commission on Unemployment Problems, *Less
Unemployment through Stabilization*, 17; Hayes, *Activities*, 141–42.

had actively participated in drafting the first Kenyon/Nolan bill in 1919.[66] But the new secretary showed no compunction about shedding his former convictions and complying with his new employer's request.

Unfortunately for Doak his task did not prove easy to accomplish. He tried to enlist the assistance of the PECE in the drafting of an alternate bill, but the committee's experts, led by Bryce M. Stewart, favored the Wagner version. In an apparent attempt to open Doak's mind to more liberal views, the AALL then proceeded to elect him a vice-president; it also circularized its several thousand members to lobby for passage of S. 3060. Doak held fast, however, and turned to Graham for help. Their combined efforts produced an amendment to the bill before the House that practically provided for a buildup of the existing USES, the only change of substance being the addition of an assistant secretary of labor.[67]

Doak could not really hope to find much sympathy for this new scheme with the advocates of federal-state cooperation. In order to leave nothing undone, however, he entered into negotiations with Wagner. Not surprisingly, the latter saw no basis for accommodation and declared himself unable to discover "even after the closest scrutiny, anything in the new proposal which materially changes the existing unsatisfactory situation" in the USES. The battle was now clearly joined, and the proponents of the Wagner bill swung into action. Behind the scenes, Woods seems to have again asked Hoover to ensure passage. The AALL sent the signatures of 150 prominent supporters to the president and persuaded many of them, including the industrial commissioners of ten states and AFL President Green, to endorse the measure publicly. This caused the indignant Doak to resign his vice-presidential position within the AALL. His hope lay with the House Judiciary Committee. He was not disappointed, as the latter, practically reversing its decision of the previous June when it had recommended the Wagner version, reported the

66 George H. Trafton, "The Wagner Bill and the Hoover Veto," *ALLR* 21:1 (March 1931), 87. Doak was an active Republican and had made a bid for a Senate seat in 1924. See on him Roger W. Babson, *Washington and the Depression: Including the Career of W. N. Doak* (New York: Harper, 1932), 92–108; and his obituary in *New York Times*, 24 Oct. 1933, p. 21.

67 Bryce M. Stewart to Woods, 19 Dec. 1930, Box 25, POUR Papers; idem, "Memorandum on Bill S. 3060 etc.," 19 Dec. 1930, Box 253, ibid.; E. E. Hunt to Woods, 23 Dec. 1930, Box 29, ibid.; J. B. Andrews to W. N. Doak, 8 Jan. 1931, microfilm, reel 43, Andrews Papers; circular letter, John B. Andrews, 5 Feb. 1931, Box 188, Legislative Files, Wagner Papers; G. S. Graham to Andrews, 10 Feb. 1931, quoted in Andrews to Wagner, 11 Feb. 1931, ibid. The text of the amendment is in *CR*, 71 Cong., 3 sess., 23 Feb. 1931, p. 5774.

amended bill out favorably. When the matter came to the House floor on 23 February, some progressive Republicans vigorously condemned the administration for acceding to the NAM's desires. Impetuous Congressman Fiorello H. LaGuardia (R-New York) denounced Doak's about face, stating that Doak, before becoming a cabinet officer, "did not peep one word" as to the bill's inappropriateness.[68] The House then proceeded to repudiate the president by voting down the Doak amendment, 182 to 84. In its stead it passed Wagner's version by voice vote. On the next day the Senate concurred in this decision, and the bill went to Hoover.

The president's dislike of the proposal had not abated. He did not have to veto it directly, though. As Congress expired on 4 March 1931, he could withhold his signature without fear of being overridden. In last minute thrusts the PECE assured Hoover that nothing was really to be feared from S. 3060, and Wagner sent a telegram asking for reconsideration. But the employers' side was equally active, and Hoover may also have had a talk with Graham, whom Bingham had urgently recommended to him as a consultant. He received a lengthy letter from Doak, who requested a presidential veto. The bill remained unsigned and did not become law.[69]

Various opinions have been voiced regarding Hoover's reasons for rejecting the Wagner measure. In a press statement of 7 March 1931, the president claimed that abolition of the existing USES would eliminate a functioning service without bringing in a substitute for months or even years. Moreover, the bill would have created forty-eight practically independent agencies, thus abandoning any interstate coordination; finally, subsidies would have been distributed, not according to economic need, but based "upon mathematical ratio to population."[70] It is easy to show

---

68 Wagner to Secretary of Labor [W. N. Doak], 6 Feb. 1931, Box 188, Legislative Files, Wagner Papers; Paul U. Kellogg to Wagner, 5 Feb. 1931, ibid.; Andrews to Wagner, 7 Feb. 1931; 10 Feb. 1931; 13 Feb. 1931, ibid.; editor's note to Fred C. Croxton, "The Federal Role in a Public Employment Service," *ALLR* 21:3 (Sept. 1931), 303; *New York Times*, 20 Feb. 1931, p. 17; *CR*, 71 Cong., 3 sess., 23 Feb. 1931, pp. 5751–77. Quotation p. 5755.

69 J. C. Lawrence (PECE) to Lawrence Richey, 5 March 1931, Box 338, Presidential Papers, Hoover Papers. Richey was Hoover's secretary. – John E. Coffin to Hoover, telegram, 25 Feb. 1931, Box 348, ibid. Coffin was president of the Merchants' and Manufacturers' Association of Los Angeles. – Hiram Bingham to Hoover, 25 Feb. 1931, ibid.; Doak to Hoover, 7 March 1931, reprinted in *Law and Labor* 13:4 (April 1931), 90–91.

70 Myers, ed., *State Papers*, I, 530–31. Wagner to Hoover, telegram, 7 March 1931, Box SM 485, Wagner Papers. See also Doak's letter to Hoover, 7 March 1931, reprinted

the flimsiness of this argumentation, and contemporaries as well as later commentators have denounced it. "The reasons offered for the exercise of the presidential veto," Green vituperated, expressing the feelings of many, "are unconvincing and unacceptable."[71]

Less clear, however, is the real motivation underlying the presidential action. At the time the suspicion was voiced that the administration was "unwilling to let credit for such a constructive law go to the Democrats." Either that, the *New Republic* wrote, or the president "was subservient to the reactionary interests which do not want systematic organization of employment." The unpublished Hoover papers do not contain any conclusive evidence in this regard, and several further explanations are possible. Irving Bernstein holds that financial considerations played the decisive role; Hoover, believing in a balanced budget, resented the additional outlay that the Wagner measure would have entailed. Schwarz rather thinks that the president was afraid of losing the political initiative to Congress and had decided to show that opposition to congressional enthusiasts was courageous and correct. There may be some virtue in these assumptions, especially so because the president's action enjoyed the backing of a substantial part of the press, including the Democratic *New York Times*. It appears, however, that Hoover also shared the more fundamental fear that the employers' organizations harbored concerning uncontrolled union penetration. The Wagner bill, he claimed in his memoirs, "would have put workers' jobs in control of political machines, such as Tammany in New York, or the Hague gang of Jersey City." The Doak amendment, though, would have greatly reduced this danger; by providing for central control from Washington, it ensured that appointments and policies were less likely to get out of hand.[72]

in *Law and Labor*, with essentially the same arguments. See also Trafton, "The Wagner Bill and the Hoover Veto," 87.

71 Ruth M. Kellogg, *The United States Employment Service* (Chicago: University of Chicago Press, 1933), 68–69; Joseph P. Chamberlain, "Facts about the Wagner Bill," *ALLR* 21:1 (March 1931), 91–93; Mary Van Kleeck, "Toward a National Employment Service," *Survey* 66:2 (15 April 1931), 88–90; Arthur W. Macmahon, "Third Session of the Seventy-first Congress, December 1, 1930, to March 4, 1931," *American Political Science Review* 25:4 (Nov. 1931), 946; Don D. Lescohier and Elizabeth Brandeis, *History of Labor in the United States, 1896–1932. Vol. III* (New York: Macmillan, 1935), 209–10; Irving Bernstein, *The Lean Years: A History of the American Worker 1920–1933* (Boston: Houghton Mifflin, 1960), 282–83; Huthmacher, *Wagner*, 84–85. Gompers is quoted in Trafton, "The Wagner Bill and the Hoover Veto," 85.

72 *New York World-Telegram* is quoted in "Why Did Hoover Veto the Wagner Bill?" *ALLR* 21:1 (March 1931), 90. See also other press quotations, ibid.; *New Republic* 64:850 (18

This latter explanation provides the answer to why the staunch resistance that the conservatives had offered to the USES extension up to this time suddenly subsided. The minority reports on S. 3060 had denounced the creation of another massive agency in Washington, but the president now moved without legislative sanction to reorganize and vastly expand the USES strictly as an executive agency headed in Washington. He obviously reasoned that if there had to be an increased service – and the substantial majorities in Congress for Wagner's bill left no doubt about feelings in the country – it was better to grasp the bull by the horns and give it the proper direction. On 12 March 1931, Hoover announced the appointment of John R. Alpine, a former AFL vice-president turned business executive, as special assistant to the secretary of labor in charge of the extension of the federal employment service, and had Congress vote an emergency appropriation of $500,000 to finance the undertaking.[73]

At this point we should cast a look at the state-run employment offices. By late 1930 nothing had materially changed from the situation in the early 1920s. Most of the state services still lacked funds to do an adequate job. As they had been hard put to function satisfactorily within their own jurisdictions, no new initiatives aiming at interservice coordination had been taken in the years before the depression. The loose ties with the USES described earlier still existed in all instances, but beyond this connection the twenty-four states that engaged in exchange activities were on their own. The number of offices and employees varied considerably, as Table 5–1 indicates.[74] The differences in size were, of course, a direct

March 1931), 109; Bernstein *Lean Years*, 284; Schwarz, *Interregnum of Despair*, 40–41; "The Wagner Veto Uproar," *Literary Digest* 108:13 (28 March 1931), 11; [Herbert Hoover], *The Memoirs of Herbert Hoover: The Great Depression 1929–1941* (New York: Macmillan, 1952), 47. See also Fausold, *Hoover*, 135, whose assertion that Hoover feared the "political machinations of local political workers" seems to support the interpretation given above. For other criticisms of Hoover's veto see ibid., 137.

73 Myers, ed., *State Papers*, I, 532–33. The Deficiency Appropriation Act for 1931 (46 Stat. 522 [1931], p. 1575) provided that if S. 3060 was passed by Congress but did not become law, an appropriation of $500,000 for the employment service would be immediately available.

74 A matter-of-fact description of the system can be found in Annabel M. Stewart and Bryce M. Stewart, *Statistical Procedure of Public Employment Offices: An Analysis of Practice in Various Countries and a Plan for Standard Procedure in the United States Made for the Committee on Governmental Labor Statistics of the American Statistical Association* (New York: Russell Sage Foundation, 1933), 220–64. In eleven additional states the USES maintained a representative in connection with its farm labor service: Arizona, Delaware, Georgia, Maryland, Montana, North Dakota, Oregon, South Dakota, Texas, Vermont, Washington.

Table 5-1. *State employment offices in 1930*

State	Year first office opened	Offices	Employees	State funds	Federal, city, county funds	Total annual expenditure
				$	$	$
Arkansas	1917	5	5	2,400	1,860	4,260
California	1915 (1895)	11	27	90,835	—	93,710
Connecticut	1901	8	16	48,114	—	50,000
Illinois	1899	20	109	266,080	—	266,080
Indiana	1909	5	15	25,000	7,970	32,608
Iowa	1915 (1891)	2	4	3,600	2,760	6,360
Kansas	1901	5	7	9,600	1,800	15,116
Maine		1	1	—	1,400	1,400
Massachusetts	1906	4	34	72,500	4,881	72,159
Michigan	1905	10	15	32,758	1,620	34,378
Minnesota	1905	3	22	35,350	9,099	44,450
Missouri	1898	3	na	na	na	na
Nevada	1923	3	3	2,000	2,123	4,123
New Hampshire	1917	1	1	3,800	960	3,733
New Jersey	1915	8	22	36,680	48,960	95,844
New York	1914 (1896)	11	96	166,280	5,280	171,560
North Carolina	1921	6	8	9,140	8,180	17,320
Ohio	1890	13	69	86,960	69,864	156,824
Oklahoma	1908	4	5	9,088	2,040	10,566
Pennsylvania	1915	13	58	100,000	8,300	102,800
Rhode Island		1	2	4,000	900	4,900
Virginia	1924	3	8	2,500	9,280	11,780
West Virginia	1901	1	2	3,000	1,440	4,440
Wisconsin	1901	10	28	50,000	19,290	58,081
Total		151	557	1,059,685	208,007	1,262,492

Source: "Public Employment Services," *Monthly Labor Review* 32:1 (Jan. 1931), 22; reports of individual state bureaus.

result of the variations in funding. In some states, little more than a so-called "mail-order system" was practiced – that is, telephone and correspondence were the sole tools of the officials[75] (Figure 5–9).

Another problem area was the still-persisting inadequacy of the personnel. "Well trained directors mean decent salaries," a knowledgeable insider complained in the *ALLR* in early 1928, "and these cannot be paid out of too meagre appropriations." The majority of states, furthermore,

75 "Public Employment Services," 11.

Figure 5-9. State employment office legislation as of 1 January 1931. Black states had no laws establishing state employment offices; shaded states had not acted on existing laws. (Source: *ALLR* 21:1 [March 1931], 94.)

did still not subject their exchange employees to civil service rules. Appointments were often "unfortunately and admittedly... of a political nature," as an observer in 1931 put it, a fact that added to the difficulty of selecting thoroughly qualified officials. But even civil service status and long tenure did not necessarily improve performance. Their effect, the Ohio Commission on Unemployment Insurance concluded in 1932, was all too often a complacent "settling into routine method of procedure and a lack of new ideas."[76]

Not surprisingly, only few businesses sought help from such agencies. The public employment offices, the Massachusetts employment stabilization commission remarked in 1931, lacked "the wide recognition and confidence of employers." Somewhat apologetically it added that this was "a characteristic they share more or less with similar agencies in most other States." Altogether the state services did offer a disheartening picture. "With rare exceptions," Douglas grieved in late 1930, "they have

76 Margaret D. Meyer, "Public Employment Bureaus: Adequate Appropriations Needed," *ALLR* 18:1 (March 1928), 85; Trafton, "The Wagner Bill and the Hoover Veto," 86; Ohio. Commission on Unemployment Insurance, *Report. Part II: Studies and Reports* (Columbus: Ohio Commission on Unemployment Insurance, 1933), 268.

Table 5-2. *United States Employment Service performance, 1919–32*

| Fiscal Year | Cooperating state services | | | USES Farm labor division placements |
	Applications	Placements	Percentage	
1920[a]	3,165,559	2,020,252	63.8	—
1921	2,433,746	1,397,738	57.4	—
1922	2,874,785	1,458,746	50.7	(75,000)
1923	2,887,697	2,156,466	74.7	113,282
1924	2,755,593	1,806,990	65.6	161,083
1925	2,663,846	1,609,977	60.4	425,548
1926	2,727,763	1,791,381	65.6	392,750
1927	2,440,640	1,688,476	69.2	na
1928	2,259,095	1,412,645	62.5	433,854
1929	na	na		559,571
1930	2,346,316	1,345,936	57.4	611,598
1931	na	1,104,136		c.670,000

[a] 1 October 1919–30 June 1920

Source: Darrell Hevenor Smith, *The United States Employment Service: Its History, Activities and Organization* (Baltimore: Johns Hopkins University Press, 1923), 61; U.S. Dept. of Labor, *Annual Reports* for the years 1923–30.

dingy quarters, are operated by low-paid and dispirited political hacks and primarily handle unskilled labor." The placement results suffered accordingly[77] (Table 5–2).

The so-called "Doak reorganization" of the USES, in actuality the handiwork of Alpine, got under way in spring 1931 amid continuing controversy.[78] The Department of Labor did not attempt to integrate the state systems into the expanding federal service, but rather endeavored to create parallel offices of its own. Until then the placement efforts of

77 Massachusetts. Special Commission on the Stabilization of Employment, *Preliminary Report* (Boston: Wright & Potter, 1932), 22; Douglas, "Connecting Men and Jobs," 253. See also Douglas and Director, *The Problem of Unemployment*, 337–42. For the reasons noted earlier, the figures in Table 5–1 have to be taken with a large grain of salt. A telling example of numbers inflation is provided by the Farm Labor Division. In 1927 it dealt with about 100,000 harvesters, whereas the placements may have been in the 400,000 range, as the same individuals were placed several times over. U.S. Dept. of Labor, *15th Annual Report, 1927*, 33.

78 See, e.g., Doak's speech on the National Radio Forum, 4 April 1931, Box 188, Legislative Files, Wagner Papers; Harvard University professor Sumner H. Slichter's rebuttal in *New York Times*, 10 April 1931, p. 24; George H. Trafton, "The Doak Plan in Operation," *ALLR* 21:2 (June 1931), 199–202; "The Week," *New Republic* 64:856 (29 April 1931), 284.

the USES had been restricted to the supply of seasonal farm hands through the Farm Labor Division and the insignificant operations of the Junior division and the recently established Veterans' Division. The service now entered the field of general direct placement, but without tying in the activities of the new offices with the work of those created earlier. These developments deeply irked Jones, who for many frustrating years had headed the anemic USES and had been known to favor the Kenyon–Wagner scheme of positive cooperation with the states, whose imminent adoption he had still expected only a few months earlier. Alpine's busy hustle left little for Jones to do, and at the end of August he resigned, not without engaging in a bitter public quarrel with the man who superseded him.[79]

The expansion had a Potemkinesque quality to it. Federal state directors were appointed in every state, and by mid-1932, 101 general placement offices had been opened. Federal appropriations for the fiscal year 1931–32 amounted to $938,780. In his report for 1932, Alpine prided himself on the job placement of a total of 2,174,174 men and women during the fiscal year, and Doak thought that this performance was "no mean accomplishment in these times of reduced work opportunities." But the figures suggested a brighter picture than reality warranted.[80] It was even doubtful that much headway was made in the effort to catch up with the private agencies. Figures for the business volume of the latter are virtually impossible to come by, but their activities must have been vastly more important than those of the governmental exchanges.[81]

79 Francis I. Jones, "Need for a Public Employment Service in the United States," IAPES, Proceedings 1924, in U.S. Bureau of Labor Statistics, *Bulletin 400* (Washington: G.P.O., 1925), 42; U.S. Dept. of Labor, *18th Annual Report, 1930*, 55; *New York Times*, 2 Sept. 1931, p. 3; ibid., 3 Sept. 1931, p. 2.

80 U.S. Dept. of Labor, *20th Annual Report, 1932*, 3; 43. Before Congressional committees Alpine stated that from 1 April to 31 Dec. 1931 the USES placed 861,653 (53%) and the "cooperative" offices 773,045 (47%) of the total of that period; from 1 April 1931 to 31 Oct. 1932 the figures were 1,842,055 (55%) and 1,536,539 (45%). Hearings on S. 2687, p. 21; Hearings on H.R. 14363, p. 81. The Farm Labor Division, which had been in existence for years and treated "directed to employment" figures as placements, was responsible for 886,605 jobs. U.S. Dept. of Labor, *20th Annual Report, 1932*, 44; Kellogg, *Employment Service*, 117. This leaves somewhat in excess of 300,000 general placements made by the USES during that period. Once allowance is made for generous padding and the fact that most jobs were only of a temporary nature (see in this context Kellogg, *Employment Service*, 121; Hearings on H.R. 14363, p. 82), the achievement is at best a minor one.

81 In 1932, when the depression had already very much depleted the ranks of the private agencies, 229 of them still did business in Chicago, 758 in New York (City), 19 in

From the start the shortcomings of the USES reorganization were relentlessly put in the pillory by those interested in the passage of the original Wagner measure. As early as May 1931 the Association of Government Officials in Industry, assembled in Boston, passed a resolution in favor of the state system "rather than an independent system of Federal employment offices." In July, representatives of ten eastern states demanded that the USES "refrain from independent operation of any direct placement offices in the states which maintain employment services."[82] A somewhat belated directive issued by Alpine aiming at interoffice cooperation did not do much good. "To date about the only thing this scheme has accomplished." the secretary of the Oklahoma Federation of Labor observed, "is to confuse matters and hamper the long-established employment service." In June the *ALLR* questioned the qualification of the federal state directors, and pointed out that fifteen of them were members of the railroad unions with which Doak had formerly been connected. At the IAPES convention in September, Leiserson condemned the new USES as "a fraud on the public and on the unemployed." The convention then formally declared that "the existing so-called reorganized Federal Employment Service is wrong in principle, has failed and cannot succeed."[83]

To keep up the pressure, Wagner made another legislative attempt in the new Congress. S. 2687 differed only in minor detail from the previous S. 3060. Again the bill was referred to Hiram W. Johnson's Committee on Commerce, which held another round of hearings in March 1932. Nothing much new came to the fore in the course of the hearings, although Wagner's relentless questioning of chief witness Alpine could have ed-

---

Buffalo, 291 in California. Kellogg, *Employment Service*, 52. The Chamber of Commerce estimated in 1932 that there were 1,150 private agencies in New York, making more than 1,000,000 placements a year. Chamber of Commerce of the United States of America. Dept. of Manufacture, *Public and Private Employment Exchanges: Report of Committee of the Department of Manufacture* (Washington: Chamber of Commerce of the United States, 1932), 15.

82 "Annual Meeting of Governmental Officials in Industry," *MLR* 33:1 (July 1931), 91; "Eastern Interstate Conference on Labor Legislation," *MLR* 33:2 (Aug. 1931), 304. The states represented were Connecticut, Delaware, Maryland, Massachusetts, New Jersey, New York, Ohio, Pennsylvania, Rhode Island, and West Virginia.

83 U.S. Dept. of Labor. Employment Service, "General Order Number 5, July 28, 1931," Box 188, Legislative Files, Wagner Papers (note the change of name of the agency); Victor S. Purdy to Wagner, 19 Sept. 1931, ibid.; Trafton, "The Doak Plan in Operation," 200–01; "State Employment Service Officials Condemn Doak 'Reorganization,'" *ALLR* 21:4 (Dec. 1931), 393.

ucated the public at large, had it cared, about the incompetence, if not downright corruption, that characterized the buildup of the service. Whereas the committee reported the bill out favorably, the authors of a minority report dreaded the end of the good work of the Doak organization. A more radical stance was taken by Senator Josiah W. Bailey (D-North Carolina), who wrote Wagner that he was "not inclined to the view that the federal government is responsible for the employment of individuals." This opinion still prevailed, as the proposal did not come up for further action during the Seventy-second Congress.[84]

But the horrible experience of the worst depression year began to have an impact. In May a committee of the United States Chamber of Commerce came out in favor of the Wagner bill. The University of Chicago, Douglas's institution, agreed to sponsor an investigation of the existing facilities. On its behalf, Ruth Kellogg undertook a twelve week fact-finding tour of sixteen states in summer and early fall 1932, visiting public employment offices and gathering data. Another indication of the changing mood was Wagner's reelection in November by the largest majority any senator had ever obtained. This event coincided, of course, with the humiliating election defeat of Hoover and his party in the country at large, a development that finally boded well for the passage of Wagner's proposal.[85]

There were indications that public opinion was now beginning to favor the reformer's cause. The result of Kellogg's survey, a book-length study published in early 1933, made up in fervent indignation what it lacked in methodicalness of presentation. Its crushing condemnation of the Doak agency culminated in the statement that the USES "fails to have any impact on the labor market – that is, does not function as a clearing place [and] has fallen prey to the spoils system." The numerous examples of ineffectiveness and corruption that it cited prepared the ground for re-

---

84 Hearings on S. 2687, pp. 8–29; 149–54. See also the excerpts of Wagner's radio address of 9 February 1932, in "Why Congress Should Enact the Employment Service Bill," *ALLR* 22:1 (March 1932), 54–55. – U.S. Senate. Committee on Commerce, *National and State Employment Service*, S.Rept. 589, 72 Congress, 1 sess. (to accompany S. 2687, 22 April 1932); idem, Part 2, 72 Cong., 1 sess. (to accompany S. 2687, 4 May 1932). The signatories of the minority report were Porter H. Dale, Roscoe C. Patterson, George H. Moses, and Hiram Bingham. – J. W. Bailey to Wagner, 11 April 1932, Box 188, Legislative Files, Wagner Papers.
85 Chamber of Commerce, *Public and Private Employment Exchanges*, 25; H. A. Millis to Wagner, 7 Dec. 1932, Box 190, Legislative Files, Wagner Papers; Huthmacher, *Wagner*, 106.

newed legislative efforts. In January 1933, the Interstate Conference on Labor Laws adopted a resolution vigorously in favor of Wagner's proposal. As the chairman of the Department of Economics at the University of Chicago remarked, Wagner's measure had "even stronger backing by people generally than ever before."[86]

"There is some hope," Douglas had written as early as December 1931, "that out of the present depression may come an adequate system of public employment services."[87] Doak's clumsy "reorganization" could temporarily forestall the adoption of the Wagner version of Kenyon's decade-old proposal. But it proved to be a rearguard action, in effect clearing the way for, rather than impeding, the ultimate establishment of a competent exchange system. The reorganization's failure demonstrated that the early promoters of a labor-exchange system had been right in reasoning that a scheme that provided for genuine federal-state cooperation was the preferable proposition. In the final analysis the reformers' protracted fight was therefore not in vain, as a perpetual rethinking and honing of the concept took place over the decades. Not only did the exigencies of a sound federal employment exchange system reach clear definition by the end of Hoover's tenure as a consequence, but the political obstacles for its institution were also visibly disintegrating. The Democratic Congress of the Roosevelt era could readily pick up from here.

IV   Public works and relief

The issue of long-range planning

Public labor exchanges, adversaries as well as proponents had emphasized as early as the 1890s, could not provide jobs where there were none. To help fill the gap, reformers had for decades advocated that public works be undertaken. In the period following World War I, neither state nor federal governments had been subject to enough pressure to implement either meaningful emergency projects or significant long-range planning

---

86 Kellogg, *Employment Service*, 171–72; "Interstate Conference on Labor Laws," *MLR* 36:3 (March 1933), 537–40. Represented were Connecticut, Maryland, New Hampshire, New Jersey, New York, Ohio, Pennsylvania, Rhode Island, and the federal Dept. of Labor. – Edwin S. Smith to Wagner, 30 Jan. 1933, Box 191, Legislative Files, Wagner Papers; H. A. Millis to Wagner, 7 Dec. 1932, Box 190, ibid. Smith was Massachusetts commissioner of labor and industries. The conference took place 27–28 Jan. 1933 in Boston.
87 Douglas, "Connecting Men and Jobs," 253.

schemes. The deteriorating employment situation toward the end of the 1920s, however, began to provide the needed incentive.

The long-range planning idea was the fiscally more innocuous one. Of course, many states, having to come to the rescue of incapacitated local authorities, found themselves forced to furnish expeditious relief. They usually opted for emergency works and disregarded the potential of the advance planning idea, because it could not yield immediate results. The federal government, on the other hand, intended not to enter the relief scene if ever it could help it or at least to keep at a distance as long as possible. Because it could not afford to ignore the relief problem fully, implementing long-range planning appeared as a perfect compromise. The concept conformed to the growing tendency to favor the control of industry in the public interest through planning. Such legislation, more-over, met the long-held expectations of the unemployment reformers. Yet the scheme did not compel the administration to undertake anything serious immediately, and a planning obligation could probably be held untroublesome. Although little movement could thus be noticed at the state level, Congress for these reasons put a full-fledged stabilization law on the statute books.

Only in a few states did long-range planning receive attention. An unsuccessful bill presented to the Massachusetts senate on 23 November 1928 proposed to establish a state reserve fund and to authorize munic-ipalities to do the same. In 1931 the state's Stabilization Commission drew up a new proposal providing for a Public Works Planning Board, but the matter was again not pursued further, perhaps because up to this time only one other state had joined California and Wisconsin in adopting such legislation. In Utah a bill was introduced in answer to Maine Gov-ernor Ralph O. Brewster's appeal, of which more will be said later. It passed, and as a consequence a planning body for new buildings and other work in the state was created in 1929. The law provided for a trial period of two years. The depression intervened, however, and the law was not extended.[88]

Elsewhere, interest in the subject did not lead beyond tentative ap-

---

88 International Labour Office, *Unemployment and Public Works* (Geneva, 1931. Studies and Reports, Series C [Employment and Unemployment], no. 15), 62; Massachusetts. Special Commission on the Stabilization of Employment, *Preliminary Report*, 31–51. Text of the bill pp. 81–89; "Communication from the Governor," 9 March 1929, pamphlet, Box 188, Legislative Files, Wagner Papers; 1929 *Utah Laws*, c. 101. See also "Utah Launches Advanced Plan for Public Work," *ALLR* 20:1 (March 1930), 22–23.

proaches. Roosevelt, as president of the American Construction Council in the early 1920s, had shown himself to be unenthusiastic about the planning idea; but when the depression struck, his Committee on Stabilization repeatedly recommended that state and municipal governments give it some consideration. A Pennsylvania committee privately appointed by gubernatorial candidate Pinchot in October 1930 proposed to plan public works six years ahead. A committee in Wisconsin advocated the creation of a stabilization fund. These initiatives certainly did not indicate a strong ground swell. To foster planning legislation in the states, in December 1932 the FESB therefore issued general guidelines that were printed in a publication sponsored by the American Engineering Council. No results came forth, of course, before the advent of the New Deal.[89]

More serious activity could be observed at the federal level. Responding to the ongoing discussion regarding the potential of public works planning, in January 1928 Wesley L. Jones (R-Washington), chairman of the Senate Committee on Commerce and author of a pertinent treatise, introduced a bill in the Senate "to create a prosperity reserve" (S. 2475). Jones, better known for his prohibition crusades and not really a progressive, was interested in the development of the Columbia River basin, and had for this reason been a long-time supporter of federal public works schemes. S. 2475 provided an appropriation of $150,400,000 in addition to the funds ordinarily available, from which the federal government was to finance building projects if the general construction volume fell abnormally.[90]

The Coolidge administration showed only lukewarm interest. Secretary of War Dwight F. Davis, whose Army Corps of Engineers executed a major part of the federally financed public works, foresaw a lack of heavy equipment. Treasury Department Acting Secretary Ogden L. Mills had

89 Mallery to Andrews, 19 Sept. 1922, microfilm, reel 27, Andrews Papers; *New York Times*, 4 June 1922, VII, p. 2; Frank Freidel, *Franklin D. Roosevelt: The Ordeal* (Boston: Little Brown, 1954), 154–55; "New York Committee on Stabilization of Industry," *MLR* 31:2 (Aug. 1930), 27; New York (State). Governor's Commission on Unemployment Problems, *Less Unemployment through Stabilization*, 5; 15; Pennsylvania. Committee on Unemployment, *Alleviating Unemployment: A Report to Gifford Pinchot, Governor* (Harrisburg, 1931), 16 and appendix; Wisconsin. Legislature. Interim Committee on Unemployment, *Report* ([Madison]: Industrial Commission, [1931]), 5; 56; 102–03; American Engineering Council, *Advance Planning of Public Works by States* (n.p., n.d.), Exhibit A.
90 Wesley L. Jones, "Federal Expenditures and the Construction Industry," Academy of Political Science in the City of New York, *Proceedings* 12 (July 1927), 735–47; Schwarz, *Interregnum of Despair*, 57.

no objection to the proposed legislation "at this time." When the Committee on Commerce held hearings on the bill in April, Hoover merely recognized that the measure contemplated would be in accord with the recommendations of the 1921 Conference on Unemployment. This studied indifference prevailed. Despite the warm advocacy of Andrews, Pepper (no longer a senator), and Dennison, the bill did not reach the floor of the Senate, and an attempt in the House (H.R. 13568) also failed. In May, Wagner introduced his S. 4307, which asked for a Federal Employment Stabilization Board to advice the president on public works acceleration. He was no more successful.[91]

There has been speculation that the complexity of Wagner's proposal was responsible for its failure. This may have been partially true. Even in liberal Senator Couzens' environment the feeling existed that "the whole work is not very satisfactory... it is so intangible." More importantly, however, the administration did not want to endorse a measure of left-wing appeal in an election year. An insider later observed that Wagner's bill "did not meet the approval of the Administration... which blocked its passage in Congress." In mid-April the Socialist Party had included in its election platform a call for an "extension of all public works and a program of long range planning of public works." At its convention in Houston in July, the Democratic Party suggested a "scientific plan" of advance-planning of public works. The Republicans preferred to remain mute on the issue, cheerfully claiming that American labor enjoyed "the highest wage and the highest standard of living throughout the world."[92]

At any rate, when the election was out of the way, the president-elect jumped on the bandwagon. Hoover probably thought that he ought to

---

91 Dwight F. Davis to W[esley] L. Jones, 7 April 1928, printed in Hearings on S. 2475, pp. 1–2; Ogden L. Mills to W[esley] L. Jones, 4 April 1928, printed ibid., 2; Hoover to Wesley L. Jones, 14 April 1928, printed in U.S. Congress. Senate. Committee on Commerce, *Creation of a Prosperity Reserve*. S.Rept. 836, 70 Cong., 1 sess. (to accompany S. 2475; 18 April 1928), 2–3; Hearings on S. 2475, pp. 5; 8; 28. See also "Bill for 'Prosperity Reserve' Now Up to Congress," *ALLR* 18:1 (March 1928), 76; Otto T. Mallery, " 'Prosperity Reserve' of Public Works Needed to Combat Unemployment," ibid., 77–80; " 'Prosperity Reserve' Bill Favorably Reported by Senate Committee," *ALLR* 18:2 (June 1928), 145–48.

92 Vernon Arthur Mund, "Prosperity Reserve of Public Works," *Annals* 149 (May 1930), 8. See also Otto T. Mallery, "Prosperity Reserves," *Survey* 62:1 (1 April 1929), 25–26. – Carson to Couzens, 18 July 1928, Box 57, Couzens Papers; Hayes, *Activities*, 53. See also Huthmacher, *Wagner*, 63. – Johnson, *National Party Platforms*, I, 275–76; 286; 292; 303–4.

build on his previous record as unemployment fighter. Intrigued by Foster and Catchings' recently published *The Road to Plenty*, he prompted Brewster to propose at the Conference of Governors in New Orleans, on 21 November 1928, the creation of a $3 billion reserve fund for public works. The money was to come from the deferral of construction projects during prosperous times. If good cooperation existed between all public agencies, Brewster promised, the device would remedy the situation "in the twinkling of an eye."[93] Blithe optimism could of course not be carried further. In 1928 the entire public construction volume of the United States amounted to about the size of Hoover's sum. The idea that projects of an equivalent value could be postponed by public authorities must have challenged anybody's imagination. Furthermore, no practicable method to pinpoint the best moment for intervention existed (Figure 5–10).

Despite the plan's manifest impracticality, however, some public interest surged up. The AFL, in convention at New Orleans at the same time as the governors' conference, incorporated Brewster's speech into its proceedings. The *St. Louis Star* called the proposal "a step in the right direction," and the *Philadelphia Record* affirmed that it was "a logical development of modern economic thought."[94] But not everybody was impressed. "A chimerical idea," the *New Haven Register* exclaimed, "tinged with socialism." In Republican circles at large the plan was generally regarded as a political blunder because it conceded the possibility of future unemployment at a time when the Republican administration had just received the American people's accolade as custodian of prosperity. The governors assembled at New Orleans decided to take no action, and Hoover did not pursue the issue further.[95]

---

93 *Commercial and Financial Chronicle*, 24 Nov. 1928, p. 2905. For press reaction, see "Hoover's 'Plan to Keep the Dinner-Pail Full,' " *Literary Digest* 99:10 (8 Dec. 1928), 507. – William Trufant Foster and Waddill Catchings, "Mr. Hoover's Plan: What It Is and What It Is Not: The New Attack on Poverty," *Review of Reviews* 79:4 (April 1929), 77.

94 AFL. 48th Annual Convention, *Proceedings 1928*, 81; 180–81; 186. See also ibid., 49–50. *Star* and *Record* quoted in "Hoover's 'Plan to Keep the Dinner-Pail Full,' " 6. See also Frank G. Dickinson, "Public Works as a Prosperity Reserve," *ALLR* 19:1 (March 1929), 89–94.

95 The *Register* is quoted in "Hoover's 'Plan to Keep the Dinner-Pail Full,' " 6–7. – E. Jay Howenstine, Jr., "Public Works Policy in the Twenties," *Social Research* 13:4 (Dec. 1946), 495; "Proposal for Three Billion Dollar Reserve Fund to Stabilize Employment," *MLR* 27:6 (Dec. 1928), 1123; Herbert Stein, *The Fiscal Revolution in America* (Chicago: University of Chicago Press, 1969), 10–12.

—Hungerford in the Pittsburgh Post-Gazette

Figure 5-10. Cartoonist's reaction to Hoover's $3 billion public works reserve proposal. (Source: *ALLR* 19:1 [March 1929], 96.)

In the next few months the idea made only small progress. During the hearings pursuant to S.Res. 219, public works planning was pushed by various interested parties, most of whom were reform-oriented or had construction business connections.[96] When the Committee on Education

---

96 Social work testimony seems to have been excluded intentionally from the hearings pursuant to S.Res. 219. *Survey* editor Kellogg had suggested the names of potential social work witnesses, but Isador Lubin of the Brookings Institution had advised Couzens that "it was better not to consult those people at all because they have the slant that

and Labor endorsed the idea, Jones reintroduced his bill in April 1929 (S. 626) after Hoover convened a special session of Congress. But the legislators were too busy dealing with problems of farm relief and tariff revision, and the attempt failed again. The administration apparently intended to bide its time. In July, Hoover's Committee on Recent Economic Changes undertook a study of "public construction as an element in any program of economic stability." There the matter rested.[97]

After the stock market collapse in October had ushered in a change in the political climate and the federal government had begun to move toward emergency measures, the prospects for legislation seemed better. Wagner resubmitted his planning bill (S. 3059), taking care this time to have it consigned, together with its two companion bills, to Johnson's Committee on Commerce. During the speedily arranged hearings, even the NAM pronounced itself in favor. The bill passed the Senate on 28 April, but things went differently in the House. Despite an array of witnessess who advocated passage, among them Frances Perkins, Graham's Judiciary Committee cut the essential Section 10, which provided for advance planning, out of the text. "The vital parts of the bill" were taken away, Representative Emanuel Celler (D-New York) protested in a seething minority report, and Wagner described the remainder as "largely an empty shell."[98]

Why Graham's committee emasculated the measure is not fully clear. At the beginning of the hearings, Graham mentioned as contentious "whether or not regulation of this kind belongs to the states or can properly

work on the unemployment problem should be started from a social viewpoint." Carson to Couzens, 21 Aug. 1928, Box 59, Couzens Papers.

97 Hearings Pursuant to S.Res. 219; U.S. Congress. Senate. Committee on Education and Labor, *Causes of Unemployment*. S.Rept. 2072, 70 Cong., 2 sess. (pursuant to S.Res. 219; 25 Feb. 1929); R[obert] P. Lamont to Secretary of the Navy, 19 July 1919, Box 508, General Correspondence, Department of Commerce Papers; President's Conference on Unemployment. Committee on Recent Economic Changes, *Planning and Control of Public Works* (New York: National Bureau of Economic Research, 1931), xx.

98 Huthmacher, *Wagner*, 72; 74. See also Johnson's voting record in Schwarz, *Interregnum of Despair*, 240; 242. – Hearings on S. 3059, S. 3060, and S. 3061, p. 108; U.S. Congress. Senate. Committee on Commerce, *Prevention of Unemployment*. S.Rept. 320, 71 Cong., 2 sess. (to accompany S. 3059; 2 April 1930); Hearings on S. 3059, S. 3060, H.R. 8374, H.R. 8655, H.R. 9560, H.R. 11414, H.R. 12550, and H.R. 12551; U.S. Congress. House. Committee on the Judiciary, *To Provide for the Advance Planning and Regulated Construction of Certain Public Works for the Stabilization of Industry, and for Aiding in the Prevention of Unemployment during Periods of Business Depression*. H.Rept. 1971, 71 Cong., 2 sess. (to accompany S. 3059; 19 June 1930).

be mingled with federal legislation." But the issue was certainly also a political one. Bernstein intimates without evidence that the White House may have prompted the committee's majority. Perhaps it did. Secretary of Labor Davis, who had earlier in private expressed strong reservations about the bill, told a radio audience in February that the government could not predict unemployment and that when it came, appropriations for public works would "mean but little." Assistant Secretary of Commerce Julius Klein, on the other hand, affirmed that "the effect of brisk and widespread construction activity in reducing unemployment is apparently so generally recognized today, that I need not dwell long on it." Maybe partisan feelings were again playing the decisive role, as a cartoon appearing in the *New York Telegram* suggested; in it several Republicans praise the Senate unemployment bill until they discover that it was introduced by a Democrat, which prompts them to condemn it to the waste paper basket (see Figure 5-8 on p. 256).[99]

Those opposed to an advance planning measure could find much vindication in the utterances of various experts. Douglas expressed doubts about the ultimate value of the device, telling the AALL that governmental agencies were in fact not likely to defer much-needed construction. Even in labor circles not everybody hewed to the official AFL line.[100] By far the most important of the skeptical statements made in mid–1930 were appearing in the report of the Committee on Recent Economic Changes. The report allegedly reflected the views of the administration, but Wolman, who was responsible for the findings, showed himself neither enthusiastic about the public works tool as such, nor about the potential of advance planning. "The increase in the volume of public works as a direct solution of the unemployment problem has historically proved a failure," he coolly observed. As for a prosperity reserve, rising costs and the construction needs of the country made the idea, in his opinion, largely illusory. The

---

99 Hearings on S. 3059, S. 3060, H.R. 8374, H.R. 8655, H.R. 9560, H.R. 11414, H.R. 12550, and H.R. 12551, p. 20; Bernstein, *Lean Years*, 271. See also the *New York Telegram* cartoon in *ALLR* 20:3 (Sept. 1930), 298. – Davis to Hiram W. Johnson, 30 Jan. 1030, Book 17, Articles and Speeches, Davis Papers; Huthmacher, *Wagner*, 74.

100 Paul H. Douglas, "Can Management Prevent Unemployment?" *ALLR* 20:3 (Sept. 1930), 279; L. E. Keller, "Efficiency and Unemployment," *American Federationist* 37:6 (June 1930), 680. Keller was a railroad union statistician. Similar doubts persisted in social reform circles. See e.g., Ralph G. Hurlin, "Use of Public Works in the Treatment of Unemployment," National Conference of Social Work, *Proceedings 1931* (Chicago: University of Chicago Press, 1931), 264–70.

Committee endorsed his views, stating that the stabilization of business should be brought about "mainly by the business community itself."[101]

It was only in late fall 1930 that the matter received official attention again. Fears arose in the administration that public clamor for some palpable action would induce Congress to pass the bill after all. A veto without offer of a substitute, Hunt wrote Woods, would leave the president "in a weak position." In January 1931, Hunt served as the president's spokesman in negotiations with Wagner. With the concurrence of the affected departments, a compromise was worked out that fixed the planning time at six years, a provision the original bill had not contained. Wagner introduced the new bill in the Senate (S. 5776); Graham sponsored an identical bill in the House (H.R. 16384). Hunt gave flanking support in public. The legislative mill now ground smoothly, and on 10 February 1931, Hoover signed the Employment Stabilization Act into law.[102]

The new act established the FESB, composed of four cabinet officers, who were to advise the president "of the existence or approach of periods of business depression and unemployment." If the president concurred, he was then to ask Congress for emergency appropriations to be expended on authorized construction projects. The act, moreover, directed federal departments and agencies to prepare six-year plans "for prompt commencement and carrying out of an expanded program at any time."

The proponents of this kind of legislation had reason to be pleased, and the *Minneapolis Tribune* felt that "sheer prime common sense" would henceforth guide federal construction. But Mallery, rather than rejoicing at the fulfillment of his durable hope, assessed the value of the measure more realistically. The Wagner Act, he wrote in the *Survey*, was just the staff of the umbrella. It would be necessary to create the ribs by passing

---

101 "Congress and Unemployment," *Congressional Digest* 10:1 (Jan. 1931), 8; President's Conference on Unemployment. Committee on Recent Economic Changes, *Planning and Control of Public Works*, xxiv–xxviii; 2–6; 174–81.

102 Bernstein, *Lean Years*, 272–73; Huthmacher, *Wagner*, 77–78; Edward Eyre Hunt, ed., "Future Planning for Public Works," in Conference on Permanent Preventives of Unemployment, *Permanent Preventives*, 79–83. The conference took place 26–27 January 1931. – Hayes, *Activities*, 53; *Commercial and Financial Chronicle*, 31 Jan. 1931, p. 770; U.S. Congress. House. Committee of the Judiciary, *Advance Planning and Regulated Construction of Public Works, Stabilization of Industry, and Aiding in the Prevention of Unemployment during Periods of Business Depression*. H.Rept. 2334, 71 Cong., 3 sess. (to accompany H.R. 16384; 22 Jan. 1931); 46 Stat. 117 (1931).

similar acts in the states, because their public works volume was substantially larger; and the fabric between the ribs would be the credit
reserves, whose creation in most cases asked for constitutional amendments. "If less," he prognosticated, "it is not an umbrella but a sieve."[103]

As became quickly evident, the federal administration did not intend
to have much recourse to the new implement to protect the people from
the rain. The lack of enthusiasm of the president, who felt that planning
should be privately financed and merely provide advice for the government, had been evident for months. As Barry D. Karl has remarked,
Hoover "appeared to object not to planning as such but to the *federal*
government's funding of the projects that were planned."[104] The president
thus took care to point out that in his view the Stabilization Act only
created "a small statistical body called the Federal Stabilization Board."
Ogden L. Mills, soon to become secretary of the treasury and therewith
ex officio member of the FESB, believed that federal public works used
as a remedial tool were "destructive to the public credit, ineffective in
reviving business and wasteful to the national resources." The reasons
for the governmental line to be followed were even more clearly spelled
out by William R. Wood (R-Indiana), chairman of the House Appropriations Committee. He advised Hoover that only the most essential programs ought to be adopted because of "the difficulties which would
confront you and those of us who are striving to curb expenditures."[105]

Decades later it was suggested that the Stabilization Act of 1931 "may

103 "New Weapons to Fight Hard Times," *Literary Digest* 108:9 (28 Feb. 1931), 9; Otto
T. Mallery, "A Program of Public Works," *Survey* 65:11 (1 March 1931), 626. Schwarz,
Interregnum of Despair, 151 uses Mallery's remark in this article that "public works can
not be extemporized" as an endorsement of the federal reluctance to initiate works
programs. This interpretation is not warranted by the context, nor by Mallery's general
attitude.
104 Barry D. Karl, *The Uneasy State: The United States from 1915 to 1945* (Chicago: University of Chicago Press, 1983), 86. For Hoover's attitude see also Frank B. Freidel,
"The New Deal: Laying the Foundation for Modern America," in Wilbur J. Cohen,
ed., *The Roosevelt New Deal: A Program Assessment Fifty Years After* ([Richmond:] Virginia
Commonwealth University, 1986), 13; and Stuart Kidd, "Collectivist Intellectuals and
the Ideal of National Economic Planning, 1929–33," in Stephen W. Baskerville and
Ralph Willett, *Nothing Else to Fear: New Perspectives on America in the Thirties* (Man-
chester, Engld.: Manchester University Press, 1985), 26–33.
105 William Starr Myers and Walter H. Newton, *The Hoover Administration: A Documented
Narrative* (New York: Scribner's Son's, 1936), 66; Bernstein, *Lean Years*, 273; William
R. Wood to Hoover, 31 March 1931, Box 338, Presidential Papers, Hoover Papers;
Hoover to Wood, 8 April 1931, ibid.

have been the most noteworthy law passed during [Hoover's] administration," because in a manner it led up to the Employment Act of 1946.
There may be some virtue in this argument in an abstract way. As a
practical measure, however, the 1931 act accomplished precious little. Its
loose wording left the initiative to those charged with its implementation,
and the administration took care to see its views carried out. Sawyer,
Hoover's choice for director of the FESB, had pleaded for advance planning as early as 1927, but had no intention of using his agency as a major
tool in the fight against human distress. "If we treat construction as an
unemployment relief measure," he told the American Academy of Political
and Social Science, "the dollar can be very much more quickly invested
in a city than it can be where its expenditure comes from the public
treasury." In July 1931 he opposed a large appropriation for federal
building, because the employment effect would not become fully noticeable until 1933 when, as he hoped, business would already have recovered.
At the end of December he told the AALL convention that progress of
the FESB's work was slow because "many interesting problems have
arisen," among them the difficulty of dealing with a large number of
construction agencies and the intricacies of federal finance. The board
therefore contented itself on the whole with assembling statistical information gathered by other agencies, until the New Deal ended its existence
in June 1933.[106]

The history of the long-range planning idea from its conception before
the war to its virtual demise in the 1930s thus apparently proved the
critics right who had claimed that the technical and political obstacles
were insuperable. But although the drive for implementation ultimately
hit a dead end, it probably nevertheless warranted the efforts spent on
it. First, it had looked like an avenue worth pursuing, and reformers could
feel justified in striking out on it; the fact that it turned out to be a blind
alley allowed concentration upon more promising routes thereafter. Moreover, the discussion about the merits of the advance planning concept
constituted the link between the unemployment reform movement and

---

106 Schwarz, *Interregnum of Despair*, 35–36. – D. H. Sawyer, "Municipal Construction as
   Unemployment Relief," *Annals* 162 (July 1932), 134; Bernstein, *Lean Years*, 273;
   Donald H. Sawyer, "Federal Planning of Public Works," *ALLR* 22:2 (June 1932), 83;
   86; U.S. Dept. of Commerce, *19th Annual Report, 1931*, 330–34; idem, *20th Annual
   Report, 1932*, 233–39; idem, *21st Annual Report, 1933*, 191–92. See also Bonnie Fox
   Schwartz, *The Civil Works Administration, 1933–1934: The Business of Emergency Em-
   ployment in the New Deal* (Princeton: Princeton University Press, 1984), 17–18.

the contemporaneous reflection on the properties of the business cycle. From the latter would result the Keynesianism of the next decades, economic behavior that would be akin to what Mallery and his sympathizers had had in mind from early on.

Emergency action in the states

Whatever the value of long-range planning schemes, the unemployment surging with the developing depression called for measures with immediate impact. The state authorities were next in line if the need arose to prop up faltering local services. They were unaccustomed to the task, as no good precedents existed for it, and they were constitutionally and administratively ill-prepared. Consequently, their responses varied, the degree of involvement in individual states depending not only on the severity of the situation at hand but also on the willingness and ability of the state's leadership to overcome the existing obstacles.

A year after the stock market crash in Wall Street, unemployment began to put considerable strain upon the established relief systems in various parts of the country. Private welfare organizations were overwhelmed with the nature and size of a problem that they were not ready to handle. Supplementing the philanthropic efforts through local public assistance did not materially change this picture. A survey undertaken by the Russell Sage Foundation in 1931 revealed that in the preceding two years the proportion of aid from public funds had greatly increased in some cities and enormously shrunk in others, whereas in a larger number there seemed to have been no remarkable change.[107]

By 1931, at any rate, the point was reached where charitable contributions in many communities could no longer be counted upon to fill the private agencies' chests sufficiently. In February the Committee for Unemployment Relief in Philadelphia announced that unless additional funds were obtained, relief activities could not be carried beyond the end of the month. In March the St. Louis Citizens' Committee on Relief and Employment issued an urgent appeal for $300,000 to keep people from starving.[108] Municipal and county treasuries for their part, relying heavily

107 Ralph G. Hurlin and Anne E. Geddes, "Public and Private Relief during the Current Unemployment Emergency," National Conference of Social Work, *Proceedings, 1931*, 436.
108 "Doleful News of 1931," *ALLR* 21:2 (June 1931), 225. For case studies of the breakdown of traditional relief methods see Bonnie Fox Schwartz, "Unemployment Relief

upon property taxes as their major revenue base, had to face the problems of shrinking property values and proliferating tax delinquencies. Property taxation "is most onerous in times of bad business and fallen values," the New Jersey Relief Administration drearily stated in January 1932, "but it is at precisely such times that the relief burden from unemployment is greatest."[109] As private and municipal funds were running out, demands for governmental help began to be heard. Although poor relief was universally understood to be a local task, municipalities and counties were political subdivisions of the states on whom responsibility presumably devolved if the former could no longer assume it. "Behind the welfare agencies stands the community," the president of the National Conference of Social Work asserted in 1931, "behind the community the state."[110]

Not all of those directly involved in the care for the destitute were eager to abandon accustomed ways swiftly. Social agencies, intent on

in Philadelphia, 1930–1932: A Study of the Depression's Impact on Voluntarism," in Bernard Sternsher, ed., *Hitting Home: The Great Depression in Town and Country* (Chicago: Quadrangle, 1970), 60–84; William W. Bremer, *Depression Winters: New York Social Workers and the New Deal* (Philadelphia: Temple University Press, 1984), 63–73; Charles M. Kimberly, "The Depression in Maryland: The Failure of Voluntarism," *Maryland Historical Magazine* 70:2 (Summer 1975), 189–202.

109 New Jersey. Emergency Relief Administration, *Unemployment and Relief Conditions in New Jersey: An Interim Report to the Governor and the Legislature* (n.p., 1932), 39. See also Hearings on H.R. 206, H.R. 6011, and H.R. 8088, p. 68; Hearings on S.174 and S. 262, p. 176. See also Joanna C. Colcord, "Unemployment Relief, 1929–1932," *The Family* 13:8 (Dec. 1932), 272. In the city and county of San Francisco the number of families aided by the Associated Charities rose from 2,914 in 1929 to 4,216 in 1930 and 9,518 in 1931; the number of meals served by community chest agencies to homeless men went from 129,970 to 190,748 to 1,379,111 during these years, the number of nights' lodgings from 100,737 to 144,556 to 347,989. California. State Unemployment Commission, *Report and Recommendations*, 286; 293. New York (State) cities of over 30,000 population showed relief expenditures of $3,835,797 in the first three months of 1929 and of $15,131,933 during the corresponding quarter of 1931. Alexander Leopold Radomski, *Work Relief in New York State, 1931–1935* (Morningside Heights: King's Crown Press, 1947), 61.

110 C. M. Bookman, "The Strategy of Relief," *Survey* 67:5 (1 Dec. 1931), 281; similarly [Franklin Delano Roosevelt] *The Public Papers and Addresses of Franklin D. Roosevelt*. Vol. I: *The Genesis of the New Deal 1928–1932* (New York: Random House, 1938), 461. For a good survey of local work relief efforts see Joanna C. Colcord, *Emergency Work Relief: As Carried Out in Twenty-six American Communities, 1930–1931, with Suggestions for Setting up a Program* (New York: Russell Sage Foundation, 1932), 33–221. Municipal relief efforts in given localities are well presented in Jo Ann E. Argersinger, *Toward a New Deal in Baltimore: People and Government in the Great Depression* (Chapel Hill: University of North Carolina Press, 1988), 21–29; and John D. Millett, *The Works Progress Administration in New York City* (Chicago: Public Administration Service, 1938), 1–13.

preserving their own turf, often had mixed feelings at seeing the state's role increased. Their reluctance was augmented by a concern that charitable contributions would dry up once the general public could assume that the state was taking care of the relief problem. These agencies were struggling to make it clear, the *Survey* on occasion observed, that a state program was "not a substitute for going efforts but an addition to them to meet abnormal needs."[111] To obviate the danger, private organizations sometimes tried, as they did in the fall of 1930 in Chicago, to distinguish between the unemployment problem, for which the state should take care, and the general relief problem, for which they alone would be responsible. But the enormity of the distress and the difficulty of maintaining a neat distinction made such attempts at differentiation futile in the long run. Andrews, although acknowledging the impossibility of arriving at clear figures, estimated that in 1930 about one half of the total relief spending in the United States was doled out to unemployment victims. As the relief load doubled in the following year, presumably three-quarters of it was spent on unemployment relief.[112]

The states were hesitant to recognize their obligation. Not only did questions of principle ask for careful consideration; constitutional and practical obstacles had also to be overcome if effective assistance should be granted. Not the least impediment was the general inertia that had characterized the states' attitude toward social affairs in the 1920s and that yielded only slowly to the insight that the unfolding depression demanded attentive involvement.[113]

State assistance to municipalities and similar subdivisions in support of social services was of course not really new. By 1930, most states had laws providing for pensions for needy widowed mothers, and several furnished aid to the elderly or the blind. A number of states had used equalization funds to maintain standards in the fields of education and health. Proponents of state relief were eager to point to these precedents, arguing that the care for persons unable to provide for themselves because

---

111 "Unemployment: Wisconsin Chips In," *Survey* 67:12 (15 March 1932), 690; Chambers, *Seedtime of Reform*, 192. The same reluctance could also on occasion be observed with regard to federal help. See the reports by community workers in various cities in "How the Cities Stand," *Survey* 68:2 (15 April 1932), 71–75; 92.

112 Gertrude Springer, "The Burden of Mass Relief," *Survey* 65:4 (15 Nov. 1930), 201; John B. Andrews, "The Cost of the American Dole," *ALLR* 21:3 (Sept. 1931), 335; Charles E. Persons, "Calculation of Relief Expenditures," American Statistical Association. *Journal* 28:181A (March 1933), Suppl., 71.

113 The states' inertia in the 1920s is summarized in Patterson, *New Deal*, 10–25.

of a proven inability to find work was in principle no different. That various states now moved to act according to this view was perhaps partially due to a growing recognition of its soundness. Acknowledgment also increased of the fact that the causes of the depression were not local in scope, and that responsibility for the consequences therefore transcended the local level. The ultimate motivation in many places, however, appears to have been the feeling that the emergency required the exercise of the police powers of the state for the protection of public health, safety, and welfare.[114]

There existed a variety of possibilities that a state could explore. One device that cost nothing at the state level was amending legislation that changed limitations of local fiscal behavior. A New Jersey act adopted in December 1930 permitted the political subdivisions to borrow and appropriate sums of money up to one eighth of one percent of the assessed valuation of real property. A New York law passed in March 1931 allowed the City of New York to float a bond issue in the amount of $10 million to finance emergency public works. Similar legislation was enacted in 1931 in Pennsylvania, Ohio (Pringle–Roberts Law), Indiana, and Minnesota. The attempt to pass a comparable act in Illinois failed in early 1932 only because the fiscal situation in Cook County suffered from such disrepute that the county's paper was considered not marketable. Another kind of statutory barrier was lowered in West Virginia, where the counties received permission to use part of their road funds for the purpose of providing food or other necessities.[115]

Measures of this kind could at best serve as temporary palliatives, and sooner or later more substantial action appeared indicated. As construction accounted for a substantial part of their expenditures, state governments, following the precedent of local administrations, sought to use this

114 James Leiby, *A History of Social Welfare and Social Work in the United States* (New York: Columbia University Press, 1978), 212–15; Josephine Chapin Brown, *Public Relief 1929–1939* (New York: Holt, 1940), 97; California. State Unemployment Commission, *Report and Recommendations*, 446.

115 1930 *New Jersey Laws*, c. 272; David M. Schneider and Albert Deutsch, *The History of Public Welfare in New York State 1867–1940* (Chicago: University of Chicago Press, 1941), 301; 1931 *Pennsylvania Laws*, c. 134. Cities of the second class obtained similar authority in c. 307. – Ohio House Bill 102, as quoted in Ohio Commission on Unemployment Insurance, *Report. Part II. Studies and Reports*, 94–95; 1931 *Indiana Laws*, c. 73; 1931 *Minnesota Laws*, c. 328; Franz Z. Glick, *The Illinois Emergency Relief Commission: A Study of Administrative and Financial Aspects of Emergency Relief* (Chicago: University of Chicago Press, 1940), 16; 1931 *West Virginia Laws*, c. 64; 1932 *West Virginia Laws*, c. 65; 1932 Ex. *West Virginia Laws*, c. 14.

instrument as soon as they opted for entering the relief scene. Spending was often stepped up or kept up in the early years of the depression despite adverse conditions (see Table 5.3). Several states also initiated special road-building programs. During the winter of 1930–31, the New Jersey State Highway Commission ran a project that at one time employed about 2,600 people. The Massachusetts legislature in 1931 appropriated over $3 million and authorized an $8.5 million bond issue for the employment of additional persons on public works construction sites.[116] Pennsylvania and Michigan similarly increased road construction. In a campaign address of October 1930, Roosevelt announced that his state would have spent by the end of the calendar year $55 million on public works, $20 million more than in the previous year. Some states even went a step further and opened work camps to take care of unemployed transients. Road building had of course often called for lodging the workers near the construction site. During the depression, however, an extra effort could be made to keep existing camps going, as was the case in Pennsylvania, which in the winter of 1931–32 ran six of them.[117]

Somewhat distinct from such arrangements were measures specifically designed to provide for nonresident jobless men. The California Unemployment Commission, which noticed the "chaotic condition" prevailing in diverse municipalities and counties, asked Governor Rolph on 13 November 1931 to consider establishing forestry camps for fire protection work. The first camp was opened on 31 December 1931, and others were set up in quick succession. By April 1932, when operations ended, twenty-eight forestry camps and two highway camps with a combined capacity of 3,352 men had been functioning for several months each. The men received board, clothing if needed, and a $5 cash bonus

116 California. State Unemployment Commission, *Report and Recommendations*, 647. See also the steps taken in Ohio in early 1930. U.S. Congress. Senate, *Stabilization of Industry*. S.Doc. 109, 71 Cong., 2 sess. (12 March 1930). – Douglas H. MacNeil, *Seven Years of Unemployment Relief in New Jersey, 1930–1936* (Washington: Committee on Social Security, Social Science Research Council, 1938), 152–53; "State Legislation for the Relief of Unemployment," *MLR* 34:6 (June 1932), 1289; Massachusetts. Special Commission on the Stabilization of Employment, *Preliminary Report*, 49.

117 Pinchot to Hoover, 18 Aug. 1931, Box 338, Presidential Papers, Hoover Papers; Arthur D. Gayer, *Public Works in Prosperity and Depression* (New York: National Bureau of Economic Research, 1935), 152–53; [Roosevelt,] *The Public Papers and Addresses of Franklin D. Roosevelt*, I, 409. For the difficulties a western state experienced in stepping up public works for relief purposes see James F. Wickens, *Colorado in the Great Depression* (New York: Garland, 1979), 17–19. – Hearings on S. 174 and S. 262, p. 214.

on discharge. In a certain way, these camps fulfilled their purpose. "The number of transient jobless entering the state," S. Rexford Black, the chairman of the state's labor camp committee, reported, "decreased rapidly after word of California's labor camp project spread east." Enough candidates were left over, though, for the state to repeat the program in winter 1932–33, and Black went to Washington, unsuccessfully as it turned out, to plead for federal support. Another type of camp was tried out in Florida, where the Jacksonville municipal authorities, with the help of the Florida National Guard, ran a program of "social reconstruction" in winter 1932–33.[118]

Road-building programs and work camps were initiated with the aim of avoiding outright relief. Remission of part of the state tax had a similar function. The Massachusetts legislature, for instance, in 1931 exempted cities, towns, and counties for a limited period from certain usual assessments for road maintenance, but at the same time appropriated $2.5 million for the next two years to be apportioned among the subdivisions for road work. This measure was patently designed to avoid setting an indisputable precedent.

A few states overcame their hesitations, however, and crossed the threshold. It is often asserted that New York was the first state to pass legislation for unemployment relief, but at least three other states, all of them with relatively small populations, acted as forerunners. In January 1931 the New Hampshire legislature granted a temporary extension of mothers' aid benefits specifically because of unemployment conditions and dedicated $75,000 to this cause. In April a Maryland law gave the governor $24,000 out of the proceeds from license fees from four special racing days for emergency unemployment relief. As this law took effect only at the beginning of 1932, Oklahoma became the first state to give direct unemployment aid. In early 1931 the legislature allocated $300,000 from unexpended funds for food, clothing, and shelter for persons destitute due to crop failures, low prices, and joblessness. A state emergency relief board was to distribute the funds to individual counties according to its own judgment.[119]

---

118 California. State Unemployment Commission, *Report and Recommendations*, 29–30; S. Rexford Black, "Report on the California State Labor Camps," in Hearings on S. 5121, pp. 8–9; 14–16; "California's State Camps for Jobless Men," *MLR* 35:5 (Nov. 1932), 1066–70; Hearings on S. 5121, pp. 2–8; *CR*, 72 Cong., 2 sess., 20 Feb. 1933, pp. 4503–04.
119 Joanna C. Colcord, "Unemployment Relief, 1929–1932," *Social Work Year Book 1933*

The New York relief program was of a far larger dimension. Various of its features were imitated in other states, and ultimately served as models for federal endeavors during the New Deal period. The measures have often been described. Roosevelt's message of 28 August to the legislature, announcing his state's willingness "to do its additional share," has over time become something of a classic.[120] The core of the plan was the Wicks Act of 23 September 1931, which appropriated $20 million. Municipalities were to receive 40 percent for direct relief and most of the remainder for work relief; the state government could use up to $1,000,000 for work projects under its own regime. In order to eliminate political influences as much as possible, the act established an independent administrative body, the TERA, which was charged with the distribution of the funds and the supervision of the program. The money was to be raised through the Dunnigan Act, passed simultaneously, which provided for a 50 percent increase in the state income tax. The original act stipulated that relief should end on 1 June 1932. As the depression persisted, amending legislation extended the life span of the program ultimately into the New Deal period. An allocation of $5 million from general revenues in March 1932 and repeated state bond issues made a continuation of the program possible.[121]

(New York: Russell Sage Foundation, 1933), 522; Brown, *Public Relief 1929–1939*, 89; Frank R. Breul, "Early History of Aid to the Unemployed in the United States," in Joseph M. Becker, ed., *In Aid of the Unemployed* (Baltimore: John Hopkins University Press, 1965), 16–17; Edith Abbott, *Public Assistance*. 2 vols. (New York: Russell & Russell, 1966), vol. II, 512; 1931 *New Hampshire Laws*, c. 1; 1931 *Maryland Laws*, c. 150; Oklahoma Senate Bill No. 23 (1931), as quoted in Federal Emergency Relief Administration, *Monthly Report*, May 1 through May 31, 1935, p. 77; 1931 *Oklahoma Laws*, c. 66, art. 10. For the general circumstances around the relief legislation see Keith L. Bryant, Jr., "Oklahoma and the New Deal," in Braeman, Bremner, and Brody, eds., *The New Deal*, II, 166–73. See also California State Unemployment Commission, *Report and Recommendations*, 448–50.

120 The most detailed account is Radomsky, *Work Relief in New York State*. See also Schneider and Deutsch, *History of Public Welfare in New York State*, 302–07. The legislative session had been called at Republican insistence to clear up an immunity problem for witnesses in the Tammany investigation. Frank Freidel, *Franklin D. Roosevelt: The Triumph* (Boston: Little, Brown, 1956), 218–19; [Roosevelt,] *The Public Papers and Addresses of Franklin D. Roosevelt*, I, 459; 465–67.

121 *New York Times*, 19 Sept. 1931, pp. 1; 20; 23; 1931 Ex. *New York Laws*, c. 798; Beulah Amidon, "Spring and Unemployment," *Survey* 66:4 (15 May 1931), 223; [Roosevelt,] *The Public Papers and Addresses of Franklin D. Roosevelt*, I, 457–68. For Roosevelt's struggle with the legislature see Bernard Bellush, *Franklin D. Roosevelt as Governor of New York* (New York: Columbia University Press, 1955), 141–47. An independent body like the TERA had been proposed in California as early as 1914. California.

Many reform-minded observers applauded Roosevelt's initiative, and a half dozen other states, with the exception of Wisconsin all of them situated in the industrialized Northeast, followed New York's example. Effective 13 October 1931, the New Jersey legislature passed an act providing for an initial expenditure of $9.6 million, to be administered by an emergency relief administration headed by a state director. The bulk of the sum was to be derived from the sale of the Camden–Philadelphia bridge and most of the rest to be transferred from the state highway fund. In December 1931 the legislature approved two bills appropriating a total of $6.5 million from the proceeds of the gasoline taxes and the motor licensing fees to be used for further unemployment relief.[122] The Rhode Island legislature on 24 November 1931 appropriated $1.5 million out of general revenues which the municipalities were to spend on direct and work relief. In April of 1932 the appropriation was increased by $1 million to be taken out of the state highway fund. The Pennsylvania act of 28 December 1931 (first Talbot Act) gave $10 million to the poor district officers of the commonwealth, rather than to a special relief administration. No special state supervision of the spending was envisaged. Governor Pinchot, disgusted at the intentional looseness of the bill, refused to sign it but nevertheless let it become law.[123]

In early 1932, three more states decided to provide aid for their jobless. The Wisconsin Highway Act of 31 March 1931 implemented a program of railroad grade-crossing elimination. The emergency relief act of 8 February 1932, which relied upon the proceeds of an emergency income

Commission of Immigration and Housing, *Report on Unemployment to His Excellency Governor Hiram W. Johnson* (n.p., 1914), 67–68. – 1931 Ex. *New York Laws*, c. 795; 1931 Ex. *New York Laws*, c. 798; 1932 *New York Laws*, cs. 566; 567.

122 1931 *New Jersey Laws*, c. 394; New Jersey. State Emergency Relief Administration, *Unemployment and Relief Conditions in New Jersey: An Interim Report*, 41; 1931 *New Jersey Laws*, cs. 397, 423, and 424; 1932 *New Jersey Laws*, c. 187.

123 1931 Ex. *Rhode Island Laws*, c. 1855; 1932 *Rhode Island Laws*, c. 1919; 1931 Ex. *Pennsylvania Laws*, c. 7E; Joseph Chamberlain, "The Legislatures and Unemployment," *American Bar Association Journal* 18:4 (April 1932), 234–35; "Constitutionality of the Pennsylvania Relief Act," *Social Science Review* 6:4 (Dec. 1932), 613–26; Arthur Dunham, "Pennsylvania and Unemployment Relief, 1929–34," *Social Service Review* 8:2 (June 1934), 249. For the background of Pinchot's struggle with the legislature see Richard C. Keller, "Pennsylvania's Little New Deal," in Braeman, Bremner, and Brody, eds., *The New Deal*, II, 45–53. A spirited debate about the political and constitutional merits of the Talbot Act is found in the Pinchot Papers. See in particular Paul B. Rice to Pinchot, 6 June 1932, Box 2550, Pinchot Papers; Pinchot to Rice, 7 June 1932, ibid.; Rice to Pinchot, 9 June 1932, ibid.

tax and emergency chain store licenses, vested administration in the state industrial commission; the main criterion for the distribution of funds was population size.[124] Legislation in Illinois resembled that enacted in New York and New Jersey, as it created a state emergency relief commission and appropriated $20 million for unemployment relief, to be financed through a combination of taxes and bond issues. The last state to make emergency appropriations before the passage of the ERCA was Ohio. In April 1932 its legislature created a state relief commission whose expenditures had to be financed, as in Wisconsin, from certain revenues, especially the gasoline and motor vehicle taxes.[125]

The early relief legislation showed disparate character, because few of the determining factors were exactly alike. "A plan that is workable in one place," a writer in the *Survey* resignedly stated, "runs into constitutional snags or local barriers of circumstance or prejudice in another." The question of conformity with the state constitution sometimes presented a difficult problem. The most important case was that of Pennsylvania, where the Talbot Act was attacked on various grounds. In May 1932 the state supreme court maintained that the support of the poor "is and always has been a direct charge on the body politic for its own preservation and protection"; as such it stood "exactly in the same position as the preservation of law and order." To expend money for this purpose thus meant performing a governmental function not controlled by a constitutional prohibition, even if the destitute were such "because of enforced unemployment."[126]

This Pennsylvania decision possessed precedent-setting character. Whereas relief legislation cases in several other states, notably Wisconsin

---

124 Don D. Lescohier and Florence Paterson, *The Alleviation of Unemployment in Wisconsin* (Madison: Industrial Commission, 1931), 103–04; 1931 *Wisconsin Laws*, c. 22; Wisconsin Industrial Commission, *Biennial Report 1930–1932*, 28; 1931–32 Ex. *Wisconsin Laws*, c. 29.

125 Illinois H.B. nos. 1, 2, 3, 4, and 5, 3d Ex. (1932); Illinois. Emergency Relief Commission, *First Annual Report, for the Year Ending February 5, 1933: Issued Jointly with a Report of the Illinois Emergency Relief Commission (Federal) Covering the Period July 27, 1932, through February 5, 1933* (Chicago, [1933]), 12; 71; 116; Illinois. Emergency Relief Commission, *First Interim Report, April 15, 1932* (n.p., n.d.), 14–35; Ohio S.B. 1, 3, and 4, 1st Ex. (1932). For the prehistory of the act see David J. Maurer, "Relief Problems and Politics in Ohio," in Braeman, Bremner, and Brody, eds., *The New Deal,*, II, 78–80.

126 Bookman, "The Strategy of Relief," 242; *Commonwealth of Pennsylvania v. Alice F. Liveright et al.*, 96 Pennsylvania Supreme Court, no. 16, May Term, 1932.

and Ohio, hinged upon technicalities and were answered by the courts on the same technical level,[127] the Pennsylvania court went beyond such reasoning and unequivocally declared unemployment relief to be within the competency and even the obligations of the state government. The other courts, of course, in sustaining the governmental side did, by implication, the same. After these decisions, exclusive local responsibility was no longer a cause of serious public advocacy.

The variety of conditions renders it unrewarding to calculate the exact amount of aid funds that these states appropriated before the enactment of the ERCA in July 1932 or to assess the possible relief effect. As pointed out, the amounts to be spent in some cases depended upon the proceeds of taxes still to be collected and the results of bond sales. Taking these circumstances into consideration, it has been estimated that between $86 million and $100 million was made available as additional relief aid. This was obviously not an insignificant amount in an age in which an unskilled laborer could earn about five dollars a day. Compared with the task to be accomplished, on the other hand, the achievement remained unimpressive.[128]

Whatever the relief sums and the mode of distribution, it is obvious that the funds could at best meet only a fraction of the need. A few

127 Rowland Haynes, *State Legislation for Unemployment Relief: From January 1, 1931, to May 31, 1932* (Washington: G.P.O., 1932), 73–74.
128 It is impossible to assess adequately in fiscal terms the need for relief, but some available figures can convey a feeling for the dimensions. Relief given by public and private agencies in New York (City) in early 1931 was over $3 million monthly. Total expenditures for charities by cities of over 300,000 inhabitants rose from $33 million in 1928 to $114 million in 1932. It is difficult to determine what proportion of the funds went into direct relief and how much was spent on work relief. New York and New Jersey were states where work on public construction played a major relief role. During the ten months from 1 November 1931 to 31 August 1932 the districts cooperating with the TERA reported a total expenditure from public funds of $48.7 million, of which $25.7 million (53%) was spent on work relief. A similar figure can be found for New Jersey, where $7.1 million, or 52% of the total relief costs, went into work programs from October 1931 through June 1932. The picture was quite different in Illinois, which spent $44.9 million from state and federal funds, excluding expenses, during the first twelve months of the state's relief activities (6 February 1932 to 31 January 1933), but only $4.3 million (9.6%) went into work relief. Andrews, "The Cost of the American Dole," 336; Social Security Board, Washington, D.C., *Social Security in America*, 359; New York (State). Temporary Emergency Relief Administration, *Report, October 15, 1932* (New York, n.d.), 22; MacNeil, *Seven Years of Unemployment Relief*, 156; Henrietta Liebman, "Work Relief in Certain States, 1930–1933," in Federal Emergency Relief Administration, *Monthly Report* (May 1936), 40, note; Illinois. Emergency Relief Commission, *First Annual Report*, 49; 65.

observations regarding the work programs support this assumption. Quite naturally the implementation of the schemes often suffered from a lack of preparation, and in various cases the weakness of state supervision further impeded effectiveness. Although officially the leash was shortest in New York and New Jersey, where the relief administrations were obliged to examine all projects and could withhold allocations, only New York's TERA could remove members of local relief bureaus whose performance did not conform to its rules. Supervision seems to have worked less well in New Jersey, where the state director had to rely on local volunteer officials. In June 1932 he felt obliged to stop payments from work relief funds for municipal or county relief wages.[129] The relief administrations in Illinois and Wisconsin confined themselves to the formulation of rules and recommendations. Pennsylvania, as has been mentioned, for a time did not provide for any specific guidance at all.

One reason for the apparent laxity of procedure in most states was that efficiency was not a very important goal. "The proportion of dollar efficiency of public made work," the untroubled New Jersey state director of emergency relief stated in January 1932, "is reported . . . to vary from 15% to 50%." He estimated that modern machinery could do the same highway construction work at about one-third of the relief work cost. The guiding ideas were all too frequently on the one hand the desire to discourage applications, and on the other the intention to supply a maximum of useful work. As a consequence, most often the authorities had recourse to light construction and road work or to repair jobs of the public improvement variety.[130] What ultimately mattered was the relief effect.

129 MacNeil, *Seven Years of Unemployment Relief*, 60.
130 New Jersey. Emergency Relief Administration, *Unemployment and Relief Conditions in New Jersey: An Interim Report*, 33. "White collar" projects were rare. In New York (State), between 1 November 1931 and 1 June 1932, they amounted to only 11% of all projects undertaken, whereas highway construction and repair commanded 40%, sanitation 16%, and park improvements 12%; work on utilities (8%), water supply systems (8%), general public improvements (3%) and miscellaneous jobs (2%) made up the remainder. A very similar distribution was found in New Jersey, where street and road work amounted to 41% of the total, water supply and sewer work to 16%; the share of clerical work, at 7.8%, was even smaller than in New York (State). Things do not seem to have been substantially different in the other states, although Wisconsin's reforestation program deserves to be mentioned. Many of these early relief projects were so inefficiently supervised and the work was "of such distasteful nature," as an observer stated, "that not much enthusiasm or effort" could be evoked from the relief workers. *Emergency Unemployment Relief Laws in the State of New York 1931–1932: The Interpretation and Application of Emergency Relief Laws by the Temporary Emergency Relief Administration Established October 1, 1931* (Albany, 1932), 180; MacNeil, *Seven*

The very fact that until 1932 only a handful of states undertook to sponsor any programs at all is indicative of the prevailing doubts.[131] The impact on the general American employment scene must of necessity have remained small. Even in the one state that emphasized work relief over direct relief – New York – state-sponsored programs were far from meeting the existing need. For June 1932 the upstate Emergency Work Bureaus reported 25,062 persons as holding employment on public projects during the month, whereas 65,917 approved applicants were waiting for work. Very conservative estimates put the number of unemployed at between 400,000 and 500,000 outside New York (City).[132]

Figures alone, of course, do not sufficiently express the importance of the efforts just described. The state payments may have been insufficient

Years of Unemployment Relief, 156. See also the project estimates for individual counties in New Jersey. Emergency Relief Administration, *Unemployment and Relief Conditions in New Jersey: An Interim Report*, 110–11; Wisconsin. Legislature. Interim Committee on Unemployment, *Report*, 28; Liebman, "Work Relief in Certain States, 1930–33," 41–42.

131 Much was made at the time of the necessity to preserve the worker's dignity through giving him work rather than a 'dole.' It is unlikely, however, that many projects lived up to this challenge. The make-work character and the work-test quality of the programs all too frequently stymied any existing eagerness. Occasionally, as in Chicago or Rochester (New York) in 1932, unions fearing the competition pressured the authorities into paying union wages. The most prevalent policy, however, was not to heed any existing wage scales. A flat hourly or daily rate, determined by the amount of funds available, was paid to all classes of labor. In Illinois food and other services were often substituted for cash. Periods worked depended on the circumstances. The method most frequently adopted was employment by two-, three-, or four-day shifts, with all workers employed the same number of hours or days. On various programs the number of dependents was taken into consideration, but even there constant employment was usually out of the question. Rather than preserving the dignity of the recipient, his participation often made the stigma of destitution manifest. New York (City). Emergency Employment Committee, *Report, October 1, 1930—July 1, 1931* (n.p., n.d.), 6; Radomski, *Work Relief in New York State*, 55; Haynes, *State Legislation*, 2; Arthur E. Burns, "Work Relief Wage Policies, 1930–1936," in Federal Emergency Relief Administration, *Monthly Report* (June 1936), 24–25; 26; 28. Liebman, "Work Relief in Certain States, 1930–1933," 36; Illinois. Emergency Relief Commission, *First Annual Report*, 14.

132 The 30,000 individuals who were given employment on relief projects in New Jersey in December 1931 constituted but 17% of the total number of 172,500 unemployed registered as seeking a job. MacNeil, *Unemployment Relief in New Jersey*, 155. See also Illinois. Emergency Relief Commission, *First Annual Report*, 49; 55; 62. In Pennsylvania the $10 million which the Talbot Act provided was considered so insufficient that in April 1932 the state's Federation of Labor demanded that $50 million should be made available. Thomas Kennedy and others to Pinchot, 11 April 1932, Box 2550, Pinchot Papers. – New York (State). Temporary Emergency Relief Administration, *Report, October 15, 1932*, 9–10.

for distress alleviation, but that they were happening at all constituted a change of historic significance. As we know, at the beginning of the depression state concern with unemployment questions had a considerable history already; nowhere in the United States, though, had a state government ever taken it upon itself to provide direct aid to able-bodied yet jobless persons. By mid-1932, on the other hand, a noteworthy number of state administrations had almost simultaneously initiated measures of this kind. The fact that most were heavily industrialized states demonstrated that government responsibility for the social consequences of industrialization was now definitely finding practical acknowledgment.

These state efforts were also important in a more immediate sense. Although unsatisfactory in size, they offered a ray of hope to desperate citizens and social workers. As they suggested that more potent government help might become available in the foreseeable future, they stiffened the resolve to endure. To reinforce local money with state funds, the executive director of the Cincinnati Community Chest remarked, meant "strengthening the public morale by the knowledge that behind the community are ranged the broader powers and resources of the state."[133]

Moreover, the early state relief legislation served a remarkable trial function. Because none of the states was able to have recourse to established and proven methods of procedure, they all had to experiment when dealing with legal and constitutional obstacles as well as when devising ways of allocation and erecting the machinery of distribution and administration. As an anonymous article in the *Survey* expressed it in April 1932, the few states with unemployment programs might have moved "fumblingly and inadequately perhaps," but they had created "at least a thin cushion for the present and a precedent for the future."[134] No doubt, various dead alleys were traveled, but the experience gained was valuable. It would handily come in once the federal government finally decided to move in the same direction.

The federal effort: Initial phase

Although the municipalities and counties, which customarily bore the relief burden, were the constitutional creatures of the states, the federal government could not entirely stand aside when the depression struck.

133 Bookman, "The Strategy of Relief," 281.
134 "How the Cities Stand," 71.

Leery of having to assume any direct responsibility for unemployment alleviation, Hoover's administration conceived of supportive measures in time-honored fashion. It felt that its task was mainly to keep the economy going at a passable step; its own direct intervention must be limited to the use of traditional instruments, of which the acceleration of regular public building appeared to be the most promising. "Public construction," the President's Conference of 1921 had concluded, "is better than relief." In accordance with this maxim, up to early 1932 federal succor to the unemployed consisted chiefly of measures to enhance, or at least maintain, federal construction volume.[135]

From the beginning of the business downturn the administration kept a confident countenance, although worries about the economic situation soon began to influence its behavior. In mid-November 1929, Hoover held several conferences with business and labor leaders, exhorting all sides to maintain a steady pace and promising that his own administration would increase construction. By telegraph he asked the state governors for an "energetic yet prudent pursuit of public works" on the state and municipal levels. He also directed Commerce Secretary Lamont to cooperate with the states in this endeavor. In December, Lamont therefore created a temporary bureau for the coordination and stimulation of construction work, which subsequently busied itself with monitoring expenditures at the various government levels.[136]

In his message greeting the newly assembled Congress on 3 December, Hoover again announced that "a special effort" would be made to expand federal construction work. He meant to remain prudent, though, conscious of his lack of control of the legislators that was soon to manifest itself distinctly in the making of the Hawley–Smoot tariff. In the face of a wave of spending bills inundating the Seventy-first Congress, he felt obliged to state that "this is not the time for expansion of general public expenditure." Accordingly, the budget for the fiscal year ending 30 June 1931, as proposed to Congress in December 1929, provided for public buildings and public works the sum of $246 million, only marginally more

135 President's Conference on Unemployment, *Report* (Washington: G.P.O., 1921), 20. For a differing interpretation, viewing Hoover's public works policy as a radical departure from past practice, see Murray N. Rothbard, "Herbert Hoover and the Myth of Laissez Faire," in Ronald Radosh and Murray N. Rothbard, eds., *A New History of Leviathan: Essays on the Rise of the American Corporate State* (New York: Durham, 1972), 133–37.
136 Myers, ed., *State Papers*, I, 137; Myers and Newton, *Hoover Administration*, 25–28; 34.

than the $245.8 million of the current budget. To this were added in March/April two government-sponsored measures that demonstrated the administration's good will. The Elliott–Keyes bill (H.R. 6210/S. 2241) increased the public building appropriation for each of the next few years by $50 million. Moreover, the Dowell–Phipps post-road bill (H.R. 5616/S. 2253), signed on 4 April 1930, raised the annual federal highway construction share from $75 million to $125 million. The president was convinced that he had therewith done enough regarding federal public works increases, as he told the disappointed Foster, coauthor of *The Road to Plenty*, who saw him in the spring.[137] Compared with the total construction volume in the United States, which in 1929 had amounted to about $10.5 billion (see Table 4-1, p. 190), the appropriated sums were of course insignificant.

As business activity did not markedly improve during 1930, calls for further federal action grew louder.[138] In November the American Association of State Highway Officials passed a resolution asking for an emergency appropriation of $250 million. In December a conference of economists at Princeton University advised the administration that the necessary borrowing could be done without any harm to the national economy. The PECE recommended a road program of regional and local character.[139]

These requests went too far in Hoover's estimation. He disliked the elimination of safeguards regarding construction costs as recommended by the highway officials and endorsed by the PECE, and he winced at the committee's recommendation, presented to him in a confidential memorandum, that he ask Congress for $350 million in additional highway funds. In his message to the legislators on 3 December he therefore merely requested an emergency appropriation of "from $100,000,000 to

137 Myers, ed., *State Papers*, I, 145; 180; Harris Gaylord Warren, *Herbert Hoover and the Great Depression* (New York: Oxford University Press, 1959), 92. Statement of 20 Feb. 1930 in Myers and Newton, *Hoover Administration*, 35. – W. T. Foster to Wagner, 9 Dec. 1930, Box 188, Legislative Files, Wagner Papers.

138 "Unemployment a Most Urgent Problem," *American Federationist* 37:8 (Aug. 1930), 914; Aaron Director, "Making Use of Public Works," *Survey* 64:10 (15 Aug. 1930), 427–28; Emergency Committee for Federal Public Works, "To Relieve Distress and Hasten Good Times," [c. Nov. 1930], pamphlet, Box 188, Legislative Files, Wagner Papers.

139 Joseph H. Willits to Woods, 3 Dec. 1930, Box 28, POUR Papers; Darwin J. Meserole, ed., "The Need for Adequate Measures," Conference on Permanent Preventives on Unemployment, *Permanent Preventives*, 76; Hayes, *Activities*, 40–43.

$150,000,000."[140] The president's suspicion that Congress would be in-
undated with extravagant spending proposals proved correct. During the
first three days of the new session no less than four emergency construction bills were introduced in the Senate alone. The bill that had the
administration's support (H.R. 14804) was presented in the House by
Wood. As the subsequent hearings revealed, some of the proposed projects were not mature, and the committee pared the requested sum of
$150 million down to $110 million. The Senate added $6 million for
forest highways, and on 20 December Hoover signed the measure into
law.[141]

This emergency appropriation did not comprise any funds designed
for public buildings construction. One reason for this was the general
understanding that the latter was hampered not so much by a lack of
money as by bureaucratic paper work. In early December 1930 a memorandum from the Treasury Department revealed that of a total of $490
million authorized for construction under the Public Buildings Act of
1926 and subsequent amending acts, including the Elliott–Keyes measure
of March 1930, only $31.7 million's worth of buildings had been com-
pleted and another $69.8 million was under contract. As a consequence,
the administration sponsored two bills (H.R. 14040; H.R. 14255) expediting the local approval process and allowing quicker construction
starts. They were enacted on 6 February and 26 February, respectively.
Moreover, another Elliott–Keyes bill (H.R. 16297/S. 5757), sponsored
by the Treasury Department, increased the limit of annual expenditures
for federal buildings construction from $50 million to $65 million.[142]

In late winter and early spring 1931, the relations between the PECE
and the administration became strained. Disagreement touched the fundamentals when Colonel Woods advocated long-term preparations for

---

140 Myers, ed., *State Papers*, I, 432–33.
141 The four emergency construction bills were S. 4783; S. 4819; S. 4938; and S. 5079.
     – Hearings [on H.R. 14804], pp. 9–10; 24; U.S. Congress. House. Committee on
     Appropriations, *Emergency Construction Appropriations, Fiscal Year 1931*, H.Rept. 2084,
     71 Cong., 3 sess. (to accompany H.R. 14804; 9 Dec. 1930); U.S. Congress. House,
     Emergency Construction of Public Works. H.Rept. 2104, 71 Cong., 3 sess. (Conference
     Report to accompany H.R. 14804; 16 Dec. 1930); 46 Stat. 19 (1930).
142 Hearings on H.R. 14040, pp. 2–16; U.S. Congress. House. Committee on Public
     Buildings and Grounds, *To Amend the Act Entitled "An Act to Provide for the Construction
     of Certain Public Buildings, and for Other Purposes," Approved May 25, 1926 (44 Stat.
     630), and Acts Amendatory Thereof.* H.Rept. 2324, 71 Cong., 3 sess. (to accompany
     H.R. 16297; 21 Jan. 1931); 46 Stat. 107 (1931); 46 Stat. 307 (1931); 46 Stat. 203
     (1931).

the forthcoming winter. The president continued to think that relief measures should not be planned for periods longer than six months, fearing their institutionalization. After Woods' resignation from the PECE chairmanship in April, no specific federal public works initiatives occurred over the next few months, and POUR chairman Gifford shared Hoover's aversion to large-scale federal relief action.[143]

But public pressure mounted. On Labor Day (6 September) 1931 the Chicago Federation of Labor asked for a $10 billion construction program. Wagner demanded $2 billion in a speech in Syracuse. As a consequence, on 25 September 1931 Hoover again exhorted the public to refrain from making money requests of the legislature. Helpfully a number of state governors had just assured him that their states were perfectly able to take care of their unemployed without outside assistance. The POUR's employment program of 29 October thus merely demanded the start of "public work already authorized and appropriated for." Large gifts by Congress for local and state public works, Gifford's agency insisted a week later, would be "unsound in principle." Concrete action, on the other hand, became an obvious necessity with every passing week.[144]

Push for federal relief

In the face of the administration's reluctance to increase its construction commitments substantially, interest thus soon focused on the ongoing struggle about substantial relief legislation. The administration, knowing itself supported by dominant elements in the business world, withstood these challenges until early 1932. By then, however, erosion set in. As demands in Congress for federal relief involvement became more insistent, the decision to distribute surplus wheat in order to bring help to individuals negated for the first time the tenet that the federal government should keep aloof from the immediate aid scene.

---

143 Hoover was backed up by the American Engineering Council. See "Engineering Works as an Emergency Relief," American Engineering Council, *Bulletin* 11:2 (Feb. 1931), 1; 20. – *New York Times*, 8 Sept. 1931, p. 1.

144 Text of the Chicago resolution in Box 189, Legislative Files, Wagner Papers. – *Commercial and Financial Chronicle*, 3 Oct. 1931, p. 2201. Cables and letters of the governors had obviously been solicited. See Box 209, POUR Papers. – "Program for Promotion of Employment," *MLR* 33:6 (Dec. 1931), 1342; "Report of the Committee on Program of Federal Public Works," 16 Dec. 1931, Box 251, POUR Papers; Myers, ed., *State Papers*, II, 47–48. For the macroeconomic reasoning underlying Hoover's attitude see Barber, *From New Era to New Deal*, 118–20.

Calls for direct federal relief involvement were heard as early as the first winter of the depression. On 1 March 1930, Progressive Republican Senator Smith W. Brookhart (Iowa) proposed that $50 million should be expended for unemployment relief through the American National Red Cross and the quartermaster general of the army (S.J.Res. 149). His call was taken up in December by Congressman George Huddleston (D-Alabama), who asked for a $50 million relief allocation (H.R. 14042). But this kind of blunt money demand did not yet have a chance. Hoover, whose administration felt simultaneous pressure for drought relief in the South, expressed the prevalent opinion when he declared that such hand-outs would bring "an inevitable train of corruption and waste such as our nation [has] never seen." Proposals by Senator Walsh (S. 5043) and Representative Benjamin M. Golder (R-Pennsylvania; H.R. 16118) for unemployment relief appropriations or loans to the several states proved equally premature.[145]

It was special-interest lobbying that overcame resistance against federal relief for the first time. Advocates of the use of agricultural surpluses opened the breach. In December 1930, Republican insurgent Senator Arthur Capper (R-Kansas), ranking exponent of the farm bloc and in the 1920s an active promoter of the McNary–Haugen bill, submitted a resolution calling for the free distribution, through relief organizations, of 40 million bushels of wheat held by the Grain Stabilization Corporation (S.J.Res. 210). The Committee on Agriculture and Forestry showed itself enthusiastic about such "an act of humanity,"[146] but after the resolution had passed the Senate on 26 January 1931, it remained stuck in the House until the session ended. Evidence of a changing mood in Congress was visible, however, as soon as the legislators reconvened in December 1931. Various proposals for the distribution of surplus goods, land settlement, and even the organization of a labor service attracted considerable

145 *CR*, 71 Cong., 2 sess., 1 March 1930, p. 4567; U.S. Congress. Senate. Committee on Education and Labor, *For the Relief of Unemployed Persons within the United States.* S.Rept. 475, 71 Cong., 2 sess. (to accompany S.J.Res. 149, 17 April 1930); [Hoover,] *Memoirs of Herbert Hoover*, 54. For the drought relief question see David E. Hamilton, "Herbert Hoover and the Great Drought of 1930," in *Journal of American History* 68:4 (March 1982), 850–75; and Nan Elizabeth Woodruff, *As Rare as Rain: Federal Relief in the Great Southern Drought of 1930–31* (Urbana: University of Illinois Press, 1985), in particular pp. 66–95; 178–81. Equally unsuccessful was the more cautious S.Res. 338. See in this context *CR*, 71 Cong., 3 sess., 4 Dec. 1930, p. 195.

146 U.S. Congress. Senate. Committee on Agriculture and Forestry, *Distribution of Surplus Wheat for Relief Purposes.* S.Rept. 1341, 71 Cong., 3 sess. (to accompany S.J.Res. 210; 21 Jan. 1931).

interest. The question of direct money allocation ultimately dominated the debate.

Capper again took up the Red Cross idea (S.J.Res. 60). The resolution passed the Senate, only to be scuttled on the House floor on 26 February 1932. But two days earlier, Senator Peter Norbeck (R-South Dakota), another insurgent, had proposed the distribution of government-owned wheat to the American Red Cross "for food for the needy and distressed people, and for feed for livestock" (S.J.Res. 110), asking for only five million bushels. He was able to produce a series of endorsements from his state, most of which stressed the plight of the cattle. After the Senate had passed the measure, a small miracle happened in the House. The Committee on Agriculture pointed out that because of interest, insurance, and storage costs, the grain would eat up its own value in less than three years. Recognizing that people and livestock were suffering equally, it increased the amount of wheat eightfold to forty million bushels. The resolution was accepted by a vote of 345 to 2, and after Senate concurrence was signed by the president on 7 March 1932. It was the first time that Congress had agreed to provide for direct relief of distress caused by unemployment. It did so at a time when several states had already moved and a few others were in the process of advancing in the same direction.[147]

Hoping to exploit the precedent, in early June Hampton P. Fulmer (D-South Carolina), later one of the authors of the Agricultural Adjustment Act, asked for the distribution of another 40 million bushels of wheat and of 100,000 bales of cotton (H.J.Res. 418). The Committee on Agriculture cut the cotton provision in half, but the Senate added another 5 million bushels of wheat. On 5 July, Hoover gave his presidential approval.[148] The prevailing distress suggested other distribution ideas. In January 1932, Couzens proposed that unemployed persons should be housed, fed, and clothed at military posts (S. 5363). Elmer T. Thomas (S.J.Res. 80) as well as La Guardia (H.R. 6746) made similar legislative attempts. However, neither these nor follow-up endeavors (H.J.Res. 422; S.J.Res. 174) got anywhere.

Equally unfruitful were efforts to get back-to-the-land or paramilitary labor service schemes going. In late summer 1931 old-time progressives

---

147 *CR*, 72 Cong., 1 sess., 4 Jan. 1932, pp. 1180; 1185–86; Hearings [Pursuant to S.J.Res. 110]; U.S. Congress. House. Committee on Agriculture, *Distribution of Government-owned Wheat for Relief Purposes*. H.Rept. 657, 72 Cong., 1 sess. (to accompany S.J.Res. 110; 1 March 1932); *CR*, 72 Cong., 1 sess., 3 March 1932, p. 5196.
148 47 Stat. 431 (1932).

Amos R. E. Pinchot and George L. Record agreed that colonization should be tried.[149] Congressman Edgar Howard (D-Nebraska) subsequently proposed a bond issue to raise funds for settling unemployed families (H.R. 7189). This bill did not advance, but it sparked proposals by Brooklyn Representative Loring M. Black, Jr. (D-New York), who in April 1932 requested the distribution of land settlement information (H.R. 11055) and $10 million "for the purpose of providing farming opportunities to destitute and unemployed persons" (H.R. 11056). Hearings before the Committee on Labor revealed that views differed. Whereas several farm movement representatives and members of charity organizations showed considerable enthusiasm, some sober criticism was voiced as well. A Department of Labor official produced an opinion that farmers already on their land "could raise more with one tractor than the whole bunch of [unemployed] Greenville people could raise in two years." The bad agricultural situation was seen as a major obstacle. "When an experienced farmer leaves a farm because he can not make a living there," Representative Oscar B. Lovette (R-Tennessee) asked rhetorically, "how can we expect a mechanic, inexperienced in farming, to go upon that same land and succeed?" Harvard economist John D. Black contended that placing the unemployed on farms "transfers the burden of feeding them and caring for them from the city to the country."[150]

Realizing that his proposal was in trouble, Black in mid-May introduced a substitute bill that omitted the money provision and merely authorized certain existing governmental agencies to coordinate the various back-to-the-farm efforts (H.R. 12097). Senator Charles L. McNary (R-Oregon) suggested that the Department of Agriculture provide guidance for would-be settlers (S.J.Res. 169). When the Committee on Agriculture and Forestry consulted with Agriculture Secretary Hyde, however, the latter showed as little enthusiasm as the Department of Labor had mustered for H.R. 11055. McNary's measure passed the Senate, but it became permanently stalled in the House.[151]

149 Eugene M. Tobin, *Organize or Perish: America's Independent Progressives, 1913–1933* (New York: Greenwood, 1986), 218.
150 Hearings on H.R. 11055, H.R. 11056, and H.R. 12097, pp. 12–13; 26; 33; 71.
151 U.S. Congress. House. Committee on Labor, *Relief of Distress Due to Unemployment.* H.Rept. 1359, 72 Cong., 1 sess. (to accompany H.R. 12097; 18 May 1932); Arthur M. Hyde to Charles L. McNary, n.d., printed in U.S. Congress. Senate. Committee on Agriculture and Forestry, *Information as an Aid to Unemployed Who Seek Opportunities in Rural Areas.* S.Rept. 799, 72 Cong., 1 sess. (to accompany S.J.Res. 169; 8 June 1932).

Failure was also the fate of a proposal aiming at the establishment of a kind of labor service that Celler, who like Black represented a Brooklyn district, introduced in December 1931 (H.R. 247). Celler sought to amend the National Defense Act so as to give the president authority to organize a special army reserve in which up to 250,000 men could enlist for up to one year. The time was apparently not yet ripe in the United States for such a scheme; the Committee on Military Affairs buried the bill without giving it any specific attention.

Heated debate

When the third depression winter loomed, the demand for large-scale federal relief assistance quickly gained prominence. Most proposals in the Seventy-second Congress did not get beyond the introduction stage. Several received intensive and prolonged consideration, however, an indication that the attitude of the congressional majority began to change. This happened against the background of a heated and acerbic debate that exhibited the distinct polarization of the views of adversaries and proponents of federal aid.

Among the most prominently discussed measures were the bills introduced on 9 December 1931 by veteran progressive Costigan (S. 174) and La Follette, son of "fighting Bob" (S. 262), which advocated cooperation between the federal government and the states for the alleviation of suffering caused by unemployment. The proposals were apparently fruits of conversations the two senators and Representative David J. Lewis (D-Maryland) had had in Costigan's office with the most important welfare organizations four weeks earlier. The bills were referred to the Committee on Manufactures, of whom La Follette was chairman and Costigan was a member. During hearings held around the turn of the year, a plethora of witnesses testified to the dire need in many parts of the country.[152] The committee decided to come out with a strong plea. It sponsored the drafting of a consolidated version (S. 3045), which provided for an appropriation of $125 million until the end of the current fiscal year and another $250 million for the next year, the money to be spent among the states (Figure 5–11). Administration was vested in a federal

---

152 Fred Greenbaum, *Fighting Progressive: A Biography of Edward P. Costigan* (Washington, D.C.: Public Affairs Press, 1971), 122–24; Schwarz, *Interregnum of Despair*, 149. Meetings took place on 7 and 11 Nov. 1931. – Hearings on S. 174 and S. 262.

—New York American

Figure 5-11. During the Hoover administration, Uncle Sam tries to prime the pump with an eyedropper. (Source: *ALLR* 23:1 [March 1933], 35.)

emergency relief board. For various features of this measure the New York TERA had obviously supplied the example.

But the majority of the Senate was not yet ready. Its spokesman on the floor, Senator Simeon D. Fess (R-Ohio), a former professor of American history with strong conservative convictions, warned that federal relief "is to create a disposition in the minds of the recipients which will demand it as a right."[153] Fear also surfaced that ordinary public works might be financed with the allotted money instead of distress relief. The bill ultimately failed to pass, and so did money demands by Huddleston (H.R. 206) and Lewis (H.R. 6011; H.R. 8088). The House Committee on Labor held hearings on the latter bills in early February. The social work lobby and several representatives of organized labor openly clashed at this occasion with the conservative witnesses, notably NAM counsel Emery; Frank L. Peckham, vice-president of the Sentinels of the Re-

153 *CR*, 72 Cong., 1 sess., 10 Feb. 1932, p. 3666.

public, a nationwide right-wing organization opposing strong federal power; and Miss Mary G. Kilbreth of the Woman Patriot Corporation. The committee reported H.R. 8088 out favorably, but it was stalled on the House floor.[154]

Either side realized in these months that not only a given congressional measure was at issue, but that the validity of the classical understanding of the "American way" was at stake. The quest for the introduction of the modern welfare state had reached the federal level. "The opposition to federal aid," one observer put it succinctly, "will be intrinsically the reluctance to tax wealth for the benefit of the poor."[155] The conservative arguments were of course as a rule not proffered in this form. Traditionalists rather insisted that the need was not great enough, and that constitutional and moral reasons prohibited change.

One sign that the situation remained under control was seen in the fact that none of the states had ever approached Congress with an official demand for unemployment relief. "Let the legislatures determine the question of need," Peckham demanded, discounting the evidence that several state administrations were seemingly reluctant, even at the cost of prolonged suffering of their citizens, to admit their own impotence. Oblivious to the fact that the majority of legislatures did not sit in 1932, he demanded that impecunious states should increase their taxation rates. Intent on rescuing the states from their own constitutional carelessness, Miss Kilbreth reminded the House Committee on Labor of John Marshall's decision in *Gibbons v. Ogden*, which had stated that Congress was not empowered to tax for purposes in the exclusive province of the states. As Emery expressed it, there existed a "traditional and organic . . . division of power of national and local government," which had to be observed since "no man can avoid the penalty of violated natural law."[156]

Good government, according to conservative understanding, was small government. There existed always the danger that the wrong people might take charge. Miss Kilbreth feared a slush fund, to be used "politically to promote the aims of a third party," which might do its "utmost to promote

---

154 U.S. Congress. House. Committee on Labor, *Cooperation of Federal Government for Relieving Unemployment*. H.Rept. 584, 72 Cong., 1 sess. (to accompany H.R. 8088; 19 Feb. 1932).
155 H. L. Lurie, "The Place of Federal Aid in Unemployment Relief," *Social Service Review* 5:4 (Dec. 1931), 538.
156 Hearings on H.R. 206, H.R. 601, and H.R. 8088, pp. 130–31; 133–34; 151; 154; 156; 161–62; 187; 233.

more radicalism." The Lewis–La Follette bills, Emery claimed, lodged larger monetary discretion in subordinate officials than had hitherto been granted to the president of the United States.[157] Even the National Catholic Welfare Conference, which in principle had no difficulty with the spending of governmental funds as such, came out in strong opposition to increased federal powers. It feared a federal board "which in all human likelihood will deprive the several states of the right to administration." The Conference's basic concern, of course, was the independence of the Catholic charities.[158]

The matter naturally had a moral dimension as well. The creation of a federal unemployment fund, Senator Otis F. Glenn (R-Illinois) said in a radio address, would weaken "the morale and the fiber of every individual, community, and state." Moreover, federal relief would "unbalance the budget on a huge scale, impair the credit of the United States Government, destroy the confidence of the people in their government, and indefinitely postpone all hope of early economic recovery"[159] (Figure 5–12).

Against the defenders of the laissez-faire order, the advocates of federal intervention emphasized humanitarian concerns. Although it has occasionally been claimed otherwise, there seems to have been little insistence on the applicability of the constitution's general welfare clause. The apparent reason for this prudence was the lack of interpretative clarity. The clause could even be used to prove the absence of any federal obligation. Overall, Emery asserted, it merely granted to the federal government a certain taxing power, and Congress was the sole judge "of what is for the general welfare." Hillman therefore on occasion stressed the "sacred trust and responsibility" of the federal government in a time of universal disaster. Columbia law professor Noel T. Dowling even claimed that the Tenth Amendment deserved no consideration respecting relief questions, because any relief program "should be considered on the merits of the program itself."[160]

157 Hearings on H.R. 206, H.R. 601, and H.R. 8088, pp. 61; 130; 149; 179–80. See also Peckham's testimony, ibid., 155. – Paul U. Kellogg, "Relief Needs: Relief Resources," *Survey* 67:9 (1 Feb. 1932), 464.
158 Hearings on H.R. 206, H.R. 601, and H.R. 8088, pp. 109–10.
159 Ibid., 189. See also Donnelly, ibid., 190; Peckham, ibid., 151; Merle Thorpe (editor of the *Nation's Business*), ibid., 205; Walter Lippman, ibid., 206–07. – *CR*, 72 Cong., 1 sess., 16 Feb. 1932, p. 4017. The date of the address was 13 Feb. 1932. See also Hearings on H.R. 12353, pp. 260–61; 263.
160 Brown, *Public Relief 1929–1939*, 113. Section 8 of the United States constitution provides that Congress shall have power to "provide for the common Defense and

—Art Young in The Unemployed

Figure 5-12. Big Business: "We may have bread lines but, thank God, no dole." Art Young in *The Unemployed*. (Source: *ALLR* 21:1 [June 1931], 223.)

The strongest interventionist arguments thus derived from the special character of the crisis, its size, and its urgency. Walter West, executive secretary of the American Association of Social Workers, understood the problem to be "national in origin, national in scope, beyond the reach of any local administrative unit or of the State in its magnitude, and therefore national." Linton B. Swift of the Family Welfare Association of America refuted the arguments for local responsibility with a disarming statement. "A dole is a dole," he advised the members of the Senate Committee on Manufactures, "whether it is given by an individual, a private charitable agency, a city, a state, or the federal government."[161]

general Welfare of the United States..." – Hearings on H.R. 206, H.R. 6011, and H.R. 8088, pp. 138–39; Hearings on S. 174 and S. 262, p. 345; Noel T. Dowling, "The Indestructible Union of Indestructible States," *ALLR* 21:3 (Sept. 1931), 294.
161 Hearings on S. 174 and S. 262, pp. 72; 103; 149. See also P. U. Kellogg, ibid., 85. – Hearings on H.R. 206, H.R. 601, and H.R. 8088, p. 134; Hearings on H.R. 12353, p. 100. See also Huddleston in Hearings on S. 174 and S. 262, p. 274. – See also Gifford Pinchot, "The Case for Federal Relief," *Survey* 67:7 (1 Jan. 1932), 347; Frank J. Bruno, "Federal Aid for Local Relief," *The Family* 13:5 (July 1932), 167.

On occasion, a radical like Rabbi Sidney E. Goldstein of the Joint Committee on Unemployment charged that the suffering jobless were "the innocent victims of an unjust system" that robbed them of "the right to work and to maintain one's self in a state of decency and self-respect." But the vast majority of aid advocates were less ready to question the political framework than the good will of the politicians in power. They rather warned of looming social disruption. Without federal aid, Karl Broders of the Chicago Workers' Committee on Unemployment affirmed in one of the hearings, "we will have starvation, misery, and probably riot and bloodshed before the end of the year." It was precisely to prevent this unrest and thus maintain the existing system that most proponents of federal intervention pleaded their cause.[162]

Federal help would come only if it could be demonstrated that the states had exhausted their means. The basic argument was that the states did not have the taxing power to tap existing sources of revenue. Up to the depression, most states had in the main relied upon property taxes for their financial needs. But increases hurt themselves against the growing impecuniousness of many property owners. A solution to the problem, it was sometimes felt, could be found through the application of an income tax, which would effect a certain redistribution of wealth. Only seventeen states had income tax laws by the end of 1931, however, and the slow process of implementation could not bring any quick results elsewhere. Even where state income tax was available, it was scarcely a cure-all. Because of absentee ownership, the taxing of revenue recipients in their state of residence did not necessarily provide financial relief to the state of business operation.[163]

The states' possibilities were thus narrowly circumscribed. Benson Y. Landis, executive secretary of the American Country Life Association, an organization endeavoring to improve rural life conditions, told the Senate Committee on Manufactures that the use of the taxing power by the federal government was "the fairest way of meeting the relief burden generally." Representative David D. Glover (D-Arkansas) gave this thought a Keynesian twist. In his view it was nonsense to tax the people for more money in times of distress; rather, he exclaimed in the House, "what we should do is ... pass this deficiency on to the general debt of

---

162 Hearings on S. 174 and S. 262, pp. 155; 185; 219; Hearings on H.R. 206, H.R. 601, and H.R. 8088, pp. 11; 38.
163 Edwin E. Witte, "The Fiscal Aspect of Federal Aid," *ALLR* 21:3 (Sept. 1931), 284. See also Pinchot in Hearings on S. 174 and S. 262, p. 217.

the Government." There existed further reasons for federal activity. The nation, tottering along on the brink of disaster, needed leadership. "Federal relief, rightly handled," Paul U. Kellogg knew, "could serve as a magnet to galvanize and organize the whole field."[164]

Advocates of federal relief legislation were eager to point out that there existed ample precedent for federal bailouts. Not only did the RFC help big business, but the United States government had also assisted Belgian refugees during the war and Russian peasants afterward. A statement presented at a Congressional hearing in early 1933 indicated that similar aid had been extended since the early nineteenth century in numerous instances to distressed foreigners as well as to residents of the United States. Victims of fire catastrophes and hurricanes, of droughts, floods, and grasshopper ravages, of earthquakes and volcano outbreaks had enjoyed the comfort of the Union government's helping hand. These people, Costigan affirmed, "did not suffer more severe or uninvited visitations" than the unemployed of the prevailing depression.[165]

Passage of the ERCA

Although argumentation and reasoning dominated congressional hearings and agitated minds in public, no substantial improvement in the unemployment situation could be felt. The conviction in both houses of Congress grew that the social effects of continued federal inaction were more regrettable than the abandonment of traditional tenets. The result was the passage of the ERCA, marking the culmination of many decades of unemployment reform.[166]

Not only the demand for direct relief, but also the quest for substantial public works appropriations met with the opposition of the traditionalist

---

164 Hearings on S. 174 and S. 262, pp. 85; 179. See also ibid., 8 and 341 for similar statements. – Hearings on H.R. 206, H.R. 601, and H.R. 8088, pp. 21 (Huddleston); 90. – CR, 72 Cong., 1 sess., 3 March 1932, p. 5197; Lurie, "The Place of Federal Aid," 533.

165 Hearings on H.R. 12353, p. 40. For a similar argument see Hearings on H.R. 206, H.R. 601, and H.R. 8088, p. 56. – Hearings on S. 174 and S. 262, pp. 9; 155; Hearings on S. 5125, pp. 547–53.

166 Frances Fox Piven and Richard A. Cloward, *Regulating the Poor: The Functions of Public Welfare* (New York: Pantheon Books, 1971), 61–72 make the case that it was fear of rising mass disorder that initiated federal relief action. This view is implicitly rejected by James T. Patterson, *America's Struggle against Poverty 1900–1985* (Cambridge, Mass.: Harvard University Press, 1986), 50–55, and by the literature cited on page 228, fn 15.

forces. Wagner submitted his Labor Day proposal to Congress as soon as the new session got under way in December 1931 (S.Res. 72), only to see it tabled. A few days later, La Follette introduced an emergency public works bill that proposed the sale of Prosperity Bonds in the amount of $5.5 billion (S. 2419). He defended this large sum by reminding the public that the federal government had borrowed "some $25 billion" in wartime for destructive purposes. But to get an adequate public works bill through Congress "in the face of the President's opposition" was difficult, as the president of the National Unemployment League rightly observed. When La Follette/Costigan's great relief bill (S. 3045) was defeated on 16 February 1932, Wagner had a substitute (S. 3696) ready the next day. The proposal did not advance beyond the committee stage. Undaunted, in mid-March Wagner presented an emergency construction bill that asked for $1 billion (S. 4076), again in vain.[167]

1932 was an election year, and much of this legislative maneuvering was already influenced by campaign considerations. On 6 May, Costigan reintroduced the measure he had proposed in January, asking for an increased sum of $500 million (S. 4592). In May and June, La Follette's committee again held hearings. This time, however, the committee did not report the bill out, possibly because still other measures were also under scrutiny elsewhere in Congress. One such proposal, submitted by former Secretary of Labor James J. Davis (R-Pennsylvania), authorized the RFC, which had been created in January to prop up credit-giving institutions and had a nationwide organization, to make loans totaling $500 million to states and municipalities (S. 4632). Another, introduced by Senate Minority leader Robinson, requested bond issues in the amount of $2.3 billion, of which $2 billion should provide construction loans to states and municipalities, "to be spent upon self-liquidating and money-making enterprises." The latter stipulation clearly originated with Baruch, who had been in touch with Robinson in this regard since March 1932.[168]

167 "Statement by Robert La Follette for Immediate Release," 23 Dec. 1931, Box 28, General Files, Wagner Papers. For the origin of the La Follette bill see Barber, *From New Era to New Deal*, 148–49. – Meserole to Wagner, 30 Dec. 1931, Box 188, Legislative Files, Wagner Papers; Paul U. Kellogg to Wagner, 3 Feb. 1932, ibid.; Wagner to Paul U. Kellogg, 15 Feb. 1932, ibid.; U.S. Congress. Senate. Committee on Manufacture, *Federal Cooperation in Unemployment Relief*. S.Rept. 347, 72 Cong., 1 sess. (to accompany S. 3696; 24 Feb. 1932). Wagner appended a list of executable construction works which had been requested on 5 Jan. 1932 through S.Res. 127; *CR*, 72 Cong., 1 sess., 14 March 1932, p. 5957. For economists' mixed views on S. 4076 see Barber, *From New Era to New Deal*, 151–55.

168 For the earlier history of the RFC see James Stuart Olson, *Herbert Hoover and the Reconstruction Finance Corporation, 1931–1933* (Ames: Iowa State University Press,

Hoover, in an apparent attempt to contain possible damage, invited Robinson and Senate Majority leader James E. Watson (R-Indiana) to the White House. The powers of the RFC should be extended, and a debenture issue of an additional $1.5 billion should augment its financial resources; up to $300 million could be loaned to states for relief purposes, but the bulk of the money was destined for "income producing and self-sustaining enterprises which will increase employment whether undertaken by public bodies or by private enterprises." To save face, the president insisted that there was a distinction "between the above purposes and [the money's] use for unproductive public works."[169]

In their countermove the Democrats remained cautious regarding loans to private enterprise. Rumor, soon substantiated, told of large sums of RFC moneys having gone to a Detroit bank in which former vice-president Dawes, now head of the RFC, had a direct interest. The bill that Wagner introduced on 25 May (S. 4755) therefore took up most of Hoover's proposal but restricted loans to "projects devoted to public use." In the House, Speaker John N. Garner (D-Texas), who was aiming for the Democratic presidential nomination, asked for public works expenditures of $2.1 billion (H.R. 12353). The shocked administration responded quickly. Treasury Secretary Mills spoke of "an unsound financial program," and Hoover denounced the plan as "the most gigantic pork barrel ever proposed to the American Congress." On 31 May he went to the Senate in person, calling for a balanced budget out of "regard for the taxpayer and the avoidance of sheer waste."[170]

Over the next few weeks a series of complicated legislative maneuvers were executed by the various interested parties to safeguard their positions. At hearings held in early June before the Senate Committee on Banking and Currency, Mills, along with Senator Carter Glass (D-Virginia), vehemently objected to S. 4755, denying that "a state has a right to exist that cannot take care of its own interests." The bill was nevertheless reported out favorably on 8 June, with the $300 million relief provision stricken out but the public works section intact. The relief clause was subsequently incorporated in another bill, introduced by three sympathetic senators, among them Tom Walsh, on the same day (S. 4860).

1977), 33–61. – CR, 72 Cong., 1 sess., 11 May 1932, pp. 9969–70; Schwarz, Interregnum of Despair, 161–62.
169 New York Times, 12 May 1932, pp. 1; 6; Myers and Newton, Hoover Administration, 204; Myers, ed., State Papers, II, 187–88.
170 CR, 72 Cong., 1 sess., 29 March 1932, pp. 7027–28; New York Times, 27 May 1932, p. 1; Myers, ed., State Papers, II, 196; 202.

The bill gained overwhelming approval on 10 June. Wagner's conciliatory attitude in adopting many of Hoover's suggestions apparently bore its fruit, as only seven Republicans, including Bingham and Felix Hebert (R-Rhode Island), together with one Democrat, voted against the measure.[171]

In the meantime the House had approved a modified version of the Garner bill (H.R. 12445) by a vote of 216 to 182. When it reached the Senate, the Committee on Banking and Currency recommended that it be substituted for S. 4755. After a spirited debate on the floor the Senate agreed, though it added a few amendments that made negotiations necessary. The conference report of 6 July had the public works provision cut down to $322 million, but still provided another $300 million for loans to the states "to be used in furnishing relief and work relief" (Title I). A stipulation in Title II (Section Five) authorizing the RFC to make loans out of the $1.5 billion fund provoked desperate resistance among some conservatives, but it passed both chambers. Hoover, though, vetoed it on 11 July, declaring that the bill was "so dangerous to public credit and so damaging to our whole conception of governmental relations to the people as to bring far more distress than it will cure."[172]

Admirers have later claimed that with this veto Hoover "asserted himself as a director of national policy." If this was the intention, his action was rather desperate. Possibly the president's almost strident opposition to substantial public works legislation before mid-June was influenced by the imminence of the Republican Party convention. In Chicago, the delegates' mind found clear expression in a platform that stressed state and local responsibility for unemployment relief and attacked the "squandering of the public resources and the unbalancing of the budget through pork-barrel appropriations." After he was nominated for another candidacy on the first ballot, however, Hoover was able to take a more conciliatory stance.[173]

171 Hearings on S. 4632, S. 4727, S. 4755, and S. 4822, pp. 11; 15; 17; 21; U.S. Congress. Senate. Committee on Banking and Currency, *Emergency Construction and Relief Act.* S.Rept. 795, 72 Cong., 1 sess. (to accompany S. 4755; 8 June 1932); *CR*, 72 Cong., 1 sess., 10 June 1932, pp. 12512–49.

172 *CR*, 72 Cong., 1 sess., 7 June 1932, pp. 12189–258; U.S. Congress. Senate. Committee on Banking and Currency, *Emergency Construction and Relief Bill.* S.Rept. 831, 72 Cong., 1 sess. (to accompany H.R. 12445; 15 June 1932); *CR*, 72 Cong., 1 sess., 17–23 June 1932, pp. 13277–787; U.S. Congress. House. Committee of Conference, *Emergency Relief Bill.* H.Rept. 1760, 72 Cong., 1 sess. (Conference Report, to accompany H.R. 12445; 6 July 1932); Schwarz, *Interregnum of Despair*, 172; Myers, ed., *State Papers*, II, 231–33.

173 Edgar Eugene Robinson and Vaughn Davis Bornet, *Herbert Hoover: President of the*

Very probably the public pressure for governmental action, finding constant echo in Congress, also played its role. Several bills were introduced in June and early July harping on the aid theme. Costigan and La Guardia offered an almost Keynesian proposal to establish a capital stock of $500 million, out of which some 7 million unemployed heads of families would each receive from $300 to $500 credit (S. 4947; H.R. 12885). Hearings were held on 6 July. Although the bill did not advance further, the fact that it was being considered showed the direction that the thinking of some parts of the public was beginning to take. Roosevelt's call in his acceptance speech at the Democratic convention on 2 July for the issuance of bonds for emergency public works and a "wide plan" of reforestation was another signal of this kind.[174]

Hoover's veto message, at any rate, hinted at possible compromise, and new relief proposals were immediately presented in Congress. A submission in the Senate took the form of an amendment to H.R. 9642. This latter bill had been introduced in February and provided for a supplemental appropriation for emergency highway construction. Hearings on H.R. 9642 had shown that all state highway departments favored such legislation. The bill had passed the House, and the Senate Committee on Post Offices and Post Roads had reported it favorably to the floor, where it still rested in July. After minor amendment, this bill was passed on 12 July by the Senate as a substitute for the measure vetoed by Hoover. Because of some resistance in the House, conferees had to be appointed twice. But on 15 July 1932 the House passed the final conference report by a vote of 286 to 48, and the next day the Senate concurred with a voice vote. On 21 July 1932, when the radical segment of the Bonus Army still camped on the capital's lawns, Hoover signed the ERCA into law.[175]

United States (Stanford: Hoover Institution Press, 1975), 225; Johnson, ed., *National Party Platforms*, I, 350.

174 For some detail on the bills see "Railway Labor's Plan for Federal Credit to Unemployed," *MLR* 35:2 (Aug. 1932), 274–75. Among the other bills were notably S. 4824; H.R. 12409; H.R. 12654; H.R. 12856. – Hearings on S. 4947; [Roosevelt,] *The Public Papers and Addresses of Franklin D. Roosevelt*, I, 653–54. On Roosevelt's switch from state action advocacy to demanding federal action see Freidel, *Franklin D. Roosevelt: The Triumph*, 27.

175 Statement of W. C. Markham in Hearings on H.R. 9642, pp. 16–18. Markham was executive secretary of the American Association of State Highway Officials. – U.S. Congress. House. Committee of Conference, *Emergency Highway Construction*. H.Rept. 1777, 72 Cong., 1 sess. (to accompany H.R. 9642; 15 July 1932). Bernstein, *Lean Years*, 469, is mistaken on the House vote. See *CR*, 72 Cong., 1 sess., 15 July 1932, pp. 15491–92. – 47 Stat. 520 (1932). A slightly more detailed account of the ERCA

The ERCA, on its surface, was truly a compromise settlement, giving neither of the antagonistic forces a full victory. The relief-minded could take satisfaction from the provision of $300 million for loans to the states to be used for unemployment relief (Title I). A petitioning governor had to certify that the resources of his state were "inadequate to meet its relief needs." Another feature substantially retained from the former bills was Title II, which authorized the RFC to give loans to states and their political subdivisions as well as to private corporations for projects that were "self-liquidating in character." For this purpose the lending power of the corporation was increased by $1.8 billion.

Less satisfactory to the reformers, however, was the federal public works program contained in Title III. The appropriation of $322 million, including a long list of authorized projects, was retained and had even been augmented by an additional $7.4 million for specific military projects. But there was now a catch. Only $120 million for highway construction and $16 million for other roads could be expended with no strings attached. The remainder could not be used if the secretary of the treasury declared that the necessary funds were unavailable. Wagner was not the only one to fear that this potential cap would in the future greatly inhibit the pump-priming effect of the program.[176]

Nobody could thus claim that the passage of the ERCA meant the adoption of a vigorous federal public works program. But the act possessed signal importance in a more philosophical sense. By providing relief loans for the states, it officially proclaimed the federal government's willingness at long last to accept a share in the provision of material aid to the unemployed. It represented, as one of the officers of the Work Progress Administration (WPA) was to acknowledge during the New Deal, "the first real step in the direction of federal assistance in the unemployment relief problem." Whereas the public works program contained in Title III did not really depart in principle from previous practice, Title I clearly did. The provision of funds for loans specifically designated for unemployment relief had no precedent. It did not matter in this respect that the money would have to be repaid by the states, or that in fact ultimately it was not.[177]

prehistory, emphasizing Hoover's basic willingness to have the act passed, is given in Olson, *Herbert Hoover and the Reconstruction Finance Corporation*, 62–72.

176 Huthmacher, *Wagner*, 101.

177 Fausold, *Hoover*, 166; Corrington Gill, *Wasted Manpower: The Challenge of Unemployment* (New York: Norton, 1939), 149. The requirement for the states to pay back the loans

It has been argued ever since the 1930s that the ERCA was basically of little importance because of its small economic impact. In the extreme view of Elliot A. Rosen, it enabled the RFC to serve "as camouflage for the achievement of federal fiscal retrenchment of a catastrophic nature." Recently, Singleton has employed considerable effort to correct this "excessively dismal picture" of federal relief endeavors prior to the New Deal by demonstrating in detail various accomplishments under the ERCA. But this kind of argumentation is not relevant to our discussion. What really mattered was not so much the size of aid furnished, however welcome greater appropriations might have been at the time. The essential point was that a precedent was established. The passage of the ERCA rewarded the exertions of a generation of reformers who had striven to induce government – and in the twentieth century that had ultimately to mean the national government – to acknowledge its responsibility for direct unemployment care. With it the federal government took the decisive step to move to the top of a welfare state hierarchy that was in the process of forming. Given the political and intellectual environment of the preceding decades, this move had the quality of a quantum leap. The road to the more generous measures of the New Deal lay now open.[178]

Hoover sensed the fiscal and administrative implications of this turn, and he feared them. Not knowing anything positive to say, he signed the act without comment. Others viewed the development more joyfully. "The administration, in the fourth year of depression," *Fortune*, certainly no enemy of American values, mused, "has come through its phases of opportunism – public works plus private charity followed by private charity without public works – to a recognition of the needs of the actual situation and an acceptance of responsibility therefore."[179]

Aftermath and evaluation

Accepting responsibility in principle, of course, was not equivalent to solving the unemployment problem for good. As will be shown, the size

---

was waived under the Federal Highway Act of 18 June 1934 (73 Stat. 584, sec. 14 [1934]).

178 Elliot A. Rosen, *Hoover, Roosevelt, and the Brains Trust: From the Depression to New Deal* (New York: Columbia University Press, 1977), 297. For earlier critical voices see Jeffrey C. Singleton, "Unemployment Relief and the Welfare State: 1930–1935," (Boston University Ph.D., 1987), 174–77. – Ibid., 178–225.

179 *New York Times*, 22 July 1932, p. 1; "No One Has Starved," *Fortune* 6:3 (Sept. 1932), 88.

of the ERCA's provisions and the speed of the act's implementation proved insufficient for this task. The second session of the Seventy-second Congress, which started in December 1932, thus saw renewed attempts at getting the now lame duck Republican government to agree to further public works programs and to increase its relief action.

Wagner still stood in the forefront of public works advocacy. A bill that he introduced on 9 January 1933 (S. 5336) aimed at augmenting the federal public works fund and facilitating the disbursement procedures. During hearings held in early February, charity workers, unemployed people, and a strong assortment of construction industry representatives testified to the desirability of such an act, whereas Charles A. Miller, president of the RFC, expressed concerns regarding the fiscal laxness of the proposal.[180] No further action occurred, possibly because La Follette/ Costigan's big relief bill was under consideration at the same time. As Congress was to adjourn within a few weeks, Wagner had apparently made his foray to keep pressure on the outgoing administration and prepare the ground for the more extensive measures of the New Deal.

Quests for relief moneys did not meet with much more success. One proposal that made headway, however, was a demand to resupply the Red Cross. By early December the organization had run out of the cotton received under H.J.Res. 418. Marvin Jones (D-Texas), chairman of the House Committee on Agriculture, requested another 350,000 bales (H.R. 13607). His chamber passed the measure quickly, and in the Senate even Bingham showed himself supportive. Conservative concurrence was clearly facilitated by the welcoming stance of the cotton merchandisers who could not see a serious diversion of business. Hoover signed the measure into law on 4 February 1933.[181]

Somewhat less fruitful was the legislature's dealing with another irksome issue. From 1931 on, the problem of transient unemployed persons had attained almost unmanageable proportions, especially in some southern and western states. The response from the states had been variegated and on the whole unsatisfactory,[182] and the federal administration con-

---

180 Hearings on S. 5336, passim.
181 Jones acted in response to a request from the Red Cross. See Robert E. Bondy to Marvin Jones, 10 Dec. 1932, printed in U.S. Congress. House, *Distribution of Government-owned Cotton for Relief Purposes.* H.Rept. 1795, 72 Cong., 2 sess. (to accompany H.R. 13607; 15 Dec. 1932), 2. – *CR*, 72 Cong., 2 sess., 3 Jan. 1933, pp. 1176; 1183; W. Ray Bell to Central Cotton Distribution Office, n.d., printed in H.Rept. 1795, p. 3.
182 For examples of state behavior see California. State Unemployment Commission, *Report and Recommendations*, 270; 302–03; 325–28; 339–45; 356–58; 379–81; 447–48;

tented itself with dispensing good advice to states and localities.[183] On 4 February 1932 a bill of La Guardia's (H.R. 6716) attempted to draw attention to the itinerant worker's plight. During the next session of Congress, one-time Bull Mooser Bronson M. Cutting (R-New Mexico), aware of the exhaustion of his own state's means, again endeavored to tackle the task with federal resources. His bill of 8 December 1932 authorized the RFC to make a total of $15 million available to states with "excessive" numbers of transients (S. 5121). At hearings in January 1933, charity workers and even a few transients themselves recounted their experiences. Grace Abbott presented statistics showing that on the Southern Pacific line alone the number of trespassers ejected from the trains had risen from 79,215 in 1929 to 683,457 in 1932.[184]

Cutting's bill was not pursued further, though, because a similar measure was under consideration at the same time. By introducing S. 5125, Costigan and La Follette had virtually repeated their daring push of a year before. The only significant difference between S. 4592 and S. 5125 was the novel provision of transient assistance. The subsequent hearings differed little from those held on S. 174. Over four dozen witnesses reiterated the by-now familiar tale of misery and human despair, whereas a few remaining opponents of federal aid briefly and perhaps somewhat less insistently stood by their former objections.[185] When the Committee on Manufactures reported back on S. 5125, it made the strongest plea

S. Rexford Black, *Report on the California State Labor Camps* (Sacramento: California State Printing Office, 1932); MacNeil, *Seven Years of Unemployment Relief*, 118–19; Donald W. Whisenhunt, *The Depression in Texas: The Hoover Years* (New York: Garland, 1983), 116–33; Joan M. Crouse, *The Homeless Transient in the Great Depression: New York State, 1929–1941* (Albany: State University of New York Press, 1986), 53–68.

183 In 1931 the U.S. Department of Commerce offered twenty thousand copies of National Association of Travelers Aid Societies, *A Community Plan for Service to Transients* (Washington, D.C.: G.P.O., 1931) to local communities. It also requested the Family Welfare Association of America to prepare a guide based on experience, later published by Robert S. Wilson, *Community Planning for Homeless Men and Boys* (New York: Family Welfare Association of America, 1931).

184 Hearings on S. 5121. The National Committee on Care of Transient and Homeless concluded on the basis of a nationwide census in January 1933 that there were 1,225,000 homeless in the United States, of whom about 50% were believed to be transient. Crouse, *The Homeless Transient*, 48. See also John N. Webb, *The Transient Unemployed: A Description and Analysis of the Transient Relief Population* (New York: Da Capo, 1971. Reprint of Washington, 1935 ed.), 7–11.

185 Hearings on S. 5125; J. M. O'Hanlon to Wagner, 23 Jan. 1933, Box 191, Legislative Files, Wagner Papers; Jos. P. Hastings to Wagner, 9 Feb. 1933, Box 213, ibid.; Karl D. Hesley to Wagner, 10 Feb. 1933, ibid.; Thomas C. Ervin to Wagner, 10 Feb. 1933, ibid.; J. O. Dowell to Wagner, 11 Feb. 1933, ibid.

for clear-cut federal unemployment aid any congressional committee had ever made. The existence of federal responsibility, it declared, was no longer open to argument after the passage of the ERCA. Because local and state resources were exhausted to an alarming degree, "the terrific burden" of unemployment relief had to be shared by the federal government. The measure encountered but little opposition on the floor and passed without a recorded vote, but reached the House too late in the session for enactment.[186]

The passage of the ERCA was thus the only substantial effort made during the Republican administration to come to grips with the distress situation created by the Great Depression. As such, its practical effects were limited enough. Not only did the allocated sums remain relatively modest, but they were also slow in coming. Title III of the act provided for the expenditure of $322 million on emergency construction, but the Treasury Department's brake functioned all too well. By the end of March 1933, only $6 million had been spent on various public works, and another $3.7 million was obligated. The bulk of the remainder was transferred to the new conservation program, as stipulated by the act that established the Civilian Conservation Corps. Title II enabled the RFC to make loans totaling $1.5 billion to states, municipalities, and corporations. By the end of calendar year 1932, projects worth $147 million had been authorized, but only $15.7 million had actually been expended. By the end of June 1933, disbursements had reached $30.2 million. The strictness of the legal requirements made it difficult for projects to be accepted. Another retarding factor was the stipulation that projects be self-liquidating. The high interest rates charged by the RFC may also have played a role.[187]

The only ERCA funds that were used up fully before the New Deal measures began effectively to get under way was the $300 million provided

186 U.S. Congress. Senate. Committee on Manufactures, *Federal Aid for Unemployment Relief.* S.Rept. 1126, 72 Cong., 2 sess. (to accompany S. 5125; 10 Jan. 1933). For an opposing voice see *CR*, 72 Cong., 2 sess., 20 Feb. 1933, p. 4490 (Lester J. Dickinson, R-Iowa).

187 Gayer, *Public Works*, 87; U.S. Congress. House, *Report of the Reconstruction Finance Corporation: October 1 to December 31, 1932, Inclusive.* H.Doc. 538, 72 Cong., 2 sess. (3 Feb. 1933), 6; idem, *Report of the Reconstruction Finance Corporation: April 1 to June 30, 1933, Inclusive.* H.Doc. 200, 73 Cong., 2 sess. (3 Jan. 1934), 8; Donald S. Watson, "Reconstruction Finance Corporation," in Clarence E. Ridley and Orin F. Noltin, eds., *The Municipal Year Book 1937: The Authoritative Résumé of Activities and Statistical Data of American Cities* (Chicago: International City Managers' Association, 1937), 381; J. Franklin Ebersole, "One Year of the Reconstruction Finance Corporation," *Quarterly Journal of Economics* 47:3 (May 1933), 481–83.

under Title I. As the act left it to the recipients to determine the specific use of the moneys borrowed, the variations among the states in the handling of relief matters were perpetuated. Far more states now became active in the relief field, though, the majority scrambling to secure a part of the federal pie.[188]

Obstacles other than the RFC's procrastination also held up the disbursement. Some states were reluctant to assume relief responsibility and did not borrow at all; others insisted that their cities apply so as to avoid

---

188 Work relief appears to have continued to play a role. In Illinois 28 out of 63 downstate counties carried on work relief programs in February 1933, employing approximately 31,000 workers. Illinois. Emergency Relief Commission, *First Annual Report*, 73. In New York (State) the work programs continued until November 1933 in the established fashion. New York (State). Temporary Emergency Relief Administration, *Five Million People: One Billion Dollars: Final Report, November 1, 1931–June 30, 1937* (Albany, 1937), 41–42. In South Dakota, where the state government had not dispensed any relief funds prior to the passage of the ERCA, work programs began in September 1932. Until the end of June 1933, $1,804,000 was spent on relief, the bulk on work relief. W. F. Kumlien, "A Graphic Summary of the Relief Situation in South Dacota (1930–1935)," *Agricultural Experiment Station, South Dakota State College of Agriculture and Mechanical Arts, Brookings, S.D., Bulletin 310* (May 1937), 17; 23; 54. In Kansas federal funds began to be available from 16 October 1932 onward; it was the "fundamental policy" of the state to provide "work relief affording applicants for relief an opportunity to give their personal service in exchange for relief." Kansas. Emergency Relief Committee, *Public Welfare Service in Kansas: A Ten Year Report 1924–1933* (Topeka, 1934), 12. Michigan, which received allotments totaling $21.8 million, devoted a part of that amount to highway construction. Michigan. State Emergency Welfare Relief Commission, *Unemployment and Relief in Michigan: First Report, July 1933–October, 1934* (Lansing, 1935), 35–36. For the comparable experience in Kentucky see George T. Blakey, *Hard Times and New Deal in Kentucky 1929–1939* (Lexington: University Press of Kentucky, 1986), 20–24.

Given the diversity among the individual states, it is not possible to establish adequately the amount of money dispensed on public works under Title I of the ERCA. The flow of funds, though, was slow to commence, even if some quick footwork in the case of Illinois in July 1932 seemed to promise overall alacrity. Illinois representatives conferred with the board of the RFC as early as 18 July, three days before the president approved the ERCA, announcing that the Cook County relief stations would have to close on 22 July if no aid were forthcoming. *New York Times*, 19 July 1932, p. 27. A few days after the signing of the act, the state was allotted an advance of $3 million. But Illinois remained an exception. By the end of July, thirteen states had applied for funds, three of whom, Pennsylvania, Louisiana, and Arizona, each asked for the maximum of $45 million. *New York Times*, 31 July 1932, p. 8. The other states were Arkansas, Idaho, Illinois, Indiana, Kentucky, Michigan, Missouri, Texas, Utah, and West Virginia. For them the well proved more difficult to tap. Pennsylvania with its record of sloppy relief-fund administration had to wait until 23 September 1932 to be allocated $2.5 million. *New York Times*, 24 Sept. 1932, p. 19. By the end of December 1932, only $79,967,042 had been apportioned.

state responsibility.[189] In various cases, legislative authorization had to be secured to take advantage of the act. Moreover, many states delayed application in order first to establish relief administrations, which frequently also required specific legislation. Politics apparently mattered too. Quite a few governors, among them New York's Roosevelt, were reported to postpone application until after the November elections, as they did not want to demonstrate a basic insolvency of their states. The greater part of the Title I funds, $219 million, was therefore expended no earlier than the first half of 1933.[190]

Because the amount of money that went into the diverse programs is unknown, not even a fair guess can be ventured as to how many unemployed were being helped. Some brief considerations show the dimensions involved, however. It has been estimated that $3.6 billion spent on public construction in 1928 gave work directly to approximately 800,000 people, which means roughly $5,000 per worker. There is also some opinion that for each worker employed directly, from one to two were given employment indirectly in the manufacture and transportation of building materials and equipment. Further employment was created through the demand of these workers for consumer goods. This secondary employment has been calculated as perhaps roughly as large again as the employment produced directly and indirectly. The spin-off in employment created by construction work would thus have been about three times the number of those employed directly on the construction site.[191]

One can use these figures in guessing the employment effect generated by the sums allocated under Title I of the ERCA, by far the largest public construction program executed before the New Deal. Funds totaling $300 million were provided for work relief and direct relief. If one half went

189 States that did not receive funds under Title I of the ERCA: Connecticut, Delaware, Massachusetts, Nebraska, Vermont, and Wyoming.
190 Robert Moses to Henry Root Stern, 30 Aug. 1932, Box GF 327, Wagner Papers. Constitutional considerations may also have played a role in the New York (State) case. Schneider and Deutsch, *History of Public Welfare in New York State*, 319, note. For the sluggish response to the ERCA in Texas see Whisenhunt, *The Depression in Texas*, 147–50. For the states' response to the ERCA see also Patterson, *The New Deal and the States*, 32–35. A good case study, detailing the intrastate difficulties bedeviling application, is Ortquist, "Unemployment and Relief: Michigan's Response," 231–35; see also idem, *Depression Politics in Michigan 1929–1933* (New York: Garland, 1982), 156–65. – Watson, "Reconstruction Finance Corporation," 378–80.
191 President's Conference on Unemployment, *Planning and Control of Public Works*, 115. Wolman calculates public works volume differently than Gayer (see Table 2–1). – Gayer, *Public Works*, 30.

to either purpose – which seems very generous for work relief – about 30,000 jobs may have been created directly, and 120,000 altogether. This would not be a negligible amount, but it is insignificant in relation to the number of unemployed, which may have been in the neighborhood of 12 million in 1932. Total expenditures for unemployment relief on the local, state, and federal levels are thought to have amounted to about $600 million in 1932. Whatever percentage of this sum went to public works and work relief, the employment effect cannot have been very pronounced.[192]

The picture is somewhat different if one also considers the conscious efforts made during the initial years of the depression to continue public activity despite, or because of, the decline of private building. Total construction volume in the United States was maintained or kept from falling further in 1930 and 1931 through the volume of public construction (see Table 4–1, page 190). Not all of it resulted from unemployment considerations, but some probably did. In 1932, however, overall volume sharply declined. Although public construction decreased less precipitately than private construction, as indicated by the percentage rise, the difference in reduction was patently insufficient to check economic disaster. The Public Works Administration (PWA) created during the New Deal under Title II of the National Industrial Recovery Act disposed of approximately $2.2 billion for public construction purposes. In comparison, the public works endeavors made by the federal government and the various states before the advent of Roosevelt's administration may at best be characterized as seminal.[192a]

However, the remarkable fact is that these efforts were being made. For over a generation unemployment reformers had endeavored to induce governments to take a hand in the alleviation of distress caused by lack of work. The states, being closer to the scene, had begun to respond, but the dimension of the need had proved larger than their means. With the implementation of the ERCA the federal government officially acknowl-

---

192 Theodore J. Kreps, "Estimates of Unemployment during the Last Four Years," American Statistical Association, *Proceedings*, 39 (March 1934), Suppl., 84; Henry J. Bittermann, *State and Federal Grants-in-Aid* (New York: Mentzer, Bush, 1938), 154. See also Paul Webbink, "Unemployment in the United States," *American Economic Review* 30:5 (Feb. 1941), Suppl., 259.

192a This sum excludes projects apart from the regular public works program of construction. Gayer, *Public Works*, 94–95. – Olson, *Herbert Hoover and the Reconstruction Finance Corporation*, 76–90, also stresses the ERCA's role as forerunner of the New Deal.

edged its duty to step in. Its action, whatever the specific volume, possessed precedent-setting character.

V   The coming of unemployment insurance

Renewed discussion

When remedies for unemployment were being debated toward the end of the 1920s and during the first years of the depression, upgrading the employment service, furnishing relief, and undertaking public works appeared to be the most promising approaches to the problem. Unemployment insurance, on the other hand, was naturally not a very prominent agenda item. As had been the case in the postwar period, it was easy to see that the long-range implications of an insurance plan made a dispassionate approach advisable and that such a scheme could not produce quick relief results. In many minds, moreover, the distinction between unemployment insurance proper and the "dole" was still blurred. As a consequence, by mid-summer 1930, public opinion seemed "almost unanimously opposed" to any form of jobless insurance, as the *ALLR* regretfully stated. But the obvious fact that the other tools at society's disposal could not satisfactorily solve the unemployment problem gave the insurance proponents reason to keep the topic under discussion. Their exertions bore remarkable fruit. In one state a government-sponsored insurance program was enacted; in various others the problem received careful scrutiny. Soon the issue was catching the attention of Congress, which gave it preliminary consideration.[193]

There existed much room for debate, all the more so because the European experience was not of much help in this regard. Detractors eagerly pointed at the complications under which the British and German insurance systems labored. Others ascribed these difficulties to faulty designs and pleaded for an adjusted "American" approach. The fronts were anything but well-defined. The amorphousness of the matter allowed planners to range in their proposals from simple permissive legislation to strictly compulsory schemes and to vary, according to their insights, important details such as occupations covered, size and periods of benefits,

---

193 "Third Unemployment Survey," *ALLR* 20:4 (Dec. 1930), 400. That public interest increased remarkably may be deducted from the fact that the *New York Times Index*, which had shown no references to unemployment insurance in 1914 and only five in 1921, had 59 in 1930 and 215 in 1931.

administration, and funding. Ideology informed the discussants as often as did actuarial knowledge, and exchanges of views were not infrequently spiced with a grain of acerbity.

Many of the former insurance proponents stayed in or rejoined the battle. Their arguments were basically no different from those employed in earlier years. They asserted the insurability of joblessness and pointed out that the payment of benefits would constitute a transfer of purchasing power from good to bad economic times. The advocates of employer reserve plans furthermore insisted that, properly devised, such plans would act as an incentive to prevent layoffs. There was general agreement in reform circles that any scheme promising large-scale results had to be compulsory, as volunteer action, in Rubinow's words, "is extremely slow in developing, includes only a small proportion of those who need it, [and] penalizes the humane employer and thrifty employee."[194]

Members of the AALL figured prominently. Andrews, Rubinow, and Epstein may not have fully acquired "the status of prophets," as a contemporary has recently asserted in his memoirs, but they certainly obtained a wider audience than in the 1920s. In addition to furnishing encouragement to other groups and lobbying on their behalf, the AALL contributed in particular to the discussion by drafting bills for both state and federal legislation. As it turned out, the state bill, labeled "American Plan" and published in late 1930, became the subject of much controversy. Although it provided for a certain pooling of funds, it was otherwise quite similar to the Wisconsin reserves plan, which stressed prevention by penalizing employers who laid off workers. It thus differed substantially from the proposal Leiserson and his friends advocated in Ohio and which, like the British or German models, focused upon the remedial aspect. By the end of 1931 Andrews had distributed 34,000 copies of his plan. His irrepressible proselytizing not only irked the Wisconsin reformers to a degree, but it especially upset Leiserson. "I hope that something will be done," the latter at one point burst out in exasperation, "to stop Andrews from interfering with what we in this state consider the best kind of legislation." The differences between the individual insurance concepts were not only dictated by philosophical predispositions, but frequently also by tactical considerations. A group of reformers might

194 For a good assessment of this argument see R. S. Meriam, "Unemployment Reserves: Some Questions of Principle," *Quarterly Journal of Economics* 47 (Feb. 1933), 320–25. – I. M. Rubinow, "The Movement toward Unemployment Insurance in Ohio," *Social Science Review* 7:2 (June 1933), 191.

concentrate on a proposal not so much because it saw it as intrinsically the best, but rather because the scheme's features looked innocent enough to make adoption by the legislature thinkable.[195]

If ease of passage was to be the criterion, permissive legislation providing a framework for voluntary employer plans was certainly the most auspicious. Such plans continued to exist, although no strong expansionary movement could be discerned. According to a survey conducted by the federal Department of Labor, in 1931 fifteen companies had programs of this kind.[196] Although the number of workers involved was small – only about 50,000 were eligible for benefits – the pioneer character of such ventures could not be overlooked. Government intervention was conceivable in various forms, the most important possibilities being the provision of tax exemptions and the establishment of mandatory guidelines. Eager reformers could see the principal value of such legislation in its wedge character; on the other hand, for those who disliked coercive schemes it offered a minimum program that testified to goodwill without imposing major obligations.

Of exemplary significance for the discussion was the plan that General Electric president Gerard Swope presented in September 1931. His scheme intended to achieve the stabilization of production and employment through the formation of trade associations with enforcement power. A national insurance system under federal supervision with unemployment insurance financed by employer and employee contributions was one of the salient features. Hoover dreaded that implementation of the Swope plan would "drive the country into fascism," but the mixed reaction of the business world included manifestations of cautious interest.[197]

---

195 Jacob Fisher, *The Response of Social Work to the Depression* (Cambridge, Mass.: Schenkman, 1980), 39. Text of the AALL bill in "An American Plan for Unemployment Reserve Funds: Tentative Draft of an Act: Submitted as a Basis for State Legislation by the American Association for Labor Legislation," *ALLR* 20:4 (Dec. 1930), 349–56. – "Report of Work 1931: American Association for Labor Legislation," *ALLR* 22:1 (March 1932), 61; Daniel Nelson, *Unemployment Insurance: The American Experience 1915–1935* (Madison: University of Wisconsin Press, 1969), 121; Leiserson to Fitch, 4 March 1933, Box 14, Leiserson Papers.

196 "Unemployment-Benefit Plans in the United States and Unemployment Insurance in Foreign Countries," in U.S. Bureau of Labor Statistics, *Bulletin 544* (Washington: G.P.O., 1931), 6. For the best-known of these plans, initiated by the General Electric Company in 1930 and the Eastman Kodak Company in 1931 respectively, see Nelson, *Unemployment Insurance*, 60–62.

197 The Swope plan is in Charles A. Beard, ed., *America Faces the Future* (Boston: Houghton Mifflin, 1932), 160–85. Business response to Swope's plan is noted ibid., 186–95; by

As for the insurance industry proper, most of it stood aloof, convinced that joblessness did not generally meet the fundamental requirements of an insurable risk. Parkinson, since 1927 president of the Equitable Life Assurance Society, told the Life Presidents' Association on 10 December 1931, that unemployment "has in it... nothing that should be done by life insurance." An exception had previously been the Metropolitan. In early 1929 it submitted a brief to Couzen's investigatory committee in which it still affirmed that if given permission by state legislatures, it would offer insurance contracts to employers. Scared by the depression experience, however, the company now changed its mind. In early 1931 it did not support the Dunmore bill in New York that basically repeated the Hastings proposal of 1924. When testifying before the Senate Select Committee on Unemployment Insurance in October, the company's actuary confirmed that his management considered further experimentation by private industries essential before it would undertake to write such insurance or favor a state scheme.[198]

In 1928, Wolman had believed that unemployment insurance "is now moving strongly in the direction of insurance by industry." But the great majority of businessmen did not think much even of experimentation. If it was not abhorrence of "paternalism" that predisposed them, it was the fear of losing competitiveness. This held especially true regarding coercive measures. As Filene at one time asserted, state legislation engendered the argument that it "handicaps the employers of the state in which it operates against the states where such legislation is not adopted." Employers' organizations were thus the most articulate and politically potent opponents of the reformers, although agrarian spokesmen often concurred. The NAM, the National Industrial Conference Board, and the United States Chamber of Commerce in particular were adamant in their refusal to consider any compulsory schemes, and so were many local businessmen's associations. Their arguments ranged from the philosophical to the practical. Unemployment was seen as not properly an insurable risk; insurance against it was "socialistic"; insurance administration would constitute an indefensible interference with individual

Nelson, *Unemployment Insurance*, 141–43; and by Edward Berkowitz and Kim McQuaid, *Creating the Welfare State: The Political Economy of Twentieth-Century Reform* (New York: Praeger, 1980), 83–84.

198 Leo Wolman, "Some Observations on Unemployment Insurance," *American Economic Review* 19:1 (March 1929), Suppl., 23; "Another Obstacle Removed," *ALLR* 21:4 (Dec. 1931), 382; Hearings Pursuant to S.Res. 219, p. 460.

liberty; the federal system of the United States presented an insurmountable obstacle; efficiently managed businesses would have to bear a burden created by less well conducted enterprises; good, productive workers would have to support the lazy and inefficient; and the excessive cost of such insurance in times of depression would hinder economic recovery. In 1931 the National Industrial Conference Board undertook a feasibility study and came to the conclusion that "unemployment is largely uninsurable (Figure 5–13).[199]

In May 1932, Charles M. Schwab, chairman of the board of the Bethlehem Steel Corporation, summed up business's attitude well enough when he warned of "rushing into some scheme for the mere sake of getting something started." A few months earlier, Emery had been blunter. Unemployment insurance was "an alien egg offered for . . . legislative incubation," he warned the American Bankers' Association in March 1931; "stripped of its philanthropic drapery, [it] remains a shameless dole, masquerading as insurance." Commons knew a palpable reason for the NAM's opposition. Its members, in his opinion, wanted to cut wages so as to be able to compete with European manufacturers; but unemployment insurance, he told a conference of religious welfare organizations, "will strengthen the resistance of labor, and labor will not accept a cut in wages."[200]

Organized labor certainly did not like wage cuts. This did not mean, however, that it strongly favored compulsory unemployment insurance, at least not during the first years of the depression. In addition to the joint-agreement plans with employers there existed forty-eight indepen-

---

199 Hearings Pursuant to S.Res. 483 (71 Cong.), p. 140. See also Vaughn Davis Bornet, "Herbert Hoover's Planning for Unemployment and Old Age Insurance Coverage," in John N. Schacht, ed., *The Quest for Security: Papers on the Origins and the Future of the American Social Insurance System* (Iowa City: Center for the Study of the Recent History of the United States, 1982), 42–43. – Edward A. Filene to Leiserson, 3 Dec. 1932, Box 14, Leiserson Papers; *Unemployment Benefits and Insurance* (New York: National Industrial Conference Board, 1931), iv. For a succinct statement of negative arguments see also John E. Edgerton, "Opposing Unemployment Insurance," in Conference on Permanent Preventives of Unemployment, ed., *Permanent Preventives of Unemployment* (Baltimore: Belvedere Press, [1931]), 46–56, in particular p. 55. Edgerton was NAM president at the time.

200 Schwab is quoted in David Brody, ed., *Industrial America in the Twentieth Century* (New York: Crowell, 1967), 113. – *Congressional Digest* 10:8–9 (Aug.-Sept. 1931), 211. See also California. State Unemployment Commission, *Report and Recommendations*, 735; John R. Commons, ed., "Favoring Unemployment Insurance," in Conference on Permanent Preventives of Employment, *Permanent Preventives*, 42.

—New York Telegram

Figure 5-13. The American public is slow to learn from experience (*New York Telegram*, 1930). (Source: *ALLR* 20:4 [Dec. 1930], 403.)

dent union plans, providing for about 45,000 persons. Officially the AFL still saw government intervention as undesirable. Over the years the organization had come to endorse public employment agencies, remedial public works, and governmental statistics gathering, after learning to reconcile these with the Gompersian philosophy of labor autonomy. But it held that governmental unemployment insurance was essentially a different matter. Unemployment, the *American Federationist* pointedly editorialized in early 1929, was "an integrated responsibility of all concerned in industry to work out its problems." The implication was that any insurance plans would have to be of a private nature.[201]

Union plans, though, had their drawbacks. "The caprices of local secretaries and the malingering of workers frequently play havoc with such funds," one observer knew, regretting that "during periods of depression [the plans] silently fold their tents and vanish." As employer plans were slow in coming, various state federations displayed interest in compulsory insurance plans. In 1931 the Conference for Progressive Labor Action drew up model state and federal unemployment insurance bills. Over time, the voluntaristic AFL attitude, as Michael Rogin has remarked, appeared "as a formalism which, in the name of abstract ideology, interfered with the workers' practical solutions to their immediate problems." At its 1930 convention, several resolutions were introduced favoring a governmental system of unemployment insurance. They did not get beyond the committee stage, but a year later similar proposals engendered considerable and acrimonious discussion, revealing a tendency among important member unions to question the official line.[201a]

Over the ensuing months it became clear that such potent bodies as the United Mine Workers and the International Association of Machinists were among the dissidents, as well as the state federations of New York, Pennsylvania, Wisconsin, California, Minnesota, Montana, Rhode Island, and Utah. An American Federation of Labor Members' League Favoring Unemployment Insurance made its appearance. In July 1932 the AFL executive council finally reversed its position and instructed its president to draw up a federal insurance plan. Green enlisted the help of Leiserson, Chamberlain, Witte, Frankfurter, Wisconsin professor Paul A. Raushenbush, Wagner, and others. The resulting program recognized the ne-

---

201 "Unemployment-Benefit Plans in the United States," 6; *American Federationist* 36:1 (Jan. 1929), 21.
201ª Theresa Wolfson, "Trade Union-Promises," *Survey* 63:8 (1 April 1929), 54; James O. Morris, *Conflict within the AFL: A Study of Craft versus Industrial Unionism, 1901–1938* (Ithaca, N.Y.: Cornell University Press, 1958), 133–34; Michael Rogin, "Voluntarism: The Political Functions of an Anti-Political Doctrine," in David Brody, ed., *The American Labor Movement* (New York: Harper & Row, 1971), 115; AFL. 50th Annual Convention, *Proceedings 1930*, 309–10; idem, 51st Annual Convention, *Proceedings 1931*, 371–98.

cessity of compulsory unemployment reserves under state administration; it advocated federal encouragement and stipulated that the cost was to be borne "by management as part of the cost of production." Despite some old guard obstruction, it received overwhelming approval in November at the Cincinnati convention.[202]

The diversity of opinions among those immediately interested in the matter reflected itself on the political scene. In 1928 the national Democratic platform remained silent on the issue, but in June 1932 in Chicago the party agreed to "advocate unemployment and old-age insurance under state laws." The Republicans, however, continued to stay aloof, merely pledging themselves to do all "that is humanly possible to see that distress is fully relieved in accordance with American principles and traditions." Groupings on the fringe were more outspoken. In 1928 the Farmer-Labor, Socialist, and Communist parties demanded national unemployment insurance legislation and were joined by the Prohibitionists in 1932.[203] Several lobbying groups supported this quest, among them the various combinations represented in the Joint Committee on Unemployment.

These advocates of governmental insurance could have found confirmation of their convictions in the attitude of the ILO. The unemployment committee of the latter's governing body met in January 1931 and urged governments to develop their unemployment insurance systems or to create such systems where they did not exist.[204] But Geneva was far away. The American business world on the whole remained doubtful about the device and watched approvingly as such bodies as the Sentinels of the Republic or the Woman Patriot Corporation defended the validity of the laissez-faire approach to social problems. Altogether, the debate certainly

202 California. State Unemployment Commission, *Report and Recommendations*, 746–47; "Ohio Looks at Insurance," *Survey* 68:4 (15 May 1932), 198; Wagner to Green, 29 Aug. 1932, Box LO 10, Wagner Papers; Green to Wagner, 30 Aug. 1932, ibid.; Green to Leiserson, 17 Oct. 1932, Box 2, Leiserson Papers; Philip Taft, *The A.F. of L. from the Death of Gompers to the Merger* (New York: Harper, 1959), 31–37; Edwin E. Witte, "Organized Labor and Social Security," in Milton Derber and Edwin Young, eds., *Labor and the New Deal* (Madison: University of Wisconsin Press, 1961), 249; AFL. 52nd Annual Convention, *Proceedings 1932*, 39–44; 325–60; 442; Lewis L. Lorwin, *The American Federation of Labor: History, Policies, and Prospects* (Washington: Brookings Institution, 1933), 292–94; Nelson, *Unemployment Insurance*, 158–60. The text of the plan is in *New York Times*, 21 Nov. 1932, p. 2.

203 Johnson, *National Party Platforms*, I, 278; 292; 304; 328; 331; 334; 338; 351–52.

204 Antony Alcock, *History of the International Labor Organization* (New York: Octagon, 1971), 100.

did not remain fruitless. One legislative proposal on the state level became law before March 1933; in other states and at the federal level the discussion was instrumental in screening the options so that subsequent legislation became a realistic prospect.

Two extremes: Wisconsin and Ohio

Unemployment insurance had made the strongest legislative advances during the 1920s in Wisconsin, and it was in this state that the first American compensation act was passed. But parallel drives were on elsewhere, most notably in Ohio, New York, Massachusetts, and Pennsylvania.

The genesis of the Wisconsin Act is well-known. The depression fully hit Wisconsin as it did other states. Reformers as well as union leaders felt that there might be virtue in a renewed push for insurance. The ailing Commons was now supported by his disciples Harold M. Groves and Raushenbush, as well as the latter's wife Elizabeth Brandeis, daughter of the United States supreme court justice. In consultation with Philip F. La Follette, a lecturer at the University of Wisconsin law school and at the time a gubernatorial candidate, Groves suggested in 1930 the maintenance of individual employer "reserve" accounts.[205] Other advocates of an insurance scheme became alarmed. Andrews and Epstein thought that the separation of funds was not needed to keep entrepreneurs activity-minded. As for labor, it felt that individual employer accounts deprived workers of the freedom of movement. The Wisconsin Federation of Labor therefore favored the Nixon bill, which insisted on a single fund under state control.[206]

During the 1931 legislative session, three bills were introduced. All were tabled, and the legislature created an interim committee to investigate the matter. The summer was filled with efforts of the reformers to advance their cause, and as a consequence the committee in its report of

---

205 The best treatment is Nelson, *Unemployment Insurance*, 118–28. – Lescohier and Peterson, *Alleviation of Unemployment in Wisconsin*, 26; John R. Commons, "Unemployment Compensation," *ALLR* 20:3 (Sept. 1930), 249–53; Elizabeth Brandeis to Andrews, 5 June 1930, microfilm, reel 42, Andrews Papers; Harold M. Groves, "Program for Unemployment Reserve Funds in Wisconsin," *ALLR* 21:1 (March 1931), 58.
206 Epstein is quoted in Roy Lubove, *The Struggle for Social Security 1900–1935* (Cambridge, Mass.: Harvard University Press, 1968), 172. – Nelson, *Unemployment Insurance*, 121.

Fig. 5-14. Governor Philip F. La Follette signs Wisconsin's Unemployment Reserve Act, 28 January 1932. Standing from left are Henry Ohl, Jr., president, State Federation of Labor; Elizabeth Brandeis, Paul Raushenbush, John E. Commons, Lieutenant-Governor Henry A. Huber, Harold M. Groves, Robert A. Nixon. (Source: *ALLR* 22:1 [March 1932], before title page.)

10 November 1931 warmly recommended unemployment reserves.[207] The conservative side sought to salvage what it could. But La Follette, who had been elected governor in the meantime, cut the wind out of the WMA's sails by securing an amendment providing that if within a year and a half enough employers should set up satisfactory voluntary plans, the compulsory features would not take effect. The assembly passed the bill on 21 December 1931, and in early January 1932 the upper chamber followed suit. On 28 January, La Follette signed the first North American unemployment compensation act into law[208] (Figure 5–14).

207 Lescohier and Peterson, *Alleviation of Unemployment in Wisconsin*, 135–36; Elizabeth Brandeis, "Labor Legislation," in Don D. Lescohier and Elizabeth Brandeis, *History of Labor Legislation in the United States*. Vol. III (New York: Macmillan, 1935), 618; Wisconsin. Legislature. Interim Committee on Unemployment, *Report* ([Madison: Industrial Commission, [1931]), 36; 39–40.
208 Wisconsin. Legislature. Interim Committee on Unemployment, *Report*, 66–69; Paul A. Raushenbush, "The Wisconsin Unemployment Compensation Law," National Conference of Social Work, *Proceedings, 1932* (Chicago: University of Chicago Press, 1932), 277; 1931–32 Ex. *Wisconsin Laws*, c. 20; Brandeis, "Labor Legislation," 619; J. Mark Jacobsohn, "The Wisconsin Unemployment Compensation Law," *Columbia Law Review* 32:2 (March 1932), 422; Nelson, *Unemployment Insurance*, 126–28. Schwarz, *Interregnum of Despair*, 209 incorrectly states that "Wisconsin had installed an unemployment insurance system in 1932." Originally 1 July 1933 was to be the starting date, but this was later amended to 1934.

Wisconsin's progressive tradition had no doubt prepared it for its avant-garde role in American unemployment insurance legislation. But the experience of the depression caused at least half a dozen other states also to examine their options and get ready for legislative action. Usually the scene was similar to that observed in Wisconsin, with reformers of one kind or another pushing for legislation and conservative circles attempting to thwart these efforts. Variations could of course be observed in the detail of the maneuvers and the degrees of success. Of more significance with regard to the ultimate advent of national legislation, however, was the fact that in the several states substantially different schemes were discussed and their merits scrutinized. Wisconsin with its plan for individual employer reserves, implementing the idea of prevention, stood at one end of the spectrum. The opposite end was occupied by Ohio, which put the emphasis upon distress alleviation. Other states sought their solutions somewhere in between these two extremes.

Ohio certainly did not lack a progressive past either, and its state employment office activities had made it an early pioneer in the unemployment field. Jobless insurance, though, was not prominently advocated until the late 1920s. Leiserson, then teaching at Antioch College and active in the Consumers' League of Ohio, basically disliked the idea of individual employer reserves as inadequate and therefore favored a bill modeled after the workmen's compensation act. Douglas, who thought along the same lines, recommended that the fund be pooled and augmented through employee contributions.[209] This idea of increased benefits appealed to the Consumers' League, which caused Marvin C. Harrison, a Cleveland attorney, to draft a bill. In January 1931 it was introduced in the legislature by veteran liberal Senator James A. Reynolds. During hearings in February and March, business resistance and the indifference of organized labor held up speedy progress. As Leiserson saw it, the Senate Committee on Labor took "the advice of the Ohio Manufacturers' Association and of the State Chamber of Commerce and killed the Unemployment Insurance bill." All that could be obtained was the creation of a commission to investigate.[210]

209 Elizabeth S. Magee, "Ohio Takes Stock," National Conference of Social Work, *Proceedings 1932*, 285; Leiserson to Magee, 7 April 1930, Box 25, Leiserson Papers; Leiserson to Commons, 18 May 1931, Box 9, ibid.; Nelson, *Unemployment Insurance*, 181. See also Douglas and Director, *Problem of Unemployment*, 490–91.
210 Paul H. Douglas, "American Plans of Unemployment Insurance," *Survey* 65:9 (1 Feb.

This body began its work in December 1931. It vigorously tackled its task, first under the chairmanship of Reynolds and after April 1932 under Leiserson. It held statewide hearings and had Rubinow work out the actuarial side of the problem. In May it decided to hold on to the pooling of funds and employee contributions. Leiserson was fully convinced by that time that the Wisconsin idea "that a two per cent cost to the employer will force him to provide steady work . . . [is] quite erroneous." When a draft bill, written up with Chamberlain's help, was ready by October, the commission presented its report.[211]

But temporary success was with the conservative side. In his message to the 1933 legislature, Democratic Governor George White recommended the postponement of legislation until the end of the depression. Rubinow declared himself "stunned," believing that the governor had made "a mistake even from a political point of view." But White remained unmoved. As an observer put it, he was afraid that the legislation in question "might affect Ohio employers adversely." Legislative action was held up in the Senate until the session came to a close. Ohio thus did not see insurance legislation enacted before the advent of the New Deal. The importance of the vigorous campaign waged by the advocates of distress alleviation rather than prevention was that this option, which later in the decade would be looked upon more favorably, received critical scrutiny and useful exposure[212](Figure 5–15).

1931), 486; Leiserson to S. P. Bush, 16 March 1931, Box 32, Leiserson Papers; Bush to Leiserson, 17 March 1931, ibid.; Magee to Leiserson, 10 Feb. 1931, Box 25, ibid.; Nelson, *Unemployment Insurance*, 181–82.

211 "Minutes of the Ohio Commission on Unemployment Insurance," 8 Dec. 1931, Box 31, Leiserson Papers; Willis Wissler to Spurgeon Bell, 23 May 1932, ibid.; Rubinow to Leiserson, 18 June 1932, Box 35, ibid.; Leiserson to Merrill G. Murray, 29 July 1932, Box 24, ibid.; Chamberlain to Leiserson, 27 Oct. 1932, Box 8, ibid.; Leiserson to Marvin C. Harrison, 15 Nov. 1932, Box 17, ibid. An elaboration on the commission's work is given in William M. Leiserson, "Ohio's Answer to Unemployment," *Survey* 68:17 (1 Dec. 1932), 643–50; 671–72.

212 Ohio. Commission on Unemployment Insurance, *Report. Part I* (Columbus: Ohio Commission on Unemployment Insurance, 1932), 89–90; 97; Magee to Leiserson, 28 Oct. 1932; 29 Oct. 1932; 16 Nov. 1932, Box 25, Leiserson Papers; George White to Charles F. Chittenden, 10 Feb. 1933, Box 14, ibid.; Rubinow to Leiserson, 10 Jan. 1932; 25 Jan. 1932, Box 35, ibid.; Leiserson to Stanley Mathewson, 29 Jan. 1933, Box 26, ibid.; William Green to Leiserson, 15 Feb. 1933, Box 2, ibid.; Leiserson to Commons, 21 March 1933, Box 9, ibid.; Marvin C. Harrison to Leiserson, 27 March 1933, Box 17, ibid. The bills were S. 46 and H. 142. – Rubinow, "The Movement

Figure 5-15. Ohio Commission on Unemployment Insurance, 1932. Seated are Senator James A. Reynolds, chairman (third from left) and Elizabeth S. Magee (second from right); standing are William M. Leiserson and Isaac M. Rubinow (second and third from left). (Source: *ALLR* 22:2 [June 1932], after p. 96.)

Efforts in other states

Reformers pushed for unemployment insurance legislation elsewhere as well. In the various legislative sessions from 1930 to 1933, 163 bills altogether were introduced in twenty-seven states; 126 of these were original bills, the rest amendment proposals.[213] Diversity characterized the detail of the specific provisions, but the most important features – namely, the administration of funds and the contribution regulations – basically situated themselves either close to the Wisconsin model, or the Ohio model, or somewhere in between. Apart from the Wisconsin proposal, none was adopted as yet, but the debates engendered by their introduction served to focus public interest and initiated the process of clarifying minds regarding pertinent measures.

In the previous decade, New York, like Wisconsin, had seen several attempts to get unemployment insurance legislation on the statute books. In the early 1930s, Roosevelt's attitude was crucial. Initially he showed little interest. Although he sensed the advisability of some dramatic action

toward Unemployment Insurance in Ohio," 224; Nelson, *Unemployment Insurance*, 185–87.
213 Tabulation in Industrial Relations Counselors, Inc., *An Historical Basis for Unemployment Insurance: A Report Prepared for the Employment Stabilization Research Institute, University of Minnesota* (Minneapolis: University of Minnesota Press, 1934), 72–73.

and appointed his unofficial Committee on Stabilization of Industry in March 1930, the latter's mandate did not mention insurance. But over the following months Frances Perkins' persistent prompting, assisted by Douglas' efforts, succeeded in persuading him of the soundness of the idea.[214] For the time being, though, he pressed ahead with the TERA, to which he clearly gave priority; he used the insurance question to gather political points and avoided committing himself outright.

Roosevelt's cautious approach followed a traceable line. In June, with an early hint at his presidential ambitions, he aired a proposal for unemployment insurance and old-age benefits, both fed by contributions from employers, employees, and the government. He repeated this suggestion before the New York Federation of Labor on 27 August. In November his Committee on Stabilization recommended joint consideration of the question "by the leading industrial states." Going beyond his own state promised broad exposure, and Roosevelt on 5 December invited the governors of Massachusetts, Rhode Island, Connecticut, New Jersey, Pennsylvania, and Ohio to meet with him. The conference, convening 23–25 January 1931 in Albany, created an interstate commission to study the problem. Wolman, who was appointed chairman, and Leiserson were among its members.[215]

General interest and the governor's seemingly favorable attitude spurred considerable activity in the legislature, the details of which Nelson has well described. Altogether twelve unemployment insurance proposals

214 Frances Perkins, *The Roosevelt I Knew* (New York: Viking Press, 1946), 103; 106–07; Paul H. Douglas, *In the Fullness of Time: The Memoirs of Paul H. Douglas* (New York: Harcourt Brace Jovanovich, 1971), 71; George Martin, *Madam Secretary: Frances Perkins* (Boston: Houghton Mifflin, 1976), 223–25. See also Roosevelt to Charles C. O'Donnell, 16 July 1930, microfilm, reel 68, General Correspondence, Governor Roosevelt Records, Roosevelt Papers.

215 *New York Times*, 1 July 1930, p. 22; Freidel, *Franklin D. Roosevelt: The Triumph*, 139. Roosevelt's motivation is analyzed in Kenneth S. Davis, *FDR: The New York Years 1928–1933* (New York: Random House, 1979), 164–66; [Roosevelt] *The Public Papers and Addresses of Franklin D. Roosevelt*, I, 224; New York (State). Governor's Commission on Unemployment Problems, *Less Unemployment through Stabilization*, 19; Martin, *Madam Secretary*, 225; Andrews to Roosevelt, 1 Jan. 1931, microfilm, reel 68, General Correspondence, Governor Roosevelt Records, Roosevelt Papers. On Roosevelt's willingness to go beyond state boundaries see Davis, *FDR: The New York Years 1928–1933*, 223. – *Proceedings of the Conference on Unemployment and Other Interstate Industrial Problems by the Governors of Massachusetts, Rhode Island, Connecticut, New Jersey, Pennsylvania, Ohio and New York* (Albany: J. B. Lyon, 1931); Bellush, *Franklin D. Roosevelt as Governor of New York*, 182–90; *New York Times*, 26 Jan. 1931, pp. 1; 3; 16; ibid., 1 Feb. 1931, III, p. 1.

were offered during the 1931 session alone. On 12 February 1932 the interstate commission published its report, recommending a plan closely modeled on the Wisconsin act. Roosevelt urged the legislature that the proposed scheme "be given a trial at the earliest possible moment." But despite various attempts, nothing substantial was achieved before the end of the 1933 legislative session.[216]

In Massachusetts and Pennsylvania, renewed discussion of the insurance issue similarly brought a softening of formerly rigid attitudes. Several abortive Massachusetts bills in 1928 and 1929 were followed by the creation of a stabilization commission in 1931. It reported in December of the following year and strongly recommended compulsory non-pooled employer reserves.[217] Hearings on two competing bills in February and March 1933 revealed such a divergence of opinions, however, that the lawmakers could not agree on either scheme. Hesitation or downright opposition from conservative interests also acted as a brake to speedy legislation in Pennsylvania. In October 1930, then gubernatorial candidate Pinchot put together a Committee on Unemployment. When it reported in February 1931, this body just noted that a choice existed between the "American" and Ohio models. Subsequent bills were killed by employer opposition, and in November 1932, Pinchot, now governor, as a consequence appointed a Pennsylvania State Committee on Unemployment Reserves. It did not report before May 1933.[218]

More or less similar developments, with only the intensity of the debate varying, could be observed in several other instances. In Connecticut,

216 Nelson, *Unemployment Insurance*, 162–73; Interstate Commission on Unemployment Insurance, *Report* (n.p., 1932), 7–8; Leiserson to Wolman, 6 Feb. 1932, Box 15, Leiserson Papers; Douglas to Leiserson, 17 Feb. 1932, Box 11, ibid. See also Douglas, *In the Fullness of Time*, 73–74; [Roosevelt,] *The Public Papers and Addresses of Franklin D. Roosevelt*, I, 469–70.
217 Stewart, *Unemployment Benefits*, 570; 577; Massachusetts. Department of Labor and Industries, *Special Report under Chapter 60, Resolves of 1930* (Boston: Wright & Potter, 1931), 58. Draft bill pp. 101–04; Massachusetts. Special Commission on the Stabilization of Employment, *Preliminary Report*, 96; Wooster to Magee, 21 April 1932, Box 25, Leiserson Papers; Nelson, *Unemployment Insurance*, 176–78; Massachusetts. Special Commission on Stabilization of Employment, *Final Report* (Boston: Wright & Potter, 1933), 4; 110–46. Draft bill ibid. pp. 192–236. – Massachusetts. Special Commission on Stabilization of Employment, *Supplementary Report* (Boston: Wright & Potter, 1934), 11–12.
218 Pennsylvania Committee on Unemployment, *Alleviating Unemployment: A Report to Gifford Pinchot, Governor* (Harrisburg, 1931), 11; 26–30; Pennsylvania. State Committee on Unemployment Reserves, *Report* (Philadelphia, 1933), 9; 54; "Report of Connecticut Unemployment Commission," *MLR* 36:2 (Feb. 1933), 279–80.

unemployed insurance bills were unsuccessfully introduced in the house during each legislative session from 1927 on. In December 1932 an investigative commission came up with the interesting idea that "dismissal wages," rather than the usual benefits, should be paid out of individual employer funds, meaning that benefits should stop only when a worker was rehired by the same employer. In Minnesota the abortive attempts of the 1920s were followed up by an insurance proposal in 1931 as well as some efforts made by Farmer-Labor governor Floyd B. Olson in 1932 to draft a bill that would please labor as well as the employers. Neither endeavor proved successful.[219] Labor-employer antagonism equally characterized the situation in California. An insurance bill introduced during the 1931 legislative session was backed by the State Federation of Labor but opposed by the Merchants' and Manufacturers' Association and made no headway. In its November 1932 report, the State Unemployment Commission recommended the creation of a system of individual plant reserves vaguely along the lines of the Wisconsin act; in 1933 the opponents of compulsory legislation, however, still had the upper hand, hindering four insurance bills from advancing. In Michigan, an Unemployment Insurance League campaigned unsuccessfully in 1930 for an unemployment insurance amendment to the state constitution. Bills submitted in 1931 and 1933 did not make headway either, nor did similar efforts in Missouri, Illinois, and Maryland.[220]

The apparent fruitlessness of all these exertions must have caused considerable frustration to the proponents of a governmental part in unemployment insurance. But even if success eluded them for the moment, their activity helped to prepare later enactments at the state level. "Only by experimentation will we arrive at sound judgment," Ohio activist Eliz-

---

219 Alvin H. Hansen and Merrill G. Murray, "Minnesota Plans for Job Insurance," *Survey* 69:2 (Feb. 1933), 58–59; "Further Hearings on Unemployment Insurance," *ALLR* 21:2 (June 1931), 220.

220 California. State Unemployment Commission, *Report and Recommendations*, 65–75; Douglas, "American Plans of Unemployment Insurance," 486; Richard T. Ortquist, "Unemployment and Relief: Michigan's Response to the Depression during the Hoover Years," *Michigan History* 57:3 (Fall 1973), 219; Carter Goodrich, "An Analysis of American Plans for State Unemployment Insurance," *American Economic Review* 21:3 (Sept. 1931), 400; Harry Greenstein to Leiserson, 7 Jan. 1931, Box 15, Leiserson Papers; William Haber to Leiserson, 4 April 1933, Box 16, ibid.; "Hearings Open at Several State Capitals on Unemployment Reserve Fund Bills," *ALLR* 21:1 (March 1931), 60. In 1931 Oregon created an investigative commission, to report in 1933, but no bills were introduced before that date. "Oregon Social Insurance Investigative Commission," *MLR* 32:5 (May 1931), 1070.

abeth S. Magee, referring to unemployment insurance, consoled the assembled social workers in 1932. "Should we, therefore, not welcome
different proposals in different states, trusting that out of them will develop
a body of experience for future action?"[221] History proved her right. The
judgment thus gained, moreover, not only benefited individual states. It
also provided intelligence useful in the quest for federal legislation.

The federal level

There could be no doubt about the ultimate need for national rather than
state unemployment insurance legislation in view of the integration of the
economic and labor markets in the United States. Initiatives in this respect
were nevertheless scarce, especially in the years before the nadir of the
depression was reached, because of the general lack of experience and
the reluctance of the federal government to get involved in social legislation. But by late 1931, change announced itself. Although the administration's emerging willingness to investigate did not yet signify a
readiness to implement, it constituted a necessary step toward that goal.

A few pertinent moves actually occurred before the depression struck.
In March 1928, Berger submitted an unemployment insurance bill in the
House, the first ever to be presented in Congress (H.R. 12205). Borrowing from the British example, it provided for a compulsory scheme
in which employers, employees, and the federal government would each
pay one-third of the cost. The bill did not advance, but only a few weeks
later the issue received greater attention in Congress when S.Res. 219
directed the Senate Committee on Education and Labor to explore the
virtue of establishing "systems of unemployment insurance or other unemployment reserve funds." During the hearings in February 1929, Commons recommended his employer reserves program; Lubin thought that
the federal government might subsidize compulsory state systems. The
committee, however, concluded that "the paternalistic and socialistic
schemes adopted in foreign countries" were not suited to the American
scene, which would be best served by private employer reserve plans;
national legislation did not seem to be indicated.[222]

Federal unwillingness to get involved did not observably alter with the

---

221 Magee, "Ohio Takes Stock," 293.
222 Hearings Pursuant to S.Res. 219, pp. 205–517; U.S. Congress. Senate. Committee
on Education and Labor, *Causes of Unemployment.* S.Rept. 2072, 70 Cong., 2 sess.
(pursuant to S.Res. 219; 25 Feb. 1929), xi–xiii.

beginning of the depression, especially because unemployment insurance was a long-range measure. Uncertainty regarding the constitutionality of federal action also worked as a brake for initiatives. Frankfurter for one felt that "the settled doctrine of the Supreme Court" made federal unemployment insurance for workers not employed in interstate commerce "clearly unattainable." In his opinion, shared by Justice Brandeis, at the very most a reserves system along the Wisconsin model had a chance in the judiciary. Lubin, on the other hand, thought that federal insurance aid to the states should be shaped after the highway construction or vocational guidance models. There were also tactical considerations. When urged in May 1930 by Andrews to offer an unemployment insurance bill, Wagner declared it unadvisable to frighten away possible support for his other three bills.[223]

That interest was nevertheless growing could be deducted from the fact that in July 1931 the federal Bureau of Labor Statistics published a well-researched study outlining in considerable detail the existing private and union benefit plans as well as government insurance schemes abroad. More tangible action came during the third session of the Seventy-first Congress when several pertinent proposals were submitted, among them a bill introduced on 15 December 1931 by Wagner that exempted employer/employee reserve funds from taxation (S. 5350). It was a modest move, taking up a suggestion that the NAM had made a few weeks earlier.[224]

Although at least the tax exemption measure was cordially welcomed by as diverse parties as Swope's General Electric Company, the federal commissioner of labor statistics, and the *New Republic*, none of these bills could realistically be expected to go beyond the committee stage. In order to keep the subject before Congress, Wagner therefore proposed the establishment of an investigative committee. After some hesitation the

223 *New York Times*, 21 July 1930, p. 17; Taft, *The A. F. of L. from the Death of Gompers*, 36; Edwin E. Witte to William Green, 24 Oct. 1932, Box 1, Witte Papers; Isidor Lubin, "The U.S. Constitution and Compulsory Unemployment Insurance," *Congressional Digest* 10:8/9 (Aug./Sept. 1931), 197; 224. On the problem of constitutionality see also Paul H. Douglas, *Standards of Unemployment Insurance* (Chicago: University of Chicago Press, 1933), 193–97. – Wagner to Andrews, 28 May 1930, Box 188, Legislative Files, Wagner Papers.

224 "Unemployment-Benefit Plans in the United States"; Hearings Pursuant to S.Res. 483 (71st Cong.), p. 266. Other bills introduced were H.R. 15269 and S. 5634. See in this context Andrews to Wagner, 10 Dec. 1930, Box 188, Legislative Files, Wagner Papers; Wagner to Andrews, 13 Dec. 1930, ibid.

Senate agreed on 28 February 1931 that the vice-president should request two majority members and one minority member to conduct "a general study of the unemployment insurance systems in use by private interests in the United States and by the foreign governments" (S.Res. 483).[225]

The New York senator's satisfaction at this success did not last. He was appointed alright, together with Republicans Hebert and Glenn. But when he met with them on 18 March, the two others proceeded to elect Hebert as chairman, not following the custom of giving this position to the initiator of the resolution. This move, they informed the Democrat, was in accordance with the president's wish. In his dislike of Wagner, Hoover was apparently willing to "play politics with human misery," to use a phrase he himself had coined. Hebert's election came shortly after the veto of the employment office bill, which seems to indicate that the president saw in Wagner's initiative another attempt to cause trouble for the administration.[226]

The committee got off to a slow start. After a brief organizational session on 2 April it decided to hold hearings in the fall. During the summer, Hebert and Glenn went on fact-finding tours to Europe. What they saw did not impress them. On his return in August and after having seen the president, Hebert publicly denounced unemployment insurance as "the first step toward the national dole." Hoover, for his part, elicited from his attorney general a legal opinion to the effect that federal unemployment insurance action was unconstitutional except with regard to interstate industries. A few days later he mentioned that he had under consideration an "employment assurance" plan, as distinguished from "employment insurance," meaning that steps might be taken to "open avenues for employment." It was quite evident that the administration was not yet willing to cede ground in the matter.[227]

If the Republican side had hoped that delay would weaken interest in the insurance question, however, the hearings in October and November 1931 proved a disappointment. Various advocates of legislation, among

---

225 J. Frank Zoller to Wagner, 26 Dec. 1930, Box 190, Legislative Files, Wagner Papers; Ethelbert Stewart to Wagner, 17 Jan. 1931, ibid.; "The Week," *New Republic* 65:840 (7 Jan. 1931), 201. S.Res. 483 is based on S.Con.Res. 36, introduced by Wagner on 9 Jan. 1931.

226 Huthmacher, *Wagner*, 85; Bernstein, *Lean Years*, 502; Nelson, *Unemployment Insurance*, 135.

227 *New York Times*, 11 Aug. 1931, p. 2; Nelson, *Unemployment Insurance*, 136; *Christian Science Monitor*, 15 Aug. 1931, as quoted in *Congressional Digest*, 10:8–9 (Aug.-Sept. 1931), 196.

them Epstein, Harvard economist Sumner H. Slichter, and Jacob Billikopf of the Federation of Jewish Charities, vigorously made their points.[228] Opponents, among whom representatives of the United States Chamber of Commerce and the Illinois Manufacturers' Association were the most articulate, denounced any governmental involvement as paternalistic. After Congress had reconvened in December, La Guardia and others proposed the creation of unemployment insurance funds (H.R. 2, H.R. 367, S. 2732).

The Republican committee members in the end showed some change of mind. In a speech on 19 December before the National Republican Club, Hebert outlined a plan for legislation by the states; it required compulsory employer reserves to be put into funds that were possibly administered with the help of the federal government. Taking up Wagner's earlier proposal, he also suggested that federal income deductions might be allowed for employer contributions. Hebert obviously felt that these concessions did not amount to any substantial commitment but had the ring of flexibility. Andrews for one was pleased, noting that Hebert's idea was "strikingly in line" with the 'American Plan' proposed by the AALL.[229]

Hebert's move took much of the wind out of Wagner's sails. The New York senator, who in February had the full text of the Wisconsin bill inserted in the *Congressional Record*, might have readily signed the majority committee report that the two other senators presented on 30 June 1932 and that basically repeated Hebert's plan. But at about this time the presidential campaign was getting under way, and Wagner could ill afford to leave the field to the Republicans. He thus added a minority report of his own, demanding that the federal government lead the way by establishing a nationwide employment service to assist the states in implementing insurance and by guiding them regarding the organization of sound systems.[230]

By mid-1932 the difference between the Republican and Democratic views of the matter had thus shrunk considerably. There was essential

228 Hearings Pursuant to S.Res. 483 (71st Cong.). Leiserson, Miss Perkins, and Wolman were not witnesses at these hearings, contrary to Bernstein's claim in *Lean Years*, 503.
229 "Senate Committee Chairman Outlines Plan for Unemployment Reserve Legislation," *ALLR* 21:34 (Dec. 1931), 374.
230 *CR*, 72 Cong., 1 sess., 10 Feb. 1932, pp. 3653–58; "Report of Senate Committee on Unemployment Insurance," *MLR* 35:2 (Aug. 1932), 268–73. See also Robert F. Wagner, "Rock-Bottom Responsibility," *Survey* 68:5 (1 June 1932), 222–24; 256.

agreement on the desirability of individual state legislation rather than federal coercion, and it seemed that even an understanding regarding the federal role could be reached over time. Because relief legislation providing instant help constituted a more pressing need, the insurance problem did not emerge any more as a prominent concern on the federal level during the Hoover administration. But the prospect was, as Douglas wrote in his competent treatment of unemployment insurance problems published in January 1933, that there might be, "within the next decade, a fairly extensive application of this [unemployment insurance] principle by our state and national governments."[231] His assessment of the general mood indicated that a remarkable change had indeed taken place during the preceding two or three years.

231 Douglas, *Standards of Unemployment Insurance*, ix.

6. Epilogue

The New Deal was doubtless more than just unemployment alleviation measures. As Romasco has pointed out, Roosevelt's administration strove to end the crippling process of deflation, lighten the burden of debt, and preserve institutions essential to the functioning of a free-enterprise economy.[1] The activities directed at solving the unemployment problem were only a part of that larger endeavor. But because they sought to bring immediate help to human beings who needed it urgently, they seem to have been watched and applauded – or decried – more intensely than those undertakings that aimed at remedying the situation in indirect ways. They were in any case significant steps on the road of the American nation toward the modern welfare state, and have for this reason justly received scholarly attention from the time of their implementation.

The most important of the New Deal's measures in this regard were the relief programs, the establishment of a functioning employment service, the public works activities, and the implementation of unemployment insurance. The bulk of the relief measures in the proper sense of the word was administered by the Federal Emergency Relief Administration (FERA), established by the Federal Emergency Relief Act of 12 May 1933. Through this act and subsequent legislation the FERA received approximately $3 billion from the federal treasury for dispensation under its terms of reference, which allowed the execution of federal work relief projects, the granting of funds to states, and other disbursements for relief purposes.[2] At the end of December 1935 the FERA ceased to operate,

---

1 Albert U. Romasco, *The Politics of Recovery: Roosevelt's New Deal* (New York: Oxford University Press, 1983), 54.
2 Arthur Edward Burns, "Federal Emergency Relief Administration," in Clarence E. Ridley and Orin F. Noltin, eds., *The Municipal Year Book 1937* (Chicago: International City Managers' Association, 1937), 404 mentions a figure of $3,088,670,625. Dorothy C. Kahn. *Unemployment and Its Treatment in the United States* (New York: American Association of Social Workers, 1937), 40, puts the amount at $2,933,107,127. Edward Ains-

superseded by a series of other agencies of which the WPA is perhaps the best known.

The FERA was practically a continuation of the ERCA's Title I program on a larger scale. In a similar way the New Deal harked back to pre-New Deal precedents when creating an employment service. Only a few days after the Seventy-third Congress convened, Wagner introduced a bill abolishing the old USES and replacing it with a new organization of the same name. The proposal had swift passage through Congress, and on 6 June 1933 President Roosevelt was able to sign the Wagner–Peyser Act into law.[3] The new service embodied the idea of a genuinely cooperative federal-state system so long advocated by the senator and his backers. Three-fourths of the annual appropriations were apportioned to the individual states on the basis of their populations. The function of the federal office was basically to promote uniformity of procedures, maintain minimum standards of operation, provide for interstate clearance of labor, and thus integrate the state services into a nationwide employment system. The buildup, fueled by an appropriation of $1.5 million for the first year and $4 million during each of the succeeding four years, went swiftly. By November 1934 the employment services of twenty-two states, comprising 75 percent of the nation's manufacturing population, had become affiliated with the new USES. After passage of the Social Security Act made the inclusion of a state into the unemployment insurance program dependent upon the existence of a public employment office system in that state, most other states quickly adhered as well, so that by 30 June 1938 the services in forty-seven states were members of the USES system.

Almost from its inception the USES had not only to fulfill the regular tasks envisaged in its constituting act, but was drafted into the employment programs of the New Deal. In June 1933 the Special Board of Public Works provided that all labor on projects of the Federal Administration of Public Works (PWA) should be referred by agencies designated by the USES. For this purpose the National Reemployment Service was created as a special division of the USES. From November 1933 the combined services were moreover charged with selecting individuals for the activities of the Civil Works Administration (CWA). During the fiscal year ending

worth Williams, *Federal Aid for Relief* (New York: Columbia University Press), 85 has $2,904,007,125.
3 "Federal Act Creating National Employment Service," *MLR* 37:1 (July 1933), 87–91.

in June 1934, they registered 12.6 million applicants and placed almost 7 million of them into positions.[4]

As just mentioned, much of the increase in the activity of the new USES was due to the implementation of the huge public works programs of the New Deal. The first of these to be implemented was the one administered by the PWA, provided for by Title II of the National Industrial Recovery Act, which was adopted on 16 June 1933. It again essentially derived from the ERCA. The new act empowered the president to undertake federal construction projects and to make loans and grants to states, municipalities, and other public bodies for building activities of their own. By July 1934, the best month, 650,000 persons were employed under it; by 1 December 1936 the PWA had allotted over $4 billion for public works on various levels.[5] In November 1933 the CWA began operations in order to supplement the PWA program, which was slow in getting work under way because of startup delays. In January 1934, CWA activity reached its employment peak of 4,264,000. When its existence ended officially in July of that year, it had spent $933 million.[6]

Government-sponsored unemployment insurance came to the United States through the Social Security Act. Discussion of the insurance issue actually continued unabated after the advent of the Roosevelt administration. Bills were still introduced and made occasional progress in a number of states, notably New York, Massachusetts, and Ohio.[7] The push for legislative action on the state level, however, was less intense than it could have been, as the country watched attentively the progress of similar efforts in Congress. On 5 February 1934, Wagner and Rep-

---

4 Committee on Economic Security, *Social Security in America: The Factual Background of the Social Security Act as Summarized from Staff Reports to the Committee on Economic Security* (Washington: G.P.O., 1937), 431–35; Raymond C. Atkinson, Louise C. Odencrantz and Ben Deming, *Public Employment Service in the United States* (Chicago: Public Administration Service, 1938), 21–37; William Haber and Daniel H. Kruger, *The Role of the United States Employment Service in a Changing Economy* (Kalamazoo: W. E. Upjohn Institute for Employment Research, 1964), 26–29.

5 B. W. Thoron, "The Federal Emergency Administration of Public Works," in Clarence E. Ridley and Orin F. Noltin, ed., *The Municipal Year Book 1937: The Authoritive Résumé of Activities and Statistical Data of American Cities* (Chicago: International City Managers' Association, 1937), 457–59.

6 Corrington Gill, "The Civil Works Administration," in Ridley and Noltin, eds., *Municipal Year Book 1937*, 419–21; Forrest A. Walker, *The Civil Works Administration: An Experiment in Federal Work Relief, 1933–1934* (New York: Garland, 1979), 133; 163. See also *Final Report on WPA Program 1935–43* (Washington: G.P.O., 1947), 2–7.

7 Daniel Nelson, *Unemployment Insurance: The American Experience 1915–1935* (Madison: University of Wisconsin Press, 1969), 171–73; 178–79; 185.

resentative David J. Lewis submitted identical bills providing for a federal unemployment tax against which 100 percent credit could be obtained by employers for contributions to a state plan that met prescribed minimum benefit standards. This proposal, although it asked for federal-state cooperation rather than centralized control, met with staunch resistance from the employer side, and no action was taken. To move the insurance matter along, Roosevelt formed the Committee on Economic Security in June 1934 to prepare legislation. Although in the course of the committee's deliberations other suggestions came up, in particular a subsidy plan that would have implemented a more centralized federal system, Roosevelt's advisors ultimately opted for a scheme similar to the Wagner–Lewis proposal. The provisions of the Social Security Act, which became law on 14 August 1935, essentially followed the committee's recommendations in this regard.[8]

The arrival of unemployment insurance meant, among other things, that at long last reasonably reliable unemployment data would become attainable. But it took years to implement the insurance plan, and during the 1930s the system could not yet supply satisfactory figures. The New Deal policy makers had thus still to rely on the methods developed earlier, but they were able to improve at least employment statistics to the point where very helpful approximations replaced the vaguer guesses used before. As early as March 1933, Frances Perkins, newly appointed secretary of labor, requested the ASA to set up an Advisory Committee on Labor Statistics. The members of this committee subsequently worked in close cooperation with the federal Bureau of Labor Statistics at improving the basis of the employment figures collected. In particular it was felt that the list of reporting firms should be expanded so as to make the data obtained more representative. As a result, in the winter of 1933–34 the Bureau of Labor Statistics, with the help of a grant from the CWA, organized a project that aimed at persuading firms to participate. Over 60,000 establishments in various lines of business were added to the existing list, improving coverage especially in southern states, but also with regard to formerly neglected lines such as wholesale and retail trades. The bureau first offered its revised indexes to the public in April 1934. They represented, in the words of an ASA expert, "a great improvement

8 William Haber and Merrill G. Murray, *Unemployment Insurance in the American Economy: An Historical Review and Analysis* (Homewood, Ill.: Irwin, 1966), 72–89; Nelson, *Unemployment Insurance*, 192–219.

over those previously issued because of many technical changes introduced, but primarily because they reflect[ed] accurately the long-time trend of employment and earnings."[9]

"The line of descent from the social justice movement of the 1900s to the New Deal," Link/Catton have written, "is clear and straight."[10] In view of the intricate advance of the reform movement described here, this pronouncement appears somewhat daring in its sweepingness. But the principal unemployment activities of the New Deal certainly corresponded very closely to the objectives that the reformers had formulated, discussed, and experimented with in the course of the preceding two generations. Far from implementing something new, the Roosevelt administration made use of the wealth of insights and experience that had been acquired in the course of earlier decades. Even a special program like the Civilian Conservation Corps had at least partially been anticipated in certain bills as well as the work camp experience before 1933. On the other hand, an idea that had not kept its original glamour under scrutiny – long-range planning of public works – did not find implementation as such in the New Deal years.

The significance of the unemployment measures of the New Deal was certainly not their novelty. A statement like Otis L. Graham, Jr.'s, that Roosevelt's social security legislation "had only the faintest roots in the pre-Depression period"[11] can clearly no longer be maintained. As for relief and public works activities, it was the dimensions that were new, and Roosevelt deserves credit for having mustered the political will to implement them on the scale he did. It also took much political resolve to adopt an unemployment insurance scheme of national scope. But in all these instances, Roosevelt built upon the experience of the foregoing years. The ineffectiveness of remedial efforts undertaken on a smaller scale had first to be proven before the country was ready for the larger endeavors of the New Deal period. Once the proof was in, public opinion graduated to the point of asking for the governmental intervention that it had formerly viewed with disfavor. The mandate that Roosevelt obtained

---

9 Aryness Joy, "Recent Progress in Employment Statistics," *American Statistical Association, Journal* 29:188 (Dec. 1934), 363. Joy was a member of the Office of the Economic Advisor to the National Emergency Council.

10 Arthur S. Link and William B. Catton, *American Epoch: A History of the United States since 1900.* 5th ed. (New York: Knopf, 1980), 59.

11 Otis L. Graham, Jr., *An Encore for Reform: The Old Progressives and the New Deal* (New York: Oxford University Press, 1967), 8.

in November 1932 offered an opportunity – and obligation – that his predecessors did not have and probably did not need, but which evolved in the time of their tenure.

During what may be called the Hoover renaissance of the last two decades, it has become very fashionable to point out that many of the measures taken during the Hoover presidency were precursors of corresponding New Deal activities. "The relationship between the Hoover administration and the New Deal is a transition rather than a watershed," Olson has thus remarked in his treatment of the RFC, meaning that the former "foreshadowed many of the programs" adopted by the latter.[12] The evidence presented here suggests that this kind of statement should probably be somewhat modified with regard to unemployment measures in particular. The point that deserves stressing is that the "transition" from laissez-faire to governmental intervention stretched much farther back than Hoover's presidential term. The Progressive Era, reaching well into the 1920s, was indubitably an integral part of this development. A period of less intensive – though still very recognizable – reform endeavor is observable in the second half of that decade, but it at best amounted to no more than an episodical three or four years. This understanding renders it advisable to abandon the concentration upon Hoover's presidency as the meritorious or nefarious precursor of the New Deal and to see it as merely a way station, albeit an important one, within that drawn-out process by which industrial society sought and seeks to come to terms with the conditions that produced it.

In the introduction of this book, the need for comparative studies on an international level has been mentioned. Acknowledging this requirement implies the recognition that the development just described came about because of the specific circumstances prevailing during its time. The fact that it happened does not entitle us to conclude that it had to happen, that it was inevitable. Any Whiggish interpretation of this kind would not only have to provide the philosophical premises for such an affirmation; it would also have to explain the phenomenon of the partially successful dismantling of governmental welfare measures witnessed by the present generation.

The growth of governmental unemployment concern before the New Deal nevertheless exemplified the emergence of a new view of the role

12 James Stuart Olson, *Herbert Hoover and the Reconstruction Finance Corporation 1931–1933* (Ames: Iowa State University Press, 1977), x–xi.

of the state. Before World War I, reformist advocacy, still influenced by the tenets of an individualistic age, stressed the need for ameliorative action and regulation; governments responded by creating locally restricted employment agencies or dabbling in small-scale public works measures. After the war, government, following prevailing public opinion, still tried to salvage the values of yore, if in modified form, by emphasizing the virtues of voluntarism and associationalism. But the insight grew that more constructive measures might be asked for, meaning that action had to be taken on the national level and on a scale with macroeconomic significance. The Great Depression brought sufficient public acceptance of these ideas to enable the New Deal to undertake their implementation. The advent of government-sponsored unemployment insurance expressed the fact that the unemployed had passed from being objects of philanthropy to being members of society entitled to adequate welfare. To express it in the image of our initial anecdote – the cheering was now theirs.

Appendix

This checklist and the checklist on page 370 covers all bills, resolutions, and hearings cited in the text and the footnotes, including those that are only quoted for reference purposes.

CHECKLIST OF CONGRESSIONAL BILLS AND RESOLUTIONS MENTIONED IN THE TEXT

(See index for page references to bills and resolutions)

S. 168	66 Cong., 1 sess.	S. 3060	71 Cong., 2 sess.
S. 174	72 Cong., 1 sess.	S. 3061	71 Cong., 2 sess.
S. 262	72 Cong., 1 sess.	S. 3078	65 Cong., 2 sess.
S. 301	65 Cong., 1 sess.	S. 3196	67 Cong., 2 sess.
S. 408	67 Cong., 1 sess.	S. 3696	72 Cong., 1 sess.
S. 510	73 Cong., 1 sess.	S. 4076	72 Cong., 1 sess.
S. 626	71 Cong., 1 sess.	S. 4157	70 Cong., 1 sess.
S. 679	64 Cong., 1 sess.	S. 4158	70 Cong., 1 sess.
S. 681	67 Cong., 1 sess.	S. 4307	70 Cong., 1 sess.
S. 688	66 Cong., 1 sess.	S. 4472	67 Cong., 4 sess.
S. 842	65 Cong., 1 sess.	S. 4592	72 Cong., 1 sess.
S. 1050	53 Cong., 1 sess.	S. 4632	72 Cong., 1 sess.
S. 1072	67 Cong., 1 sess.	S. 4727	72 Cong., 1 sess.
S. 1442	66 Cong., 1 sess.	S. 4755	72 Cong., 1 sess.
S. 1790	64 Cong., 1 sess.	S. 4783	71 Cong., 2 sess.
S. 2241	71 Cong., 2 sess.	S. 4819	71 Cong., 3 sess.
S. 2253	71 Cong., 2 sess.	S. 4824	72 Cong., 1 sess.
S. 2419	72 Cong., 1 sess.	S. 4860	72 Cong., 1 sess.
S. 2475	70 Cong., 1 sess.	S. 4938	71 Cong., 3 sess.
S. 2543	68 Cong., 1 sess.	S. 4947	72 Cong., 1 sess.
S. 2587	63 Cong., 1 sess.	S. 4968	65 Cong., 2 sess.
S. 2687	72 Cong., 1 sess.	S. 5043	71 Cong., 3 sess.
S. 2732	72 Cong., 1 sess.	S. 5079	71 Cong., 3 sess.
S. 2749	67 Cong., 1 sess.	S. 5121	72 Cong., 2 sess.
S. 3045	72 Cong., 1 sess.	S. 5125	72 Cong., 2 sess.
S. 3059	71 Cong., 2 sess.	S. 5180	63 Cong., 2 sess.

S. 5336	72 Cong., 2 sess.	H.R. 367	72 Cong., 1 sess.
S. 5350	71 Cong., 3 sess.	H.R. 544	66 Cong., 1 sess.
S. 5363	72 Cong., 2 sess.	H.R. 1473	66 Cong., 1 sess.
S. 5397	65 Cong., 3 sess.	H.R. 1577	71 Cong., 1 sess.
S. 5634	71 Cong., 3 sess.	H.R. 4305	66 Cong., 1 sess.
S. 5757	71 Cong., 3 sess.	H.R. 5141	45 Cong., 2 sess.
S. 5776	71 Cong., 3 sess.	H.R. 5616	71 Cong., 2 sess.
S. 6205	64 Cong., 1 sess.	H.R. 5783	64 Cong., 1 sess.
S. 7725	63 Cong., 3 sess.	H.R. 6011	72 Cong., 1 sess.
S.Con.Res. 21	65 Cong., 2 sess.	H.R. 6176	66 Cong., 1 sess.
S.Con.Res. 22	65 Cong., 2 sess.	H.R. 6210	71 Cong., 2 sess.
S.Con.Res. 25	65 Cong., 2 sess.	H.R. 6559	69 Cong., 1 sess.
S.Con.Res. 36	71 Cong., 3 sess.	H.R. 6665	72 Cong., 1 sess.
S.J.Res. 60	72 Cong., 1 sess.	H.R. 6670	72 Cong., 1 sess.
S.J.Res. 80	72 Cong., 1 sess.	H.R. 6716	72 Cong., 1 sess.
S.J.Res. 110	72 Cong., 1 sess.	H.R. 6746	72 Cong., 1 sess.
S.J.Res. 112	67 Cong., 1 sess.	H.R. 7009	66 Cong., 1 sess.
S.J.Res. 149	71 Cong., 2 sess.	H.R. 7026	66 Cong., 1 sess.
S.J.Res. 169	72 Cong., 1 sess.	H.R. 7189	72 Cong., 1 sess.
S.J.Res. 174	72 Cong., 1 sess.	H.R. 7222	65 Cong., 2 sess.
S.J.Res. 210	71 Cong., 3 sess.	H.R. 7438	53 Cong., 2 sess.
S.Res. 72	72 Cong., 1 sess.	H.R. 7463	53 Cong., 2 sess.
S.Res. 126	67 Cong., 1 sess.	H.R. 8088	72 Cong., 1 sess.
S.Res. 127	72 Cong., 1 sess.	H.R. 8374	71 Cong., 2 sess.
S.Res. 140	67 Cong., 1 sess.	H.R. 8655	71 Cong., 2 sess.
S.Res. 147	70 Cong., 1 sess.	H.R. 9237	67 Cong., 2 sess.
S.Res. 219	70 Cong., 1 sess.	H.R. 9560	71 Cong., 2 sess.
S.Res. 338	71 Cong., 3 sess.	H.R. 9642	72 Cong., 1 sess.
S.Res. 354	69 Cong., 2 sess.	H.R. 11011	72 Cong., 1 sess.
S.Res. 378	69 Cong., 2 sess.	H.R. 11055	72 Cong., 1 sess.
S.Res. 382	65 Cong., 3 sess.	H.R. 11056	72 Cong., 1 sess.
S.Res. 409	71 Cong., 3 sess.	H.R. 11329	64 Cong., 1 sess.
S.Res. 483	71 Cong., 3 sess.	H.R. 11414	71 Cong., 2 sess.
H.R. 2	72 Cong., 1 sess.	H.R. 12097	72 Cong., 1 sess.
H.R. 20	45 Cong., 1 sess.	H.R. 12139	65 Cong., 2 sess.
H.R. 110	45 Cong., 1 sess.	H.R. 12205	70 Cong., 1 sess.
H.R. 153	65 Cong., 1 sess.	H.R. 12353	72 Cong., 1 sess.
H.R. 206	72 Cong., 1 sess.	H.R. 12409	72 Cong., 1 sess.
H.R. 247	72 Cong., 1 sess.	H.R. 12443	68 Cong., 2 sess.

H.R. 12445	72 Cong., 1 sess.	H.R. 16187	65 Cong., 3 sess.
H.R. 12550	71 Cong., 2 sess.	H.R. 16297	71 Cong., 3 sess.
H.R. 12551	71 Cong., 2 sess.	H.R. 16384	71 Cong., 3 sess.
H.R. 12654	72 Cong., 1 sess.	H.R. 17017	63 Cong., 2 sess.
H.R. 12856	72 Cong., 1 sess.	H.R. 19015	63 Cong., 2 sess.
H.R. 12885	72 Cong., 1 sess.	H.R. 21331	63 Cong., 3 sess.
H.R. 12946	72 Cong., 1 sess.	H.R. 21332	63 Cong., 3 sess.
H.R. 13415	65 Cong., 3 sess.	H.R. 21386	63 Cong., 3 sess.
H.R. 13316	67 Cong., 4 sess.	H.R. 25680	62 Cong., 2 sess.
H.R. 13568	70 Cong., 1 sess.	H.Con.Res. 20	67 Cong., 1 sess.
H.R. 13592	65 Cong., 3 sess.	H.Con.Res. 53	65 Cong., 2 sess.
H.R. 13607	72 Cong., 2 sess.	H.Con.Res. 54	65 Cong., 2 sess.
H.R. 13870	66 Cong., 2 sess.	H.J.Res. 87	71 Cong., 1 sess.
H.R. 13901	70 Cong., 1 sess.	H.J.Res. 144	66 Cong., 1 sess.
H.R. 14040	71 Cong., 3 sess.	H.J.Res. 159	64 Cong., 1 sess.
H.R. 14042	71 Cong., 3 sess.	H.J.Res. 203	62 Cong., 2 sess.
H.R. 14185	67 Cong., 4 sess.	H.J.Res. 250	64 Cong., 1 sess.
H.R. 14255	71 Cong., 3 sess.	H.J.Res. 289	70 Cong., 1 sess.
H.R. 14363	72 Cong., 2 sess.	H.J.Res. 290	70 Cong., 1 sess.
H.R. 14450	71 Cong., 3 sess.	H.J.Res. 418	72 Cong., 1 sess.
H.R. 14454	70 Cong., 2 sess.	H.J.Res. 422	72 Cong., 1 sess.
H.R. 14804	71 Cong., 3 sess.	H.Res. 25	67 Cong., 1 sess.
H.R. 15008	69 Cong., 2 sess.	H.Res. 276	68 Cong., 1 sess.
H.R. 15269	71 Cong., 3 sess.	H.Res. 452	65 Cong., 2 sess.
H.R. 15422	66 Cong., 3 sess.	H.Res. 463	65 Cong., 2 sess.
H.R. 15672	65 Cong., 3 sess.	H.Res. 463	65 Cong., 3 sess.
H.R. 15993	65 Cong., 3 sess.	H.Res. 525	65 Cong., 3 sess.
H.R. 16118	71 Cong., 3 sess.	H.Res. 529	65 Cong., 3 sess.
H.R. 16130	63 Cong., 2 sess.	H.Res. 608	66 Cong., 3 sess.

CONGRESSIONAL BILLS AND RESOLUTIONS MENTIONED IN THE TEXT
[The order followed is that of the *Congressional Record*]

45 Cong., 1 sess.

A Bill to Extend the Scope and Efficiency of an Act Entitled "An Act to Secure Homesteads to Actual Settlers on the Public Domain," Approved May 20, 1862. H.R. 20 (29 Oct. 1877, Nathaniel P. Banks)

A Bill Supplemental to an Act Entitled "An Act to Secure Homesteads to Actual Settlers on the Public Domain," Approved May 20, 1862. H.R. 110 (29 Oct. 1877, Hendrick B. Wright)

45 Cong., 2 sess.

A Bill for the Relief of the Industrial Classes, for the Prompt Settlement of the Public Lands, and for the Better Protection of the Frontier from the Indians. H.R. 5141 (10 June 1878, Benjamin F. Butler)

53 Cong., 1 sess.

A Bill to Provide for the Employment of Labor and the Prosperity of the People of the United States, and for Other Purposes. S. 1050 (6 Oct. 1893, William A. Peffer)

53 Cong., 2 sess.

A Bill to Provide for the Improvement of Public Roads, and for Other Purposes. H.R. 7438 (12 June 1894, Henry A. Coffeen)

A Bill to Provide for Public Improvements and Employment of the Citizens of the United States. H.R. 7463 (15 June 1894, Thomas J. Geary)

62 Cong., 2 sess.

A Bill to Provide for the Employment of All Willing Workers, and for Other Purposes. H.R. 25680 (10 July 1912, Victor L. Berger)

A Joint Resolution Requesting the Secretary of Commerce and Labor to Investigate and Report to Congress the Wisdom and Practicability of Establishing Labor Exchanges. H.J.Res. 203 (5 Jan. 1912, Martin W. Littleton)

63 Cong., 1 sess.

A Bill to Provide for the Organization of the Unemployed into an Industrial Army of the United States, and the Maintenance of Same. S. 2587 (21 June 1913, Miles Poindexter)

63 Cong., 2 sess.

A Bill to Authorize the Postmaster General of the United States to Establish Employment Exchanges at all Presidential Post Offices. S. 5180 (8 April 1914, Moses E. Clapp)

A Bill to Establish in the Department of Labor a Bureau to Be Known as the Bureau of Employment, and for Other Purposes. H.R. 16130 (29 April 1914, Victor A. Murdock)

A Bill to Provide for the Establishment of a National Employment Bureau under the Direction and Supervision of the Secretary of Labor. H.R. 17017 (3 June 1914, William J. MacDonald)

A Bill to Provide for the Establishment of a National Employment Bureau in the Department of Labor. H.R. 19015 (29 Sept. 1914, William J. MacDonald)

63 Cong., 3 sess.

A Bill to Provide for the Establishment of a National Employment Bureau in the Department of Labor. S. 7725 (23 Feb. 1915, Moses E. Clapp)

A Bill to Amend an Act Entitled "An Act to Create a Department of Labor," by Providing for a Bureau of the Unemployed. H.R. 21331 (4 March 1915, H. Robert Fowler)

A Bill to Provide for the Unemployed, Strengthen the National Defense, and for Other Purposes. H.R. 21332 (5 Feb. 1915, George W. Loft)

A Bill to Establish in the Department of Labor a Bureau to Be Known as the National Bureau of Labor Exchanges, and for Other Purposes. H.R. 21386 (9 Feb. 1915, Raymond B. Stevens)

64 Cong., 1 sess.

A Bill to Authorize the Postmaster General of the United States to Establish Employment Exchanges at All Presidential Post Offices. S. 679 (7 Dec. 1915, Moses E. Clapp)

A Bill to Provide for the Organization of the Unemployed Into an Industrial Army of the United States and the Maintenance of Same. S. 1790 (13 Dec. 1915; Miles Poindexter)

A Bill to Provide for the Establishment of a National Employment Bureau in the Department of Labor. S. 6205 (26 May 1916, James D. Phelan)

A Bill to Provide for the Establishment of a National Employment Bureau in the Department of Labor. H.R. 5783 (15 Dec. 1915, John I. Nolan)

A Bill to Authorize the Secretary of Labor to Cooperate with Other Departments of the Government in Fostering, Promoting, and Developing the Welfare of the Wage Earners of the United States, by Creating New Opportunities for Permanent and Profitable Employment, and for Other Purposes. H.R. 11329 (11 Feb. 1916, Robert Crosser)

A Joint Resolution for the Appointment of a Commission to Prepare and Recommend a Plan for the Establishment of a National Insurance Fund and for the Mitigation of the Evil of Unemployment. H.J.Res. 159 (19 Feb. 1916, Meyer London)

A Joint Resolution to Provide for the Appointment of a Commission to Prepare and Recommend a Plan for the Establishment of a National Insurance Fund and for the Mitigation of the Evil of Unemployment. H.J.Res. 250 (30 June 1916, Meyer London)

65 Cong., 1 sess.

A Bill to Provide for the Organization of the Unemployed Into an Industrial Army of the United States and the Maintenance of Same. S. 301 (4 April 1917; Miles Poindexter)

A Bill to Provide for the Establishment of a National Employment Bureau in the Department of Labor. S. 842 (6 April 1917, James D. Phelan)

A Bill to Provide for the Establishment of a National Employment Bureau in the Department of Labor. H.R. 153 (2 April 1917, John I. Nolan)

65 Cong., 2 sess.

A Bill to Promote the Welfare of Industries and Wage Earners of the United States, to Extend the United States Employment Service in the Department of Labor, and for Other Purposes. S. 3078 (7 Dec. 1917, Joseph T. Robinson)

A Bill to Provide for the Creation and Establishment of a Federal Commission on Reconstruction, and for Other Purposes. S. 4968 (3 Oct. 1918, Lee S. Overman)

A Concurrent Resolution Creating a Committee to Be Known as the Joint Congressional Committee on Reconstruction. S.Con.Res. 21 (27 Sept. 1918, John W. Weeks)

A Concurrent Resolution to Authorize and Create a Committee on Reorganization for the Purpose of Making Investigations and Recommendations upon the Reorganization Required for a Return to the Occupations of Peace. S.Con.Res. 22 (28 Sept. 1918, Robert L. Owen)

A Concurrent Resolution to Provide for the Appointment of Certain Joint Congressional Committees on Reconstruction. S.Con.Res. 25 (21 Nov. 1918, Albert D. Cummins)

A Bill to Promote the Welfare of Industries and Wage Earners of the United States, to Extend the United States Employment Service in the Department of Labor, and for other Purposes. H.R. 7222 (7 Dec. 1917, Edward Keating)

A Bill to Create a Commission to Investigate the Problems of Reconstruction. H.R. 12139 (16 May 1918, George W. Edmonds)

A Concurrent Resolution for the Appointment of a Joint Committee of Congress to Investigate and Report on Certain Questions. H.Con.Res. 53 (2 Oct. 1918, Martin B. Madden)

A Concurrent Resolution Creating a Committee to Be Known as the Joint Congressional Committee on Reconstruction. H.Con.Res. 54 (4 Oct. 1918, Meyer London)

A Resolution to Initiate the Necessary Steps to Open Opportunities for Employment to All Workers in the United States Who Face Enforced Idleness. H.Res. 452 (21 Nov. 1918, Ernest Lundeen)

A Resolution to Initiate the Necessary Steps to Open Opportunities for Employment to All Workers in the United States Who Face Enforced Idleness. H.Res. 463 (3 Dec. 1918, Horatio C. Claypool)

65 Cong., 3 sess.

A Bill to Provide for the Commencement or Prosecution of Public Works in Order to Provide Increased Opportunities for Employment during the Period of Demobilization and Industrial Readjustment, and for Other Purposes. S. 5397 (21 Jan. 1919, William S. Kenyon)

A Bill Making Appropriations to Supply Deficiencies in Appropriations for the Fiscal Year Ending June 30, 1919, and Prior Fiscal Years, and for Other Purposes. H.R. 16187 (27 Feb. 1919, Swagar Sherley)

A Resolution Directing the Committee on Education and Labor to Recommend to the Senate Methods of Promoting Better Social and Industrial Conditions along Lines Suggested and Indicated Herein. S.Res. 382 (11 Dec. 1918, William S. Kenyon)

A Bill to Provide for the Present Emergency Arising Out of the Demobilization of Soldiers and Sailors by Securing for them Opportunities for Permanent and Profitable Employment through the Settlement, Colonization, and Development, upon a Systematic and Comprehensive Basis, of Agricultural Lands, and of the Forest, Mineral, and Other Natural Resources, within the United States and Alaska, and for Other Purposes. H.R. 13415 (17 Dec. 1918, M. Clyde Kelly)

A Bill to Amend an Act Entitled "An Act to Create a Department of Labor" by Providing for a Bureau of the Unemployed. H.R. 13592 (2 Jan. 1919, Ernest Lundeen)

A Bill to Provide for the Emergency Arising Out of the Demobilization of Soldiers, Sailors, and Marines, and the Discharge of Workers from War Industries and Other Occupations, by Securing Therefor Permanent Opportunities for Profitable Employment by Means of a National Construction Service Organized for the Systematic Extension of Useful Public Works and the Development of Natural Resources, and for Other Purposes. H.R. 15672 (5 Feb. 1919, M. Clyde Kelly)

A Bill Providing for Cooperation between the United States and State Governments in the Rural Settlement of Soldiers, Sailors and Marines, and to

Promote the Reclamation of Lands, and for Other Purposes. H.R. 15993 (5 Feb. 1919, Edward T. Taylor)

A Bill Making Appropriations to Supply Deficiencies in Appropriations for the Fiscal Year Ending June 30, 1919, and Prior Fiscal Years, and for Other Purposes. H.R. 16187 (27 Feb. 1919, Swagar Sherley). 41 Stat. 6 (1919)

A Resolution to Initiate the Necessary Steps to Open Opportunities for Employment to All Workers in the United States Who Face Enforced Idleness. H.Res. 463 (3 Dec. 1918, Horatio C. Claypool)

A Resolution to Initiate the Necessary Steps to Open Opportunities for Employment to All Workers in the United States Who Face Enforced Idleness. H.Res. 525 (27 Jan. 1919, Ernest Lundeen)

A Resolution to Initiate the Necessary Steps to Open Opportunities for Employment to All Workers in the United States Who Face Enforced Idleness. H.Res. 529 (27 Jan. 1919, Horatio C. Claypool)

66 Cong., 1 sess.

A Bill to Create a Commission to Investigate and Report to Congress a Plan on the Questions Involved in the Financing of House Construction and Home Ownership and Federal Aid Therefor. S. 168 (20 May 1919, William S. Kenyon)

A Bill to Provide for a National Employment System. S. 688 (23 May 1919, Joseph T. Robinson)

A Bill to Provide for the Establishment of a National Employment System and for Cooperation with the States in the Promotion of Such System, and to Regulate the Expenditure of Moneys That Shall Be Appropriated for Such Purposes. S. 1442 (6 June 1919, William S. Kenyon)

A Bill to Provide for the Establishment of a National Employment Bureau in the Department of Labor. H.R. 544 (19 May 1919, John I. Nolan)

A Bill to Provide for Public Improvements, Needs, and Employment of Discharged Soldiers, Unemployed, and Other Citizens, through Issue of Legal Tender Notes. H.R. 1473 (21 May 1919, Isaac R. Sherwood)

A Bill to Provide for the Establishment of a National Employment System and for Cooperation with the States in the Promotion of Such System, and to Regulate the Expenditure of Moneys That Shall Be Appropriated for Such Purposes. H.R. 4305 (31 May 1919, John I. Nolan)

A Bill Making Appropriations for Sundry Civil Expenses of the Government for the Fiscal Year Ending June 30, 1920, and for Other Purposes. H.R. 6176 (18 June 1919, James W. Good)

A Bill to Provide Legal Tender Money without Interest for Public Improvements, Needs and Employment of Discharged Soldiers, Sailors, Marines, Unemployed, and Other Citizens of the United States. H.R. 7009 (8 July 1919, Isaac R. Sherwood)

A Bill Providing for Employment for Returning Soldiers and Sufferers from the Drought, by the Construction of Irrigation Projects. H.R. 7026 (8 July 1919, Carl W. Riddick)

A Joint Resolution Authorizing and Directing the Secretary of Labor to Make an Investigation and Report Regarding Insurance Against Unemployment and Old Age. H.J.Res. 144 (14 June 1919, Adolph J. Sabath)

66 Cong., 2 sess.

A Bill Making Appropriations for Sundry Civil Expenses of the Government for the Fiscal Year Ending June 30, 1921, and for Other Purposes. H.R. 13870 (30 April 1920, James W. Good). 41 Stat. 235 (1920)

66 Cong., 3 sess.

A Bill Making Appropriations for Sundry Civil Expenses of the Government for the Fiscal Year Ending June 30, 1922, and for Other Purposes. H.R. 15422 (29 Dec. 1920, James W. Good). 41 Stat. 161 (1921)

A Resolution Directing Investigations for the Relief of the Unemployed in the United States. H.Res. 608 (8 Dec. 1920, William E. Mason)

67 Cong., 1 sess.

A Bill to Establish a Department of Social Welfare. S. 408 (12 April 1921, William S. Kenyon)

A Bill for the Establishment of a National Employment System and for Co-operation with the States in the Promotion of Such System and to Regulate the

Expenditure of Moneys That Shall Be Appropriated for Such Purposes. S. 681 (13 April 1921, William S. Kenyon)

A Bill to Amend an Act Entitled "An Act to Provide That the United States Shall Aid the States in Construction of Rural Post Roads and for Other Purposes," Approved July 11, 1916, as Amended and Supplemented, and for Other Purposes. S. 1072 (21 April 1921, Lawrence C. Phipps)

A Bill to Prepare for Future Cyclical Periods of Depression and Unemployment by Systems of Public Works. S. 2749 (19 Nov. 1921, William S. Kenyon)

A Joint Resolution Instructing the Committees on Labor of the Senate and House to Investigate the Cause and Remedy for the Existing Unemployment of the United States. S.J.Res. 112 (23 Aug. 1921, Edwin F. Ladd)

A Resolution Directing the Secretary of Labor to Advise the Senate as to the Estimated Unemployment in the Several States. S.Res. 126 (5 Aug. 1921, Medill McCormick)

A Resolution Directing the Committee on Education and Labor to Investigate the Causes, Effects, and Character of the Prevalent Unemployment. S.Res. 140 (24 Aug. 1921, David I. Walsh)

A Concurrent Resolution Creating a Joint Commission on Unemployment. H.Con.Res. 20 (27 May 1921, Meyer London)

A Resolution Directing Investigations for the Relief of the Unemployed in the United States. H.Res. 25 (11 April 1921, William E. Mason)

67 Cong., 2 sess.

A Bill to Encourage the Development of the Agricultural Resources of the United States through Federal and State Cooperation, Giving Preference in the Matter of Employment and the Establishment of Rural Homes to Those Who Have Served with the Military and Naval Forces of the United States. S. 3196 (24 Feb. 1922, Charles L. McNary).

A Bill Making Appropriations to Supply Deficiencies in Appropriations for the Fiscal Year Ending June 30, 1922, and prior Fiscal Years, Supplemental Appropriations for the Fiscal Year Ending June 30, 1922, and Subsequent Fiscal Years, and for Other Purposes. H.R. 9237 (21 Nov. 1921, Martin B. Madden)

67 Cong., 4 sess.

A Bill to Make an Investigation of the Needs of the Nation for Public Works to Be Carried on by Federal, State, and Municipal Agencies in Periods of Business Depression and Unemployment. S. 4472 (3 Feb. 1923, Joseph S. Frelinghuysen)

A Bill Making Appropriations for the Departments of Commerce and Labor for the Fiscal Year Ending June 30, 1924, and for Other Purposes. H.R. 13316 (11 Dec. 1922, Milton W. Shreve). 42 Stat. 24 (1923)

A Bill to Make an Investigation of the Needs of the Nation for Public Works to Be Carried on by Federal, State, and Municipal Agencies in Periods of Business Depression and Unemployment. H.R. 14185 (3 Feb. 1923, Frederick N. Zihlman)

68 Cong., 1 sess.

A Bill to Make an Investigation of the Needs of the Nation for Public Works to Be Carried on by Federal, State, and Municipal Agencies in Periods of Business Depression and Unemployment. S. 2543 (19 Feb. 1924, Royal S. Copeland)

A Resolution for the Appointment of a Select Committee to Inquire into the Need and Form of a Nationwide System for the Distribution of Labor and to Report Thereon, and for Other Purposes. H.Res. 276 (30 April 1924, Scott Leavitt)

68 Cong., 2 sess.

A Bill to Provide for the Establishment of a National Employment System and for Cooperation with the States in the Promotion of Such System and to Regulate the Expenditure of Moneys That Shall Be Appropriated for Such Purposes. H.R. 12443 (28 Feb. 1925, Mae E. Nolan)

69 Cong., 1 sess.

A Bill to Provide for the Construction of Certain Public Buildings, and for Other Purposes. H.R. 6559 (4 Jan. 1926, Richard N. Elliott)

69 Cong., 2 sess.

A Bill Making Appropriation for the Department of Agriculture for the Fiscal Year Ending June 30, 1928, and for Other Purposes. H.R. 15008 (13 Dec. 1926, Walter W. Magee). 44 Stat. 39 (1927)

A Resolution Relative to the Stabilization, during Periods of Business Depression, of Employment and Industry by the Construction of Public Works. S.Res. 354 (15 Feb. 1927, George W. Pepper)

A Resolution for an Investigation into the Economic Conditions of the Agricultural and Cotton Producing Industries and the Extent of Unemployment. S.Res. 378 (28 Feb. 1927, David I. Walsh)

70 Cong., 1 sess.

A Bill to Create a Prosperity Reserve and to Stabilize Industry and Employment by the Expansion of Public Works during Periods of Unemployment and Industrial Depression. S. 2475 (11 Jan. 1928, Wesley L. Jones)

A Bill to Provide for the Establishment of a National Employment System and for Cooperation with the States in the Promotion of Such System. S. 4157 (20 April 1928, Robert F. Wagner)

A Bill to Amend Section 4 of the Act of March 4, 1913, entitled "An Act to Create a Department of Labor." S. 4158 (20 April 1928, Robert F. Wagner)

A Bill to Provide for the Emergency Construction of Certain Public Works for the Relief of Unemployment during Periods of Business Depression. S. 4307 (1 May 1928, Robert F. Wagner)

A Resolution to Investigate the Extent of Unemployment in the United States and Methods Collecting Statistics Thereof. S.Res. 147 (15 Feb. 1928, Robert F. Wagner)

A Resolution Providing for an Analysis and Appraisal of Reports on Unemployment and Systems for Prevention and Relief Thereof. S. Res. 219 (2 May 1928, Robert M. La Follette, Jr.)

A Bill to Authorize the Establishment of a Bureau of Unemployment Insurance in the Department of Labor, to Provide for the Creation of a System of Compulsory Unemployment Insurance for the Purpose of Insuring Wageworkers against the Hardships Caused by Unemployment, and for Other Purposes. H.R. 12205 (19 March 1928, Victor L. Berger)

A Bill to Create a Prosperity Reserve and to Stabilize Industry and Employment by the Expansion of Public Works during Periods of Unemployment and Industrial Depression. H.R. 13568 (5 May 1928, Henry R. Rathbone)

A Bill to Provide for the Establishment of a National Employment System and to Regulate the Expenditure of Moneys That Shall Be Appropriated for Such Purposes. H.R. 13901 (19 May 1928, Henry R. Rathbone)

A Joint Resolution Creating a Joint Committee of Congress to Gather, Analyze, and Appraise Information Available Concerning Unemployment. H.J.Res. 289 (26 April 1928, Meyer Jacobstein)

A Joint Resolution Calling for an Investigation Relative to Information Available Concerning Unemployment. H.J.Res. 290 (26 April 1928, Meyer Jacobstein)

70 Cong., 2 sess.

A Bill to Provide for the Establishment of a National Employment System and for Cooperation with the States in the Promotion of Such System. H.R. 14454 (3 Dec. 1928, John J. Casey)

71 Cong., 1 sess.

A Bill to Create a Prosperity Reserve and to Stabilize Industry and Employment by the Expansion of Public Works during Periods of Unemployment and Industrial Depression. S. 626 (25 April 1929, Wesley L. Jones)

A Bill to Provide a Record of Employment through the Census. H.R. 1577 (20 April 1929, M. Clyde Kelly)

A Joint Resolution Providing for Investigation of the Unemployment Problem by the Department of Commerce and the Department of Labor, and the Collection of Information by the Bureau of the Census in Connection Therewith. H.J.Res. 87 (28 May 1929, William A. Pittenger)

71 Cong., 2 sess.

A Bill to Amend the Act Entitled "An Act to Provide That the United States Shall Aid the States in the Construction of Rural Post Roads, and for Other Purposes," Approved July 11, 1916, as Amended and Supplemented, and for Other Purposes. S. 2253 (3 Dec. 1929, Lawrence C. Phipps). 46 Stat. 105 (1930)

A Bill to Provide for the Advance Planning and Regulated Construction of Certain Public Works, for the Stabilization of Industry, and for the Prevention of Unemployment during Periods of Business Depression. S. 3059 (9 Jan. 1930, Robert F. Wagner)

A Bill to Provide for the Establishment of a National Employment System and for Cooperation with the States in the Promotion of Such System, and for Other Purposes. S. 3060 (9 Jan. 1930, Robert F. Wagner)

A Bill to Amend Section 4 of the Act Entitled "An Act to Create a Department of Labor," Approved March 4, 1913. S. 3061 (9 Jan. 1930, Robert F. Wagner)

A Bill to Amend the Act Entitled "An Act to Provide for the Construction of Certain Public Buildings, and for Other Purposes," Approved May 25, 1926 (44 Stat. 630); [etc.]. S. 2241 (3 Dec. 1929, Henry W. Keyes). 46 Stat. 99 (1930)

A Bill Making an Appropriation to Establish an Emergency Fund to Be Used for the Purpose of Accelerating the Construction of Certain Public Works to Aid in Relieving Unemployment. S. 4783 (2 Dec. 1930, Otis F. Glenn)

A Joint Resolution for the Relief of Unemployed Persons in the United States. S.J.Res. 149 (1 March 1930, Smith W. Brookhart)

A Bill to Amend the Act Entitled "An Act to Provide That the United States Shall Aid the States in the Construction of Rural Post Roads, and for Other Purposes," Approved July 11, 1916, as Amended and Supplemented, and for Other Purposes. H.R. 5616 (2 Dec. 1929, Cassius C. Dowell). 46 Stat. 105 (1930)

A Bill to Amend the Act Entitled "An Act to Provide for the Construction of Certain Public Buildings, and for Other Purposes," Approved May 25, 1926 (44 Stat. 630); [etc.]. H.R. 6210 (3 Dec. 1929, Richard N. Elliott). 46 Stat. 99 (1930)

A Bill to Provide for the Establishment of a National Employment System. H.R. 8374 (9 Jan. 1930, John L. Cable)

A Bill to Provide for the Establishment of a National Employment System. H.R. 8655 (15 Jan. 1930, James M. Mead)

A Bill to Provide for the Advance Planning and Regulated Construction of Certain Public Works, for the Stabilization of Industry, and for the Prevention of Unemployment during Periods of Business Depression. H.R. 9560 (5 Feb. 1930, James M. Mead)

A Bill to Provide for the Advance Planning and Regulated Construction of Certain Public Works, for the Stabilization of Industry, and for the Prevention of Unemployment during Periods of Business Depression. H.R. 11414 (4 April 1930, Charles J. Esterly)

A Bill to Provide for the Establishment of a National Employment System and for Cooperation with the States in the Promotion of Such System, and for Other Purposes. H.R. 12550 (22 May 1930, Martin J. Kennedy)

A Bill to Provide for the Advance Planning and Regulated Construction of Certain Public Works, for the Stabilization of Industry, and for the Prevention of Unemployment during Periods of Business Depression. H.R. 12551 (22 May 1930, Martin J. Kennedy)

71 Cong., 3 sess.

A Bill to Authorize an Increase in the Appropriation for Federal-aid Highways for 1932 and 1933. S. 4819 (2 Dec. 1930, Smith W. Brookhart)

A Bill Providing for the Construction and Improvement of Post Roads in the Several Counties in the United States for the Relief of Unemployment and for Other Purposes. S. 4938 (2 Dec. 1930, Kenneth McKellar)

A Bill to Reimburse the States and Their Political Subdivisions for Certain Relief Expenditures. S. 5043 (3 Dec. 1930, David I. Walsh)

A Bill Making an Appropriation to Provide for an Emergency Construction Fund for Public Works during the Remainder of the Fiscal Year Ending June 30, 1931. S. 5079 (4 Dec. 1930, Wesley L. Jones)

A Bill to Amend the Revenue Act of 1928 in Regard to Unemployment Relief Trusts, and for Other Purposes. S. 5350 (15 Dec. 1930, Robert F. Wagner)

A Bill to Provide for Cooperation with the Several States in Providing Insurance against Unemployment. S. 5634 (9 Jan. 1931, Robert F. Wagner)

A Bill to Amend an Act Entitled "An Act to Provide for the Construction of Certain Public Buildings, and for Other Purposes," Approved May 25, 1926 (45 Stat. 630) and Acts Amendatory Thereof. S. 5757 (17 Jan. 1931, Henry W. Keyes). 46 Stat. 203 (1931)

A Bill to Provide for the Advance Planning and Regulated Construction of Public Works, for the Stabilization of Industry, and for Aiding in the Prevention of Unemployment during Periods of Business Depression. S. 5776 (19 Jan. 1931, Robert F. Wagner)

A Concurrent Resolution Establishing a Joint Congressional Committee To Make a General Study of the Unemployment Insurance Systems in Use by Private Interests in the United States and by Foreign Governments. S.Con.Res. 36 (9 Jan. 1931, Robert F. Wagner)

A Joint Resolution to Authorize the Distribution of 40,000,000 Bushels of Surplus Wheat for Relief Purposes. S.J.Res. 210 (2 Dec. 1930, Arthur Capper)

A Resolution Creating Special Select Committee on Emergency Relief Legislation. S.Res. 338 (2 Dec. 1930, Elmer T. Thomas)

A Resolution Requesting a Copy of the Metropolitan Life Insurance Co.'s Report on the Unemployment Survey, S.Res. 409 (20 Jan. 1931, Robert M. La Follette, Jr.)

A Resolution Establishing a Select Committee to Investigate Unemployment Insurance Systems. S.Res. 483 (28 Feb. 1931, Robert F. Wagner)

A Bill to Enable the Secretary of the Treasury to Expedite Work on the Federal Building Program Authorized by the Act of Congress Entitled "An Act to Provide for the Construction of Certain Public Buildings, and for Other Purposes," Approved May 25, 1926 and Acts Amendatory Thereof. H.R. 14040 (2 Dec. 1930, Richard N. Elliott). 46 Stat. 107 (1931)

A Bill Authorizing an Appropriation for Relief of Destitution in the United States. H.R. 14042 (2 Dec. 1930, George Huddleston)

A Bill to Expedite the Construction of Public Buildings and Works Outside the District of Columbia by Enabling Possession and Title of Sites to Be Taken in Advance of Final Judgment in Proceedings for the Acquisition Thereof under the Power of Eminent Domain. H.R. 14255 (3 Dec. 1930, George S. Graham). 46 Stat. 307 (1931)

A Bill Making an Appropriation to Provide an Emergency Construction Fund for Public Works during the Remainder of the Fiscal Year Ending June 30, 1931. H.R. 14450 (4 Dec. 1930, William R. Wood)

A Bill Making Supplemental Appropriations to Provide for Emergency Construction on Certain Public Works during the Remainder of the Fiscal Year Ending June 30, 1931, with a View to Increasing Employment. H.R. 14804 (4 Dec. 1930, William R. Wood). 46 Stat. 19 (1930)

A Bill to Provide for an Employment Commission, the Creation and Maintenance

of an Unemployment Insurance Fund, and Raising Necessary Revenue Therefor.
H.R. 15269 (16 Dec. 1930, Fiorello H. La Guardia)

A Bill to Provide for Loans to States for Drought and Unemployment Relief.
H.R. 16118 (13 Jan. 1931, Benjamin M. Golder)

*A Bill to Amend an Act Entitled "An Act to Provide for the Construction of
Certain Public Buildings, and for Other Purposes," Approved May 25, 1926
(45 Stat. 630) and Acts Amendatory Thereof.* H.R. 16297 (17 Jan. 1931,
Richard N. Elliott). 46 Stat. 203 (1931)

*A Bill to Provide for the Advance Planning and Regulated Construction of Public
Works, for the Stabilization of Industry, and for Aiding in the Prevention of
Unemployment during Periods of Business Depression.* H.R. 16384 (20 Jan.
1931, George S. Graham). 46 Stat. 117 (1931)

72 Cong., 1 sess.

*A Bill to Provide for Cooperation by the Federal Government with the Several
States in Relieving the Hardship and Suffering Caused by Unemployment, and
for Other Purposes.* S. 174 (9 Dec. 1931, Edward P. Costigan)

*A Bill to Provide for Assisting the Several States and Their Political Subdivisions
in Meeting the Expense of Emergency Relief Activities, and to Provide for Relief
of the Unemployed.* S. 262 (9 Dec. 1931, Robert M. La Follette, Jr.)

*A Bill to Accelerate Construction during the Present Emergency, to Provide
Employment, to Create the Administration of Public Works, to Provide for the
More Effective Coordination and Correlation of the Public Works Activities of
the Government, and for Other Purposes.* S. 2419 (22 Dec. 1931, Robert
M. La Follette, Jr.)

*A Bill to Provide for the Establishment of a National Employment System and
for Cooperation with the States in the Promotion of Such System, and for Other
Purposes.* S. 2687 (6 Jan. 1932, Robert F. Wagner)

A Bill Creating an Unemployment Fund. S. 2732 (7 Jan. 1932, Elmer T.
Thomas)

*A Bill to Provide for Cooperation by the Federal Government with the Several
States in Relieving the Hardship and Suffering Caused by Unemployment, and
for Other Purposes.* S. 3045 (15 Jan. 1932, Edward P. Costigan and Robert
M. La Follette, Jr.)

A Bill to Provide for Cooperation by the Federal Government with the Several States in Relieving the Hardship and Suffering Caused by Unemployment and for Other Purposes. S. 3696 (17 Feb. 1932, Robert F. Wagner)

A Bill to Provide for Emergency Construction of Certain Authorized Public Works to Aid in Increasing Employment, and for Other Purposes. S. 4076 (14 March 1932, Robert F. Wagner)

A Bill to Provide for Cooperation by the Federal Government with the Several States in Assisting Persons, Including Veterans of the World War, Who Are Suffering Hardship Caused by Unemployment, and for Other Purposes. S. 4592 (6 May 1932, Edward P. Costigan)

A Bill to Authorize the Reconstruction Finance Corporation to Make Loans to States and Municipalities. S. 4632 (11 May 1932, James J. Davis)

A Bill to Amend the Reconstruction Finance Corporation Act for the Purpose of Providing for Employment through the Construction of Works of a National Character, to Provide Funds Therefor, and for Other Purposes. S. 4727 (23 May 1932, W. Warren Barbour)

A Bill to Provide for Grants and Loans for the Several States to Aid in Relieving Unemployment, to Facilitate the Construction of Self-liquidating Projects, to Provide for the Construction of Certain Authorized Federal Public Works Projects, and for Other Purposes. S. 4755 (25 May 1932, Robert F. Wagner)

A Bill to Further Unemployment Relief by Authorizing the Secretary of War and the Secretary of Agriculture to Make Available the Personnel and Equipment of Their Respective Departments in Aid of Such Organized Programs for Unemployment Relief as May Be Approved by Them, Respectively, and by Extending All Powers Heretofore Granted to the Reconstruction Finance Corporation, and to All Farm Loan Agencies so as to Include and Confer upon Them, Respectively, the Power to Make Loans in Furtherance of Such Organized Programs for the Location of Unemployed on Farms as May Be Approved by Such Respective Agencies. S. 4824 (4 June 1932, John H. Bankhead)

A Bill to Provide for Loans or Advances to States and Territories for the Relief of Distress Arising from Unemployment, and for Other Purposes. S. 4860 (8 June 1932, Robert J. Bulkley, Key Pittman, and Thomas J. Walsh)

A Bill to Provide Emergency Financing Facilities for Unemployed Workers, to Relieve Their Distress, to Increase their Purchasing Power and Employment, and for Other Purposes. S. 4947 (1 July 1932, Edward P. Costigan)

A Joint Resolution Authorizing the Distribution of Government-owned Wheat to the American National Red Cross and Other Organizations for the Relief of People in Distress. S.J.Res. 60 (17 Dec. 1931, Arthur Capper)

A Joint Resolution Authorizing the Secretary of War to Furnish Equipment, Goods, and Supplies to Governors and Acting Governors for Use in Aid of Distressed Citizens. S.J.Res. 80 (15 Jan. 1932, Elmer T. Thomas)

A Joint Resolution Authorizing the Distribution of Government-owned Wheat to the American National Red Cross and Other Organizations for Relief of Distress. S.J.Res. 110 (24 Feb. 1932, Peter Norbeck)

A Joint Resolution to Provide Information and Direction to Individuals and Agencies Concerned with Relieving Unemployment Through Finding Opportunities for Subsistence in Rural Areas. S.J.Res. 169 (3 June 1932; Charles L. McNary)

A Joint Resolution Providing for Issuance of Army Rations to Unemployed World War Veterans. S.J.Res. 174 (9 June 1932, Smith W. Brookhart)

A Resolution Requesting the Transmission to Congress of Supplemental Estimates of Appropriation for the Purpose of Inaugurating an Emergency Public Works Program. S.Res. 72 (14 Dec. 1931, Robert F. Wagner)

A Resolution Calling upon the Federal Employment Stabilization Board for a List of Construction Projects Which Should Be Entered upon within Six Years, Together with Certain Information Pertaining Thereto. S.Res. 127 (5 Jan. 1932, Robert F. Wagner)

A Bill to Provide for an Employment Commission, the Creation and Maintenance of an Unemployment Insurance Fund, and Raising Necessary Revenues Therefor. H.R. 2 (8 Dec. 1931, Fiorello H. La Guardia)

A Bill Authorizing an Appropriation for the Relief of Destitution in the United States. H.R. 206 (8 Dec. 1931, George Huddleston)

A Bill to Relieve the Unemployment Emergency by Amending the National Defense Act so as to Organize a Special Army Reserve, in Which Unemployed Men to the Number of 250,000 May Enlist for a Period of Not to Exceed One Year. H.R. 247 (8 Dec. 1931, Emanuel Celler)

A Bill Creating an Unemployment Fund. H.R. 367 (8 Dec. 1931, James V. McClintic)

A Bill to Provide for Cooperation by the Federal Government with the Several States in Relieving the Hardship and Suffering Caused by Unemployment, and for Other Purposes. H.R. 6011 (16 Dec. 1931, David J. Lewis)

A Bill to Establish a Public Works Administration and Transfer to and Consolidate and Coordinate Therein All the Public Works Activities of the Government. H.R. 6665 (4 Jan. 1932, William Williamson)

A Bill to Accelerate Public Construction in Periods of Business Depression through the Creation of an Administration of Public Works, and to Provide for a More Effective Coordination and Correlation of the Public-Works Functions of the Government, and for Other Purposes. H.R. 6670 (4 Jan. 1932, John J. Cochran)

A Bill to Provide Relief for Unemployed Itinerant Workers Having No Permanent Residence. H.R. 6716 (4 Jan. 1932, Fiorello H. La Guardia)

A Bill for the Protection of the Public Health by Providing Clothing for Unemployed and Destitute Citizens. H.R. 6746 (4 Jan. 1932, Fiorello H. La Guardia)

A Bill to Authorize the Issue of Bonds to Meet Expenditures for Aiding the Unemployed and Others to Establish Homes on 5 to 40 Acre Tracts of Land. H.R. 7189 (7 Jan. 1932, Edgar Howard)

A Bill to Provide for Cooperation by the Federal Government with the Several States in Relieving the Hardship and Suffering Caused by Unemployment, and for Other Purposes. H.R. 8088 (20 Jan. 1932, David J. Lewis)

A Bill to Authorize Supplemental Appropriations for Emergency Highway Construction, with a View to Increasing Employment. H.R. 9642 (23 Feb. 1932, Edward B. Almon)

A Bill to Establish a Public Works Administration and Transfer to and Consolidate and Coordinate Therein All the Public Works Activities of the Government. H.R. 11011 (31 March 1932, John J. Cochran)

A Bill to Encourage the Utilization of Farming Opportunities by Certain Destitute or Unemployed Persons. H.R. 11055 (1 April 1932, Loring M. Black, Jr.)

A Bill to Provide Farming Opportunities for Certain Destitute and Unemployed Persons. H.R. 11056 (1 April 1932, Loring M. Black, Jr.)

A Bill for the Relief of Distress Due to Unemployment, to Create a Committee for Federal, State, and Local Cooperation in Placing Qualified Unemployed Persons on Unoccupied Farms for the Purposes of Growing Subsistence Food Crops during the Continuance of the Unemployment Emergency. H.R. 12097 (16 May 1932, Loring M. Black, Jr.)

A Bill to Relieve Destitution, to Broaden the Lending Power of the Reconstruction Finance Corporation, and to Create Employment by Authorizing and Expediting a Public Works Program and Providing a Method of Financing Such Program. H.R. 12353 (27 May 1932, Henry T. Rainey)

A Bill to Provide for Advances to States for the Relief of Distress Arising from Unemployment, and for Other Purposes. H.R. 12409 (1 June 1932, Willis C. Hawley)

A Bill to Relieve Destitution, to Broaden the Lending Powers of the Reconstruction Finance Corporation, and to Create Employment by Authorizing and Expediting a Public-Works Program and Providing a Method of Financing Such Program. H.R. 12445 (3 June 1932, Henry T. Rainey)

A Bill to Provide for Loans for the Relief of Distress Arising from Unemployment, and for Other Purposes. H.R. 12654 (15 June 1932, Ralph Horr)

A Bill to Provide for Loans for the Relief of Distress Arising from Unemployment, and for Other Purposes. H.R. 12856 (29 June 1932, Ralph Horr)

A Bill to Provide Emergency Financing Facilities for Unemployed Workers, to Relieve Their Distress, to Increase Their Purchasing Power and Employment, and for Other Purposes. H.R. 12885 (1 July 1932, Fiorello H. La Guardia)

A Bill to Relieve Destitution, to Broaden the Lending Powers of the Reconstruction Finance Corporation, and to Create Employment by Providing for and Expediting a Public Works Program. H.R. 12946 (12 July 1932, Henry T. Rainey)

A Joint Resolution Authorizing the Distribution of Government-owned Wheat and Cotton to the American National Red Cross and Other Organizations for Relief of Distress. H.J.Res. 418 (6 June 1932, Hampton P. Fulmer)

A Joint Resolution to Provide for a Survey to Determine the Amounts of Surplus Cloth Held by the Government, and to Provide for the Free Distribution of Such Surplus to Unemployed People of the United States. H.J.Res. 422 (7 June 1932, Jed Johnson)

72 Cong., 2 sess.

A Bill to Amend Title I of the Emergency Relief and Construction Act of 1932, Approved July 21, 1932 (47 Stat. L. 709) by Authorizing Cooperation by the Federal Government with the Several States and Territories in Relieving Distress among Unemployed Needy Transients. S. 5121 (8 Dec. 1932, Bronson Cutting)

A Bill to Amend the Emergency Relief and Construction Act of 1932. S. 5125 (8 Dec. 1932, Edward P. Costigan)

A Bill to Amend the Emergency Relief and Construction Act of 1932. S. 5336 (9 Jan. 1933, Robert F. Wagner)

A Bill to Provide for the Housing, Feeding, and Clothing of Certain Unemployed Persons at Military Posts of the United States. S. 5363 (10 Jan. 1933, James Couzens)

A Bill to Authorize the Distribution of Government-owned Cotton to the American National Red Cross and Other Organizations for Relief of Distress. H.R. 13607 (13 Dec. 1932, Marvin Jones). 47 Stat. 43 (1933)

A Bill Making Appropriations for the Departments of State and Justice and for the Judiciary, and for the Departments of Commerce and Labor, for the Fiscal Year Ending June 30, 1934, and for Other Purposes. H.R. 14363 (21 Jan. 1933, William B. Oliver)

73 Cong., 1 sess.

A Bill to Provide for the Establishment of a National Employment System and for Cooperation with the States in the Promotion of Such System, and for Other Purposes. S. 510 (20 March 1933, Robert F. Wagner). 48 Stat. 113 (1933)

CHECKLIST OF CONGRESSIONAL HEARINGS MENTIONED IN THE TEXT

(See index for page references to hearings)
Hearings

on S. 168	66 Cong., 1 sess.
on S. 174 and S. 262	72 Cong., 1 sess.
on S. 688, S. 1442, and H.R. 4305	66 Cong., 1 sess.
on S. 2475	70 Cong., 1 sess.
on S. 2687	72 Cong., 1 sess.
on S. 2749	67 Cong., 1 sess.
on S. 3059, S. 3060, and S. 3061	71 Cong., 2 sess.
on S. 3059, S. 3060, H.R. 8374, H.R. 8655, H.R. 9560, H.R. 11414, H.R. 12550, and H.R. 12551	71 Cong., 2 sess.
on S. 4592	72 Cong., 1 sess.
on S. 4632, S. 4727, S. 4755, and S. 4822	72 Cong., 1 sess.
on S. 4947	72 Cong., 1 sess.
on S. 5121	72 Cong., 2 sess.
on S. 5125	72 Cong., 2 sess.
on S. 5336	72 Cong., 2 sess.
on S. 5397	65 Cong., 3 sess.
Pursuant to S.Res. 219	70 Cong., 2 sess.
Pursuant to S. Res. 382	65 Cong., 3 sess.
Pursuant to S. Res. 483 (71st Cong.)	72 Cong., 1 sess.
[Pursuant to S.J.Res. 110]	72 Cong., 1 sess.
on H.J.Res. 159	63 Cong., 2 sess.
on H.J.Res. 679	75 Cong., 3 sess.
on H.R. 206, H.R. 6011, and H.R. 8088	72 Cong., 1 sess.
on H.Res. 452 and H.Res. 463	65 Cong., 3 sess.
on H.R. 1473	66 Cong., 1 sess.

on H.R. 5783	64 Cong., 1 sess.
on H.R. 6176	66 Cong., 1 sess.
on H.R. 6665 and H.R. 6670	72 Cong., 1 sess.
on H.R. 9642	72 Cong., 1 sess.
on H.R. 11055, H.R. 11056, and H.R. 12097	72 Cong., 1 sess.
on H.R. 11329	64 Cong., 1 sess.
on H.R. 12353	72 Cong., 1 sess.
on H.R. 13316	67 Cong., 4 sess.
on H.R. 13870	66 Cong., 2 sess.
on H.R. 14040	71 Cong., 3 sess.
on H.R. 14185	67 Cong., 4 sess.
on H.R. 14363	72 Cong., 2 sess.
on H.R. 14450	71 Cong., 3 sess.
[on H.R. 14804]	71 Cong., 3 sess.
on H.R. 15422	66 Cong., 3 sess.
on H.R. 16130	63 Cong., 2 sess.
on H.R. 16187	65 Cong., 3 sess.
on H.R. 17017	63 Cong., 2 sess.

CONGRESSIONAL HEARINGS MENTIONED IN THE TEXT

63 Cong., 2 sess.

House. Committee on Labor, *National Employment Bureau*. Hearings on H.R. 16130 (5 June 1914)

House. Committee on Labor, *National Employment Bureau*. Hearings on H.R. 17017 (12 June–13 July 1914)

64 Cong., 1 sess.

House. Committee on Labor, *National Employment Bureau*. Hearings on H.R. 5783 (3–17 Feb. 1916)

House. Committee on Labor, *National Colonization Bill*. Hearings on H.R. 11329 (18 May–15 June 1916)

House. Committee on Labor, *Commission to Study Social Insurance and Unemployment*. Hearings on H.J.Res. 159 (6–11 April 1916)

65 Cong., 3 sess.

Senate. Committee on Education and Labor, *Emergency Public Works Board*. Hearings on S. 5397, (29 Jan.–7 Feb. 1919)

Senate. Committee on Education and Labor, *Social and Industrial Conditions in the United States*. Hearings Pursuant to S.Res. 382 (3–24 Jan. 1919)

House. Committee on Appropriations, *Third Deficiency Appropriation Bill, 1919*. Hearings on H.R. 16187 (14–22 Feb. 1919)

House. Committee on Rules, *Employment of Soldiers and Sailors*. Hearings on H.Res. 452 and H.Res. 463 (11 Dec. 1918)

372

66 Cong., 1 sess.

Senate. Committee on Appropriations, *Sundry Civil Appropriation Bill, 1920*. Hearings on H.R. 6176 (24 June 1919)

Senate. Committee on Education and Labor, *Financing House Construction and Home Ownership*. Hearings on S. 168 (7 June 1919)

House. Committee on Banking and Currency, *Employment on Public Improvements through Issue of Legal Tender Notes*. Hearings on H.R. 1473 (25 June 1919)

Joint Committees on Labor, *National Employment System*. Hearings on S. 688, S. 1442 and H.R. 4305 (19 June–25 July 1919)

66 Cong., 2 sess.

House. Committee on Appropriations, *Sundry Civil Appropriation Bill, 1921*. Hearings on H.R. 13870 (12 March–3 April 1920)

66 Cong., 3 sess.

House. Committee on Appropriations, *Sundry Civil Appropriation Bill, 1922*. Hearings on H.R. 15422 (4 Dec. 1920)

67 Cong., 1 sess.

Senate. Committee on Education and Labor, *Relieving Periods of Unemployment by a System of Public Works*. Hearings on S. 2749 (21–22 Dec. 1921).

67 Cong., 4 sess.

House. Committee on Appropriations, *Departments of Commerce and Labor, Appropriation Bill, 1924*. Hearings on H.R. 13316 (14–21 Nov. 1922)

House. Committee on Labor, *Needs for Public Works to Be Carried on by Federal, State, and Municipal Agencies*. Hearings on H.R. 14185 (17 Feb. 1923)

70 Cong., 1 sess.

Senate. Committee on Commerce, *Expansion of Public Works during Periods of Unemployment and Industrial Depression*. Hearings on S. 2475 (12 April 1928)

70 Cong., 2 sess.

Senate. Committee on Education and Labor, *Unemployment in the United States*. Hearings Pursuant to S.Res. 219 (11 Dec. 1928–9 Feb. 1929)

71 Cong., 2 sess.

Senate. Committee on Commerce, *Unemployment in the United States*. Hearings on S. 3059, S. 3060, and S. 3061 (18 March–1 April 1930)

House. Committee on the Judiciary, *Unemployment in the United States*. Hearings on S. 3059, S. 3060, H.R. 8374, H.R. 8655, H.R. 9560, H.R. 11414, H.R. 12550, and H.R. 12551 (11–12 June 1930)

71 Cong., 3 sess.

House. Committee on Appropriations, *Appropriation Bill for 1931*. Hearings on H.R. 14450 (5–6 Dec. 1930)

House. Committee on Appropriations, *The Emergency Construction Appropriation Bill for 1931*. Hearings [on H.R. 14804] (5–6 Dec. 1930)

House. Committee on Public Buildings and Grounds, *Public Buildings and Grounds*. Hearings on H.R. 14040 (11 Dec. 1930)

72 Cong., 1 sess.

Senate. Committee on Banking and Currency, *Unemployment Relief*. Hearings on S. 4632, S. 4727, S. 4755, and S. 4822 (2–13 June 1932)

Senate. Committee on Commerce, *National and State Employment Service*. Hearings on S. 2687 (24 March–31 March 1932)

Senate. Committee on Manufactures, *Unemployment Relief*. Hearings on S. 174 and S. 262 (28 Dec. 1931–9 Jan. 1932)

Senate. Committee on Manufactures, *Federal Cooperation in Unemployment Relief*. Hearings on S. 4592 (9 May 1932)

Senate. Committee on Manufactures, *Emergency Financing for Unemployed Workers*. Hearings on S. 4947 (6 July 1932)

Senate. Select Committee on Unemployment Insurance, *Hearings Pursuant to S.Res. 483 (71st Cong.)* (2 April–13 Nov. 1931)

House. Committee on Agriculture, *Wheat Distribution*. Hearings [Pursuant to S.J.Res. 110] (4 Jan.–1 March 1932)

House. Committee on Expenditures in the Executive Department, *Public Works Administration*. Hearings on H.R. 6665 and H.R. 6670 (1–12 March 1932)

House. Committee on Labor, *Unemployment in the United States*. Hearings on H.R. 206, H.R. 6011, and H.R. 8088 (1–12 Feb. 1932)

House. Committee on Labor, *Relief of Distress Due to Unemployment*. Hearings on H.R. 11055, H.R. 11056, and H.R. 12097 (29 April–6 May 1932)

House. Committee on Roads, *Roads*. Hearings on H.R. 9642 (23–24 Feb. 1932)

House. Committee on Ways and Means, *National Emergency Relief*. Hearings on H.R. 12353 (31 May–2 June 1932)

72 Cong., 2 sess.

Senate. Committee on Banking and Currency, *Further Unemployment Relief through the Reconstruction Finance Corporation*. Hearings on S. 5336 (2–3 Feb. 1933)

Senate. Committee on Manufactures, *Relief for Unemployed Transients*. Hearings on S. 5121 (13–25 Jan. 1933)

Senate. Committee on Manufactures, *Federal Aid for Unemployment Relief*. Hearings on S. 5125 (3 Jan.–3 Feb. 1933)

House. Committee on Appropriations, *Department of Labor Appropriation Bill for 1934*. Hearings on H.R. 14363 (16 Dec. 1932)

75 Cong., 3 sess.

Senate. Committee on Appropriations, *Work Relief and Public Works Appropriation Act of 1938*. Hearings on H.J.Res 679 (16–18 May 1938)

MANUSCRIPT COLLECTIONS CONSULTED

Andrews Papers
John B. Andrews Papers. New York State Library of Industrial and Labor Relations, Ithaca, New York.

Commission on Industrial Relations Papers
United States Commission on Industrial Relations Papers. RG 174, National Archives and Records Administration, Washington, DC.

Commons Papers
John R. Commons Papers. State Historical Society of Wisconsin, Madison, Wisconsin.

Couzens Papers
James Couzens Papers. Library of Congress, Washington, DC.

Davis Papers
James John Davis Papers. Library of Congress, Washington, DC.

Department of Labor Papers
United States Department of Labor Papers. RG 174, National Archives and Records Administration, Washington, DC.

Department of Commerce Papers
United States Department of Commerce Papers. RG 40, National Archives and Records Administration, Washington, DC.

Draper Papers
Ernest G. Draper Papers. Library of Congress, Washington, DC.

FESB Papers
Federal Employment Stabilization Board Papers. RG 187, National Archives and Records Administration, Washington, DC.

Harding Papers
Warren G. Harding Papers. Ohio Historical Society, Columbus, Ohio.

Hoover Papers
Herbert C. Hoover Papers. Herbert Hoover Library, West Branch, Iowa.

Huber Papers
Henry A. Huber Papers. State Historical Society of Wisconsin, Madison, Wisconsin.

Leiserson Papers
William M. Leiserson Papers. State Historical Society of Wisconsin, Madison, Wisconsin.

Pinchot Papers
Gifford Pinchot Papers. Library of Congress, Washington, DC.

POUR Papers
President's Organization on Unemployment Relief Papers. RG 73, National Archives and Records Administration, Washington, DC.

Roosevelt Papers
Franklin D. Roosevelt Papers. Franklin D. Roosevelt Library, Hyde Park, New York, New York.

Van Kleeck Papers
Mary Van Kleeck Papers. Archives of Labor and Urban Affairs, Walter P. Reuther Library, Detroit, Michigan.

Wagner Papers
Robert F. Wagner Papers. Georgetown University, Washington, DC.

Walsh Papers
Thomas J. Walsh Papers. Library of Congress, Washington, DC.

Witte Papers
Edwin E. Witte Papers. State Historical Society of Wisconsin, Madison, Wisconsin.

Woods Papers
Arthur Woods Papers. Library of Congress, Washington, DC.

Index

Page references to bills, resolutions, and hearings mentioned in the text or footnotes.

Congressional bills and resolutions

Congressional hearings